SECOND EDITION

INTRODUCTION TO
PHYSICAL
EDUCATION
A Contemporary Careers Approach

ROBERT A. PESTOLESI
Professor Emeritus
California State University, Long Beach

CINDI BAKER
Regional Sales Manager
PHOENIX/BFA Films and Video, Inc.

SCOTT/FORESMAN/LITTLE BROWN HIGHER EDUCATION
A Division of Scott, Foresman and Company
Glenview, Illinois   London, England

To our spouses, Marilyn and John, for their unending support.

Library of Congress Cataloging-in-Publication Data

Pestolesi, Robert A.
  Introduction to physical education : a contemporary
careers approach / Robert A. Pestolesi, Cindi Baker. — 2nd
ed.
    p.   cm.
    ISBN 0-673-16719-4
    1. Physical education and training — Vocational guidance.
  2. Physical education and training — Study and teaching
(Higher) I. Baker, Cindi. II. Title
GV362.P46   1990
613.7'023 — dc20   89-27161

All photographs not credited are property of the authors.   **31,** This chart is reprinted with permission from the *Journal of Physical Education, Recreation & Dance,* Jan., 1988, 69–71. The *Journal* is a publication of the American Alliance for Health, Physical Education, Recreation and Dance, 1900 Association Drive, Reston, VA 22091;   **33,** Courtesy California State University, Dominquez Hills;   **39–42,** Elementary hierarchical objectives chart prepared by Dr. Daniel D. Arnheim for School Evaluation Project, University of California, Los Angeles, Center for Study Evaluation;   **44,** Robert Drea;   **52,** Steve Lissau;   **63,** Courtesy of the Metropolitan Museum of Art, Gift of Thomas F. Ryan, 1910;   **83,** The Granger Collection;   **87,** The Granger Collection;   **91,** Alice Austen;   **99,** Focus on Sports, Inc.;   **114,** (both) Don Cabrall;   **115,** (top and middle) Don Cabrall;   **118,** Courtesy California State University, Dominquez Hills;   **170,** Harold Edgerton;   **204,** California State University, Dominquez Hills;   **176, 178–179, 183,** The American Alliance for Health, Physical Education, Recreation and Dance, 1900 Association Drive, Reston, VA 22091;   **208,** Courtesy California State University, Dominquez Hills;   **216,** Mario Del Curto/Gamma-Liaison;   **229,** Focus on Sports, Inc.;   **241,** Don Klumpp/The Image Bank;   **298** Courtesy of the Boy Scouts of America;   **310,** NASA;   **381,** Keza/Gamma-Liaison;   **389,** PEPI is a project of the National Association for Sport and Physical Education, Recreation and Dance, 1900 Association Drive, Reston, VA 22091;   **402,** Jean-Claude LeJeune.

Preface

Introduction to Physical Education: A Contemporary Careers Approach, Second Edition, is designed to give college students an insight into the foundations of physical education as well as the many diverse careers that can result from studying physical education. Too often students choose an academic major without adequately considering how the selected course of study can lead to employment and without being aware of the range of current and future job opportunities. Because the importance of physical fitness, sport, outdoor recreation, and leisure time is being increasingly recognized, the student who will become a specialist in one of the human movement professions needs to be aware of the variety of exciting careers that could develop from our changing lifestyles.

Part One provides an overview of the physical education profession and discusses the challenge of using multiple means to meet individual needs in our sedentary society. The importance of seeking a career that is appropriate to the student's own interests and abilities is emphasized to encourage the student to establish a career objective that is a personal goal.

Part Two describes the foundations of the physical education profession and includes a survey of the historical, philosophical, biological, sociological, and psychological aspects of the profession as well as their field applications. The relationship between the humanities and physical education and sport is discussed along with the importance of measurement and evaluation. The role of athletics is presented in its broadest sense — as activities open to competitors of all ages and levels of skill.

Part Three allows students to discover their personal talents and preferences and shows how these factors relate to developing a career path. Many career options are described with an emphasis on nonteaching career opportunities. Numerous vocational biographies describe firsthand a variety of successful careers in physical education, sports, and related fields. The career search is carefully described to provide students with the tools and techniques required for success in the job market. Part Three concludes by examining the responsibilities of the professional physical educator and by showing how to plan for future career mobility.

At the conclusion of each chapter are challenging, motivational class activities that summarize key points and are designed to encourage further study. Figures, tables, and checklists help the student organize essential information and record short-range and long-range career goals.

This text aims to help the student majoring in physical education major (1) to have a sound understanding of the foundations of the profession, (2) to select a career path that reflects personal interests and abilities, (3) to establish and follow a curricular path that leads toward a career goal, and (4) to pursue employment that is personally rewarding and that allows further professional development.

No single job alternative should be overlooked in the search for professional careers in sport and fitness. Our aim is to make students aware of the many exciting career opportunities available and to prepare students to accept, with enthusiasm and creativity, whatever career they choose in physical education.

We would like to thank the following professionals for their comments and suggestions during manuscript development of both editions of *Introduction to Physical Education: A Contemporary Careers Approach:* Waldean Robichaux, University of Colorado; J. Tillman Hall, University of Southern California; Michael Stewart, University of Nebraska— Omaha; Neil Hattlestad, The University of Central Arkansas; Elizabeth Crilley, Long Beach City College; Sam Winningham, California State University—Northridge; Carolyn Cody, University of Northern Colorado; Billie Jo Jones, The Florida State University; Elizabeth Hall, Texas Tech University; and Roy Clumpner, Western Washington State University.

R. A. P.
C. B.

Contents

Introduction to
the Profession

1. The Physical Education Profession

Chapter Outline

How Healthy Are We?
A Nation at Risk
Implications of Educational Reform
Adult Fitness
Government and the Nation's Health
Defining Physical Education
Defining Terms
Justifying Physical Education
Image of the Modern Physical Educator
Student Activities
Suggested Readings
References

Objectives

Chapter 1 is designed to enable you to:

- Develop an awareness of the challenges that face physical educators as we approach the turn of the century.
- Relate the implications of education reform for public school physical education.
- Define *physical education*
- Examine the variety of career options and responsibilities regarding the nation's fitness.

WITH the twenty-first century looming before us, professionals from many walks of life are involved in attempting to predict the future. There are many factors that contribute to the study of the past and of current behaviors and the application of these factors as indicators of Future America. For example, the senior adult population grew twice as fast as the rest of the American population in the last two decades (Brown, Cundiff, and Thompson, 1989). Today, approximately 40 percent of the elderly population is age 75 or older. By the year 2000, it is projected that at least half of the senior population will be older than 75. By the middle of the next century, the resulting "very old" population (85 years or more) will be seven times larger than it is today. This surge will have tremendous implications for physical education programs and careers. As a prospective physical educator, you are concerned with your future career and the direction that it will take. Questions are developing daily as you make decisions that will have a profound effect on your life. As you begin your study of physical education, it will be important to examine aspects of your career choice with a positive and enthusiastic desire to learn the fundamentals of the discipline

As many Americans are living longer, it is increasingly important that they develop sound health, fitness, and recreational habits.

in order to provide yourself with a firm foundation for your future career path.

How Healthy Are We?

As one views American society as a whole, it appears that enthusiasm for exercise, nutrition, and physical fitness is at an all-time high. The public has been saturated through the media with an incredible amount of fitness information and propaganda. People have spent large amounts of money on exercise programs, fitness-related equipment, athletic clothing, and diets. The commercial side of fitness interests has blossomed into exercise clubs and health spas in almost every community in the United States. The crossing of gender and age barriers in exercise and sports programs appears to occur much more frequently among white-collar than blue-collar workers. The characteristics of the exercising population can skew the application of facts and figures for the population as a whole. However, despite the amount of activity, it is difficult to determine whether the exercising public is responding to a fad such as oat-bran diets or whether they are making sound educationally based lifestyle decisions. The negative commercial side of fitness also exists, as evidenced by the number of fitness programs that are developed without concern for basic principles of exercise: The administrators of such programs are concerned solely with monetary gain and impressive membership rosters, despite the language of their advertisements.

In 1980, the U.S. government published a report titled "Promoting Health/Preventing Disease: Objectives for the Nation" (Wilmore, 1982). The report focused on the hope that increased levels of physical fitness may contribute to reduced heart and lung disease rates, possibly to reduced injuries among the elderly and, more broadly, to an enhanced sense of well-being which may reinforce positive health behaviors in other areas. The following objectives were delineated by the federal government for the year 1990, since they were not achieved in accordance with the projected timeline.

Reduced Risk Factors
- The proportion of children and adolescents participating regularly in appropriate physical activities, particularly cardiorespiratory fitness programs which can be carried into adulthood, should be greater than 90 percent.
- The proportion of children and adolescents participating in daily school physical education programs should be greater than 60 percent.

- The proportion of adults ages 18 to 65 participating regularly in vigorous physical exercise should be greater than 60 percent.
- Fifty percent of the adults 65 years and older should be engaging in appropriate physical activity such as regular walking, swimming, or other aerobic activity.

Improved Services and Protection
- The proportion of employees of companies and institutions with more than 500 employees offering employer-sponsored fitness programs should be greater than 25 percent, compared with approximately 2.5 percent in 1979.

Improved Surveillance and Evaluation Systems
- Methodology for systematically assessing the physical fitness of children should be established, with at least 70-percent participation in such assessment.
- Data should be available with which to evaluate the short- and long-term health effects of participation in programs of appropriate physical activity.
- Data should be available to evaluate the effects of participation in programs of physical fitness on job performance and health care costs.
- Data should be available for regularly monitoring national trends and patterns of participation in physical activity, including participation in public recreation programs in community facilities.

Why are the 1990 exercise objectives so important? Rising health care costs and the enormous economic toll inflicted on business and industry through lost workdays are enough to justify the need for exercise-related behavioral changes. This is predicted on the general belief that the benefits of regular exercise can partially affect the medical and economic burdens that often accompany the aging process (Brown, Cundiff, and Thompson, 1989).

> By the year 2020, our nation's population will be made of more old timers than ever before — a serious implication for health care costs.
> *(Brown, Cundiff, and Thompson, 1989)*

The 1990 objectives should serve as a challenge to current and future professionals in the fields of health, physical education, and recreation (Wilmore, 1982). These objectives can be attained if current trends in health and fitness programming into corporate, commercial, and community settings continue, with trained professionals implementing these programs.

A Nation at Risk

In 1981, another U.S. government study was published titled "A Nation at Risk." The focus of this study was on the status of the nation's public education system. It is important to note, however, that physical education was not included in the major issues, despite the previous publication from the Office of Disease Prevention and Health Promotion. The dichotomy between the mind-body relationship has not been overcome by professionals in physical education. Alarm sounded across the country regarding the lack of quality teaching and quality achievement in young people. Reform was the cry heard across the land in school board meetings and state capitols. Curriculum reform in reading, language arts, mathematics, social studies, and the sciences focused on the concept of mastery learning. The quality of teaching was also addressed in the evaluation of criteria for certification in teaching and the development of teacher competency testing programs in many states. Despite the abundance of research regarding the health and fitness of our youth, it rarely surfaces in debates among curriculum specialists, educational administrators, and local school boards. What does the future hold for our children's health, fitness, and leisure lifestyle? What about the quality of physical education instruction?

As educational reform became a critical issue in the public forum, our children's health and fitness were being overlooked. Could it be that we in the United States are becoming complacent regarding the existence of cancer and heart disease? There are probably very few families in our society that have not been affected by either disease. Have we accepted their existence simply as a fact of life, or are we truly committed to a healthier lifestyle? The jury is still out as researchers continue to gather data. Nonetheless, when America does not perform well in worldwide sports competition, the general public does take notice. Our winter Olympic team's performance at the 1988 Calgary games was very disappointing. The paucity of medals won received much attention and emphasized the need for increased funding and training for future Olympians. However, no connection was made to the overall level of fitness and skill development of average American children.

As a result of U.S. government reports and with increasing concerns for the fitness level of our children, the National Children and Youth Fitness (NCYF) Study (Ross and Gilbert, 1985) was initiated to determine how fit and how active fifth through twelfth graders are. The study had three main objectives: (1) to describe the current fitness status of American young people, (2) to describe patterns of participation in physical activity, and (3) to evaluate the relationship among physical activity patterns and measured fitness. In 1982, the Office of Disease Prevention and Health Promotion convened a panel of experts to design a battery of tests. The data were collected between February and May 1984. As a result of this lengthy process, a new fitness test was developed, though the test items evoked controversy between various programs. The conclusions of the study were that (1) American young people have become fatter since the 1960s, (2) students performing below average on the fitness tests experience the greatest reduction in physical activity during the nonsummer months, (3) enrollment in physical education positively affects fitness, but of greater importance is the nature of the program (variety of activities; weekly activity time), and (4) the greater the number of physical activities in which students have participated during the year, the better the performance on physical fitness tests (Ross and Gilbert, 1985). These results illustrated the need for a well-coordinated effort between schools, community organizations, children, and their parents to improve the health and fitness levels of our nation's young people. However, as we prepare for the twenty-first century, we must acknowledge the fact that data gathered in 1984 did not influence the nation to demand increased funding for quality physical education programming.

According to Mark Pitman, M.D., Chief of Sports Medicine at the Hospital for Joint Diseases in New York City (1987), the lack of fitness in our children has become a problem partly because of the prevailing attitudes toward athletics. He continues by stating that the purpose of sports, especially for children, should be to make healthy people healthier. The concept of team sports has failed to do this. Rather than learning to interact and cooperate with others, youngsters are taught to compete. Pitman concludes by stating that team sports have only reinforced the notion that the team on top is the winner and that all others are losers. This approach may not make sports appealing to many children, and some, especially among the less fit, burn out by the time they are 12 years old (Pitman, 1987). If we assume that there is truth to this statement, then our elementary physical education programs as well as our community youth sports programs are failing the individual child.

According to David Griffey (1987) of the University of Wyoming, "We have failed to provide an experience that our students perceive as meaningful. The sense of mastering something important is denied most students in secondary physical education programs." He contends that the profession has an inability to communicate to students, parents, administrators, fellow teachers, and the community what is distinct about what physical education has to offer. Large classes make it difficult to individualize the teaching of basic motor development skills and concepts. Class management or discipline becomes a major task and often discourages the good teacher from pursuing a lifetime career in the elementary field where the profession needs high-quality instructional programs. Without quality programs at the elementary level, middle school and high school programs often suffer.

Educational reform has failed to address the needs of physical education in the school curriculum. In Texas, the state legislature passed a reform bill in 1985 mandating the content of the curriculum and the allotted time per week per course of study. Although physical education time was mandated based on the total amount of minutes per week per grade level, the amount of time provided did not allow most children to master the skills and concepts taught.

The report, "A Nation at Risk," cites as one example of decline in academic performance "the fact that 25 percent of the credits earned by general track high school students are in such courses as physical and health education." This directly implies that the physical education curriculum has lost the credibility it once had of being an important part of the general high school curriculum. The following suggestions have been made for the physical education program to align itself with current changes in other subjects:

1. Emphasize the cognitive learning of the concepts and principles that underlie a physical activity.
2. Integrate the physical education curriculum into the general high school curriculum.
3. Encourage learning for mastery on fewer activities.

(Taylor and Chiogioji, 1987)

Emphasizing the academic connections between programs would make integrating physical education into the general high school curriculum more likely, in turn making physical education more credible at a time when the stress is on academic achievement.

Results of reported studies continue to indicate that what is happening with our nation's children and youth is not good. The available data also suggest that inadequate childhood fitness habits might carry over into adulthood. Cardiovascular heart disease and obesity remain major health problems for children and adults. Pemberton and McSwegin (1989) believe that we have failed to motivate children and youths to engage in physical activity that promotes physical fitness. These facts indicate that the challenge of fitness is not just in getting our children and youth physically fit but in getting them fit and educating them to stay fit for life.

Adult Fitness

"American Health" magazine in 1985 revealed that information polls and general surveys can lend some insight into people's perceived values or how they feel they should respond; however, the information gathered is not "research data." Polls can often manipulate statistics to achieve specific marketing objectives of concepts or products. What people say, what they actually do, and to what degree they do things can be very different. Gallup polls are often used to obtain opinions. The editors of "American Health" magazine conducted such a poll in 1985 which suggested that 54 percent of Americans exercised regularly. It also appeared that people who exercised were more likely to change their diets and improve their health habits. People also stated that they tended to feel better about themselves in general. Two years later, Gurin and Harris (1987) decided to conduct another poll to determine whether this was a perceived fad or a major trend. In later 1986, a Gallup poll of 1,022 adults revealed that the number of Americans "exercising" had jumped to 69 percent; more than two-thirds of Americans were "exercising regularly" (Gurin and Harris, 1987). These polls cannot accurately ascertain the level of knowledge that respondents have regarding the concept of quality exercise.

Are adults really convinced that physical activity is essential to their health, or is the public's affair with an active lifestyle merely a form of flirtation rather than a serious commitment (Seefeldt, 1987)? Additional information provided by Gurin and Harris (1987) reported that only 10 to 20 percent of adults are *sufficiently active* to derive the cardio-respiratory benefits of activity. Their update also illustrated that another 40 percent are somewhat active, and 40 to 50 percent are completely sedentary. If actions are truer indicators than words or surveys, then we can understand the public apathy for school-based physical education programs.

Although physical fitness professionals are committed to the benefits of physical activity, it appears that the vast majority of the adult population is not. We need to consider the questions these skeptics pose to us:

1. What are the objectives of physical education programs and where is the evidence that these objectives are not being met in school-based programs?

2. What are the short- and long-term effects of specific activity programs and how are these effects mediated? Are they the result of enhanced physical fitness, metabolic changes, psychological effects, some other mechanisms, or a combination of these?
3. What prescriptions of exercise are prudent for the various segments of our society in order for us to acquire the maximum health benefits? Are the results of an activity program sufficiently general to benefit all individuals?
4. What are the patterns or determinants of lifestyles during childhood that predispose individuals to a physically active lifestyle as adults?
5. What are the risk factors and injuries associated with specific kinds and intensities of exercise programs? Are these risk factors uniform across the age span or is this occurrence selective?

(Seefeldt, 1987)

These questions illustrate the inadequate delivery system that exists for the dissemination of data regarding a healthy lifestyle for both young people and adults. Until relevant answers can be provided to these questions, we are not likely to persuade skeptics that physical education in the schools, community programs, or health clubs provides either short-term or long-term benefits for all participants. Historically, physical educators have shown themselves more adept at defending their failures in times of educational reform rather than proposing strong defensible programs. The importance of implementing quality public relations programs has never been more evident. Physical education has the opportunity to respond to the challenge of the public schools. Programs need to be redirected so that the health-related benefits of physical activity are presented.

Government and the Nation's Health

Government leaders have recognized the value of physical activity and sports for our nation's health. In 1955, the first governmental agency established for the fitness of school-aged Americans, now called the President's Council on Physical Fitness and Sports, was founded by President Dwight Eisenhower. In 1961, the National Conference on Youth Fitness was called by President John F. Kennedy, whose enthusiasm for physical fitness was shared, and whose example of participating in physical activity and sports was followed, by people of all ages.

The first National Conference on Physical Fitness and Sports for All was called in 1980 by President Jimmy Carter, who linked recent drops in death rates and increases in life expectancy to improved exercise habits. Research had verified that good diet and exercise were vital to good health. However, President Carter cautioned that we still have more progress to make before our children are fully involved in a healthy lifetime lifestyle. When time permitted during President Reagan's busy schedule, he would visit his ranch in California and enjoy horseback riding as well as chopping wood. He served as a role model for maintaining annual physical examinations with his doctors for preventive medicine.

Recently, the U.S. government has shown even greater interest in the status of youth fitness. During the Youth Fitness Hearings of 1984, Senator Richard Lugar of Indiana stated, "There is a strong connection between the decline in academic test scores and the sorry state of fitness and health among our young people. We really have to indicate that physical education is clearly one of the important studies" (Hayes, 1984). As a result of the nationwide hearings, the President's Council on Physical Fitness and Sports recommended that all children in grades kindergarten through 12 (1) participate in daily physical education that emphasizes both fitness and skills, (2) be tested twice yearly in fitness, (3) understand and be able to apply exercise science principles, (4) have posture checks, routine health screenings, and appropriate follow-ups, (5) receive remedial attention as needed, and (6) if they are disabled, be identified and provided with appropriate programs (Hayes, 1984).

These hearings stimulated the development of legislation at both the federal and state levels that directly addressed the quality and quantity of physical education in our schools. Due to the amount of time involved in establishing committees, developing legislative proposals, presenting such proposals before legislative bodies, and implementing timelines of approved legislation, a joint resolution for daily physical education requirements in grades kindergarten through 12, first presented to Congress in 1986, was not passed until the spring of 1988. The concurrent resolution is presented in Figure 1.1. It is important to note, however, that although this resolution indicates a degree of awareness, it does not reflect any financial commitments to assist states and local educational agencies in the development and implementation of physical education programs.

The government has the potential to play an important role in improving the nation's health. With diligent efforts from physical education professionals to work with their government representatives, new funding commitments from the various levels of government may become a reality during the next century.

Figure 1.1 Concurrent Resolution

100TH CONGRESS
1st SESSION # H. CON. RES.97

To encourage State and local governments and local educational agencies to provide high
quality daily physical education programs for all children in kindergarten through grade 12.

IN THE HOUSE OF REPRESENTATIVES

CONCURRENT RESOLUTION

To encourage State and local governments and local educational agencies to provide high quality daily physical
education programs for all children in kindergarten through grade 12.

Whereas physical education is essential to the development of growing children;

Whereas physical education helps improve the overall health of children by improving their cardiovascular endurance, muscular strength and power, and flexibility, and by enhancing weight regulation, bone development,
posture, skillful moving, active lifestyle habits, and constructive use of leisure time;

Whereas physical education increases children's mental alertness, academic performance, readiness to learn, and
enthusiasm for learning;

Whereas physical education helps improve the self-esteem, interpersonal relationships, responsible behavior, and
independence of children;

Whereas children who participate in high quality daily physical education programs tend to be more healthy and
physically fit;

Whereas physically fit adults have significantly reduced risk factor for heart attacks and strokes;

Whereas the Surgeon General, in Objectives for the Nation, recommends increasing the number of school mandated
physical education programs that focus on health-related physical fitness;

Whereas the Secretary of Education in First Lessons—A Report on Elementary Education In America, recognized
that elementary schools have a special mandate to provide elementary school children with the knowledge,
habits, and attitudes that will equip the children for a fit and healthy life; and

Whereas a high quality daily physical education program for all children in kindergarten through grade 12 is an
essential part of a comprehensive education: Now, therefore, be it

Resolved by the House of Representatives (the Senate concurring), That the Congress encourages State and
local governments and local educational agencies to provide high quality daily physical education programs for all
children in kindergarten through grade 12.

Defining Physical Education

The term *physical education* is used to define many different programs
and is sometimes perceived as an inaccurate description of the academic
nature of our field. It is important to clarify its meaning as you begin
the study of physical education as a career. It is also essential to understand other terms that are connected with our profession.

First, let us examine the term *physical education*. The word *physi-*

cal refers to the body. It is often used to refer to bodily characteristics such as strength, endurance, flexibility, health, coordination, and appearance. It usually contrasts the body to the mind. The term *education* when used in conjunction with the word *physical* refers to the process of education that develops the human body, specifically fitness and movement skills. The term *education* supports our existence primarily as a teaching field, which fuels the misconception that physical educators are not qualified to pursue careers outside of education. Although teaching and coaching remain the more prominent aspects of our profession, the description of physical education requires a much broader scope.

Physical education has been known by other titles in the past. *Gymnastics* was the earliest name attached to our field of study in the nineteenth century. As the nature of the activities grew, however, that was no longer appropriate. *Hygiene* was another term substituted for or used in close association with *physical education* in the nineteenth century. In modern times, we can see that hygiene has developed into health education. *Physical culture* was another name used to describe the profession. The term *physical education* has contributed to the growth and development of the discipline more than any other name that preceded it. This is evidenced in the quality and quantity of educational programs as well as the training of qualified professionals.

However, there are many leading physical educators who have criticized the adequacy of this title. Other terms that have been suggested as descriptive titles for our field include *human movement, sport science, kinesiology, movement education, art and science of human movement, human kinetics,* and *health* (Table 1.1). *Wellness* is also a contemporary term that the lay public identifies with physical education and fitness. None of these terms have been acceptable to all contemporary physical educators. To appease the various sides of this issue, perhaps a change of focus is needed. It has been suggested that the discipline needs to attend more to the proper interpretation of physical education and its major objectives. Practicing physical educators, such as Word (1988), still like the name *physical education* and perceive the problem as one of image or association. If we can change people's perceptions through their experiences, the name *physical education* will continue to exemplify the nature of the discipline.

Physical education attempts, through research and the application of knowledge, to understand and predict the effects of human movement on people. Human movement includes exercise, games, sports, aquatics, and dance. While at Oregon State University at Corvallis, Lambert (1980)

Table 1.1 Names or Titles Suggested as Alternatives
for Physical Education

TITLES	PROPONENTS	MAIN ARGUMENT
Human Movement or Movement Studies or Human Movement Studies	Peter Karpovich (1969), Jagger (1977), Groves (1977)	Movement is a fundamental characteristic of life. It gives physical education a unifying focus and makes possible an identification of its knowledge structure.
Movement Arts and Sciences	Metheny (1967)	The arguments of the proponents of this title are similar to the one proposed above. The main aim of its proponents is to identify physical education as a discipline.
Movement Education	Porter (1969), Kirchener et al. (1970)	Movement Education is conceived as capable of giving an extended meaning to what is now known as physical education and enables a better understanding and appreciation of the values of physical education. However, *movement education* has been used to refer to a program of physical education. It has also been used to refer to a method of instruction involving movement exploration. It seems that this term itself carries with it the multidimensional meaning which has

Table 1.1 (continued)

TITLES	PROPONENTS	MAIN ARGUMENT
		made physical education vulnerable to criticism.
Kinesiology or Anthropokinesiology	Mackenzie (1969)	*Kinesiology* is proposed as the science of human movement, the study of man in motion. Proponents of this title see it as an option for elaborating the structure of knowledge of physical education as a distinctive field of scholarly inquiry, which in turn supports, nourishes, and informs vocational or professional interests and services. The philosophical framework undergirding this title is similar to that of *human movement studies* and *movement arts and sciences*.
Sports Education and Sports	Sheenham (1968), Ziegler (1964)	The advocates of this title believe that *sports* as a title for the field of physical education provides a rallying point and focus of study. It is further argued that physical education does not fully portray the significance of sports. Preferably, therefore, the title for the field should either be *physical*

TITLES	PROPONENTS	MAIN ARGUMENT
		education and sports or _sports science._ However, there is a very strong feeling against the use of the word _sports_ as a title for the field. Some feel that sport is one of the activities included in physical education. Furthermore, experience with sport has shown that it is characterized by unwholesome practices that may pollute or adulterate the meaning and significance of physical education.
Developmental Motor Performance	Emanates from AAHPER (1972) Publication, _Tones of Theory_	Physical education is viewed as a field concerned with motor performance and its development. Hence, _developmental motor performance_ is seen as a suitable title for the field of physical education. (Ojeme, 1984)

E.O. Ojeme, "How the Name Physical Education Outlived Its Usefulness," _The Physical Educator_, December, 1984: 192. Reprinted with permission.

stated that if you define physical education only as "the teaching of sports, dance, and exercise in the public schools," you limit your job opportunities because you think it is the only thing you can do with your college education. Lambert (1980; p. 76) suggests that the physical education major should examine the following definitions: Physical education is the art and science of human movement,

sports education,

fitness education and the effects of physical stress upon the human body,

preventive and rehabilitative medicine,

the study of play,

perceptual-motor development,

the study of human energy, and

an academic discipline that investigates the uses and meanings of physical activities to understand their effects and interrelationships with people and their culture.

Your definition of physical education may be the key to finding your professional niche after graduation.

Defining Terms

As you begin your study of physical education, an understanding of the meaning of the following terms that are frequently used within the profession will be an asset.

Physical Fitness. According to current practices in the profession, *physical fitness* is considered to be either performance-related or health-related. The health-related component of physical fitness is concerned with the development of the body to provide protection against diseases such as coronary heart disease and obesity. Performance-related fitness is associated with developing the attributes necessary for improved performance in sports and other physical activities such as endurance, strength, and speed. Both components involve similar knowledge of bodily function, but the degree of knowledge varies.

Motor Learning. *Motor learning* is concerned with the process of how one learns various motor skills. The learning process consists of a variety of perceptual and motor responses acquired through practice and repetition. Eventually, the learner develops a set of motor responses into an integrated movement pattern of skill.

Short Pedagogy. *Sport pedagogy* is the art, science, or profession of physical education that includes formal study and research in the areas of curriculum, teaching methodology, teacher education, evaluation, organization, and administration.

Sport Psychology. Psychology is concerned with the individual. He or she is the unit of analysis, and the outcome of the interaction of the individual with stimuli is the focus. _Sport psychology_ is an attempt to understand the how and why underlying sport behavior. The central focus is on the application of psychological principles to learning sport skills, performing skills in both competitive and noncompetitive situations, coaching, and to personality factors.

Sport Sociology. _Sport sociology_ is study of the role of social behavior in a sport setting. Groups and institutions, including athletes, spectators, sports organizations and cultural groups, are the focus of analysis. The influence of the mass media on sports groups and institutions has become an area of increased study for the sport sociologist.

Sports Medicine. Sports medicine is concerned with the scientific study of the effects of physical activity on the human body as it affects sports performance. The influence of drugs, the environment, emotions, and growth parameters are some of the elements included in sports medicine. The prevention of disease and injury as well as rehabilitation associated with athletic training programs are also included.

Health. The term _health_ refers to total physical and mental health and not the mere absence of disease. The emphasis is now on wellness rather than illness and on preventive medicine.

Recreation. _Recreation_ comprises leisure activities performed by an individual during nonworking hours. Educating people to use their leisure time wisely with a variety of activities is the focus of community recreation programs and various groups within the community including the Young Men's Christian Association (YMCA), scouting programs, and the arts.

These are only a few of the terms and concepts that will be introduced to you in greater detail in later chapters. Physical education is more complex than is perceived by many people who are not directly involved in our field. As we continue to examine the impact of physical education on people's lives, from birth through the senior years, opportunities for professional growth will expand to exciting dimensions as we prepare to enter a new century.

Justifying Physical Education

As we examine the plight of physical education in the schools and the physically degenerate American society, it is ironic that we have more

Modern sport facilities enhance quality instructional programs.

information today about the benefits of physical activity than ever before. Our knowledge regarding the relationship between health and physical activity is incredible when compared to the early decades of the twentieth century. Many agencies and commissions are recommending that individuals of all ages become involved in physical activity. The inconsistency between federal policy, recommendations, and local implementation requires additional study.

It appears that only a small number of Americans currently enjoy their nearly full capacity for health. The failure of people to make use of this capacity appears to be the major contributor to many of our illnesses. People are aware of the incidence of various diseases but, according to Bloomfield (1984), they need a new vision of the fully functioning person, a new model of health and fitness. He calls his model "positive wellness." People enjoying positive wellness are

Trim and physically fit; full of energy and vigor; rarely tired.

Free from destructive lifestyle habits.

Free from minor complaints such as indigestion, constipation, headaches, or insomnia.

Aware and alert; able to concentrate and think with great effectiveness.
Radiant in appearance, with clear skin, glossy hair, and sparkling eyes.
Able to relax easily, free from worry and anxiety.
Self-assured, confident, optimistic, active and creative.
Satisfied with work and the direction of their lives.
Fulfilled and at peace with themselves.

(Bloomfield, 1989)

Whatever career path you choose to follow in the field of physical education, the challenge is immense. The potential to influence the degree of positive wellness in the lives of young, mature, or aging Americans is there. Contrary to popular belief, the average person need not remain at the mercy of many of today's worst illnesses. We must instill a commitment to maximum wellness in all Americans by developing quality programs in all areas of physical activity. In addition, we must be proactive to draw all constituencies to our support.

Image of the Modern Physical Educator

Despite the many advances in physical education research and technology and improved skill levels of a talented group (athletes), the image of the modern physical educator as a professional is far from ideal. The public and often our peers within the school setting view physical educators as less academic and, therefore, less important than educators in other disciplines. The idea that some physical educators function mainly as playground supervisors, coaches, or baby-sitters persists and is encouraged by some whose behaviors warrant such criticism. Those professionals who do not reflect negative behaviors are often frustrated by criticism engendered by others. Even those professionals who are dedicated to their career should examine their behavior periodically to see what opportunities exist to integrate physical education more fully into a total school program.

The following questions are offered for reflection on your past experiences as a physical education student and for consideration as you develop your professional goals.

1. Did students enjoy their physical education experiences?
2. What percentage of students do you believe applied what they learned in class to their daily lives (i.e., sports, exercise programs, dance)?
3. Was your physical education teacher an example of physical fitness?

4. Are your parents regular exercise and sport participants?
5. Was your high school physical educator a recreation director or a teacher?
6. Did you feel that other teachers in your high school believed that physical education was important?
7. Are there facilities and programs in your community for exercise and sports participation?
8. Were any of your school or community programs (e.g., class tournaments, *Pop Warner*, Little League) structured to eliminate anyone from participating?
9. Does the medical community in your hometown advocate exercise and nutrition programs?
10. Are there any examples of business or industrial fitness programs in your community?
11. Can you remember any public relations programs for the support of school physical education or cooperative community-school health and fitness programs?
12. If you were to return to your high school and conduct your own poll, what comments about physical education classes would you expect?

Creating a positive image as a professional is important in establishing positive lines of communication with individuals and groups within our society who impact the status of physical education programs in our schools, businesses, hospitals, and communities. We need to remain committed to our ideals. However, the implementation of programs to achieve those ideals is dependent on what others around us think about us individually and collectively as a profession. Each of us must do our part to ensure that physical education regains status as an integral part of childhood education to foster the development of a healthy lifestyle throughout an individual's life span.

The challenge is clear: Physical education professionals must be more reflective about our mission to turn the tide of public dissatisfaction with our programs and meet the objectives for the nation for the twenty-first century.

Student Activities

1. Develop your personal definition of *physical education.*
2. Develop a statement that best describes your current perception of your proposed physical education career.

Quality instruction enhances a positive attitude toward living a physically active life.

3. Recall your high school days and imagine what physical education activities might be included in the curriculum in the year 2050. Be prepared to share the list with your class.
4. Discuss the pros and cons of the following statement: "Professionals must make a personal commitment. How can we be effective in promoting health and fitness if our bodies are not living testimonies of our commitment? What we are communicates more than what we say (Wilmore, 41–43)!"
5. Read your local paper for at least one week. Clip out the articles related to athletics, disease, and physical education. Is there more information on one of the above topics than the others? Why or why not?
6. When you meet other college students, do you introduce yourself as a physical education major? If not, why not?

Suggested Readings

Cooper, R. K. 1989. *Health and fitness excellence: the scientific action plan.* Boston: Houghton Mifflin Co.

Hoffman, H. A. 1987. Images of quality for elementary school physical education, *Journal of Physical Education, Recreation and Dance:* 36–42.

Massey, B. H., and T. G. Lohman. 1985. A fit America in the coming decade 1985–1995—introduction. *Journal of Physical Education, Recreation and Dance:* 24.

Pemberton, C. and P. J. McSwegin. 1989. Goal setting and motivation. *Journal of Physical Eduction, Recreation and Dance:* 39–42.

Word, C. 1987. Letters—change perception not name. *Journal of Physical Education, Recreation and Dance:* 15.

Ziegler, E. F. 1983. Sculpting the future—our challenge for the 80's. *Journal of Physical Education, Recreation and Dance:* 14–15.

References

Brown, S. P., D. E. Cundiff, and W. R. Thompson. 1989. Implications for fitness programming—the geriatric population. *Journal of Physical Education, Recreation and Dance:* 18–23.

Griffey, D. C. 1987. Trouble for sure, a crisis—perhaps: secondary school physical education today. *Journal of Physical Education, Recreation and Dance:* 20–21.

Gurin, J. and G. T. Harris. 1987. Taking charge—the happy health-confidents. *American Health*, March: 53–57.

Hayes, A., 1984. Youth physical fitness hearings: an interim report from the President's council on physical fitness and sports. *Journal of Physical Education, Recreation and Dance*, Nov/Dec: 29–40.

Pemberton, C. and P. J. McSwegin. 1989. Goal setting and motivation. *Journal of Physical Education, Recreation and Dance:* 39–42.

Pitman, M. I. 1987. Health and fitness. *Time* 2/23: 43.

Ross, J. G. and G. G. Gilbert. 1985. The national children and youth fitness study—a summary of findings. *Journal of Physical Education, Recreation and Dance*, Jan: 3–8.

Seefeldt, V., ed. 1987. Selling the potential rather than the record. *Journal of Physical Education, Recreation and Dance*, Sept: 42–43.

Taylor, J.L., and E.N. Chiogioji, 1987. Implications of educational reform on high school programs. *Journal of Physical Education, Recreation and Dance*, Feb: 22.

U.S. National Committee on Health, 1987. Promoting health/preventing disease: objectives for the nation. Government Printing Office, Washington, D.C.

U.S. National Committee on Excellence in Education, 1983. A nation at risk: the imperative for educational reform. U.S. Department of Education, Government Printing Office, Washington, D.C.

Wilmore, J. H., 1982. Objectives for the nation—physical fitness and exercise. *Journal of Physical Education and Recreation,* Mar: 41–43.

2. Contemporary Physical Education

Chapter Outline

Impact of Educational Reform
Principles of Physical Education
Aims of Physical Education
Objectives of Physical Education
Physical Education Model
Future Directions
Professional Experience as a Learning Tool
Student Activities
Suggested Readings
References

Objectives

Chapter 2 is designed to enable you to:

- Appreciate the leadership role of the physical educator.
- Understand the need for educational reform in physical education.
- Realize that quality programs are based on a solid foundation of principles, aims, and objectives.

W HERE is physical education as a profession? The answers vary depending on the respondents and their environments and experiences. Most adults have experienced physical education as part of their schooling. The quality of their experiences in their youth and the relevancy of those experiences to their current lifestyles are the major factors influencing people's perceptions and support of contemporary programs in schools and related settings. Unfortunately, on the whole, physical education has not met its goals for the nation in terms of physical fitness or lifetime skills for the pursuit of an active leisure lifestyle. Despite the influence of the medical community and the media, parental apathy toward physical education in the schools is abundant. Parents' personal lifestyles indicate an increase in sedentary habits (see Chapter 1).

Where is the profession's leadership? The importance of strong, positive, and effective role modeling by teachers and exercise specialists is well known and widely accepted for successful instruction in physical education (Whitley, Sage, and Butcher, 1988). "Rather than accepting the primary responsibility for the low level of cardiorespiratory fitness of our school children, many physical education instructors have assigned the major blame for this condition on such societal factors as television, lack of physical work and improper diet" (Whitley, Sage, and Butcher, 1988). As a result of their leadership positions, physical educators in schools, health clubs, and community settings automatically become role models for the clients they serve. Whether or not we are aware of or accept the responsibility, our potential influence on the physical and social behavior of others cannot be denied. We may continue to argue that the fundamental problem remains with our society's traditionally negative view of physical education and our resistance to change in educational organizations.

Change will not come easily, but as the price of parental apathy and professional arrogance deepens the demise of American physical education, the need for reform will become all too obvious (Wilcox, 1987). Quality training in physical education theory and practice to meet these demands has never been more available. Training professionals who can adapt to changes in society's needs and who are committed to quality programs is critical to the survival of the profession. Our educational requirements for physical educators are constantly changing, but current needs include knowledge of the following:

- Early childhood programming and day-care needs
- Elementary physical education

- Secondary physical education
- Adult fitness
- Adult leisure activities
- Cardiac and sports injury rehabilitation
- Hotel and resort management and fitness programs
- Sports marketing and information
- Sports business
- Athletics
- Special populations
- Gerontology
- Research

Impact of Educational Reform

The call for educational reform in the mid-eighties focusing on the concept of effective schools provided an impetus for the self-study of physical education. Taylor (1986) suggested that reform in physical education is noticeably absent in the discussions about school reform and is not subject to debate in the numerous professional organizations to which physical educators belong. In addition, the current philosophical debates widened the gap between the educational reform movement and physical education.

Why have we failed to educate taxpayers and educational leaders that physical education is an important course of study? The failure to be accepted is caused by not instructing students in physical education or not getting them physically educated. Researchers have clearly shown that physical education instruction in the average kindergarten through grade 12 class is used as a teaching method for less than 6 percent of the allotted class time and that students are physically active less than one-third of the time (Kneer, 1987). School principals, teachers of other school subjects, and students all have varied reactions to the subject of physical education. The most compelling observation is made by Lawson (1987), who states that it is easy to locate different versions of gym class in the same school based on the quality of the "gym teachers," instruction, and class organization.

The majority of physical education teachers are hard-working and dedicated individuals. Many of these people work long hours in less than ideal settings for modest salaries. However, they voice consistent concerns about large heterogeneous classes and about the inadequacy of facilities and equipment. Attempting to educate children physically under these conditions is difficult and supports the low levels of activity and instruction as revealed in research studies. Many of our professionals feel ignored by their principals and peers. The public does not perceive a need for employing physical educators when teacher aides can be assigned with fewer budgetary demands.

It should not surprise anyone examining the current status of teaching that some teachers are choosing one of four popular alternatives: (1) Forget about class and concentrate on coaching; (2) pursue the credentials that are appropriate for a principalship; (3) abandon teaching for another career; and (4) start what amounts to an early retirement program while remaining on the job. As a newcomer to the profession, you have probably encountered a variety of professionals who fit the descriptors of this statement. There are many issues and problems confronting the profession, but there are also many exciting challenges for those committed to physical education reform.

Oliver (1988), in his concern for reform in our profession, suggests that we seriously consider these findings:

1. Twenty-five percent of the nation's fifth graders will not make it through high school (35 percent and 25 percent, respectively, for Hispanic and black youth).
2. One in four children entering school over the next couple of years will come from families living in poverty.
3. Fourteen percent of the children entering school will have teenaged mothers.
4. One in five children live with a mother, with no father present (56 percent of these are poor).
5. Forty percent of the children entering school will live in a broken home by the age of 18.
6. California, New Mexico, Texas, Louisiana, Alabama, Georgia, and Mississippi have approximately 35-percent minority student enrollment. Arizona, Florida, New York, North Carolina, Virginia, and others have 25- to 34-percent minority enrollment.
7. The number of black teachers in the nation's schools is decreasing at such an alarming rate that some researchers have suggested that within 10 years the number of blacks in the nation's teaching force will be less than 1 percent!

It is this type of data and the declining health and fitness of America's school-aged population that suggest we are dealing with a different child-family structure and a different school system than we dealt with 10 years ago. If reform in education, particularly in physical education, is to achieve the level of excellence expected, these simple demographic facts must be considered.

The potential contribution that parents, even single parents, might make to the physical education of their children has been neglected. Schools in the United States have chosen not to involve those citizens who are later called on to vote on educational bond and political issues. It is somewhat ironic to note that athletics, which are accused of being a detriment to physical education, clearly show the rewards of parental support. Wilcox (1987) states that while one might hope to find a positive image and optimum degree of involvement in physical education, the most likely scenario appears to be one of parental cynicism and apathy toward reform. We need to embark on an aggressive campaign to disseminate clear and accurate information through carefully planned parent education activities to facilitate attitude change and support.

The complexity of the schooling process in our country and the vast differences between and among local and state reform efforts make it difficult to summarize what has been done. The five major areas of concern and their proposed changes can be seen in Table 2.1. This movement provides us with a unique opportunity to improve the quality of our programs by getting involved and demonstrating leadership. Very few curriculum areas have as much versatility as physical education in terms of expanding the scope of learning activities. The nation's interest in competitive sports, fitness, and health promotion enhances our potential.

The most effective physical education programs that bring about dramatic change in their target populations are those that have been developed on a solid foundation of goals and objectives. The discussion of objectives that follows shows how several professionals view physical education. You need to understand these perspectives in order to develop your own personal beliefs about your objectives in physical education. The objectives you develop should respond to the multifaceted needs of society and allow you to adapt to future changes. The major emphasis of physical education may continue to be in the schools, but alternative settings are becoming increasingly important. Your objectives should be based on sound principles. The foundation of principles is needed to provide a permanent base for the development, implementation, and assessment of aims and objectives.

Principles of Physical Education

Physical education is based on scientific facts. These facts lead to basic beliefs that serve as general principles to the professional. Basic beliefs that have been verified by science are the foundation of any discipline or profession, and a physical educator's principles are no exception. *Principles* are truths or general concepts based on facts that are used as guides

Table 2.1 Educational Reform

AREA	PROPOSED CHANGES
Teachers	Teacher compensation
	Career ladders
	Merit pay
	Competency testing
	Performance evaluation
	Alternative credentialing
	Special incentives to teach
Students	Academic preparation for college
	Basic skills
	Broaden curriculum
	Competency tests
	Graduation requirements
	Homework emphasis
	Increased graduation requirements
	Increased time
	Policies on athletics and extracurricular activities
School organization	Extend school year or day
	Reduce teaching loads
	Role and training of administration
	Community and industry partnerships
	Alternative schools
Funding	Expanded state financial support
	Scholarship programs
	Financial incentives for school personnel
	Increased taxes
	Incentive programs for educational quality
Teacher education, higher education	Recruitment and admission to teacher education programs
	Scholarships for teachers
	Content of programs
	Faculty involvement in public schools
	Redesign of teacher education programs
	Establish links with public schools
	Greater involvement of liberal arts
	Alternative credential programs
	Minority recruitment

for taking action and making choices. By the very nature of physical education, the professional physical educator is called on in many situations to make decisions and take action. Our general principles form the basis for our daily decisions and actions.

Principles are more permanent than aims or objectives. Principles based on scientific facts are more universally acceptable than philosophically based principles and ideas about short-term or long-term goals. Principles based on faith and personal experience are more tentative and changeable.

Physical education draws its principles from at least three fields— the physical sciences, humanities, and social sciences. Among the physical sciences are biology, anatomy, physiology, and biomechanics. In the field of humanities, history and philosophy are pertinent to physical education. Psychology, sociology, and anthropology are social sciences with which physical education is concerned. These three general fields are interrelated, and as a result of their interaction, scientific and philosophical concepts are revealed and principles are developed. When developed by experts in a field these principles often become the core of the discipline. All professionals within the discipline are obliged to put the principles into action as part of their professional work. Some professionals are more overt than others in stating their principles. The Hippocratic oath in the medical field is a strong statement of the principles of the professional behavior expected of doctors. Every professional will face career crises of varying magnitudes that will challenge his or her dedication to principles. Each situation will warrant careful analysis so that principles are rarely, if ever, compromised. Physical education teachers who simply "roll out a different ball" each season in their classes are clearly ignoring the principles of their profession. Health clubs who hire untrained exercise leaders to develop and assist in the implementation of personal exercise programs for clients are not truly concerned about the quality of their business. Their unprofessional conduct does tremendous injustice to those professionals who truly care as well as to students and clients.

Listed below are some potential principles of physical education:

- Equal opportunities in all competitive sports should be provided for both boys and girls.
- Exercise improves our body's efficiency.
- Physical education contributes to the development of the whole child.
- The aging process can be slowed down by a carefully designed wellness program.

Aims of Physical Education

An *aim* is defined as a general philosophical statement of purpose derived from principles. It serves as a guide to developing and selecting general and specific objectives that are more readily attainable. The aim of any discipline is first in the hierarchy of purposes that describe specific subject areas in the total school curriculum. In 1918, the Educational Policies Commission restated the purposes of education in American democracy. Of the seven cardinal principles of education that the Commission described, physical education contributed directly to three: health, worthy use of leisure time, and ethical character. More recently (U.S. Bureau of Education, 1981), the central purposes of education were reduced to four: self-realization, civic responsibility, economic efficiency, and improved human relations. It is important for children of all ages to understand their strengths and weaknesses in order to develop a positive and accurate self-image. The physical education curriculum also provides a variety of socially oriented activities. Children learn how to interact in group situations in a socially acceptable manner. Playing with others in structured activities and coping with stress factors introduced into the action helps prepare children for the dynamic world in which they live (U.S. Bureau of Education. Bulletin No. 35. Washington, D.C.: U.S. Government Printing Office, 1981: 5–10).

Through the years, professional physical educators have expressed the aim of physical education in a variety of ways, but interpretations of their statements show how similar their aims are.

Competitive games help children cope with stress and strive for success.

Hetherington (1922)   Physical education is that phase of education concerned first with the organization and leadership of children in big-muscle activities, to gain the development and adjustment inherent in the activities according to social standards, and second with the control of health and growth conditions naturally associated with the leadership of the activities, so that the educational process may go on with or without handicaps.

LaPorte (1955)   The ultimate aim of physical education may well be to so develop and educate the individual through the medium of wholesome and interesting physical activities that he or she will realize his or her maximum capacities, both physically and mentally, and will learn to use those powers intelligently and cooperatively as a good citizen even under violent emotional stress.

Williams (1964)   Physical education should aim to provide skilled leadership and adequate facilities that will afford an opportunity for the individual or group to act in situations that are physically wholesome, mentally stimulating and satisfying, and socially sound.

Bookwalter (1969)   An aim of physical education is the optimum development, integration, and physical, mental, and social adjustment of the individual through guided instruction and participation in selected total-body sports and in rhythmic and gymnastic activities conducted according to social and hygienic standards.

Nixon and Jewett (1980)   The aim of organized physical education programs is the creation of an environment that stimulates selected movement experiences, resulting in desirable responses that contribute to the optimum development of the individual's potentialities in all phases of life.

Nixon (1980) and others   Organized physical education should aim to make the maximum contribution to the optimum development of the individual's potentials in all phases of life by placing one in an environment as favorable as possible and promoting muscular and related responses or activities that will best contribute to the purpose.

Graham (1987)   Physical education is obviously more than motor skill acquisition. However, learning to move efficiently and effectively is a major aim of physical education programs.

We propose that the primary aim of physical education is to facilitate optimum growth and development of each individual through sequential, guided instruction and participation in sports and games, rhythms, and individual physical activities presented in a balanced manner, leading toward the fulfillment of those physical, emotional and social needs acceptable in today's society.

Objectives of Physical Education

Professionals in the field have not agreed completely on the objectives of physical education, which accounts for the range of objectives found in the literature, making it difficult for physical educators to develop a united front in times of adversity and reform. Current professionals recognize that many objectives of the past are not as relevant in today's world and are contributing factors to misperceptions about our legitimacy as a discipline and a profession.

An *objective* might well be defined as a statement of purpose that is more immediate and specific in nature than an aim but is in harmony with the established aim and more likely to be attained. In an effort to justify the profession, too many objectives attempting to reach all people have been developed. Excessive numbers of objectives weaken the position of physical education. Objectives should be realistic, supported by research and experience, but responsive to a changing world.

Barrow (1977) reminds us that the diversity of opinion regarding the objectives of physical education is the result of the perspective of the practitioner (teacher, coach) and the scientists (exercise physiologists, biomechanists). For an objective to be meaningful, it should represent the application of a tested scientific thought. Our discipline is enlarging not only our knowledge base but also the distance between the researcher and the practitioner. Understanding recent research can help keep our program objectives current and relevant. Many objectives have been presented within the discipline; some are truly unique to physical education, whereas others are shared with other disciplines.

Barrow (1977) suggests four major groups of objectives derived from previous writings in the literature:

1. Organic development, including fitness
2. Psychomotor domain, including sports skills
3. Cognitive domain, including knowledge and understanding associated with sports, exercise, and dance
4. Affective domain, including emotional and social development

The value of an objective depends on its implementation. Physical education is a vast expanse of knowledge and activities. Physical educators must become more selective in developing their objectives and prioritize the objectives based not only on the values of the community but on our changing society. The ability to express objectives clearly and accurately will help others understand the discipline and relate to the more general aims of the program.

Parks (1980) presents an informative historical summary of core objectives. Her investigation of the professional literature published since 1930 reveals three primary schools of thought relative to the objectives of physical education:

1. Physical education as education through the physical
2. Physical education as education of the physical
3. Physical education as education for human movement

Supporters of the "education through the physical" philosophy support the contention that physical education is more than physical development of the body. The point of view that education of the mind may occur through the education of the body is a central component of this concept and helps justify the existence of physical education in the school curriculum.

Jay B. Nash and Jesse Feiring Williams, two prominent physical educators of the 1930s, believed in educating the whole child through the medium of physical activity. Physical education as "education for life" was Williams's core concept. Additional objectives have been suggested by other professionals committed to education through the physical. Some of these include social development, moral development, development of cooperation, enrichment of life, development of self-image, and development of sportsmanship. Although their perception of the direct outcomes of physical education programs varied, the concept of the whole person underlies this basic objective.

Charles McCloy, a pioneer in physical education, is credited with being the key supporter of the core physical education objective as "education of the physical." This point of view substantiates the adequate training and development of the body as the profession's reason for existence. Physical education was justified in the schools on the basis of its unique physical contribution to the education of the whole child. Early programs primarily stressed exercises for the development of the physical body. McCloy implies that many professionals in the field felt inferior to their intellectual peers. He challenges physical educators to return to the basic purposes of the field as stated in its name _physical education_. Although this viewpoint was short-lived early in the twentieth century, there are significant examples of physical fitness and disease prevention. Contemporary professionals are lending renewed credibility to and respect for the word _physical_ in the definition of the discipline.

Eleanor Metheny, a proponent of "education for human movement" as a major objective of physical education, defined this concept as follows:

> If we define the totally educated person as one who has fully developed his ability to utilize constructively all of his potential capacities as a person in relation to the world in which he lives, then we may define the physically educated person as one who has fully developed the ability to utilize constructively all of his potential capacities for movement as a way of expressing, exploring, developing, and interpreting himself and his relationship to the world he lives in.
>
> _(Parks, 1980, p. 31)._

A new objective of physical education has been formulated: the concept of movement education as a lifelong process. This concept emphasizes individualized programs of motor development in which participants become aware of their physical abilities and learn to use them effectively through problem-solving techniques. It is significant for physical education both within the educational framework and in alternative career paths. This approach contains parts of earlier theories and binds them together as a contemporary objective of physical education.

With the emphasis in the late 1980s on improving the fitness levels of Americans and with the development of a new health-related fitness test by the American Alliance for Health, Physical Education, Recreation, and Dance, one definitive goal of physical education programming is being emphasized: improving the physical fitness levels of school-aged youths in cardiorespiratory efficiency, flexibility, strength, and body density.

As we move into the next century, more scientific data will be available for professionals to continue to refine the objectives of physical education. Such objectives will enhance the quality of both school-based and alternative-site physical education experiences.

Physical Education Model

From the author's perspective, there are three general aspects of physical education: (1) physical development, (2) knowledge and understanding, and (3) attitude and appreciation. Table 2.2 is a model for a balanced approach to physical education. Each general objective has been divided into two subcategories that are listed as intermediate objectives of physical education.

Physical Development

The general objective of physical development can be divided into the intermediate objectives of general motor control and skill development. General motor control includes as a major objective physical efficiency (development of muscular strength and endurance, cardiorespiratory endurance, joint flexibility, and postural control). Another major objective of motor control is that of basic motor control. People need to develop balance, large-muscle coordination, small-muscle coordination, and eye-hand coordination. These basic motor controls enable the child to participate successfully in sports, games, dance, and aquatics. The development of a solid foundation of basic motor controls will permit the individual to learn more complex motor skill patterns essential to participating in more sophisticated activities throughout his or her leisure lifetime.

The intermediate objective of skill development can be subclassified into the specific objectives of basic motor skill patterns and basic play skills. The various modes of locomotion such as walking, jumping, hopping, skipping, crawling, climbing, rolling, and sliding should be developed. Adequate postural control for proper stature should also be learned.

People must be able not only to control their own personal movements but also to control objects in activities of throwing, catching, kicking, striking, pulling, pushing, stopping, and carrying. These skills enable people to participate successfully in basic play activities. Many children and adults often prefer to be spectators rather than participants in an

Table 2.2 Elementary Hierarchical Objective Chart

GENERAL AND INTERMEDIATE OBJECTIVES	COMPONENTS

Physical development
  General motor control
	Physical efficiency
	  Muscular strength and endurance
	  Cardiorespiratory endurance (stamina)
	  Flexibility (static and dynamic)
	  Efficient postural control
	
	Basic motor control
	  Balance (static and dynamic)
	  Large-muscle coordination (agility)
	  Small-muscle coordination (dexterity)
	  Eye-hand and eye-foot coordination
	  Rhythmic coordination
	
	Basic motor skill patterns
	  Locomotor patterns
	  Postural control
	  Object control

Skill development	Basic play and skill activities
	  Throwing
	  Catching
	  Kicking
	  Striking
	  Rhythmic
	  Aquatic

(cont.)

Table 2.2 (continued)

GENERAL AND INTERMEDIATE OBJECTIVES	COMPONENTS
Physical education knowledge and understanding Understanding the value of physical activity, games, and sports	Values of socialization Learns: why children play together how children play together when children play together where children play together Values in relation to growth and developmental process Understands how activity relates to: muscle girth and strength performance of various skills organic vigor Values of self-expression Learns to: develop spatial awareness explore the environment express feelings create through movement Values of tension reduction and relaxation Understanding muscular tension and relaxation Learns how to reduce muscular tension through physical activity Learns the values of rest and sleep
Understanding how to play games and sports	Rules, regulations, and terminology Knows: rules of various games and sports regulations of various games and sports terminology of various games and sports

(cont.)

GENERAL AND INTERMEDIATE OBJECTIVES	COMPONENTS
	Objectives, strategies, and self-analysis
	Knows: playing objectives of various games and sports
	playing strategies of various games and sports
	how to suggest ways to improve performance
	Adaptations, modifications, and innovations
	Knows how to: adapt games and sports according to player needs
	modify games and sports to playing conditions
	think up games and activities
	Conduct in group activities
	Ability to: cooperate and take turns
	win and lose gracefully
	follow and lead
	show allegiance to the team
	follow rules and regulations
	Consciousness of safety to others
	Respect for the differences in others
	Personal conduct
	Develops: emotional self-control
	honesty and integrity
	consciousness of safety to self
Attitude and appreciation	
Sportsmanship	

Table 2.2 Elementary Hierarchical Objective Chart

GENERAL AND INTERMEDIATE OBJECTIVES	COMPONENTS
	In participation
	Learns: enjoyment of physical activity
	playing with abandon
	enjoyment of striving for excellence
	about the importance of esprit de corps
	In leisure
	Learns to: relax by engaging in physical activities
	enjoy participating in out-of-school activities
	enjoy watching a variety of games and sports
	appreciate the excellence of high-level performance
	In history and culture
Appreciation	Learns: influence of sport on our heritage
	influence of sport throughout history
	cultural influence of sport today

activity owing to their failure to develop these basic skills and their current feelings of inadequacy and embarrassment.

Knowledge and Understanding

Understanding the value of physical activity, games, and sports, and knowing how to play games and sports are two more intermediate objectives of physical education. Understanding the values of physical activity can be further subdivided. The value of self-expression is often lost in our society where conformity is the norm. Through physical activity, students have the opportunity to explore the environment and learn to express their feelings through creative movement. The value of tension reduction and relaxation through physical activity is an important awareness for a world that is becoming not only more stressful but also more dependent on artificial and often harmful means of alleviating stress and inducing relaxation. The value of socialization whereby children and adults learn to participate successfully with people of different backgrounds is an important objective. If we can play together, we should be able to work together and increase the quality of life for everyone. The value of physical activity in relation to the growth and development process and continued vitality throughout life is another important objective.

Knowing how to play games and sports is divided into more specific categories including (1) rules, regulations, and terminology, (2) strategies and self-analysis, (3) adaptation, modification, and innovations, (4) attitude and appreciation, and (5) sportsmanship. A thorough knowledge of the rules of various activities and strategies for achieving the objectives of an activity is an important cognitive skill necessary to successful performance. To complete one's understanding of games and sports, players need to know how to adapt games to players' needs, to playing conditions, and to playing facilities.

Attitude and Appreciation

Children who learn to enjoy physical activity in a variety of properly supervised situations should grow up to become adults who participate in playful and active leisure activities. Program excellence plays an important role in developing positive attitudes toward the role of exercise and sports in one's life. The individual needs to appreciate his or her own capabilities and to enjoy striving for personal excellence in lieu of continually comparing oneself to the performance of others. As children we can learn to develop a healthy balance of free play, relaxation activities, and competitive activities. One should develop an appreciation of high-level athletic skill by observing others. In an era of increasing spectator violence, the development of a healthy attitude as a spectator is important. Added cultural appreciation of various sports throughout history and the appreciation of contemporary sport on the national and international level should be learned.

Sportsmanship is not inherent in physical education activities but must be planned for by the teacher, coach, or director. Emotional self-control, a sense of honesty and integrity, cooperation, learning to win and lose gracefully, and respect for others are important components of this objective.

Future Directions

Sports and exercise programs have reached unprecedented levels of popularity both for participants and observers. According to Lawson (1987), whereas the school was once the primary or exclusive organization offering opportunities for sport and exercise, it is now just one of many, and it may not be the most important one. At the same time that elementary physical education programs, staffed by physical education specialists, remain the exception rather than the rule, sports op-

Participating in sports and games that are guided by the physical educator can help children understand the value of physical activity while learning how to interact in group situations in a way that is socially acceptable.

portunities for young children have multiplied in the communities. Numerous physical activity programs exist, such as dance for pre- schoolers, aerobicize or jazzercise programs for people of all ages, com- munity swimming and tennis programs, and sports camps. Physical education is happening outside the school and it is happening before children and youth ever enter an organized physical education class.

There are many questions that need to be addressed by both current professionals and people, such as yourself, just entering the field. Lawson (1987) continues to probe our minds with the following examples:

1. Can physical education programs remain unchanged in the face of these ever-present and increasing opportunities for instruction and participation that are outside the school?
2. Given these opportunities, what is unique about physical education?
3. Why should a student who participates outside the school be required to participate in a school physical education class?
4. How can a physical education teacher tell a seventh grader that phys- ical education class will provide him or her with a lifetime sport at the very time that the 13-year-old has already completed 8 years of competitive tennis?

Oberle (1988) proposes that we physical educators need to define our existence so that we know what we are about and how to control our own destiny, for if we do not establish quality control, then others will do it for us. The Alliance for Health, Physical Education, Recreation, and Dance uses a well-known slogan—"You are either part of the prob- lem or you are a part of the solution"—in its Physical Education Public Information program.

Every profession has problems with apathy. In our profession, ineffec- tual people need to make a new commitment to the profession or make room for those who want to contribute positively. Debbie Walsh, as- sociate director of the educational issues department at the American Federation of Teachers, stated that "by 1992, we will need to replace half of 2.2 million teachers—the average teacher is now 46 years old" (Morris, 1988). Carnegie Forum's 1988 report, "A Nation Prepared: Teachers for the 21st Century," mobilized public opinion and spurred career improvements. Some states and school districts, including those of Rochester, Toledo, Memphis, and Houston, are leading the way to- ward raising teaching's professional status by offering career ladder plans by which salaries for "master teachers" can go as high as $70,000.

Opportunities for employment in the nineties and into the next cen- tury will be in the health-related and education fields. Health and fitness will continue to become more personalized. Entrepreneurship in exercise physiology is creating small businesses that provide personal fitness assessment and exercise prescription and monitoring on an individual basis at a small clinic, small health club, or mobile unit that travels to the homes of clients. An ever-increasing population of active people in their sixties and beyond is a challenge to the profession. Community recreation programs, hospitals, and religious organizations are developing health-related activities that extend into populations that do not have the means to participate in more costly membership clubs. Learning to adapt physically and emotionally to an increasingly more populated society requiring smaller personal living spaces may be the profession's greatest challenge in the very near future. Helping to implement the concept of positive wellness may well be your major focus in whichever professional career path you select.

Will physical educators seize the opportunities available to them? Will you, as an undergraduate, commit yourself to becoming a strong new professional leader? Together we can meet today's challenge and convert traditional programs into dynamic experiences based on sound principles and objectives that will provide the base for quality of life in the twenty-first century. Oberle (1988) is convinced that physical education professionals can accomplish all of this by hard work, rededication, and mastering the new technologies in a world of the future. We will:

- Use telecommunication networking to store and disseminate information.
- Develop research equipment that will replace manual manipulation and interpret findings through computer technology.
- Create programs that deal with high technology and space exploration.
- Increase the base knowledge of movement, exercise science, wellness, and human awareness.
- Propagate lifelong learning.
- Redesign teaching technologies.

Professional Experience as a Learning Tool

From this chapter you should have a basic understanding of the universality of basic principles, aims, and objectives that are based on scientific facts and tested philosophical beliefs. One must remember that professionals do modify these principles to meet personal needs and values that may conflict with the profession's more esteemed values. It is important as a physical education major that you begin to analyze your perceptions of principles as you experience a variety of physical activities including fitness, sports skills, and dance.

The more professional experiences in which you can become involved as a student, the stronger you will be as a career professional. Part-time coaching jobs, officiating jobs, camp counseling, teacher aiding, teaching at sports camps, working in sporting goods sales and health clubs, and other opportunities will increase your contact with active professionals. Such contacts will allow you to observe these individuals applying their principles in their careers. A variety of experiences with professionals in the field will afford you an opportunity to prioritize your aims of physical education and will contribute to your ability to develop, verbalize, uphold, and modify your understanding of the sound principles of physical education. One should not minimize the value of time committed to this aspect of professional development.

The ability to verbalize the professional principles in which you believe and, more importantly, practice will help you select the appropriate career path. Employers are interested in committed applicants who know who they are, what they are about, and where they would like to go. This is true of education, the health sciences, public agencies, and private businesses. The greater challenge, however, is to continue to grow professionally and remain open to modifying principles, aims, and objectives when scientific research has substantiated new evidence for change in the discipline. There is security in sticking with the old but adventure in taking the calculated risk with the new.

Student Activities

1. Interview physical educators in different or similar career roles. Ask them to state their principles of physical education and state one objective in which they apply that principle. Compare responses.
2. List your personal principles of life and physical education. Are they compatible? Which career path do your principles seem most to represent?
3. List a general principle, long-range aim, and several objectives for your life. Is there a core principle or set of objectives that you use as a basis for your daily decisions and actions? Discuss how this relates to your physical education career.

Suggested Readings

Barel, B., et al. 1985. Physical education shapes up. *The Physical Educator* Win: 194–195.

Bloom, A. 1987. *The closing of the American mind.* New York: Simon and Schuster.

Kneer, M. E. 1987. Where is the "education" in physical education? *Journal of Physical Education, Recreation and Dance* Sept: 70–72.

Maeroff, G. I. 1982. *Don't blame the kids — the trouble with America's public schools.* New York: McGraw-Hill.

Oberle, G. H. 1988. A future direction plan for our professionals. *Journal of Physical Education, Recreation and Dance* Jan: 76–77.

Oliver, B. 1988. Educational reform and physical education. *Journal of Physical Education, Recreation and Dance* Jan: 68–71.

Simons–Morton, B., et al. 1988. Children and fitness: a public health perspective, reaction to reactions. *Research Quarterly for Exercise and Sport* 59 (2): 177–179.

Whitley, J. D., J. N. Sage and M. Butcher. 1988. Cardiorespiratory fitness — role modeling by P.E. instructors. *Journal of Physical Education, Recreation and Dance* Sept: 81–86.

Wilcox, R. C. 1987. Promoting parents as partners in physical education. *The Physical Educator,* 19–23.

References

Annarino, A. A. 1977. Physical education objectives: traditional vs developmental. *Journal of Physical Education and Recreation* Oct: 22–23.

Barrow, H. M. 1977. *Man and movement.* Philadelphia: Lea & Febiger.

Bookwalter, K. W., and H. J. Vendersway. 1969. *Foundations and Principles of Physical Education.* Philadelphia: W. B. Saunders.

Gallup, A. M., and M. Elam. 1988. The 20th annual Gallup poll of the public's attitudes toward the public schools. *Phi Delta Kapper* Sept: 33–48.

Graham, G. 1987. Motor skill acquisition — an evential goal of physical education programs. *Journal of Physical Education, Recreation and Dance* Sept: 44–48.

Grant, G. et al. 1983. Today's children are different. *Educational Leadership* 40:4–9.

Hetherington, C. W. 1922. *The School Program In Physical Education.* New York: World Book.

Kneer, M. E. 1987. Trends — physical education. *Educational Leadership* Feb: 93–94.

Kozol, J. 1981. *On being a teacher.* New York: Continuum.

LaPorte, W. R. 1955. *The Physical Education Curriculum,* 6/e. Los Angeles: University of Southern California.

Lawson, H. A. 1987. Teaching the body knowledge. *Journal of Physical Education, Recreation and Dance* Sept: 70–72.

Morris, M. 1988. 25 hottest careers in 1988. *Working Women* July: 55–66.

Nixon, J. E., L. Flanagan, and F. S. Frederickson. 1964. *An Introduction to Physical Education,* 6/e. Philadelphia: W. B. Saunders.

Nixon, J. E., and A. E. Jewett. 1980. *An Introduction to Physical Education.* Philadelphia: Saunders College.

Postman, N. 1983. The disappearing child. *Educational Leadership.* 40:10–17.

Taylor, J. L., and E. N. Chiogioji. 1987. Implications of educational reform on high school programs. *Journal of Physical Education, Recreation and Dance* Feb: 22.

Williams, J. F. 1964. *The Principles of Physical Education.* Philadelphia: W. B. Saunders.

3. Exploring Your Potential

Chapter Outline

Lifestyle and Your Career
Personal Attributes
Alternative Pathways
The Planning Process
Student Activities
Suggested Readings

Objectives

Chapter 3 is designed to enable you to:

- Relate the importance of self-concept to exploring career paths.
- Appreciate the interrelationship between lifestyle preferences and one's career path.
- Begin to assess personal attributes as they relate to a career in physical education.
- Develop an appreciation for the career-planning process.

To bridge the gap between who you are and what you want to be and between where you are and where you would like to be, your attitude provides 90 percent of the result. The hope of success in a career hinges on your perception of your natural abilities and your desire to work as hard as necessary to develop them. The more you know about yourself and use this information in a positive manner to pursue career alternatives and get advice, the more career experiences will be possible. Learning about yourself and about career opportunities is directly related to the development of active listening skills. People often develop a mindset about what is right or possible for them in career planning and do not pay enough attention to what others have to offer. College advisers, former teachers or coaches, other professional people, and even parents may appear to talk *at* you, instead of sharing *with* you, but they may have valuable advice. Active listening is important to maintaining a healthy positive attitude and remaining open to explore a variety of alternatives while building on a core career concept.

Asking others how they perceive you and your strengths will help you understand yourself and where you are going. Very often the result of actively listening and interacting with others is a heightened sense of competence that enlarges your realm of career possibilities. Your attitude is vital to this process. Do not block communication channels and restrict your potential simply because throughout high school you developed a plan to be perhaps a physical education teacher at a community college without examining all the other possible routes that complement such a career plan.

Work has historically been considered a survival mode, the way to feed, clothe, and shelter an individual or family. The Puritan work ethic, which still operates in American society, is illustrated by those who advocate work over idleness or, in extreme cases, believe that leisure time is idle time. This concept of work is undergoing many changes as more people look to their careers for rewards greater than money, a shorter workweek, or moral responsibility. Work as an end in itself does not satisfy the needs of many individuals. People appear to desire an opportunity to make choices throughout their careers instead of feeling trapped in a given position or environment. Your educational background and personal experiences shape the number and kind of choices that will be available during your lifetime. Your personal history to this date has shaped the direction of your life in the workplace. What you are now is probably a result of how family, friends, and school experiences influenced your growth and development.

Leisure time does not have to be idle time. The professional physical educator helps others develop a variety of skills for a healthy, vigorous lifestyle.

People have traditionally entered college to prepare for a career that they imagine will last a lifetime with minimal changes. Society's rate of change and the influence of change on the individual is now resulting in several career moves during the average person's working years. No longer can the student focus unequivocally on a single career. We are subject to changes now that have never before been experienced. Technology, the availability of environmental resources, and the expanding world population are only a few of the countless influences on our lives and careers. People are living longer and healthier lives. Retirement from one profession to pursue another as a senior citizen is becoming more common. The desire to contribute is even drawing people out of retirement after several years of leisure.

As we discuss careers, our focus will be on how you can discover and design your own career path, one that leads somewhere desirable and lets you continue to grow professionally. Along the way career choices, smaller pathways that branch off to the side, will give you alternative routes to follow. Your decisions will contribute to the development of a personal career choice that is uniquely yours and never ending. Your career is a journey, not a destination.

Lifestyle and Your Career

Let us examine some lifestyle components that must be considered in planning your career path. What do you want out of life? The type of lifestyle that you plan on enjoying is an economically important factor. As an educator, you should not expect to reap major economic rewards. In 1988, a first-year teacher's salary averaged $16,595 before taxes, retirement benefits, and insurance. Does that salary meet your personal lifestyle expectations for home, family, and travel? If there is a major discrepancy between desired and actual projected salary, perhaps alternative careers in the realm of human movement should be examined, with business-related opportunities in mind. However, in working with children, the personal satisfaction of a job well done, for example, provides many rewards greater than monetary gain. In addition, summer vacation provides an opportunity for alternative personal growth and recreation and so adds an attracive dimension to a teaching career that is absent from most full-time positions.

A second very important factor is how you relate to people. Do you like people? Do you enjoy being with many people or only a few? Do you truly like children? If so, which age group do you prefer? Are you capable of and do you enjoy working with a multitude of skill levels or only the highly skilled? Do you enjoy helping others rehabilitate themselves? These questions may seem mundane, but it is amazing how many physical education majors complete their course work and enter student teaching or, in the case of adult fitness majors, accept internships only to find that they heartily dislike the experience. In most cases, such students have prepared for a one-track career and find themselves in a very frustrating position as graduating seniors.

Some people who end up as physical education teachers and coaches discover that their sole interest and reward is working with the highly skilled on varsity teams. Often their physical education classes suffer from the leader's lack of interest, enthusiasm, and planning, which is unfair to students. Such teachers might better have been counseled to enter related careers with an opportunity to coach the highly skilled in youth sports leagues, Amateur Athletic Union (AAU) sports, or higher education.

With the growing emphasis on adult fitness and health clubs in the United States, some physical education majors are being prepared to perform solely in those areas, only to discover they would rather work with young people. Unfortunately, if the student failed to obtain a teaching certificate as an undergraduate, he or she has a difficult choice to make between returning to school or staying in the current career path.

Another consideration is the level of accountability and stress that you can accommodate in a job. Does having six or seven 30-minute classes of thirty-five students each that meet only once weekly in an elementary school frustrate you to the point of destroying your enthusiasm and robbing you of the belief that you can make a difference? How important is it that you feel your peers respect what you are doing or truly care about your program? Physical educators often feel alienated from teachers of more academic subjects. Administrators often display behaviors that imply they do not care what goes on in the gym. Despite these attitudes, will you be able to maintain a positive and enthusiastic outlook on the job? How does the apathy of many high school students affect you? Can you handle the fate of your job depending on your most recent win and loss record? Do you prefer the challenge of attaining a sales quota in a line of sporting goods or health club memberships? Can you handle the stress of working with the disabled, in which patience is a premium and progress is slow?

The quality of our lives is becoming increasingly dependent on our ability to handle stress. Stress affects each person differently. Everyone possesses different coping mechanisms which determine the amount of stress that either motivates one to achieve or is a detriment to one's physical and emotional health. The world of sports, for example, has built into it high levels of stress in many occupations. It is important to determine the amount of competition and degree of stress that meets your needs. You may thrive on the accountability required of the varsity coach at a large institution, on encouraging people to play for the fun of it in a recreation setting, or on working with the handicapped.

What about working hours? Are you an 8-to-3 or 9-5 person? Do you prefer a rigid schedule or flexible hours that change as in sales, therapy, or health clubs? Are you a night person or a morning person? Do you mind working long overtime hours for minimal pay as is common in supervising recreational facilities and coaching? Is having weekends off important to your lifestyle? Would you like a career that involves a lot of travel, as is found in professional sports and work in sports media? It is important to examine your working preferences in relation to career and economic growth. Are you willing to work odd hours to acquire the needed experience for upward mobility?

Working hours directly influence your family plans and leisure lifestyle. Long working hours and travel could take you away from family, friends, and recreation. Some good career paths involve incorporating weekends into your workweek and would pose some adjustments to family lifestyle. Yet there are advantages to a work schedule that allows you to pursue leisure experiences during the average person's workday.

Women are still faced with greater lifestyle pressure than men, despite the achievements of job equity. A traveling woman who is away from home on sales trips or extended competitive tours may find it more difficult to marry, raise a family, and maintain her career choice than the woman who pursues a more traditional teaching and coaching position. These factors should be carefully considered in designing your career path.

Figure 3.1 gives you the chance to determine what your current lifestyle preferences are. In Chapter 16, you will have the opportunity to assess your personal strengths and correlate them with this description of your lifestyle preferences to help complete the design of your career path.

Figure 3.1 Lifestyle Preference Chart

Carefully review the following lifestyle criteria to determine what you now prefer:

Location
Where in the United States would you most like to work?
East ____   West ____   North ____   South ____   Midwest ____
Northeast ____   Northwest ____   Southeast ____   Southwest ____
Alaska ____   Hawaii ____

Community Size
In what kind of community would you most enjoy working?
Rural ____   Suburban ____   Large urban ____   Small urban ____

Family Life
What type of family life do you prefer?
None ____   Spouse or companion ____   1 child ____   2 children ____
3 or more children ____

Travel
How much travel do you want in your job?
None ____   Local trips ____
1 week per month out of town ____
2 or more weeks per month out of town ____

Interpersonal Contact
What age group would you most like to work with?
Early childhood ____   Elementary ____   Secondary ____   Adult ____
Later life ____

Figure 3.1 (continued)

In what kind of situation do you hope to encounter people?
Individually ____   Small group (5–9) ____   Medium group (10–29) ____
Large group (30 or more) ____

Work Schedule
What days do you want to work?
Monday–Friday ____   Weekends ____   Every day ____
Varied workdays ____
What hours do you want to work?
7–3:30 P.M. ____   8–3:30 P.M. ____   8–5:30 P.M. ____   9–5 P.M. ____
Varied hours ____

Stress
How much stress can you handle daily?
Few decisions; minimal responsibility ____
Some decisions; some responsibility ____
Many decisions; numerous responsibilities ____

Salary
What salary do you think you will need to support your desired lifestyle?
$15,000 or less ____ $15,000–$25,000 ____ $25,000–$50,000 ____
$50,000–$75,000 ____ $75,000 or more ____

Fringe Benefits
What fringe benefits do you need your work to provide?
None ____   Health insurance, retirement plan ____
Health insurance, dental coverage, retirement plan ____
Health insurance, dental coverage, retirement plan, travel allowance ____

Vacation
How much vacation time do you want each year?
1 week ____   2 weeks ____   3 weeks ____   1 month ____
2 months ____   3 months ____

After you determine your preferences on the chart above, summarize in
twenty-five words or less what your lifestyle would now be like if you
achieved them.

Personal Attributes

Another factor you must consider is your personal skills and interests,
not only now as you design your career path but along the way as alternatives arise. It is important to realize that simply because you are
skilled or talented in one phase of physical education and sport, your
skills are not necessarily transferable to another career. For example,
a good teacher does not necessarily make a good administrator. A

Your personal interest in sport activities can guide you in the selection of a career such as professional golf shop management.

talented athlete does not always make a good coach. A good coach may not have the skills needed to be the athletic director over a sports program that deals with diverse sports and varied personalities of other coaches. A physical fitness promoter may not have the sensitivity and patience to work with those who are not committed to daily exercise. It is very important to examine your personal skills and interests in physical education and to decide objectively where your talents can best be used. For example, your personal competitiveness may be so strong that you expect too much of others and put too much pressure on younger competitors in a public school situation; AAU-level competition or private clubs may be a better arena in which you could exercise your commitment and enthusiasm. Conversely, if you are more interested in participation for the exercise and fun of it, club sports could be the place for you. Neither option is better than the other. You are simply attempting to optimize all your strengths and to minimize your weaknesses by selecting a career path that will be successful and rewarding.

Assessing yourself should begin now and include both self-analysis and active listening. You may possess skills and talents that can be applied to a career path in a manner that you have never considered. One of the most difficult tasks is to project where you would like to be several years from now on your career path.

Alternative Pathways

As you follow your career path, you will discover several alternatives that branch off to the sides. Your decision to accept or reject these alternatives will ultimately influence your career choice. Throughout your career you will be confronted by some choices that will involve greater personal and financial risks than others, and such risks can help make a career exciting.

What keeps you motivated and challenged while preparing and pursuing your career are unique personal factors that you should identify and monitor to avoid boredom, low productivity, and an unsatisfying growth rate. The personal factors that influence your attitude toward a career are illustrated in Figure 3.2. For a teacher, changing grade levels or changing schools may help maintain the challenge and excitement of the gymnasium. For a coach, becoming a professional umpire can add a refreshing dimension to your favorite sport. For a college physical educator, a new research project can be professionally stimulating. An athletic trainer may decide to pursue physical therapy in a hospital setting for a change of pace. As you design your career path, it is important to build in some skills and training that can be used in later years as career options.

Whether a pathway will be open to you depends on what you bring with you, what education, experiences, interests, skills, and abilities you have. Identifying these qualities probably sounds difficult now, but exposure to the foundations of physical education in the next several chapters will help you begin the self-assessment process and start planning your career path.

The Planning Process

Planning for your future is an important ongoing process that is vital to creating opportunities for yourself. It is important to plan and not rely on luck to set appropriate goals that enable you to make progress. The evidence indicates that those who set daily goals are more apt to achieve their desired objectives. Goals should be renewable, dynamic, and realistic. Once goals are attained, they lose their appeal and should be updated.

Figure 3.2 Aspects of Career Development that Influence Attitude

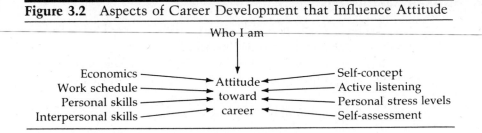

Goals should not be viewed as endings. This concept is often difficult to accept as we tend to set up goals as "the accomplishment" or "the desired end." The quest for the storybook happy ending is ultimately frustrating. It is important to set goals that are stepping-stones and not obstacles to further career development.

It is also important to set short-range and long-range goals and to include alternatives. What goals have you set for yourself today? Minigoals can be helpful. For example, one minigoal should be to explore as many careers as possible during this course. Another short-range goal might be to participate in three very different career experiences during the academic year, perhaps including sports writing for the student newspaper, working as a team manager, or coaching a youth sport. A long-range goal could be to graduate with a double major in physical education and business administration.

Even if what interests you now seems vague, start building your assets by gaining professional experiences and completing relevant course work so that choices will be available to you when you are ready to make a decision. Reading is an invaluable tool. Expand your reading to include both professional and nonprofessional materials. Ideas for career possibilities surface from a variety of sometimes surprising resources. It is important to consider even studying subjects that you do not think you will like: You may discover that you do like the subject after all and that the skills taught may be valuable someday. For example, a bilingual physical education professional is more likely to find opportunity for rewarding sport careers both nationally and internationally.

The foundations of physical education are important to the design of your career path, but do not be afraid to diversify. Declaring a double major, for example, may require you to go the second mile, but you may reap untold rewards by increasing your career choices in such related areas as communication, business, and science. Above all, remember that career planning is an ongoing challenge that you can enjoy.

Student Activities

1. List twenty adjectives that describe your current career choice. What other careers could these words describe?
2. Write a 300-word essay describing your lifestyle goals. Remember to include economics, family, travel, recreation, and daily work patterns.
3. Interview a classmate and actively listen to his or her perception of future career goals. List several other career alternatives in sports and physical education for your classmate to consider.
4. Practice goal setting. Begin with relevant short-term goals and keep track of your progress in a journal. When your deadline for the realization of your goal arrives, assess the effectiveness of your timeline by the steps achieved and any modifications you needed to make.

Suggested Readings

1979. *Alternative professional preparation in physical education.* Washington, DC: National Association for Sport and Physical Education, AAHPERD.

Bolles, R. N. 1982. *What color is your parachute?* rev. ed. Berkeley, CA: Ten Speed Press.

Campbell, D. 1974. *If you don't know where you're going, you'll probably end up somewhere else.* Allen, TX: Argus Communications.

American Alliance for Health, Physical Education, Recreation and Dance. Careers in physical education and sport. Brochure of AAHPERD Publications Sales, 1900 Association Drive, Reston, VA 22091.

Sage, G.H. 1980. Sociology of physical educator/coaches personal attributes controversy. *Research Quarterly for Exercise and Sport* 51:110–121.

PART TWO

Foundations of Physical Education

4. The Essence of Philosophy

Chapter Outline

Defining Philosophy
Traditional Philosophies
Educational Philosophy
Philosophical Perspectives in Physical Education
Sport Philosophy
Student Activities
Suggested Readings
References

Objectives

Chapter 4 is designed to enable you to:

- Appreciate the importance of philosophy in physical education and sport.
- Understand the traditional philosophies of life.
- Relate educational philosophy to physical education.

As we examine our contemporary society, change is everywhere. In order for our profession to survive, there must be a firm philosophy of physical education to support our programs. Physical educators need to ask themselves some important questions: What do Americans value regarding their health and fitness? What do Americans value as leisure activities? What can we do to maintain our relevancy as a profession in meeting society's needs?

Before we can intelligently address these questions, it is critical that we understand the nature of philosophy and the terminology associated with it. Philosophical inquiry attempts to help people evaluate their relationships to their world, their universe. Philosophy is an organized study of human thought and behavior that seeks to give us a knowledge base for dealing with the basic problems of life, to explain life and guide our behavior. Our values form the foundation of our philosophy of life. Our professional and personal behaviors are inextricably woven around our value system.

Bucher (1983) summarizes some of the concerns of philosophers in the following questions:

- What is the role of human beings on this earth?
- What is the origin and nature of the universe?
- What constitutes good and evil, right and wrong?
- What constitutes truth?
- Is there a God?
- Do human beings have souls?
- What is the function of education in society?
- What relationship exists between mind and matter?

Defining Philosophy

Philosophy generally refers to the organized study of human thought and conduct. Its very nature insists on the identification and development of laws and principles that underlie all human knowledge and perceptions of reality. Philosophy becomes a tool that we use to explain the nature of our universe and our attitudes to direct and control human life. Zeigler (1977) defines *philosophy* as "that branch of learning (or that science) which investigates, evaluates, and integrates knowledge of reality as best as possible into one or more systems embodying all available wisdom about the universe."

According to Burke, ". . . the content of philosophy is a rational, consistent, systematic set of pervasive general principles which explain existence, perceived facts, and causations. It provides a framework, a rational theory, a logical method, a penetrating explanation, and a uni-

Contemplating:
What you are now
is where you were
when!

versal guide for the problems of human existence" (Nixon and Jewett, 1980).

For many people, _philosophy_ is best defined as the "Who am I?" question. However, the study of philosophical inquiry is much more sophisticated and often overlooked as a serious course of study. There are generally five major branches of philosophy: (1) metaphysics, the nature of reality; (2) epistemology, the nature of knowledge; (3) logic, the relationships between ideas; (4) axiology (ethics), the nature and sources of values; and (5) aesthetics, the nature of beauty. Within these branches are a variety of subdivisions that may be more familiar to you. These include, but are not limited to, idealism, realism, humanism, pragmatism, and existentialism.

Traditional Philosophies

The three traditional philosophical systems are idealism, realism, and pragmatism. Existentialism is a more modern approach to reality. These philosophies have affected educational philosophies for many centuries.

However, most contemporary physical education philosophies fit closely into one traditional philosophy. Sport and physical education have undergone dramatic changes throughout the years. Yet one must remember that current philosophies have been influenced by the past. It is important to present an overview of these philosophies so that, as an emerging professional, you can reflect on the importance of your philosophy as it affects your professional development.

Idealism extends beyond the time of the Greeks, but Plato was its recognized leader. The idealist believes that reality depends on the mind for existence, that one can only know mental states. Reality is spiritual rather than physical. Idealists believe that ideas and intuitive thought are reality, not the physical self or physical environment. The physical world, therefore, exists only in the mind. The universe can be known only through the cognitive processes. The perfect ideas are truth, goodness, and beauty. René Descartes is one of the most famous idealist philosophers. His oft-cited quote, "I think, therefore I am," is the basis of idealist philosophy. As applied to physical education, idealism would lead the contemporary coach to believe that all coaches value the wellbeing of the athlete more than winning. Knowledge of performance such as the correct angle of impact for a tennis serve is another function of idealism.

Realism was also inherited from the Greeks. Aristotle was its first champion, followed over the centuries by Thomas Aquinas, John Locke, and Rousseau. There are many facets of realism, but basically realists view reality in terms of the physical world and scientific facts. Trust is knowledge obtained through experimentation. Realism deals with nature—its rules, laws, and order: the scientific method. Contemporary realism in adult fitness is illustrated by increasing one's cardiovascular capacity so that one can be more productive in society.

Pragmatism views ultimate reality as something that is experienced. A pragmatist sees no absolutes. Reality cannot be stated because it evolves from experiences that are constantly changing. Therefore, reality is dynamic. Truth is that which is discovered by experience. Truth is relative and changes according to the situation. Truth must be functional and provide answers. The pragmatic coach would modify coaching strategies to accommodate player abilities and would perceive the coaching role as a strong motivator.

Existentialism is a much newer philosophy. Sartre was a strong existialist in the twentieth century. This philosophy embraces reality as something that lies within our experience as human beings. People have a freedom of choice for their moral selves. The individual is more important than society. The reality is there before meaning can be attached to it. Truth is something arrived at by the individual from within, through personal experience. Truth is personal because it is one's choice. The burden of responsibility for one's choices must be understood and accepted. Existentialism in teaching would provide a variety of activities to meet individual needs and interests.

These four philosophies—idealism, realism, pragmatism, and existentialism—have affected educational philosophy in major ways. There have been many different educational philosophies, but we will briefly describe only a few. In future courses, you may have the opportunity to discuss these in greater depth and relate them to your own professional philosophy.

Educational Philosophy

Educational philosophy must examine the fundamental assumptions about the nature of humankind and society that are the foundations of educational practice. The educational philosopher must raise basic questions and articulate them clearly so that educational change can proceed with a well-developed plan. The report on education in 1983 "A Nation At Risk" raised many such questions:

- What is the status of learning in our schools?
- What should be taught?
- How do we assess student mastery?
- What are effective teaching models?
- How is the curriculum related to the needs of the student?
- How does discipline management affect learning?
- What attributes make a competent teacher?
- How do we assess teaching effectiveness?
- What responsibility does the school have for social development?
- What is the role of parents in the educational process?

Traditional Philosophies Applied to Education

Educational philosophy is a specialized area of philosophy that investigates the aims and practices of educational organizations. Traditionally, educational philosophers set out to describe major schools of thought and then related them to a concept for improvement in practices or tried to clarify educational problems in terms of the basic branches of general philosophy. The effects of the traditional philosophies on education can be summarized as follows.

Idealism as applied to education focuses on the development of the personality as the primary aim of education. The mind and spirit are critical to character education and the search for the good life. The development of the physical is held in high esteem if it contributes to the development of some of the enduring virtues such as self-discipline and courage. The student is perceived as a creative being that is guided by the teacher.

In the philosophy of realism, providing the student with the type of training necessary to meet successfully the realities of life is foremost. Realistic education depends on the basic sciences and proved facts. Historically, realism was seen in physical education when physicians were some of the first practicing physical educators.

The primary aim of pragmatic education is to provide opportunities to experience life problem-solving in order to develop a better member of society. It is education based on doing. Experiential education, often in wilderness settings, and movement education are pragmatic in nature.

In existentialism, the focus is on the student and his or her self-actualizing independent self. The student must make choices and accept the responsibility of these choices. The curriculum is centered on the individual, and the teacher acts as stimulator.

Progressive Education

John Dewey, the great philosopher of education, developed the concept of progressive education, in which basically pragmatism is applied to education. Life adjustment education, the concept of the child as a whole, and the child-centered approach were developed by Dewey. Progressivism rebelled against the traditional education with its strict discipline and dull methodology. Dewey advocated problem-solving skills, cooperation instead of competition, and recognition of individual differences. Progressivism stressed the child experimenting and gaining experience through democratic processes.

This philosophy has been criticized because its emphasis was on the student and not the subject matter, an attitude often considered too permissive. Progressivism did influence curriculum development at all levels, including higher education. The basic courses were replaced by novel courses in all subject areas. The launch of the Russian Sputnik led to the decline of progressivism. The fear of falling behind the Russians again placed more emphasis on mathematics, science, physical education, and prudent discipline. However, human rights legislation in the 1980s renewed the emphasis on progressivism.

New Approaches

In recent years, philosophical analyses have been made of important educational problems to clarify the search for more effective strategies for administering educational practices. Contemporary education may be operating from an essentialist perspective. Essentialism's main concept is that there is a core of knowledge, skills, and values essential for all students to learn. This is often referred to as the "back to basics" movement. Both reading and mathematics test scores at all levels in the United States have dropped dramatically during recent decades. With all the educational technology available today, teachers, administrators, and the public are searching for answers. Funding for the social sciences, art, music, and physical education has in some cases decreased because of the high cost of technology.

Table 4.1 cites ten educators who made major philosophical contributions to education based on their schools of thought. The table should assist you in understanding the important role one's philosophy of life plays in educational practices.

Table 4.1 Educational Philosophers and Their Contributions

TEN EDUCATORS	SCHOOLS	CONTRIBUTIONS
Bagley, W. C.	Essentialist	Knowledge may be background as well as instrument. Concerned with permanent values. Defended Essentialist Manifesto. Criticized seven vicious trends influential in radio education.
Bode, B. H.	Pragmatist	Function of school is cultivating habit of relying on foresight of consequences rather than on authority. Progressive education must *not* rely on immediate interests. Wanted stated university to promote scientific subjects. Cooperative intelligence is function of higher learning.
Breed, F. S.	Realist	New Realism uses only experience and explains knowledge in terms of scientific data. Content is concern of administrator. Education must adapt men and women to their environment.
Counts, G. S.	Pragmatist	Educators should not wait for all the facts before acting on a social problem; teachers should grasp for power. In "Dare the Schools Build a New Social Order?" proposed a frame of reference: (1) affirm values deeply rooted in America's past, and (2) recognize the coming industrial society.

Table 4.1 (continued)

TEN EDUCATORS	SCHOOLS	CONTRIBUTIONS
Dewey, John	Pragmatist	Life is a relationship between the individual and his or her society. Experiences in school should be educative, with indirect teacher guidance and pupil purpose. Teachers should have a part in school administration.
Hutchins, Robert	Idealist	Believes in pursuit of knowledge for its own sake. Resents professionalism. Leave experiences to other influences. Wants a book-centered college with formal discipline. Tried his idea at St. John's College.
Judd, C. H.	Realist	Regards school subjects as institutions of society to which a child must adjust. Conservative. Does not think school is proper organ for social reconstruction. Scientific educators need ideal conditions.
Kilpatrick, William	Pragmatist	Popularized Dewey. Criticized meaningless drill. Seventh grade should reflect organization of sixth. Pupils should work on mutual problems three-quarters of time, remaining on special interests. Part of time to be spent with home room teacher. Wants teachers to participate in policy making. School should (1) engage in socially useful activities and (2) study live social issues. Sees trend toward cooperative activities.
Morrison, H. C.	Realist	Unit teaching: exploration, presentation, assimilation, organization, and recitation. Centered in courses of study and texts. Pupil adjusts to his or her environment by adaptations to nature, humankind, and social institutions. Called *mastery teaching*. Individual must adjust himself or herself to the environment.
Thorndike, E. L.	Realist	Made objective studies of adult in-

TEN EDUCATORS	SCHOOLS	CONTRIBUTIONS
		terests and learning abilities. Found adults learn best at 25 years of age and only fall off 1% each year until 45. Showed differences between individuals is greater than between age groups. Motivation factor strong.

Philosophical Perspectives in Physical Education

You are unique. You are the culmination of generations of experiences and beliefs. Your family tree, if analyzed, can provide you with tremendous insights about your race, your religion, your ancestors, and the historical events that affected your ancestors throughout the centuries. All of this historical information accounts for much of who you are today.

Intertwined with your biological makeup and historical events is the development of your current philosophy of life, education, and physical education. The values and beliefs that you have inherited have evolved through the centuries. Your immediate family background, physical environment, and social relationships have also exerted an overwhelming influence on your current philosophical perceptions and behavior patterns. Your decision to become a physical education major and to select this career path was based on your historical and philosophical past. The following list is only a sample of the factors from your personal history that have contributed to your decision to become a physical educator:

Your parents' philosophy about and participation in sport
Family health and fitness values and practices
Family leisure patterns
Effects of sex roles on sport participation
Your grandparents' participation and values
Cultural influences
Socioeconomic influences
Peer relationships
Inherited physiological and emotional traits
Religious and spiritual influences

As you begin to analyze the history and philosophy of physical education and sport as it relates to your professional goals, the following

Artemis, goddess of the hunt, epitomized female strength and skill as shown in this Greek sculpture (about 400 B.C.). Except as mythological figures in art and legend, women historically have been relegated to only passive roles in sports events, primarily as spectators, and when allowed to participate, were until recently given only limited opportunities.

list of questions may help you become an historical and philosophical critic, a qualified contemporary physical educator:

What is the current status of physical education in America?

Do American adult health and leisure patterns reflect quality school programs?

What is your former high school's philosophy of the relationship between physical education and athletics?

Does the physical education curriculum in today's schools reflect the three major categories of sports, dance, and gymnastic exercises?

What is your personal philosophy regarding competition? Of winning and losing? Who influenced the development of your philosophy?

What is your philosophy of sport participation and sport leadership for both sexes? Can you identify how you developed this philosophy?

What is your philosophy of physical fitness? Does your behavior reflect
   your philosophy?
What is your favorite sport? Can you trace its historical development
   including changes in rules, equipment, and dress?

Philosophy is a critical part of the process of developing physical education programs. Scientific findings provide quantitative descriptions
of what is, whereas philosophy suggests what should be. Philosophy in-
terprets what is known (facts) through the various stages of development until we arrive at the actual policies and procedures that will be
used in administering a physical education program. Philosophical thinking processes are used to develop goals and objectives.

   The highest level of discussion involves asking questions relative to
what is really true, valuable, right, or real. Our value systems are very
personal, and such discussions can be enlightening professionally if we
can contain the emotions that arise from challenges to our value systems. Currently, because the field of physical education is in a state
of flux, such discussions may not produce clear-cut solutions to problems but may steer a course toward problem resolution.

   Some philosophical questions for physical educators might be:

Is coeducational physical education improving the quality of instruction for boys and girls?
To ensure the success of every student, should we eliminate competitive experiences from the curriculum?
Should I, as the exercise specialist, insist on increasing an adult's cardiovascular condition if he or she has set his or her own goal and is
   satisfied at that level?
How much involvement do I really want from parents of my swim team
   members?
In our community's youth ice hockey program, how much aggressive
   behavior should be allowed?
What is relevant to geriatric patients in a nursing home regarding their
   physical fitness and maximizing their potential?

There are many such situations in the profession that merit philosophical discussion. A philosophy of physical education is not simply a statement; it guides action. Philosophy helps the professional to determine
the aim, objectives, and principles and goals of programs in all physical
activity settings. A sound philosophy is the foundation for improving
our practices and setting our future direction. A well-defined philosophy of physical education enables us to communicate the worth of our
profession to the public more effectively.

In everything, including physical education, philosophy is the source of all goals, objectives, criteria, and standards. The physical educator's philosophy serves as the foundation for one's behavior because philosophy determines life values and behavior, teaching style, and coaching values. Whatever career path in physical education and sport that an individual follows, personal philosophy dictates a system of values responsible for selecting alternatives. As a physical educator, you can profit from a study of the classical philosophies as they relate to education, physical education, and sport according to truth, value, and reality.

Physical educators have philosophized about their field of study both verbally and in writing for a very long time. The educational and personal philosophies held by a teacher or coach and the instructional methods and curriculum designs used are inseparable. All educators must realize that how they teach and coach depends on their basic philosophical beliefs and values. Although our physical education philosophy is seldom written out, it operates in every interaction we have with students and athletes. The process of periodically taking time to review and describe one's professional value systems will better enable professionals to interact with young people consistently and effectively. This will enhance the fulfillment of the best experience possible for each student or athlete.

As a physical education major, you may enroll in a course to study in detail the history and philosophy of physical education and sport.

Sport Philosophy

As the concept of physical education as a discipline developed in the early 1960s, interest in the scholarly study of sport grew. The attempt to define and explain sport began to absorb more scholars' attention during the early 1970s as they considered the meanings of such critical terms as *play, games, sport,* and *athletics.* The major early questions were: How is *sport* defined? What is its significance in culture? What is the sport experience?

Harold Vander Zwaag and Thomas Sheehan (1978) suggested that the sport experience has three basic characteristics: (1) It is an emotional experience for both participant and spectator, (2) it is intensely personal, and (3) the experience depends on the situation. Basically, the sport experience cannot be prescribed or structured. No two people will react to the same thing in the same way or draw the same lesson from it. Although it is meaningful, it is not any more meaningful than the other parts of one's life.

The sport philosopher attempts to define and clarify sport and the sport experience to determine the significance of sport in our lives. The philosophical study of sport has its own methodology, which you may wish to explore in greater depth.

Harper (1978) suggests the following three reasons for the study of sport philosophy: First, we can learn what we really know about sport, including play, games, exercise, and athletics. Our culture has many beliefs, but which beliefs are really proved? Second, serious thinking about sport can provide answers that may be useful in planning what we will try to do in sport for the future of sport. Third, our knowledge and understanding of sport are minimal. We need a deeper understanding of sport to learn more about humanity. From these three major reasons for studying sport philosophy come several major contemporary issues, which may be familiar to you (Freeman, 1982):

1. What is the nature of sport? What is and what is not sport?
2. How do people really understand, approach, and use sport?
3. What is the relationship among the mind, body, and soul?
4. What is a "meaningful" or "peak" sport experience?
5. What is the relationship between sport and physical education?
6. When does a sport's phenomenon have the quality to be considered a work of art?
7. Are values taught in sport settings? Are they inherent in sport or in games?
8. How does one define *fair play* and *sportsmanship?*
9. How do we conceptualize the amateur athlete versus professionalism, especially during Olympic years?
10. What is the value of international competition?

Sport philosophy is a relatively new focus of study, and the questions to be answered are pertinent today though the issues have existed throughout sport history. The scholarly study of these issues may provide us with critical information that enhances the quality of the sport experience in the next century.

Student Activities

1. Describe your
   a. philosophy of life.
   b. philosophy of education.
   c. philosophy of physical education.
   d. philosophy of sport.

2. Abstract an article from either the *Journal of Philosophy of Sport* or *Quest*. Discuss the content of the article in relation to your philosophies.

3. Write a 300-word essay either to support or to negate the following statement: "The physical educator does a disservice to his field to use Plato's historical dualistic conception of mind and body as justification for today's physical education program" (Nixon and Jewett, 1980).

Suggested Readings

Davis, E. C. 1961. *The philosophic process in physical education.* Philadelphia: Lea & Febiger, p. 26.

Freeman, W. H. 1982. *Physical education and sport in a changing society,* 2nd ed. Minneapolis: Burgess Publishing Company.

Gerber, E. W., and W. J. Morgan. 1978. *Sport and the body: a philosophical symposium,* 2nd ed. Philadelphia: Lea & Febiger.

Harper, W. 1978. The philosophical perspective. In R. S. Revenes, ed. *Foundations of physical education: a scientific approach.* Boston: Houghton Mifflin.

Vander Zwaag, H. J., and T. J. Sheehan. 1978. *Introduction to sport studies: from the classroom to the ball park.* Dubuque, IA: William C. Brown.

References

Bucher, C. A. 1983. *Foundations of physical education and sport.* St. Louis: Mosby.

Dewey, J. 1930. *The quest for certainty.* London: George Allen Junior, Ltd.

Nixon, J. E., and A. E. Jewett. *An introduction to physical education.* Philadelphia: Saunders College Press, pp. 68–73.

Ziegler, E. F. 1977. *Physical Education and Sport Philosophy,* Englewood Cliffs, N.J.: Prentice-Hall, Inc.

United States National Commission on Excellence in Education. 1983. A nation at risk: the imperative for educational reform: a report to the nation and the secretary of education, United States Department of Education, Washington, D.C.: Supt. Documents, U.S. G.P.O. Distributor.

5. Historical Time Capsule

Chapter Outline

Early Civilizations of the Ancient World
Physical Education in Ancient Greece
Roman Physical Education
Physical Education in the Middle Ages
The Renaissance
European Influence on Physical Education in America
Developing Physical Education in the United States
Physical Education in the United States in the Twentieth Century
Student Activities
Suggested Readings
References

Objectives

Chapter 5 is designed to enable you to:

- Identify the main difference between Greek and Roman physical education.
- Explain why asceticism and scholasticism impeded the progress of physical education.
- Explain why the European gymnastic systems were not fully adopted by physical educators in the United States.
- Identify some outstanding leaders in physical education.
- Draw implications from the profession's history to guide one's physical education career.
- Project future professional developments based on contemporary issues and trends.

As long as humankind has existed, education has had a major impact on its survival. We can gain insight into our struggle to survive and trace the role of education as societies evolved through the study of peoples who lived before there were written records. From earliest history, the way humankind was viewed and how various cultures exercised mind and body has had tremendous impact on society as a whole.

The analysis of historical developments in physical education and sport enhances our understanding of societal factors that are currently affecting the status of physical education and laying the foundation for the public's conception of the profession in the twenty-first century.

Early Civilizations of the Ancient World

During prehistoric times, the world underwent long periods of major climatic changes. The harshness of these primitive environments made survival the major focus of daily life. The basic aim of education during this era was individual and group survival. Instinct motivated adults to teach male youths good hunting and fighting skills so they could feed their people and provide protection from other forces. There was also a strong belief in many gods.

Little is known about the games of prehistoric times, although some artifacts that have been discovered are similar to present-day toys. From observations of some contemporary less advanced cultures, such as the African Bushmen, we can assume that the children of early civilizations obtained much of their education through imitation of such skills as archery, spear and rock throwing, and stalking animals. Survival skills included running, jumping, and swimming, while wrestling was the major fighting skill.

Play and dance activities had a major role in the lives of primitive people. Dance was used as a means of communication with nature and forces that could not be explained. Nearly every ceremonial occasion had an appropriate dance which was handed down in detail from one generation to another.

As societies grew more advanced and life became easier, recreational activities developed. The earlier survival skills evolved into gamelike activities for both children and adults. As games developed, ball activities became popular. Despite geographical differences, recreational games around the world were similar because they continued to serve as training activities for the youth.

Egyptian Physical Education

Egypt was the site of one of the first cultures to emerge from barbarism. Situated in the Nile valley, the ancient Fertile Crescent provided soil and water for farming. The Egyptians are generally considered the predecessors of Western civilization. Their culture dates back thousands of years but reached its zenith in approximately 1500 B.C. when the Egyptians controlled most of the Middle East. These people were very advanced for their times. The Egyptians made advances in science, farming, irrigation, building, and household items. Some of their accomplishments, such as pyramid building and embalming, remain a mystery. They also developed a primitive form of paper writing, the 12-month calendar, mathematical concepts, and the arts. Egyptian culture was founded on religious values, and life after death was an important facet of their belief system. Their society was one of the first to elevate women to a status nearly equal to that of men.

Most of the education in early Egypt was aimed at professional training, and so little emphasis was placed on physical education. The peaceful Egyptians were more interested in the recreational and religious use of physical activity. Therefore games and sports were very popular; swimming was especially important for their life was based on the river.

Gymnastic activities, ball games, and dance were also popular. Wrestling was well developed among warriors as conditioning and among professionals for entertainment. Archaeological digs have discovered all types of play equipment for young children, such as dolls, tops, hoops, balls, and marbles.

Chinese Physical Education

According to historians, Chinese civilization predates Christianity by approximately 2,500 years. Although it had almost no effect on the development of Western civilization, it remained stable well into modern times, making it one of the longest-lasting of history's civilizations.

The aim of education in Chinese civilization was to maintain stability of the state and the family by training each person for his or her prescribed duties in the feudal system. The educational process, which was mainly for the upper classes, became formal and book-oriented with a system of rigorous examinations. This left no time for physical activities.

In many societies, the defense needs of the nation promoted physical education, but this was not true of the Chinese. Their natural geographical barriers, such as the Himalaya mountains and the Gobi Desert, provided protection. The Great Wall was erected to protect those borders not sheltered by a natural barrier. Nonetheless, some sports were developed for Chinese warriors, such as wrestling and charioteering. Archery and horsemanship were also practiced. Boxing was developed after the period of Buddhism in approximately A.D. 527, from which evolved a series of movements and forms that stressed self-discipline in life.

Football is one of China's oldest sports. The football began as a round hair-filled ball made of eight pointed strips of leather, but by the fifth century the inflated ball was introduced. The game was probably performed more for the amusement than the training of soldiers and remained popular for centuries. At about the time of the T'ang Dynasty (A.D. 618 to 907), a game evolved with two goalposts. Later, a game using only one goalpost in the form of an open arch became popular. More than seventy types of kicks could be made in a Chinese football game.

Polo probably came to China by way of Persia and Tibet in approximately A.D. 700. This was played primarily by noblemen. The Chinese were also fond of many types of gambling, including cockfighting and dice. Hunting, fishing, swimming, and flying kites were other popular activities. Kite flying and kite fighting were highly developed skills around A.D. 1070. Organized hunts using dogs and hawks were practiced as early as 100 B.C. Kung fu, a system of light exercises, was developed to prevent disease, which the Chinese believed could result from being physically inactive. Dancing, although used primarily for ceremonies, was also popular in its recreational forms.

Physical Education in India

Although India was not a major contributor to the development of Western civilization, it is an important ancient culture. The primary religion and the foundation of India's social system was Hinduism. The caste system within the social framework became very rigid and placed severe limits on the development of India's culture. People could not move out of their caste and so life was unchanging.

Education was based on training for one's caste with the aim of being virtuous. Emphasis was placed on one's future life through reincarnation. There was little interest in physical education because exercise of the body was not a major concern of Hinduism. However, personal cleanliness and health were means of achieving spiritual well-being. Cities that existed 5,000 years ago had closed drainage systems, and homes had bathrooms. Religious exercises were part of early worship. Modern yoga, although somewhat different in exercise format, can be traced back to India in approximately 200 B.C. Dancing was widely practiced and closely associated with the religion. Most games were discouraged as they did not meet the needs of the Hindu lifestyle. However, children had some toys, and adults enjoyed various types of gambling and wrestling.

Physical Education in Ancient Greece

Greece is considered the birthplace of Western culture. It was the first European land to become civilized due to its geographical location as a peninsula jutting toward Asia Minor. Additionally, the environment proved excellent for the development of an agrarian economy. The sea provided a pathway to the cultures of other peoples, and the climate allowed the Greeks to enjoy a vigorous outdoor life.

Greece was not a united nation but an assortment of small governmental units known as city-states. Of them, Athens and Sparta are usually studied as the two distinct and contrasting city-states of the Hellenic culture. Greek society was based on class stratification. Citizenship came with birth and education. Only the citizens were free to participate in government, own land, and become educated.

Serving the state was the devotion of every Greek citizen. In city-states that encouraged education, the Greeks made remarkable contributions in sculpture, poetry, architecture, music, oratory, history, science, mathematics, drama, philosophy, and gymnastics. The names of Homer, Socrates, Plato, and Aristotle should be familiar as some of the world's earliest and greatest thinkers. Greek society was very progressive, but its character changed with each of the following generations.

Homeric Greeks

The earliest record of the Homeric Greeks' more primitive lifestyle is preserved by Homer in *The Iliad* and *The Odyssey*. Homeric Greeks lived a rustic life cultivating fields and shepherding their flocks. Religion was very important to Greek life. It provided the base for much of their education and arts. They worshiped many gods, but their gods were idealized humanity and were not considered all-powerful. This directly affected the Greeks' educational goal of individual excellence, which might be achieved through the emulation of their gods.

Physical education was undertaken to develop the physical fitness necessary for a soldier. The qualities stressed were strength, endurance, agility, and bravery. Body massiveness was not important. However, it was in body symmetry that the Greeks surpassed other cultures; the beauty of the body was adored.

The Iliad and *The Odyssey* help us picture the role of athletic sports. Chariot racing, boxing, upright wrestling, foot racing, and javelin and discus throwing were the most common activities. Dancing was another important activity for Greek citizens.

Spartan Greeks

The Spartans were a totalitarian society. Their entire life was concerned with military objectives. The Spartan constitution designed an educational system that would ensure a constant supply of manpower to maintain and protect the state. Instilled in youths was the desire to be obedient soldiers, capable commanders, and conscientious citizens. While boys were drilled as soldiers, girls were being physically conditioned to bear strong children. Mothers were not allowed to express maternal affection. Everything was for the state. As a result of their excessive preoccupation with militaristic goals, intellectual and aesthetic growth ceased. Every precaution was taken to avoid anything that might weaken the Spartan state.

As would be expected in such a society, physical education had only one purpose—training for war. The education of the child was the responsibility of the state. Children went through a variety of state-controlled experiences from age 7 to 20. At age 7, young boys left their homes to live in barracks for training. At 20, young men began actual warfare. As military men, they continued to live in the barracks until they were 30, at which time they were permitted to marry. Men remained active in the military until the age of 50. Spartans were taught never to admit defeat. The education of Spartan women was similar. Girls were divided into classes and participated in the same exercises as the boys, but they had separate training grounds and continued to live at home. They continued their program until they were nearly 20 years old, when they generally married and stayed in the home.

The Olympic Games provided opportunities for the Spartan youth to exhibit their skills. Of the first eighty-one victories recorded in the Olympics, forty-six were won by the Spartans.

Whereas the Spartans were trained for war, they were not equipped to survive peaceful times. Their unbalanced approach to education led to their eventual conquest by the Romans.

Early Athenians

Athens contrasted to Sparta in several ways. The Athenian state had begun as an oligarchy, but it evolved into a democratic society oriented toward the individual rather than the state. Still, despite the claim of

Competitive sports have played a major role in society even in ancient times.

democratic process, 95 percent of Athenians were slaves, leaving only 5 percent free to participate in government. It is also important to note that the Athenian concept of democracy basically did not allow women to be educated.

In Athens the first system of education that we think of as modern was developed. Physical educators especially value it for its emphasis on physical education. It was the first educational system to be concerned with the all-around development of an individual. "A sound mind in a sound body" is a familiar quotation that expresses the balance in their educational system. The ideal characteristics of the Athenian citizen included aesthetic sensibilities, knowledge, physical skills, and a strong sense of ethics. The physical skills included educational gymnastics, track and field activities, classical dance, and ability to participate in the events of the Olympic Games.

Since the Greeks were concerned with artistic standards, much greater emphasis was placed on the form of a physical performance than on the establishment of records of strength, speed, or endurance. Physical education had to be a perfectly balanced program that completely harmonized with other aspects of education. There was also more emphasis on the formation of character than on the development of strength and athletic prowess.

The *gymnasium* was the term for the training school for older men. It was large, to accommodate running and throwing activities, and was built outside the city. A smaller facility, the *pasestra* or wrestling school, was located within the city. The physical exercise teacher was called a *paidotribe* and was similar to today's physical educator. Coaches were called *gymnastes* and were often retired champions. The basic aim of the educational process at the gymnasium was not the development of the physical body for its own sake. Rather, it was the development of the best qualities of the individual through physical activity. As a result of this balance, physical education was better integrated into the educational process than in any other culture.

Later Athenians

Athens had become the commercial cosmopolitan capital of an empire. With increased leisure time among its citizens and contact with other cultures, the city underwent a great cultural revolution. The Golden Age of Athens provided the state with the growth of democracy, unity, and an abundance of scholars. The forms of inquiry that developed caused people to question tradition, which led to extreme individualism. Socrates, Plato, and Aristotle recognized the problems this created but also realized that it was impossible to return to the old social processes. Therefore, they developed new educational concepts combining the needs of the individual with the interests of society. During this time, schools became more concerned with developing the intellectual component of the individual, almost to the exclusion of the physical component.

Professionalism emphasizing specialization by paid athletes replaced the earlier Athenian ideal of all-around excellence for service to the state in times of both war and peace. Coaches (gymnastes) were in great demand for aspiring professional athletes. These coaches determined in what sport a person would be most successful and then designed training programs for that individual. As time passed, active participants in gymnastic and athletic activities waned. Professionalism took its toll, and people now preferred to be spectators rather than participants. The baths became recreational centers. Many of the old sports, such as wrestling, became exhibitions of brute strength rather than a harmony of grace and skill. Professional athletes trained year-round for the Olympic Games, but their careers were short-lived. Such athletes had no other education on which to fall back in pursuit of new career options; they had devoted themselves entirely to physical training.

Plato, Aristotle, and Hippocrates were critical of the changes. However, the Athenians did not listen and continued to move farther away from their ideals. The long Peloponnesian War severely weakened the Athenians, and they were eventually conquered by the Macedonians and then the Romans.

Olympic Games

The Olympic games were the greatest Greek festival, celebrated in honor of Zeus, the Greeks' chief god. The festival lasted 5 days in late August and was held every fourth year (hence the term *olympiad*). The first recorded games took place in 776 B.C. in Western Greece. A month-long peace every 4 years was declared around the time of the games. No women were allowed to view or compete in the Olympic Games, but eventually there were separate competitions for women. Historical records indicate that a festival of Hera was held every 4 years at the Olympic Stadium at a time separate from the Olympic Games.

Originally, the games were held on a field beside the statue of Zeus, at whose base the footraces began. The "stade" race was the only event in the early games. As the games evolved, there were many races of varying lengths, but the shortest was the most important. Other events were added, including the discus throw, the javelin throw, the long jump, several styles of wrestling, boxing, the rough pankration, chariot and horse racing, and the pentathlon. The prize for an Olympic victory was a wreath or crown of olive leaves. The victorious athletes were treated as heroes when they returned home.

When professional athletes in the late Athenian period began to compete, the Olympic Games fell into disrepute. The professionalism became even more obvious after the Romans conquered the Greeks. In A.D. 394, the emperor of the Byzantines abolished the games, in part because the emperor was a Christian and considered the games to be pagan events as they were held to honor the Greek gods.

Roman Physical Education

The Roman Empire has left an eternal imprint on civilization, especially in terms of efficient government, large conquests, precise laws, and large-scale organizations. It is difficult to generalize about the Romans because their total society, its rise and fall, lasted for nearly 1,300 years. Several different eras over these years brought severe changes to the Roman way of life.

It has been said that Rome was not built in a day. Likewise, it did not decline in a day. The eventual decline of the empire was attributed to the consequences of the wealth and grandeur accumulated through the Romans' many conquests. While they admired the Greeks for their classical culture, the Romans never developed the Greek philosophy of the all-around development of the individual.

For the Romans, physical development was a practical matter based on military motive. The Greek ideals of beauty and harmony of movement were considered frivolous. In the early days of the empire, Roman education was designed to train youths to be citizen-soldiers who would serve the state, conduct their businesses and farms, and revere their gods and parents. The Romans had the first athletic trainers as we know them. By the third century B.C. the common people were enjoying the highest degree of political and economic freedom.

The Roman curriculum was designed to develop strength of body, courage in battle, agility in arms, and obedience to command. In becoming the ruler of the ancient world, Rome acquired tremendous wealth and prestige. This opulence was to contribute to the fall of the empire. The common people lost their political and economic rights. To satisfy the populace, the professional athlete was created, and gladiator combats and chariot racing were provided as entertainment. These contests were characteristically very brutal, violent, and bloody as compared to the fair play and skilled performance so respected by the Greeks. (There are critics of life in the United States who maintain that our tremendous enthusiasm for professional sports and the violence and aggression within them is similar to that of the spectators of Roman times. These critics suggest that we need to reevaluate sports in America to avoid the pitfalls of the Roman era.) During the latter part of the empire's reign, the Romans' attitude toward physical development became more positive. Some of the components of Greek education were incorporated into their programs.

A major facet of Roman life was the *thermae,* the public bath. The baths served a societal function for Romans similar to that of the gymnasium for Greeks. In the United States, golf clubs, tennis clubs, and health spas serve similar functions today. The city of Rome lacked space for physical activity and recreation (which is a common problem for American cities). Therefore, most Romans participated in sports and games only as spectators.

The Roman Empire declined, and finally fell to barbarians from northern Europe, primarily because of the internal moral and physical decay of its people. The empire's vastness changed its way of life dramatically, and sensual pleasure created moral and biological decay.

Physical Education in the Middle Ages

The period known as the Middle Ages is often misperceived, as illustrated by the sobriquet, the Dark Ages. Basically, the Middle Ages comprised a transition period between the reign of a large and powerful civilization, the Roman Empire, and the Renaissance, during which nations acquired stability.

The fall of the Roman Empire in the fourth century A.D. was the beginning of the medieval period. The invasions of the Teutonic barbarians brought about the lowest level in literature and learning known to history. The outdoor life of the nomadic invaders contributed to strong and physically fit bodies. Their lifestyle helped to develop a robust society for future generations. The Middle Ages lasted approximately 1,000 years. Following the downfall of Rome, feudalism developed as a way of life. Groups of peasant families gathered together with noblemen to form social units. The noblemen would provide a place to live and protection for the peasants in return for the peasants' labor and goods. Scholasticism, which focused on facts as the most es-

The longevity of a medieval community often depended on the physical prowess of its defenders.

sential items in one's education, had a major influence on the history of physical education. Developing one's intellectual capacities was emphasized while the physical was deemed unimportant and unnecessary.

The Catholic church in the late Middle Ages continued to exert much control over the peoples of Europe. The exact view of the church regarding physical education is not clear. However, the traditional view is that the church was opposed to physical education for three specific reasons (Freeman, 1982):

1. The church was disturbed by what it considered the debased character of the Roman sports and games.
2. It closely associated the Roman games with pagan religions and was intolerant of other faiths.
3. A growing concept of the evil character of the body was developing in the church. Body and soul were viewed as two separate entities.

Along with the growth of Christianity, asceticism thrived. Asceticism supported the belief that this life should be spent in preparation for the next world. Physical education was deemed foolish because it was designed to improve the body, which was evil. Ascetics preached separation of the mind and body and believed that neither entity had a bearing on the other. In A.D. 394, the Christian emperor Theodosius abolished the Olympic Games. The practice of subordinating the evil body to the pure spirit as truth spread: People were encouraged to torture their physical bodies to purify their spirits. Such practices led to poor health. Although the church's narrow view of humankind regarding the denial of the body's needs existed throughout the Middle Ages, the church remained the foundation of education. The monasteries preserved much of the learning and played a major role in education.

Feudalism consisted of only two vocations for the young noble man: He could become a clergyman or a knight. The early knight's training and behavior were very militaristic. As time passed, the influence of the church gave rise to the morals and codes associated with chivalry. The young knights were well trained in horsemanship, warfare, social graces, and customs appropriate to their nobility. Physical education existed only for the noble youth in the form of military training. Centuries passed, and the age of chivalry reached its peak under the direction of the church. The Crusades were the finest cause a knight could defend. The feudal aristocracy became very well developed and shunned all undesirable types of sport and conduct promoted by the Romans. (The motion-picture industry has glorified the lifestyle of the feudal aristocracy; "Camelot" is a prime example. However, feudal castles and court life were not as pleasant as portrayed in films.)

The Renaissance

The Renaissance was a period between the fourteenth and seventeenth centuries. During the Middle Ages, many advances in learning were accomplished. In the Renaissance, education flourished. Renaissance culture placed less supremacy on the church and God and more emphasis on the individual's relationship to others. This new philosophy was called *humanism*. During the Renaissance, science was introduced and universities were established. The Reformation created less reliance on the authority of the church. Another influential social class evolved—the middle class, led by the merchants.

Europe was making the transition to modern times. The feudal system gave way to the more powerful monarchies. Governments were gradually being centralized. The birth of nationalism (English, French, and German) completely changed the complexion of European affairs.

During the Renaissance, education was enhanced by the invention of the printing press because the need for literacy increased tremendously. This was a period of discovery of the outside world by exploration on land and at sea.

During this era, the Athenian ideal of unity of mind and body was revived, and health and physical exercise were stressed. Young men were taught to appreciate the graceful coordinated body rather than pure strength. As a result, the concept of the "whole man" evolved. The goal of Renaissance educators was to develop an all-around person with a balanced education. Girls and women were encouraged to participate in activities such as horseback riding and dance, but intelligent spectating of, rather than participation in, sport games was expected of women. Education was considered valuable for its own sake, regardless of its immediate practicality.

In the sixteenth century, Martin Luther and others protested against many of the beliefs and actions of the Roman Catholic church. As a result of the Reformation, new churches were started. The Protestants were more supportive of physical activities than was the Catholic church. They believed that such activities would help prevent corruption of the body and were, therefore, of moral value. The humanistic philosophy moved, during this era, to a rigid moralism, with a revolt against the church. Once again, there was separation of church and state leading to Puritanism, which would greatly affect the American colonies. The philosophy of realism arose to combat the Puritan ethic. The realists in general supported a place for the human body within the educational system, but not since the Greeks had anyone so stressed the unity of mind and body.

European Influence on Physical Education in America

With the ending of the Renaissance, strong national states developed under monarchies. Each national state possessed its own complex culture and structure. Various schools of thought in physical education emerged. Several major leaders in Europe contributed to the creation of exercise practices that would influence the shaping of the modern physical education curriculum.

Great Britain

The British inspired much debate of the value of physical education between church representatives and government leaders. This conflict continued to the period when early colonists emigrated to the New World. Although British educators did not recognize physical education and sport as educational or scholarly in any way, the powerful heritage of British sports influenced the emergence of sports as we know them in colleges and universities today. Archibald Maclaren (1820 to 1884) was a major early influential leader. He proposed a gymnastic-based physical program. Most importantly, he stressed a balance between recreational activities and educational physical activities as part of regular classes in the total educational program. Although Maclaren's ideas were never adopted, they did eventually influence British physical education in the late 1800s.

Germany

The Germans produced three major contributors to the development of modern physical education. Gymnastics was the first modern school physical education curriculum. Guts Muth (1759 to 1839), the "grandfather of German gymnastics," was a pioneer in the field and published the first books by a specialist in physical education. Freidrich Jahn (1778 to 1852) earned the title of "Father of Gymnastics." Jahn saw the need for a strong and vigorous youth for his native state. His system of gymnastics became known as the Turner movement, which eventually spread throughout the world. Jahn introduced such modern apparatuses as the vaulting horse, parallel bars, and horizontal bar. His gymnastics were practiced in clubs known as turnvereins. However, it was Adolph Speiss (1810 to 1858) who introduced gymnastics into the schools of the country. Speiss devised a system of free exercises that required almost no apparatuses. He also used musical accompaniments for these activities. An important concept was the need for professionally trained teachers. Many of the ideas of these three men were brought to the United States by German immigrants and are still visible today in modern physical education (Van Dalen and Bennett, 1971).

Sweden

Swedish gymnastics were founded by Per Henrik Ling (1776 to 1839), who had visited the German gymnasiums and had set as his goal the search for a scientific basis for gymnastic programs. The Swedish system challenged the German system and initiated a controversy throughout Europe and the United States that continued for several decades. Ling had a great influence on equipment. His system included stall bars, rings, swinging ladders, climbing ropes, and hand apparatuses (Indian clubs and wands). His emphasis on simple, fundamental movements and exercises was a dramatic change from Jahn's complicated program of activities. Although Ling's medical and military gymnastics were successful, it was his son, Hjalmer Ling, who had an enormous impact in the educational arena of the Socialist system. The Swedish gymnastic system was introduced in America in 1891.

Denmark

Franz Nachetegall (1777 to 1847) is considered the father of physical education in Denmark. He was inspired by the writings of Guts Muth

Influence of Swedish gymnastics in Miss Daisy Eliot's gymnasium in late 1800s.

and rose to a leadership position in Denmark's gymnastic and physical training programs. He was the director of the newly established Military Gymnastic Institute, which offered a teacher preparatory programs. Today this is the oldest institution training gymnastic instructors in Europe. Nachetegall did not design his own system but had a tremendous impact on the development of Denmark's school programs as well as influencing Ling's Swedish system of gymnastics.

Developing Physical Education in the United States

To understand the development of physical education in the United States, we must examine the events that shaped our developing nation. It is also important to consider how the Europeans influenced the development of our programs as well as how the American system evolved.

Colonial Period

In the Colonial period of our history (1607 to 1783), physical education did not exist as we now know it. Although the colonists attempted to start some schools, physical survival was paramount. The focus of what little education they had was on the basics — reading, writing, and arithmetic. Reading was considered the most important skill to be learned so that settlers could read their Bibles and worship freely in the New World.

Of the many diverse groups that settled in the colonies, the Puritans and Quakers were the most negative in their views of physical activities, which were deemed pleasurable and therefore leading to sin. Recreational activities were perceived as nonproductive and hedonistic. As other groups, such as the Dutch, arrived in the colonies, some appreciation of such activities developed.

The Revolutionary War did little to unify the nation. The colonies were farspread, and there was little spirit of nationalism until the War of 1812.

Colonial schools were copies of the European schools of the time. Physical education did not serve as an official function of a colonist's education, although unorganized games and sports for recreation became more acceptable. Some prominent men did support physical education; Thomas Jefferson and Benjamin Franklin are the most notable.

Physical Education for Nationalism

Nationalism (1787 to 1865) grew slowly until the War of 1812, when it emerged fully. The conflict between colonialism and nationalism gave birth to an American spirit that assisted in the cultivation of defense and economic strategies to protect the developing nation. With increasing national stability, expanding education not only in academic content but also to include more Americana became an important thrust.

The first attempts to put physical education in the curriculum were made in the 1820s and 1830s. Schools were opening under the direction of people who had been influenced by the changes in European schools. Physical education before the Civil War was affected by the growth of women's education, the movement of religious groups into education, and the growth of sports before 1860.

The German gymnastic system was brought to America by German immigrants. Three immigrants in particular appear to have had the greatest impact on spreading this system in our physical education program before 1900. They were Charles Beck, who taught at Round Hill School in Massachusetts, and Charles Follen and Frances Leiber, both of whom taught at Harvard.

The Round Hill School, a college preparatory school that provided a classical education, opened in Northampton, Massachusetts, in 1823. It was the only school of its day that focused on individualized instruction and also recognized the importance of physical activity as part of the educational program. The founders had observed the German system and decided to found a school on those principles. Charles Beck taught Latin and gymnastics at the Round Hill School from 1825 to 1830. Following Jahn's system, he started the first outdoor school gymnasium and the first school gymnastics program in the United States. The Round Hill School closed in 1834. Like other secondary-level schools of the day, it was a private tuition-based academy, though public schools had begun to open at the elementary level. The Round Hill School had experienced financial difficulties, but the main reason for its closing was that it differed so dramatically from other schools of this period. Its students were much better prepared for college work; in fact, they often were ready to enter their senior collegiate year directly. However, colleges required students to pay fees for all 4 years, regardless of the number of years matriculated. Therefore, it was not advantageous to attend and pay for the Round Hill School program. By the mid-1880s, society was leaning toward totally free education for both sexes.

Catherine Beecher was a prominent supporter of physical education for women during the period preceding the Civil War. She promoted sports, games, and exercise for the improvement of health. However, she was very puritanical in other areas. She was more interested in preparing women for their role in the home than for other intellectual activities. Since women were struggling for their rights at this time, her ideas were not extremely popular.

It appears that the most influential factor in the development of physical education in the United States in the last 10 years before the Civil War was the German gymnastic societies known as the Turners. At this time there was an influx of Germans to the United States owing to unstable political conditions between the German states in Europe. The German gymnastic societies served dual purposes as physical and social clubs.

A major figure in nineteenth century physical education history was Dr. Edward Hitchcock (1828 to 1911). (Freidrich-Cofer, 1984) As a graduate of Harvard's medical school, he was hired as a professor of hygiene and physical education at Amherst College in Massachusetts. This was the first recognized position for a physical educator in college in the United States and indicated growing acknowledgement of the value of physical education in a college's educational program.

In 1861, with the outbreak of the Civil War, the United States began its shift from an agricultural to an industrialized nation. This would profoundly affect the demand for the quality and quantity of physical education programs.

Physical Education after the Civil War

As the Civil War ended, many changes were taking place. Dio Lewis (1823 to 1886) became a major leader in the development of physical education. He devised his own system of gymnastics, which he called the new gymnastics. His concern was the development of the upper body for all people, and his program consisted of free exercises and light apparatus. Lewis started the first teacher-training institution for physical education in Boston in 1861. The Normal Institute for Physical Education remained open until 1868 and trained more than 300 teachers.

The German Turners also formed a school to train teachers. It began as a 1-year course and included the history and aims of physical education, anatomy, first aid, dancing, gymnastics, and teaching methods. Over the years, it evolved into a 2-year program in Milwaukee. The Turners decided they wanted to extend their program beyond the German community, and so they offered a more diversified curriculum and moved the new 4-year program to Indianapolis, where it later became affiliated with Indiana University.

Expansion of Schools and Programs

In the minds of many who were associated with the newly emerging field of physical education, the goals of physical training and athletics were hygiene and educative. The first goal was especially concerned with bodily health, hygiene, and fitness of the muscular, circulatory, digestive, and excretory functions. This aspect of physical education was strongly influenced by antebellum health reform movements but drew also from newer discoveries in the biological sciences, especially the physiology of the circulatory, respiratory, and digestive systems. The second goal emphasized development, a vague and variously used term that meant, among other things, the ways in which the organism grew, how character was formed, and the way in which the human species had evolved (Park, 1987).

Dr. Dudley Sargent (1849 to 1924) developed the Sargent System at Harvard University (Park, 1989). It was based on a thorough medical examination and was a combination of both the German and Swedish systems. His school, the Sargent School for Physical Education, eventually merged with Boston University. Sargent was a prominent leader, along with Dr. Hitchcock of Amherst College, in the development of modern American physical education.

The Swedish system grew in popularity under the leadership of Hartwig Nissen and Niles Posse. The flexibility of the Swedish system afforded it more adaptability than the American programs based on the German system.

In 1866, California was the first state to pass a law requiring physical education in public schools. It was not until 1882 that Ohio followed suit. More states followed their example near the turn of the century.

In 1885, the Association for the Advancement of Physical Education was formed (Park, 1989). Dr. William Anderson of Adelphi College in Brooklyn, New York, wanted to learn from others about their physical training programs. He invited a group of people to his school to discuss the content and promotion of physical training programs, and thus the association was born. Dr. Hitchcock assumed the leadership role for the young association. By this time, the battle between the German and Swedish systems was at its climax. At the 1889 association meeting, it was suggested that an American system should be developed to meet the public's needs rather than to adopt either of the existing systems. By the 1890s, few Americans looked back across the Atlantic for their inspiration in sports or anything else.

Physical Education in the United States in the Twentieth Century

The twentieth century witnessed a rapid growth in physical education in the United States. Early in the 1900s, remarkable leadership and professional contributions were provided by many individuals, including Luther H. Gulick, Clark W. Hetherington, Jesse Feiring Williams,

Jay B. Nash, Charles McCloy, Jessie Bancroft, Robert Tait McKenzie, Mabel Lee, Anita Turner, Delphine Hanna, and Edwin Henderson. Henderson was the first black man appointed as a physical educator in the U.S. public school system.

Before 1900, a philosophy of dualism was present in our schools: Educating the mind and training the body were viewed as separate processes. A major leader in the move to unify the teaching of the mind and body was John Dewey (1859 to 1950), who suggested that a major reason for the success of the Greek educational system was that it did not try to separate the mind from the body in the educational process (Park, 1974). Dewey's teachings included the concept of the "whole child," which led to a gradual shift in the aim of United States programs from a health-centered objective to a focus on all educational values — toward a unified picture of the child and educator. Dewey considered schools to be social institutions and believed that physical education should be an integral component of the socialization process; he believed in "learning by doing" through both play and organized experiences.

Today's children have a variety of apparatuses on which to climb and learn to balance.

The New Physical Education

Dewey's work in physical education was carried on by many others. Thomas Wood began to develop the new physical education during the first decade of the twentieth century. Games, sports, and other new nonstructured physical activities were included in his program under the name *natural gymnastics*.

Clark Hetherington was strongly influenced by his association with Wood at Stanford University (Thomas, 1985). His contributions included a better comprehension of children's play activities in terms of survival, continued participation, and athletics. Jay B. Nash succeeded Hetherington as physical education department chairperson at New York University and helped make the program there a leader in teacher training.

In the teacher preparation field of physical education, higher standards were established. The 2-year normal school became a thing of the past as 4-year programs became required. The trend changed from concentration on hygiene to a broader education including child growth and development, psychology of learning, and specialized training in physical education.

When World War I ended, the public had an opportunity to study the medical examiner's report for the men who had been called to duty. One-third of the men had been found physically unfit, and many more lacked basic physical skills. Furthermore, a 1918 survey by the National Council of Education showed that American children were in poor physical shape (Van Dalen and Bennett, 1971). These facts resulted in the passing of legislation in many states to upgrade physical education programs in the schools.

The 1920s saw a rise in popularity of the new physical education. The times supported a less formal program than the European system, and games, sports, and free play rose in popularity. Discussion was lively in professional circles, as the new system integrated the belief that physical education had greater worth than simply the building of physical qualities. The concept that physical education could contribute to the whole individual began to develop.

During these years, there was an increase in both intramural and interscholastic athletics. Women's programs also grew in number and variety. The depression years saw many setbacks for physical education as a result of strict limits in funding. A large percentage of programs in the schools were dropped completely. However, the number of recreational programs sponsored by agencies for the unemployed increased, with a trend toward less formal programs.

Impact of World War II—The Physical Fitness Movement

Analysis of the U.S. selective service physical examinations during World War II made apparent once again the need for a national program of physical fitness. President Roosevelt appointed John B. Kelly to the position of National Director of Physical Training. The war years saw the development of several organizations and political appointees to physical fitness posts (Freeman, 1982). The impact on programs of physical education in the schools was great. Daily physical education classes were instituted in many elementary schools, and there was also an increase in the number and frequency of secondary-level classes. The programs became more formalized to meet the physical conditioning objectives for the existing national emergency. These programs spanned gender and age barriers.

After the war, the federal government continued its involvement in the health and fitness of the nation, as evidenced here:

1955   President Dwight Eisenhower established the President's Council on Youth Fitness.

1961   President John F. Kennedy renamed the council the President's Council on Physical Fitness.

1965   President Lyndon Johnson once again changed the council's name to the President's Council on Physical Fitness and Sports and appointed Captain James Lowell, Jr., U.S.N., to lead it.

1980   President Jimmy Carter called the First National Conference on Physical Fitness and Sports for All.

1981   President Ronald Reagan appointed George Allen to lead the council.

1989   President George Bush began his administration with Dick Kazmar chairman of the President's Council on Physical Fitness and Sports for All.

Gender Equity for Excellence in Physical Education and Sports

Title IX was passed by the U.S. Congress in 1972 to assure equal rights for both men and women in educational and career opportunities. In physical education and athletics, girls and women were not receiving equal funding, equal leadership roles, equal facilities, or equal program opportunities. As a result of this legislation, sex equity workshops were conducted to develop an awareness of the extent of sex role stereotyp-

Getting to the top: Quality coaches for talented athletes.

ing in our entire educational system from textbooks to instructional methodology.

Since Title IX was enacted, there has been a significant increase in the number of coeducational physical education classes offered at all levels. Physical education departments, including those in institutions for higher education, now have men and women working together to maximize the physical education programs for boys and girls.

However, all is not well in the coeducational gym. With respect to gender, equity exists in physical education only on the surface. The overall picture shows that both female and male teachers interact differently with girls and boys and thereby continue to reinforce limiting gender typing. These interactions are replicated in children's interactions with one another in the gymnasium where generally boys only are allowed to engage in physical and psychological harassment. It is no wonder that girls are bored in physical education classes or are too self-conscious to participate actively in coeducational classes (Talbot, 1986). Attention to equity in physical education classes could raise the quality of education for all. There is much work yet to be accomplished regarding the sensitivity of individual and group similarities and differences.

According to the 1980 U.S. Commission on Civil Rights report on Title IX, boys are still favored over girls in school athletics. From 1970 to 1979, the number of girl athletes increased to 570 percent, whereas the number of boy athletes increased only 13 percent according to the government study. One of the greatest remaining barriers is that girls generally do not compete in two of the five most popular sports: football and wrestling. There remain rare discrepancies in the availability of less popular sports, which are offered to boys far more frequently than to girls. According to the U.S. Commission on Civil Rights (1980), the barriers to equality that still exist include (1) sex stereotypes of sports, (2) the myth that sports "masculinize" women and girls, and (3) discrimination in allocating facilities, equipment, and budgets to female teams.

Although recently they have acquired additional financial support and developed higher levels of competitive skill and intensity of competition, women's programs have inherited some of the problems that evolved in men's programs. The financing of highly competitive teams for success is extremely costly. Longer and more intense preseason and postseason practice schedules, equipment, number of coaches, length of competitive season, travel budgets, and intensity of student athletic recruitment are all factors to be considered in every competitive sport program offered by an institution. Consequently, the requirement for increased funding of all teams is often difficult or impossible to obtain. Decisions to eliminate various competitive sports are difficult but often necessary. Some programs are eliminated to support the "more visible" or "more traditional" or more "income-producing" sports, thereby reducing opportunities for greater participation. The sports generally affected by budget cuts are golf, gymnastics, tennis, softball, synchronized swimming and, in some areas, soccer and field hockey.

According to Hasbrook (1988), young members of society must have the opportunity to observe a significant number of women, not just an isolated few, in positions of power and status within the sporting world if society is ever to view sport, participation in sport, and sporting careers as unrelated to one's gender. Her available data suggests a dramatic decline in the percentages of female intercollegiate and interscholastic coaches between the 1970s and the early 1980s. There is no single explanation for these losses. A variety of explanations may be plausible, although none to date are scientifically based. The common assumptions are that female coaches are less qualified, less willing to travel and recruit, less likely to apply for positions, and more likely to be concerned with time constraints due to family responsibilities. The fact is that these assumptions are not generally true but reflect gender typing. Other possibilities are that it is more acceptable, with Title IX, for men to coach women's teams, the salaries for coaching women's teams are comparable, and men may enjoy the enthusiasm of female athletes and a less stressful coaching environment.

Sex equity in physical education and sports continues to be an element of concern for the overall quality of programs and opportunities for all individuals to participate at any desired level.

Physical Education for the Special Student

Another legislative decision that improved opportunities for participation in physical education was the Education for All Handicapped Children Act: PL94-142 stated the provisions for physical education. During the summer of 1979, a series of public meetings were held to help clarify this law, which states that physical education must be included in every child's individualized educational program (IEP). Four separate levels of programs are described in detail in the law, as follows:

- Regular physical education with other, nonhandicapped students (for example, for students with a speech impairment)
- Regular physical education with adaptations (for example, using a bowling rail for blind students)
- Specifically designed physical education for a particular need (for example, for an orthopedic condition)
- Physical education in special settings (for example, in a residential school or hospital)

The mainstreaming of handicapped children into regular physical education classes is a tremendous challenge that can be rewarding to the handicapped child, the nonhandicapped peers, and the teacher. Athletic opportunities have increased greatly for the handicapped through the Special Olympics, Beep Baseball, Adapted Floor Hockey Leagues, and many other programs. However, mainstreaming can be very taxing and impose severe restrictions on class organization. There are teachers who prefer to keep disabled students in their own special class for ease of instruction and for the least disruption of general class organization.

Youth Sports

Little League baseball was once the only highly organized youth sport on a national level. Within the last two decades, youth sport programs as well as concern for the young athlete have increased dramatically. Pop Warner football, AAU swimming, gymnastics, tennis, ice hockey, softball, and the recent soccer boom are indicative of the American addiction to sport.

Youth sport has had many positive outcomes, but a broad range of still unresolved criticism has also developed. Concern over physical injuries to Little League pitchers, for example, led to new rules to limit the number of innings pitched during a given time, but research evidence on "Little League elbow" is still controversial. Proper bone development, cardiovascular development, sociopsychological development, and risk of injury are highly debated topics. The effects of overzealous parents, untrained coaches, the emphasis on winning, and the effects of cutting youngsters from teams are only a few criticized issues of youth sport. Coaches at the high school level and even some Olympic coaches are concerned that young athletes exposed to too much highly organized sports training and development "burn out." Child development specialists are concerned about the lack of free play opportunities for children. Youth sports will undoubtedly be around for years to come, and more research is needed to provide guidelines for quality programs.

Adult Fitness

The increased developments in medical research regarding cardiovascular disease and health risk factors have prompted more adults to adopt lifestyle changes for longevity. To implement medical exercise prescriptions, adult fitness in both the private and public sectors has provided an expanding career marketplace in related exercise physiology activities. Americans continue to focus on remaining youthful and maintaining a good appearance. Health spas, diet and nutrition spas, and aerobics programs exist throughout the United States. Wellness career opportunities can provide physical educators with immediate feedback on contributing to increasing a person's level of physical health.

The graying of America will have serious implications for the nation's health care delivery system. Piscopo (1985) states that according to a current demographic movement, one of every five persons in the United States will pass the age of 65 by the year 2020. Fitness programming for an aging population will become increasingly more important.

Research

There is an increased emphasis on research in physical education and sport. More graduate programs are training highly qualified researchers. Colleges and universities are providing larger research facilities with sophisticated laboratories and equipment for scholarly work. The specificity of research projects is overwhelming.

The practitioner in the field needs to be able to apply research findings. Attempts are now being made to translate these findings into principles and guidelines that teachers and coaches can follow. The major research areas include biomechanics, growth and development, health, history and philosophy, measurement and research, design, neurophysiology, pedagogy, psychology of sport, recreation, sociology of sport, and teacher preparation, curriculum development, and instruction.

Student Activities

1. Write a short biography of one of the following American leaders in physical education: Edward Hitchcock, Dudley Allen Sargent, William G. Anderson, Mabel Lee, Catherine Beecher, Luther H. Gulick, Clark W. Hetherington, Jesse Feiring Williams, Jay B. Nash, Charles McCloy, Robert Tait McKenzie, Anita Turner, or Edwin Henderson.

2. Select a recent article from the *Journal of the Philosophy of Sport* or the annual *Proceedings of the North American Society for Sport History*. Write an abstract of the article.

3. Interview people at a shopping mall or supermarket. Ask them how they feel about physical education in the public schools. Then ask which athletic philosophy they might represent. Identify an historical personality that reflects their opinions.

4. Select four professional journals of interest to you. Go to the library and obtain a recent copy of each one. Review the journal and summarize the objectives of the periodical.

Suggested Readings

Anderson, G. 1985. AAHPERD from the beginning. *Journal of Physical Education, Recreation and Dance* Apr: 94–96.

Freeman, W. H. 1982. *Physical education and sport in a changing society*, 2nd ed. Minneapolis: Burgess Publishing Company.

Hasbrook, C. A. 1988. Female coaches — why the declining number and percentages? *Journal of Physical Education, Recreation and Dance* Aug: 59–63.

Lawson, H. A. 1982. Looking back from the year 2082. *Journal of Physical Education, Recreation and Dance*, Apr: 15–17.

Van Dalen, D. B., and B. L. Bennett. 1971. *A world history of physical education*, 2nd ed. Englewood Cliffs, NJ: Prentice-Hall.

References

Barney, R. K. 1979. Friedrich Ludwig Jahn revisited — a report on the International Jahn Symposium. *Journal of Physical Education and Recreation* 50: 58.

Freidrich-Cofer, L. K. 1984. The legacy of Edward Hitchcock. *Journal of Physical Education, Recreation and Dance* Nov/Dec: 24–29.

Park, R. J. 1989. Physiologists, physicians, and physical educators: nineteenth century biology and exercise, hygiene and education. *Journal of Sport History* 14(1): 28–57.

Park, Roberta J. 1974. The philosophy of John Dewey and physical education. *Dimensions of Physical Education*, 2/e. St. Louis: Mosby.

Piscopo, J. 1985. *Fitness and aging.* New York: Wiley.

Talbot, M. 1986. Gender and physical education. *British Journal of Physical Education* 17: 121–122.

Thomas, D. L. 1985. Clark W. Hetherington: persuasive and philosophic. *Journal of Physical Education, Recreation and Dance* Nov/Dec: 74–75.

U.S. Commission on Civil Rights. 1980. More hurdles to clear. Publications Warehouse, 621 North Payne, Alexandria, Virginia 22314.

6. The Humanities in Physical Education

Chapter Outline

Literature and Physical Education
Art and Physical Education
Music and Dance
Communication—An Art and a Technology
Sport Film
Integrating Disciplines
Student Activities
Suggested Readings
References

Objectives

Chapter 6 is designed to enable you to:

- Become aware of the relationship between sport and the humanities.
- Appreciate the skill and talent required to produce sport art.
- Become aware of the variety of sport literature available to schools and the general public.
- Appreciate sport film as an important aspect of American social history.

THE fine arts and sport have contributed to the culture of societies over the centuries. Historians have recorded sporting events of the past and the arts preserve memories and reflections of the role of sport in culture. Sport and the humanities are a means of communication between past, present, and future societies.

Art, sculpture, literature, dance, and music have historically reflected the influence of sport and human movement. However, professionals in the human movement disciplines have not recognized their important contributions until recently. Course work for the undergraduate physical education major seldom addresses the complexity of the humanities. The concepts have been given lip service in traditional activity classes such as modern dance, folk dance, and square dance.

It is important for the emerging professional to recognize the pervasiveness of sport in our society that is reflected in the study of the humanities. During the 1960s, colleges and universities witnessed an upheaval in general education requirements, which resulted in a decreased emphasis on the liberal arts. These same institutions in the 1980s were beginning to reinstate humanities courses in the required general education framework. The concept of the fully educated person goes beyond the ability of an individual to function in a specified career path.

The connection between liberal arts and technology has vast implications for the impact of sport on our culture. We once had only painting and sculpture as ways to represent our world visually. Photography then was introduced in the early 1800s. In the 1870s and 1880s, American and French photographers began to investigate animals and humans moving through time and space and produced the first overlapping photographic images in a sequence. Motion pictures were born. Since then, cinematography has allowed millions to witness excellent performances of sporting events. Film, videotape, television, and computer graphics have increased public awareness of physical education and, in the profession, have become important tools for the study of human movement.

Literature and Physical Education

Prose and poetry have been important communication tools throughout humankind's existence. Prior to the written word, athletic contests and heroes were praised and legends, poems, and songs about their achievements were passed from generation to generation as an oral tradition.

Physical excellence, similar to the qualities of the gods, was highly valued in Greek culture. Poets were eager to sing the praises not only of victors in battle, as in Homer's *Iliad*, but also of victors in athletic contests of skill and strength. The great poet Pindar wrote odes in memory of the winners of athletic contests who were given the laurel or wild olive wreath. This laudatory tradition survived for centuries, inspiring the poetry of the Golden Age of Greece. The first recorded Olympic games by our calendar were held in 776 B.C. Literature has evolved to record sporting events and athletes in poetry, fiction, and nonfiction prose, autobiographies, biographies, and sports magazines, as well as plays and film scripts. Contemporary sports literature still includes how-to books and rule books but has come also to have a major impact on the reading material of the American public. For example, Neil Berman has written a book entitled *Playful Fictions and Fictional Players* (Port Washington, New York: Kennikat, 1981), a critical analysis of five recent American novels that have a form of sports as their subject matter. This is an important addition to sports literature.

The impact of sports and physical education on our youth and educational system is reflected in the reading materials adopted by school districts for students. Major publishing companies include stories about athletes and sports in their reading series because of the high level of interest young readers have in these topics. The authors of children's books recognize the important role of sports in our society. Figure 6.1 on pages 109–111 is a partial list of forty-seven review copies of sport books for kindergarteners through twelfth graders that were included in a book exhibit sponsored by the Instructional Media Service Department, Houston Independent School District, Houston, Texas, in 1982. This is only a brief representative sample list of the many books about sports that are available for children.

The Athletic Institute in Florida is a publishing and production company that has expanded its collection from loop films to a variety of paperback books, films, and videotapes on specific sports skills and physical fitness. The variety of literature available to young people that focuses on sports, sport techniques, and sport heroes can be a valuable resource for teachers, coaches, parents, and youth sponsors. It is important to be aware of current educational materials that are relevant to the curriculum. These materials can be used to reinforce motor skills, can function as motivational tools, and can provide an accessible avenue by which to integrate physical education with the basic-skills curriculum in the classroom. Sport technique books begin at the primary level and focus on soccer, gymnastics, tennis, skiing, and other sport activities. Intermediate-level materials include books on physical fitness, running, and stories about athletes, both fiction and nonfiction. Biographies and autobiographies of sports heroes more frequently feature female athletes today and can be highly motivational for young athletes. Poetry is also very inspirational. Coaches and parents find poems such as this one to be very effective in encouraging youngsters to be good sports and give their all.

"The Game Started"

The game started
   and we held nothing back.
For just a moment
   we knew, each of us,
   the secret terror of being all
     alone . . .
   on the line . . .
And then we tumbled into the fray.
The pain, the excitement,
   the order and confusion,
   the precision of seeing—
   for just a moment—
   everything in crystal clarity.
We have done it all;
   lived a lifetime in minutes—
been the best we could be,
   and now it is done
     this competition thing.
And now that it is finished you are here;
   you cheered me—you stood by me
     my friend,
       my father,
         my family.
I am no longer alone
   but am content to rest
   in the love you give
which cares not for the score—
   but commemorates only the doing
     of this wonderful thing.

("The Game Started" by Bonnie Beach
from Journal of Physical Education,
Recreation and Dance, *March 1982, vol.*
53, no. 3. Reprinted by permission.)

Young adult and adult literature includes such psychological and philosophical items as Tim Galloway's *Inner Game of Tennis* and George Leonard's *Ultimate Athlete.* The popularity of physical fitness has created growing interest in books on exercise, nutrition, relaxation techniques, outdoor recreation, and stress management. The medical profession has contributed such notable authors as Dr. George Sheehan, who wrote *Running and Being—The Total Experience.* The biographies and autobiographies of professional athletes sometimes make bestseller lists.

Figure 6.1 Book Exhibit, Houston Independent School District, 1982

Grade Level Indications
P   Primary (Grades K–3)
E   Elementary (Grades 4–6)
J   Junior High (Grades 7–9)
S   Senior High (Grades 10–12)
YA Young Adult (For mature senior high or college students, not for elementary or junior high libraries)

Sports and Physical Education
Anthony, J. *Winning Combination.* (Scribner 1980) $12.50, JS
   Tennis is one of the fastest growing sports for children today. Book shows parents how they can make tennis a game that will bring self-fulfillment to their children. Good photos.
Barnes, B. E. *Beginner's Guide to Better Boxing.* (McKay 1980) $7.95, EJ
   Illustrated guide to boxing, including equipment, conditioning, basic forms, blows, defenses, rules, injuries, and style.
Barrett, F. *How to Watch a Football Game.* (Holt 1980) $7.95, JS
   Excellent book, written through interviews with numerous players, coaches, and officials, gives wealth of information not readily found in other football books.
Christeson, B. *First Olympic Games.* (Silbur 1978) $7.35, EJ
   A description of the ancient Olympic Games, as seen through the eyes of a young Greek boy, is accompanied by a history of the games from ancient times to the present.
Egbert, B. *Cheerleading and Songleading.* (Sterling 1980) $11.69, JS
   Outstanding book to be used in the physical education department along with booster clubs and cheerleading. Excellent diagrams and illustrations.
Fassi, C. *Figure Skating with Carlo Fassi.* (Scribner 1980) $17.95, SYA
   This basic, well-illustrated comprehensive guide for both beginning and more advanced skaters has specific, easy-to-follow instructions.
Fisher, L. *Sports.* (Holiday 1980) $7.95, EJ
   While discussing the development of athletic competition in

Figure 6.1 (continued)

nineteenth-century America this well-known author sprinkles the text with colorful figures and major events of the sporting world.

Fleming, G. H. *Unforgettable Season.* (Holt 1981) $16.95, S
An unusual account of a baseball series for the pennant more than 10 years ago. Exciting narrative. Lot of material taken from newspaper.

Hatfield, F. C. *Weight Training for the Young Athlete.* (Atheneum 1980) $8.95, JS
An up-to-date book on weight lifting for young people written on their level. Stresses the need for moderation in any type of exercise.

Holmes, B. *World's First Baseball Game.* (Silbur 1978) $7.35, PE
Describes the development of rules for baseball and the first game played "by the rules" in Hoboken, New Jersey, on June 19, 1846. Good format, full of drawings in full color.

Kaneko, A. *Olympic Gymnastics.* (Sterling 1976) $7.95, EJS
This well-illustrated book starts with exercises to use even before you mount the equipment and goes on to develop a complete training program for beginning male gymnasts.

Laklan, C. *Golden Girls.* (McGraw 1980) $8.95, EJ
Brief biographies of women athletes who became Olympic winners. Shows the changing role of women in sports. Useful biographical information and also good history of the Olympic Games.

Orr, R. *Swimming Basics.* (Prentice 1980) $8.95, EJ
Text and illustrations introduce the fundamentals of competitive swimming with emphasis on different types of strokes and breathing techniques. Good systematic coverage.

Pollock, R. *Soccer for Juniors.* (Scribner 1980) $9.95, JS
Well-done, illustrated book for everyone interested in youth soccer— parents, players and coaches. Gives many good pointers.

Ryan, F. *Jumping for Joy.* (Scribner 1980) $7.95, EF
Discusses the history and techniques of the four jumps featured in track and field events: the high jump, the pole vault, the long jump, and the triple jump.

Sullivan, G. *Cross-Country Skiing.* (Mesner 1980) $8.49, JS
Comprehensive discussion of cross-country skiing, the equipment, clothing, basic techniques, preparations, and precautions. Lists places to ski and the names of skiing guidebooks. Very useful for beginners.

Swinburne, L. *America's First Football Game.* (Silbur 1978) $7.35, PE
A history of American football from the first college game in 1869 between Princeton and Rutgers.

Thomas, A. *Volleyball Is for Me.* (Lerner 1980) $5.95, E
Follows the members of a volleyball team as they learn volleyball fundamentals including serving, blocking, spiking, and passing. Factual without being too technical. Excellent photographs and simple language.

Whitehead, N. *Conditioning for Sport.* (Sterling 1980) $10.39, JS

Figure 6.1 (continued)

Starts with exercises that will benefit anyone interested in sports, then zeroes in on exercises and training schedules to meet specific needs. Practical guide with good instructions and photographs.

Willcox, I. *Acrobats and Ping-Pong.* (Dodd 1981) $8.95, JS

Highlights various forms of recreation enjoyed by the people of China. Good photographs enhance the book. Probably will have little interest to anyone except sports enthusiast.

Examples of current literature available to the public on sports include the following:

Angell, R. 1989. *The summer game.* New York: Ballantine Books.

Chesnov, M. 1988. *Healing sport injuries.* New York: Ballantine Books.

Conner, F. 1989. *This date in sports history.* New York: Warner Books.

Daly, M. 1974. *Daly's billiard book.* New York: Dover Publications.

Diamond, H., and M. Diamond. 1987. *Fit for life.* New York: Warner Books.

Dunham, J. 1988. The art of the trout fly. San Francisco: Chronicle Books.

Fancher, T. 1984. *Racquetball 1–2–3.* North Palm Beach, FL: Athletic Institute.

Gunther, M., and B. Carter. 1988. *Monday night mayhem.* New York: Beach Tree Books.

Hoose, P. M. 1986. *Hoosiers.* New York: Vintage.

Katz, J. 1987. *Swimming for total fitness.* New York: Doubleday

Krugel, M. 1989. *Michael Jordan.* New York: St. Martin's.

Loehr, J., and E. J. Kahn III. 1989. *The parent-player tennis training program.* New York: Stephen Greene Press.

Lorer, S. 1988. *Soccer match control.* New York: Penguin Books.

Mason, B. 1984. *Path of the paddle.* Toronto: Key Porter Books.

Pepe, P. 1988. *The wit and wisdom of Yogi Berra.* New York: St. Martin's.

Player, G. 1988. *Golf begins at 50.* New York: Simon and Schuster.

Portugues, G., and J. Vedrel. 1986. *Hard bodies.* New York: Dell.

Prudden, B. 1986. *Bonnie Prudden's after fifty fitness guide.* New York: Ballantine Books.

Raymond, S. 1988. *The year of the angler.* New York: Simon and Schuster.

Savage, B. 1983. *Miles from nowhere: round-the-world bicycle adventure.* Seattle: The Mountaineers.

Souza, K. 1989. *Biathlon training and racing techniques.* Chicago: Contemporary Books.

The interdependence of sports and literature goes beyond the paperback book to newsstand magazines. *Sports Illustrated* and *Sport* are two of the most successful magazines in this genre. However, a well-stocked newsstand will also carry magazines on individual sports. The list is extensive and includes such periodicals as *Golf Digest, PRI, The Runner, Spray's Water Ski, Cross Country Ski, Racquetball Illustrated, Skiing,* and *Runner's World.*

Art and Physical Education

Sport art captures for all time the inspiring performances of athletes. In art, the traits of power, agility, and skill are all timeless. Sport art is achieving national and international prominence.

Founded in 1959 under charter of the New York State Board of Regents, the National Art Museum of Sport, New Haven, Connecticut, holds pursuit of excellence as its prime purpose, reaching out to the sports-minded public with sports expressed in fine art. By promoting these two universal languages—sport and art—the museum seeks to be instrumental in establishing a stronger and more vital art tradition in the United States. Prominent personalities in the world of sports helped establish the museum: H. H. S. Phillips, Jr., publisher of *Sports Illustrated;* the late Robert J. H. Kiputh, who was a Yale and Olympic swimming coach and curator of Yale University's sport art collection; Joseph Brown, Princeton University professor of sculpture and boxing coach; Allison Danzig, *New York Times* sportswriter and director of the National Football Foundation and Hall of Fame and the Lawn Tennis Hall of Fame; Stewart Klinis, president of the American Fine Arts Society; and the late Paul J. Sacks, professor emeritus of Fine Arts at Harvard University and honorary patron of the National Art Museum of Sport.

In 1967, the National Art Museum of Sport found a home at Madison Square Garden. The collection grew and remained there until its relocation 10 years later to its current home at the University of New Haven. Throughout the museum's sport history, it has reached a variety of audiences through traveling shows and separate exhibits such as the 1980 Master Sports Art Exhibition at Lake Placid, New York, in conjunction with the Master Olympics. The museum has presented approximately 100 art exhibits to date and is playing a vital role in developing sport art in the United States and internationally.

In 1979, a study on the role of sport in society, financed by a grant from the National Endowment for the Humanities, was completed by the National Art Museum of Sport. The study concluded:

> Sport portrayal through art can help preserve the American heritage visually and beautifully for the education and enjoyment of the public. . . . It can also help bring people of all ages together from all walks of life, lessening the social tensions that often threaten our country. . . . We seek to inspire artists and sports-minded art patrons to participate in an exciting movement for a better society while providing lasting commentary on the American scene.
>
> *(National Art Museum of Sport, 1980)*

The appreciation of sport performance through art enhances both sport and the humanities in our culture. The National Association for Sport

Unity, *a bronze sculpture by Gene Logan, at the national office of the American Alliance for Health, Physical Education, Recreation and Dance.*

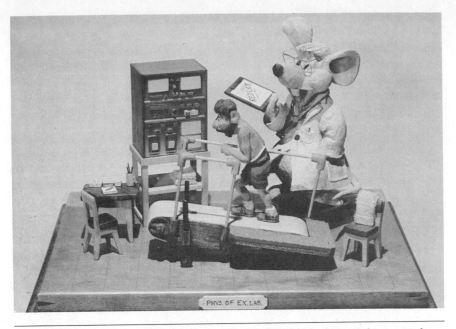

PHYS. OF EX. LAB.

Sport can be a theme in art as this sculpture by Bob Sorani shows. Other examples follow.

Joggers *by Bob Sorani.*

Hockey Player *by Bob Sorani.*

Gymnast *by Bob Sorani.*

The Athlete and Sport *by Robert Pestolesi.*

and Physical Education, an affiliate of the American Alliance for Health, Physical Education, Recreation and Dance (AAHPERD), has begun sponsoring the Sport Art Academy, which is comprised of physical education and recreation professionals who are either sport artists or sport-art patrons. The academy has hosted a sport art exhibit at recent national conventions of AAHPERD. In 1981, the exhibit included pastel paintings, art on canvas, charcoal sketches, lithographs, photography, and poetry. The National Art Museum of Sport contributed several pieces of art for exhibit, but most of the exhibit represented the talent of practicing physical educators.

Leroy Neiman established a name for himself in the art world through his sport-art pieces. The 1976 Olympics launched an impressive art career for him. Since then, much of his artwork has focused on golf, sailing, and skiing.

The Wolffe Collection of Sculpture by R. Tait McKenzie is an impressive and important collection of bronze sculptures gathered by the late Joseph B. Wolffe over a 25-year period. Wolffe's interest in collecting McKenzie's work went beyond the appreciation of artistic ability. As a physician, Wolffe agreed with McKenzie that physicians and physical educators need to extend their cooperative efforts in the use of physical activity as a tool for preventive medicine. As one of the founders of the American College of Sports Medicine, Wolffe was active in fusing medicine and exercise science to promote total health for all citizens.

R. Tait McKenzie (1867 to 1938) was internationally known for his sculpture of athletes. He was recognized as a very gifted person because he demonstrated outstanding talent as a physician, physical educator, and sculptor. His experience with anatomy and sports gave him a deeper understanding of his ability as a sculptor. The Wolffe Collection of R. Tait McKenzie's work is a good representative sample of the nearly 400 sculptures by this great man. The works of this sculptor of athletes are on permanent display at the University of Tennessee at Knoxville.

Another art form that is engaging the interest of sport enthusiasts is artwork on postage stamps and hunting stamps. There is a large annual competition between artists to be selected as the designer for the National Duck Stamp. States are beginning to sponsor their own stamp competitions. For the first time in its history, the U.S. Postal Service in 1981 issued stamps honoring sports figures. The first American athletes so honored were golfer Bobby Jones and track star and golfer Babe Didrickson Zaharias. Football great Jim Thorpe and baseball slugger George Herman ("Babe") Ruth are being considered for future stamps. The U.S. Postal Service will not honor a celebrity unless he or she has been dead at least 10 years.

Humor, movement, and sport performance can be appreciated both through physical activity itself and through the world of art. Education can play an important role in fostering this relationship. The William R. Roberts Physical Education Elementary Magnet School program in Houston, Texas, is an example of what can be done. At the school, components of the art curriculum coincide with physical education activities. When students study physical fitness, they also draw life-size replicas of their bodies, including bones and muscles. When specific sport skills are being learned, the students construct papier-mâché figures performing a selected skill. These activities foster in young people an appreciation for sport and art. It is important to examine our personal talents beyond physical activity itself to discover the creativity within us and to foster an early artistic development in the child.

Music and Dance

Music and dance are additional disciplines in the humanities that have an influence on art and human movement, and they are so interrelated that we will discuss them together. Many musical melodies and lyrics are used in elementary physical education in rhyming games and dances. Basic motor skills and rhythms are taught using tambourines, drums, pianos, and children's records. Some basic melodies that you may remember from elementary school are "Skip to My Lou," "This Old Man," and "She'll Be Coming 'Round the Mountain." Two comprehensive guides to music and movement for young children are Patty Zeitlin's *A Song is a Rainbow* (1982) and Ann Lief Barlin's *Teaching Your Wings to Fly* (1979). Rhythmic gymnastics and adult home exercise routines, accompanied by a variety of music from classical pieces to contemporary jazz, are also now available as records and videotapes.

What is dance? As bodily activity, dance shares many movement elements with other physical activities. Hayes (1964) states that the key to its distinction is that the dancer's immediate concern is not lifting weights, transporting oneself through water, balancing on skates or skis, or winning a game, but rather with movement that has been consciously given form and rhythmic structure to provide physical, emotional, or aesthetic satisfaction. A lot of fundamental motor skills are taught in the name of dance but should actually be classified as basic movement. Dance is much more than basic movement. Although mastery of the fundamentals of movement is a prerequisite to success in dance, movement becomes dance only when the mover is free enough of mechanical considerations to be able to enjoy and create movement for its own sake.

Most dances are performed with musical accompaniment. Ballet and ballroom dancing are still enjoyed by many patrons of the arts and reflect the continued impact of the classical forms of dance and music. Other dance forms that are taught and performed are tap, ballet, modern dance, folk dance, square dance, ethnic dance, jazz, disco, and country-western. The early 1980s witnessed a national trend in the United States toward the lifestyle of the Old West, most evident in the popularity of western clothes and music, with country-western dancing using the two-step and the "cotton-eyed Joe" performed in "kicker clubs" across the country. In the late 1980s, a wave of nostalgia swept the country, with renewed interest in both the big band sounds of ballroom dancing and early rock and roll from the 1950s and 1960s.

For many centuries people from all nations have danced. Ethnic dance is dance that is performed in its original form, just as it was performed by the group of people who created it. On the other hand, folk dance describes a dance that was originally an ethnic dance but that often has undergone some changes over the years. Ethnic dance is a form of cultural transmission through which one learned to appreciate peoples of other cultures. It is not enough to know the steps and patterns of an ethnic dance; the dancer must also know what type of dance it is and from where it came. The spirit and meaning of the dance must be captured.

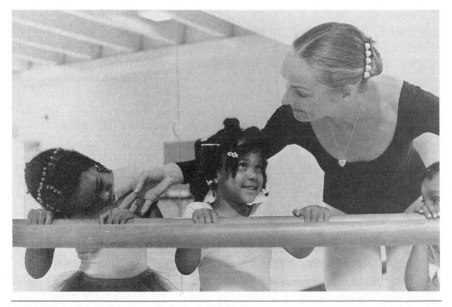

Dance can be learned and enjoyed by all ages.

The United States is no longer advocating the melting-pot concept of a place where cultures all blend as one. Cultural pluralism is becoming increasingly evident. Peoples of various ethnic backgrounds are emphasizing their cultural uniqueness. Music and dance are integral parts of a culture, and physical educators can provide meaningful physical activity and social development programs by including more dance in the curriculum.

For many years, dance education had been the stepchild of the arts curriculum (McLaughlin, 1988). If dance education was part of any formal curriculum, it was buried in physical education programs, and basic instruction included some folk dances and possibly an introduction to American square dancing. If dance was not appreciated by the teacher or the teacher had little training in dance, it may not have been included in the curriculum. Private dance instruction was the only route for those seriously interested in jazz, modern dance, or ballet. However, for young people with talent whose parents could not afford lessons, opportunities were lost.

During the 1970s, new interest in dance developed across the United States. Dance companies were rejuvenated and new dance groups emerged. People began to enjoy watching dance performances. Aerobic dance and jazz became the style for exercise and leisure. American choreography established itself and competed equally with the Russian ballet. The defection of Mikhail Baryshnikov assisted the United States in the further development of ballet. The National Council for the Arts and the National Endowment for the Arts supported this rebirth of dance.

Dance education, as a result of national interest, began to appear again in school curricula and in field trips. In the late 1970s, economic crunches resulted in cutbacks in arts education, but concern over this surfaced in discussions of educational reform. Arts education includes the fields of dance, music, visual arts, creative writing, and theater. The increasing lack of cultural literacy in America is becoming a growing concern as we prepare to enter the next century. Dance is an integral part of our profession as physical educators, and we should support dance education and dancing in all sectors of physical activity.

Ironically, one of the major events supporting dance in the late 1980s was the film *Dirty Dancing*. The star, Patrick Swayze, developed a major following that resulted in the adoption of dance classes to teach this new style, which appealed to more than the teenaged population. Adults of all ages were interested in learning how to do some of the so-called dirty dances. Ballroom dance teachers incorporated some of these new techniques to add flair to more traditional dance steps.

The time is ripe for the promotion of serious dance education. Partnership efforts with dance groups, local dance artists, and university dance departments in the public schools or community groups can assist in promoting an appreciation of dance as well as in developing dance education in the school curriculum and dance classes in local community recreation departments or similar civic organizations. Dance should be an integral part of the education of every child.

Communication—An Art and a Technology

As we discussed earlier, photography in sport has come a long way: From 8-mm films to computerized cinematographic motor-skill analyses, sport and visual communications have been joined hand in hand. A technological development that revolutionized the use of video in sport was the instant replay. It is difficult to imagine watching sports on television without the instant replay. Some spectators bring tiny portable televisions to a televised game just so they can see the instant replays. Sport competition of all kinds contributes many hours to television programming. Monday Night Football on television helped create a new social lifestyle.

Another communication phenomenon for sports is the use of satellites to broadcast national and international competitions live in your home. The Olympic Games are an excellent example of international telecommunications via satellite. The cost of obtaining television rights for major sporting networks is astronomical. As a result, the American Broadcasting Corporation (ABC), which developed the concept and televised the Olympics for years, bowed to the Columbia Broadcasting System (CBS) for the 1988 summer Olympic Games in Seoul, South Korea. With CBS' intent to re-establish their position in the sports marketplace, they then won the bid for the 1992 Winter Games.

The increased emphasis on televised sports has resulted in an increased need for individuals trained in various aspects of sports broadcasting. The national cable television sports network ESPN provides daily 24-hour sports broadcasting, which enables spectators to watch sports in the comfort of their homes around the clock. Turner Broadcasting System (TBS) set records for both ratings and household delivery with its schedule of thirty-one National Basketball Association playoff contests in 1988. The number of households viewing the playoffs (slightly more than 2 million) in that year was up 52 percent over the previous year. There are also electronic television games based on various sports such as baseball, basketball, football, and hockey. Atari and

Intellivision are major products currently vying for business, but many other products are becoming available.

Sport Film

The impact of film in sports is more extensive than televised sporting events. The cinema or movie theater is an established major cultural vehicle that attracts members of every social class. According to Crawford (1988), movies, especially American ones, have portrayed the United States as the nation wants to see itself. Athletic activity in film may not be representative of a real world but will perhaps reflect stereotypes or symbols. The movie _Knute Rockne_, in which an athletic coach is glorified, is exemplary of this rarefied view of sports in America.

Up to the end of World War II, film portrayal of sports and athletic activity were frequently characterized by the unerring innocence of a Knute Rockne and the aesthetics of Esther Williams (Crawford, 1988). Fred Astaire and Ginger Rogers displayed their athleticism in their brilliantly choreographed romantic films. Following the war, athletic movies began to change from innocence to the darker side of competitiveness, as in _Rollerball_, a movie that exploited the commercial side of sport and also introduced the science fiction aspect of entertainment. The Tarzan era with Johnny Weismuller helped develop the strongman character in the 1950s. Sylvester Stallone, with his series of _Rocky_ films about boxing, capitalized on another strongman perception in the 1970s and 1980s. In the early 1970s, Bruce Lee emerged as an international star, using the martial arts to defeat the bad guys. These were followed by the less violent _Karate Kid_ in the 1980s, in which Pat Morita played the role of the martial arts teacher.

Film also portrays the athlete as folk hero, which has been economically successful. According to Crawrod (1988),

> Many other conceptual issues need to be incorporated into the examination of sports films, such issues as the antifeminism of the traditional sports film _(Requiem for a Heavyweight)_, the social dynamics of sport in small-town America _(Hoosiers)_, nationalism and jingoism with sport as a propaganda tool _(Rocky IV)_, women in sport _(Personal Best)_, sport as metaphor and allegory _(That Championship Season)_, athletic activities as powerful weapons for "rational recreation" _(The Longest Yard)_, cross-cultural studies exploring the historical, social significance, and impact of athletic excellence on national character: _Chariots of Fire_—England, _The Boy in Blue_—Canada, and _Phar Lap_—Australia.

Integrating Disciplines

Sport and physical education influence many aspects of our society. The humanities reflect the pervasiveness of sport in our culture. An art patron or artist can extend communication between societies and between generations.

As American society puts more emphasis on sport, the role of sport in the humanities will undoubtedly increase. Hence, physical educators need to consider the humanities as a part of total physical education, while especially emphasizing lifetime leisure activities to fill the need for physical activity when the days of hard physical competition are no longer practical. Patrons of art, literature, music, dance, and video communication can be creatively included by supporting or managing programs in need of financial aid or experienced guidance. The full potential of the integration of physical education and the humanities has only begun to be explored. As an emerging professional, your experience in the humanities can broaden your perspective and may prove to be an asset in your career.

Student Activities

1. Visit a local art museum and look for classical art masters and contemporary sport artists such as Leroy Neiman and Joni Carter.
2. Visit a local newsstand and develop a list of current sports magazines, listing them by category.
3. Describe an art form related to sport.
4. Write a poem using a sport theme.
5. Review the movie *Dirty Dancing* and explore the evolution of modern popular dance.
6. Karate epitomizes mental discipline and judicious use of physical strength. View the movie *The Karate Kid* and comment on the effectiveness of the conflict resolution model of the story line.

Suggested Readings

Barlin, A. L. 1979. *Teaching your wings to fly.* Glenview, IL: Scott, Foresman.

Hayes, E. R. 1964. *An introduction to the teaching of dance.* New York: Ronald Press.

John, T. 1978. *The great song book.* Garden City, NY: Doubleday, Bens Book Collection.

Joukowsky, A. M. 1965. _The teaching of ethnic dance._ New York: Lowell Pratt.

Kazar, A. J. 1975. _R. Tait McKenzie: sculpture of athletes._ Knoxville: University of Tennessee Press.

McLaughlin, J. 1988. A stepchild comes of age. _Journal of Physical Education, Recreation and Dance_ Nov/Dec:58–60.

References

Beach, B. 1982. The game started. _Journal of Physical Education, Recreation and Dance_ 53(3):42.

Crawford, S. A. G. M. 1988. The sport film—its cultural significance. _Journal of Physical Education, Recreation and Dance_ Aug:52–58.

Kazar, A. J. 1978. The Wolffe Collection of Sculpture by R. Tait McKenzie. _Journal of Physical Education and Recreation_ Mar:60–61.

National Art Museum of Sport. 1980. Brochure of the 1980 Master Sports Art Exhibition at Lake Placid, New York.

National Art Museum of Sport. 1980. Newsletter, vol. 1, no. 1.

National Art Museum of Sport. 1981. Newsletter, vol. 2, no. 2.

Seeger, R. C. 1948. _American folk songs for children._ Garden City, NY: Doubleday.

Zeitlin, P. 1982. _A song is a rainbow._ Glenview, IL: Scott, Foresman.

7. Scientific Foundations

Chapter Outline

Anatomy and Physiology
Locomotor System
Body Types
Kinesiology
Mechanics of Sport Activity
Sport Skill Analysis
Exercise Physiology
Methods of Conditioning
Strength Training
Student Activities
Suggested Readings
References

Objectives

Chapter 7 is designed to enable you to:

- State the basic reason for the science core in physical education.
- Discuss the implications of sport balance, sport motion, and sport force.
- Be familiar with three methods of sport skill analysis.
- Know the difference between interval, Fartlek, and continuous training methods.
- Know the difference between isotonic, isometric, and isokinetic strength training.

P HYSICAL education majors often have difficulty understanding the purpose of pursuing a scientific base for teaching and coaching activities. Why do professional preparation programs require anatomy, physiology, kinesiology, and exercise physiology as a basic core for the physical education major? Is it necessary to take kinesiology and exercise physiology? Can one teach skills without understanding the biomechanics of movement? Can one adequately ensure the development of fitness by timing runners and obtaining results during the training period?

If we are to be true professionals and teach for mastery or high-level performance, we must have a thorough knowledge of the human beings with whom we work. One must understand not only the principles of training and motor development, but also how external forces and their effects act on the learner or competitor. The contemporary professional preparation curriculum places an increased emphasis on the sciences as related to health, physical fitness, dance, and sport performance.

There is a unique body of knowledge related to movement that includes exercise physiology, kinesiology, motor performance, biomechanics, and physical fitness. Physical educators are an important adjunct to the medical profession.

It seems incomprehensible that one would try to teach a movement skill (1) without knowledge of the growth and development of the individual participating, (2) without understanding the mechanics involved in the skills being learned, (3) with the expectation that the human machine will perform at high levels for extended periods of time but without assurance that the human body is well tuned, and (4) without specific knowledge of the skill or activity to be performed. Unfortunately, there are still numerous professionals in the physical education field who fail to apply the scientific information learned to their daily lessons, whether they be in coaching, teaching, or leading exercises.

Today, participants at all levels cannot achieve their potential unless the teacher or coach uses the knowledge obtained in the science core to facilitate efficient learning or training modes in either the instructional or competitive program. It is important to be able to distinguish accurately between levels of fitness and good and poor sports performance techniques. It is also important to recognize causes and faults in performance as one observes an individual demonstrating a skill. By selecting proper teaching or coaching techniques, based on sound motor-learning principles of length, frequency, and style of practice, the instructor can introduce the proper type of physical training program that will complement the techniques required.

The purpose of this chapter is to acquaint you with the biological areas to be studied; it is not designed to teach the principles involved in each area except by example. The authors believe that, for a true understanding of the scientific bases of sport, the physical education major must be aware of the scientific foundation of the discipline.

Anatomy and Physiology

Most physical education major science courses require a lower-division course in anatomy and physiology. Selected institutions offer anatomy and physiology courses in different ways. Some offer combined courses, and others offer separate courses with a laboratory experience in each. Either way, and regardless of whether the course is taught in the physical education department or the biology department, the purpose is to acquaint the physical education major with the musculoskeletal systems of the body and the physiological functions of the organs and cardiorespiratory system. Add to this a knowledge of the nervous system and the growth and development patterns of the individual from birth through death and one is prepared to develop activity programs appropriate for individuals of all ages. The human body is a mechanical genius that for top performance must have its physiological systems fine-tuned to the highest degree possible. This highly complex organism consists of billions of cells, all performing specialized functions. The proper interaction of the musculoskeletal system with the circulatory and nervous systems is what enables humans to move with the greatest efficiency.

Locomotor System

The locomotor system is composed of a skeleton consisting of 206 bones, which represent approximately 20 percent of your total body weight. These bones of various shapes and sizes are held together by ligaments that connect the body joints. Between the ligaments is the muscle mass that moves the bony levers. This function of movement is the result of nearly 650 muscles, which represent approximately 43 percent of your weight. For the body to move efficiently on a continual basis, a cardiorespiratory system effectively transports nutrients and oxygen to the muscular structure through the blood. Only by studying these functions in detail can the physical educator intelligently prescribe fitness activities or teach skills appropriate to an individual's needs.

The three major body types, or somatotypes, that the physical educator should be able to recognize are (left to right) the endomorph, mesomorph, and ectomorph.

Body Types

Coaches and physical education instructors should strive to understand as much as possible about the individual involved in sport skills or general fitness activities, in order for effective instruction to take place. All of us are different in size and shape. Our body composition, body configuration, proportions, strength, power, speed, and flexibility should be measured before instruction begins. We will not attempt to discuss all these factors now but will acquaint you with the major body types or *somatotypes.*

The most common arrangement of body types was developed by Sheldon, who identified three basic forms: the *mesomorph* or muscular type; the *ectomorph* or slim, linear type; and the *endomorph* or obese type. Further study in this area will result in degrees of refinement for each body type based on direct body or anthropometric measurement (comparative measurement of the human body) of height, weight, skin folds, limb girth, and bone width. The coach can use this information to help select players or assign positions in competitive sport programs.

There is considerable information available (e.g., Carter, 1984) with respect to which body types are best suited for specific sports, specific events, or certain playing positions within selected sports. Most kinesiology texts indicate the advantages of specific body types to successful performance, but there are always exceptions to the rule. Regardless, basic anatomical information is essential to effective coaching and teaching techniques. Developing a good background in this area provides the foundation for more sophisticated study later in one's career.

Kinesiology

Kinesiology is often defined as the study of human motion. The laws of mechanics and physics are studied as they relate to human movement. Logan and McKinney (1977), two noted kinesiologists, state that "for the physical education major, kinesiology specifically means the study of the diversified human motions one observes in the field of sports, dance, and exercise" (p. 1). The physical education major pursues knowledge in this area for purposes of understanding the mechanics of, and improving the performance skills of, individuals participating in sport, dance, and general movement activities.

Fundamental movement can be described as a continuum that runs from the general type of movement abilities necessary to carry out tasks in daily life to the highly specialized sport or dance skills found in competitive or high-performance programs. These highly specialized movements are individual in nature and unique to the restrictive forces that act on and are found within the human body structure.

In movement associated with sport skills, an organized pattern of movement activities is developed. For the most part, these patterns come in the area of gross motor skills or in the more delicate area of fine motor skills related to activities requiring finesse. Gross motor skills involve using the large fundamental muscles of the body required for locomotor activities and selective posture. The fine motor skills involve manipulation often found in less active movements but requiring sensitivity and precision. Many activities articulate fine motor skill performance with the framework of locomotion or postural gross motor activities to complete a movement skill.

Since movement is complex and requires an orchestration of a variety of skills, students of kinesiology must understand how this interaction is related to the performance of the actions of the muscles and how it is achieved through successful sport skill acquisition. After completing course work in kinesiology, the teacher or coach should be able to analyze effectively the technique involved in a sport skill and suggest corrections that will result in improved performance.

By understanding the scientific bases of sport performance, the physical educator can operate beyond the limits of personal coaching experience, mimicry of the style of contemporary champions, or individual preference or personal style. Although these aids are useful, the professional must integrate style with sound principles of movement if optimum performance is the goal.

Mechanics of Sport Activity

If one is to teach the most effective movement technique required for successful performance, it is necessary to understand what effect balance, motion, force, and momentum have on the skill being learned.

Sport Balance

Balance is related to the individual's center of gravity and base of support during sport activity. Balance may need to be maintained over an extended period of time in such sports as archery, or may be fleeting in others such as striking a tennis ball. Each sport skill is unique, and maintaining balance is mandatory for the duration of the action required in a given sport if effective recovery and body position are to be accomplished.

The traditional ready position—with the weight on the balls of the feet and the knees flexed—places the body in a balanced stance that enables the individual to move in any direction with quickness as required by the specific sport. Variations in balance will enhance movement in limited directions.

Sport Motion

In sport skill techniques, linear motion (motion along a straight line) and angular motion (movement about an axis of rotation) are integrated to achieve object velocity. Whether throwing a football or striking a tennis ball, learning the correct technique will enhance sport performance. By studying efficient movement patterns, the teacher can instruct the student, using a scientific basis for discussion.

Sport Force

Force in sport is most simply defined as push or pull. In certain sports such as wrestling, this exertion comes solely from muscular force on the skeleton, which moves the body. Other sports introduce an implement, such as a golf club or tennis racquet, to combine this movement with an extended lever (the club or racquet) to increase speed at impact.

An understanding of Newton's laws of motion is required if one is to pursue excellence in teaching sport activity:

- _Law 1_ A body remains in a state of rest or uniform motion in a straight line unless acted upon by a force.
- _Law 2_ The total force of a body is the product of the mass of the body and its acceleration.
- _Law 3_ To every action there is an equal and opposite reaction.

Careful study of these laws will permit one to detect errors in performance through visual observation and interpretation.

Summation of Forces

Summation of forces relates to the correct sequence of a combination of forces to achieve the desired result. As an example, in golf, if the proper sequential use of legs, arms, and hands is not followed in the downswing, club head speed at impact will be reduced and distance shortened. Whether throwing a ball or striking an object, applying force in the proper sequence is necessary to produce maximum controlled velocity.

Sport Momentum

Momentum is the amount of motion possessed by a moving object. Body momentum is the product of body weight and velocity. In contact sports such as football, the lighter, faster player may develop the same momentum as a heavier, slower player and become just as effective. Of course, we all look for the heavy, fast player for our teams.

Momentum also plays an important role in activities such as putting the shot in track and field. By moving quickly in the confines of the ring, the shot has begun to move forward and the straight movement of the upper body is more effective as the muscles contract in sequence to achieve the summation of forces. Proper leg angles and body position are critical to establishing initial sport momentum.

Anything that moves—whether a football, tennis ball, hockey puck, or person—obeys Newton's laws of motion.

Sport Skill Analysis

For one who teaches sport skills, it is most enjoyable to possess the knowledge that enables one to analyze a movement skill and suggest modes of improvement. Much satisfaction is gained when errors in performance can be recognized and corrected so that the learner can progress. Having the knowledge of correct mechanics and how individuals learn motor skills is the basis for teaching effective movement acquisition in all sport or fitness activities. To teach for sport skill mastery, to teach someone to master a skill, this knowledge is essential.

Observation Analysis

There are various methods used to analyze sport skills, the observation approach being the most common. It requires no special equipment and is the simplest of all methods. When observing a sport skill, the instructor assesses (1) the skill level of the performer, (2) performance consistency, and (3) individual performance style. After the observation, suggestions for improvement are made based on the instructor's knowledge of correct playing form and the learner's movement characteristics *or* result of the action.

Some suggestions for developing sport skill analysis techniques through observation include the following:

- Become as knowledgeable as possible about the skill to be taught.
- Focus on one thing at a time when observing skill development.
- Progress from individual to small-group to total-group observation when teaching large classes.
- Develop a checklist for developmental progress in learning skills.
- Refer to high performance standards to check on the accuracy of observational techniques.

Although subjective in nature, observation becomes more objective as the instructor gains experience and develops a thorough understanding of correct movement patterns.

Film and Videotape Analysis

For the most part, videotape has replaced film with respect to ease of use and cost effectiveness in skill analysis. Videotape and film analysis has become a sophisticated method of determining proper skill performance. Whether in the laboratory or on the playing field, filmed or videotaped performance provides a permanent record that can be stored and retrieved for further study and comparison.

The use of videotape photography allows for immediate feedback to the learner, because a student can observe his or her own performance for a more thorough understanding of the changes needed to improve the skill. Through slow-motion or stop-action pictures, the instructor can more accurately point out performance faults. When the skill is photographed in front of a grid with a timer in the picture, accurate movements can be recorded to show speed, lever action, and angle of performance. Usually, students enrolled in kinesiology classes will have their first experience with videotaping or filming a sport skill and analyzing the performance.

Computerized Skill Analysis

In the more advanced classes of biomechanics, one may use computerized skill analysis to examine an individual's performance. This sophisticated technique will soon become more readily available as the professional becomes more comfortable with the computer. The computer is commonplace in most institutions and is also found in many fitness centers.

One of the most advanced operational centers for computer analysis is the Cota Research Center under the direction of Dr. Gideon Ariel and Vic Braden in Trabuco Canyon near Irvine, California. Ariel, the researcher, and Braden, the "scientific" tennis coach, share a zealous interest in learning more about what obstructs the development of opti-

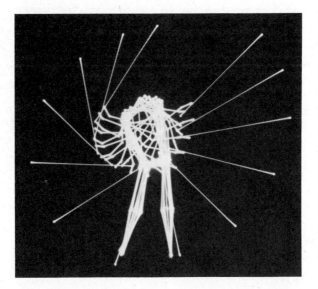

The sophisticated technique of computerized skill analysis enables the physical educator to analyze performance when human movement is too fast to watch closely. Here the golf drive of former president Gerald Ford is shown on the display screen of a computer. The correct sequential use of legs, arms, and hands determines the proper speed and direction of the golf club as it strikes the ball.

mum performance. At the research facility, Dr. Ariel, believing in the old adage that "the hand is quicker than the eye," contends that the body moves too fast for the human eye to discern what the body must do to perform a skill as perfectly as possible. The analysis begins with slow-motion cinematography that records action up to 10,000 frames per second. From this film, each frame is taken separately and the athlete's action traced from joint to joint. This information is transferred into a series of stick figures on the computer display screen, resulting in a continuous series of body positions in each critical phase of action. The resulting analysis enables one to compare any subject's performance to the "theoretically perfect" skill performance of champions. The computer also communicates how and where the subject should modify or change performance to achieve optimum results.

This type of analysis is currently limited; but we may soon see modifications of this system in simplified form in our public schools, colleges, and universities. The growing use of computer skill analysis indicates a need to expand one's knowledge of computer systems and their application to sports.

Exercise Physiology

If you are to teach the values of maintaining efficiency of the human body systems, then you must understand the study of exercise physiology. Too often coaches conduct the conditioning phase of a sport program without a complete knowledge of the sport or activity requirements. One may also discover that the fitness director in a health club may "look the part" but may have little knowledge about designing an individualized fitness program appropriate to the client's needs. For professional instruction to be successful, sound principles of conditioning must be applied.

The Overload Principle

For one to improve one's fitness level, it is necessary to participate in a training program in which the intensity of the activity exceeds that to which the body is usually accustomed. When the training load meets this criterion, the body adapts and will require a greater load if further improvements are desired. If no overload occurs, increased fitness levels will not be achieved. In the case of muscular overload, as is found in weight training, the muscles will increase in size as adaptation occurs to achieve greater strength. If the training load is too light, no increase in performance will result and, in some cases, a deterioration will take place.

It is the instructor's or coach's responsibility to determine scientifically whether training programs are too light, too heavy, or just right for proper development or maintenance without strain or fatigue. Athletes differ greatly in their ability to assimilate hard training, and the coach or teacher should constantly monitor participants for signs of fatigue or strain.

The Principle of Specificity

Exercise programs for sport training should be tailored to the demands of the sport. The muscle groups involved should be exercised if performance gain is to be achieved. A knowledge of the muscle groups used in a baseball swing, for example, should tell the coach what kind of a weight program is best for developing that particular skill. Although general physical conditioning is good for all sports, running alone will not eliminate soreness of the muscles used in specific activities. As an example, in the game of tennis, the stretching and reaching used in the game should be part of the design of the training program.

The same principle applies to sprint activities versus endurance programs. Training limited to one or the other will not necessarily prepare the body to undertake the performance requirements of a specific sport. The coach or teacher must design a program that specifically overloads the muscles or cardiorespiratory requirements involved in the movement patterns of the sport being taught. However, one may vary the workout with nonspecific movements from time to time, without detrimental effect, if this approach is followed for only a limited time and is used primarily as a practice motivator.

Methods of Conditioning

There are now many different types of conditioning programs available for sport and fitness activities. In professional preparation programs, the student will study in detail the strengths, weaknesses, advantages, and disadvantages of each training method. This information will enable the teacher or coach to select the training program best suited to the participant and requirements of the sport or fitness activity. The most common methods of sport conditioning are interval training, Fartlek training, and continuous training.

Interval Training

Interval training is simply a series of repeated exercise bouts alternating with periods of rest. Proponents of the interval training method believe the participant should accomplish all physical work in alternate periods rather than continuously. Many claim more work can be accomplished with less fatigue using this method of conditioning. Successful training using this approach depends on the ability of the coach or teacher to select the proper intensity of the exercise followed by a correct rest period. A sample interval workout plan follows:

Set 1 Warm-up
2-mile jog
15-minute stretch
16 × 110 yards easy (called *shakes*)

Set 2 3 × 550 yards, relaxed pace, good form, diagonal recovery
2-lap job recovery

Set 3 8 × 150 yards downhill, good pace (sprint action downhill)
Jog recovery to start
2-lap jog recovery

Set 4 1-mile cross-country course for time—full (hard)
1-lap jog/walk
880 yards for time—full
1-lap jog/walk
440 yards for time—full
2-lap jog recovery

Set 5 3 × 440 yards—(1) good form
(2) extension/leg extension
(3) good pace

Set 6 3 × 150 yards—alternate relaxed pace/good form
2-lap jog

Cool down 16 shakes
1-lap walk/jog

Progress in training is verified through performance measurement, and the program is adapted as appropriate to the participant. The variables that can be manipulated are (1) duration of the exercise event, (2) intensity of the work, (3) length and type of recovery period, and (4) repetitions of the interval sequence. The recovery phase of the interval program usually consists of light exercise such as walking or slow exercise movements. Interval training is applicable to both distance and endurance activities and selected sport skill drills of either a team or individual nature.

Fartlek Training

The Fartlek training system involves short bursts of speed interspersed between long sessions of continuous training. These short bursts usually last from 5 to 10 seconds and are repeated every 2 to 3 minutes in a 30-minute training session. This system may be viewed as a modified interval training approach to conditioning, with continuous regular exercise rather than intermittent rest periods. This approach to training, sometimes referred to as *speed play,* is effective in running events that are usually a maximum of 1 mile long.

Continuous Training

The continuous training method is activity over extended periods of time. Usually the training bout ranges from 15 minutes to 1 hour and may extend to 2 or more hours for long-distance or marathon runners. The goal of the continuous training participant is to maintain a heart rate between 80 and 85 percent of the maximum during a workout. Therefore, it is critical to know the participant's maximum heart rate in order to regulate the training pace intelligently. A simple method for determining a person's maximum heart rate is to subtract his or her age (in years) from 220.

Continuous training is used for long-distance runners, swimmers, and cyclists. Training for long periods helps the individual get accustomed to the requirements of a sport activity involving extended lengths of participation.

Understanding the different methods of conditioning and their application to various sport and fitness activities is a necessary requirement if effective teaching or coaching is to be achieved.

Strength Training

There are three basic types of training methods commonly used in strength development programs: the *isotonic,* the *isometric,* and the *isokinetic* strength systems. The overload principle is followed closely in strength development programs, as the weight or repetitions are increased to develop muscular power. A closely related development procedure is the progressive resistance system, which is sometimes used as an alternate approach to strength training.

Isotonic Training

Traditional weight-training programs utilize the isotonic system, in which the participant moves the weight in an exercise pattern throughout the range of motion. An example of this approach to strength training would be a bench press using a barbell. The program usually consists of three sets of ten repetitions each. The first set is done at 50 percent of one's maximum, the second at 75 percent, and the third at the repetition maximum. The repetition maximum is determined by trial and error as the participant works ten repetitions with the highest weight possible before becoming fatigued. Obviously, the maximum will vary from individual to individual.

A well-balanced strength program will work all parts of the body. Specific muscle groups should be exercised more if required for high performance in a selected sport.

Isometric Training

Isometric training can be accomplished without weights. In this approach to strength training, there is no range of motion as the individual holds a maximum muscle contraction for 5 seconds and then relaxes. These contractions should be repeated five or six times. The resistance can be obtained by pushing against oneself or by pushing or pulling against an immovable object such as a door jamb. It is important to select the angle of exercise that is appropriate to the sport skill required, as strength will be developed at the angle of pressure exerted.

Isokinetic Training

Isokinetic strength training is comparatively new and requires the use of some expensive equipment. The Nautilus System®, Orthotron®, and Cybex® devices work on the isokinetic principle; exercise is done at a constant speed against a resistance that changes to meet differences in the movement.

The advantage of isokinetic exercise over isotonic exercise is the assurance that the muscles are overloaded at all stages of the movement. Specialized equipment allows the participant to simulate or duplicate the specific movement used in sport activities such as the throwing motion of a baseball pitcher. Slow-speed training bouts with heavy resistance usually consist of three sets of ten repetitions, whereas high-speed movements, in which the resistance is decreased, usually consist of three sets of twenty repetitions. The rate of strength gain has been shown to be the fastest with isokinetic exercise compared to either the isotonic or isometric systems.

New and specialized conditioning equipment is attractive and encourages adherence to personal workouts.

Plyometrics

Plyometric exercise, first discovered by the Europeans, initially was identified as *jump training*. The essence of the exercises is the ballistic eccentric-concentric loading of the elastic components of one's muscle tissue. Designed to enable the muscle to reach maximum strength in the shortest period of time, this type of training is best employed by athletes requiring quickness and vertical leaping abilities, such as in basketball and volleyball. It should be used as a supplement to regular strength training programs for such athletes.

To develop quick response to floor contact, an exercise would consist of 50 to 100 sequential foot contacts with the ground surface using a quick response time between each contact. This training method should be used twice weekly in preseason and once weekly during the sport season, as overuse could result in trauma to the participant. To avoid injury, the contact surface should be soft, and a sound base of personal strength training should be achieved before an individual participates in plyometric exercises.

An example of a plyometric exercise would be to jump down from a box elevated to approximately chair height and quickly jump up to the same height. The number of repetitions would be determined by each individual's initial strength base. Plyometric exercises are designed to be sport- or movement-specific. Exercises can be designed to improve arm and hand quickness, as for the basketball pass, by using a weighted ball.

A thorough study of cardiovascular and strength training systems should be a part of the physical education major's formal course work in the science core. Attention to scientifically based systems of physical conditioning will provide the practitioner with the knowledge required to plan successful programs designed to improve individual sport performance or general health maintenance.

Student Activities

1. Research in detail the major somatotypes and determine your personal body type.
2. Investigate three sport movements and determine the proper movement sequence that is necessary to achieve a favorable summation of forces.
3. Select a sport you enjoy and compare your performance style with that of a champion.
4. Investigate in detail one of the methods of conditioning described in this chapter.
5. Evaluate your personal fitness level and design a plan for individual improvement or lifetime maintenance.

Suggested Readings

Chu, D. A. 1985. Plyometrics for basketball. *Shot Doctor Basketball.* (Fall 1985):10–11.

Garhammer, J. 1986. *Sports Illustrated strength training.* New York: Harper and Row.

Magill, R. A. 1988. *Motor learning—concepts and applications.* Dubuque, IA: William C. Brown.

Shephard, R. J. 1987. *Exercise physiology.* Philadelphia: B. C. Decker.

Stortz, N. S., and W. H. Greene. 1983. Body weight, body image and perception of fad diets in adolescent girls. *Journal of Nutrition Education* 15:15–17.

Wilmore, J. H., and D. L. Costillo. 1988. *Training for sport and activity,* 3rd ed. Dubuque, IA: William C. Brown.

References

Carter, J. E. L. 1984. "Physical structure of olympic athletes," Part II of *Kinanthropometry of Olympic Athletes.* Basel: Karger.

Logan, G. A., and W. C. McKinney. 1977. *Anatomic kinesiology,* 2nd ed. Dubuque, IA: William C. Brown.

Sheldon, W. H., S. S. Stevens, and W. B. Tucker. 1940. *The varieties of human physique.* New York: Harper and Brothers.

8. Sociological and Psychological Foundations

Objectives

Chapter 8 is designed to enable you to:

- Understand the importance of the learning process in physical education.
- Be familiar with the general definitions of terms used in the sociological and psychological foundations.
- Describe the difference between learning and performing a motor skill.
- Be aware of the variety of learning theories that exist.
- Relate to anthropology, comparative physical education, motor learning, sport pedagogy, sport psychology, and sport sociology as they apply to your physical education career.

HISTORICALLY, the emphasis in physical education and sports performance has been on the physiological components of the human body and the mechanics of movement and motor skills. As a motor skill performer, you have probably paid a lot of attention to the health and training of your physical body. The development of higher skills became a function of understanding the most effective mechanics to achieve the desired goal. Then came the commitment to practice and more practice through daily training sessions.

The application of psychological or learning theory to the learning involved in physical education and sport did not command the attention of educational psychologists for many years. Even today, few investigators outside our discipline care much about motor skill development and performance in light of psychological and sociological phenomena. Unfortunately, many physical educators do not integrate psychological and sociological phenomena in motor skill situations to the extent that is possible. Nonetheless, motor learning, sport psychology, sport pedagogy, and sport sociology are recognized within the profession as integral components.

Most learning emphasizes the acquisition and use of verbal and mathematical skills. Since this learning is so important to human affairs, this emphasis is well founded. However, the acquisition and use of motor skills should be equally important. Physical education professionals realize the importance of a healthy well-trained body to the development and use of verbal skills; yet the back-to-basics movement focuses solely on reading, writing, and arithmetic. The current focus on critical thinking skill development is based in the academic part of the curriculum. However, we know that the ability to perform high-level motor skills consistently well in a variety of situations requires advanced thinking skills. The development of basic motor skills is ignored unless a deficiency happens to be noticed. Competency-based teaching and testing programs are now the vogue. Many students across the United States are required to pass competency tests before they are allowed to graduate from high school. Physical education is not a competency that is generally tested, owing to the low value placed on fitness and basic motor skills by the curriculum decision makers. In an age of increasing educational accountability, we need to be prepared to justify and promote our discipline as a basic skill worthy of some form of competency testing. Before students are allowed to move from the required to the elective program, specific fitness parameters, motor skills, knowledge, and attitudes should be tested. Periodic retesting during an elective program should be undertaken to supervise maintenance levels. Our greatest accountability lies in the failure of many Americans to exercise or participate in active sports and recreational activity.

Importance of Behavioral Sciences to Physical Education

The outcome of physical education programs are generally stated in terms of three domains: motor, cognitive, and affective. Although researchers have attempted to provide information to assist teachers in setting motor skill objectives and designing instructional programs to help children meet them, there is less information available in physical education for the cognitive and affective objectives. It appears that while we continually expound on the social and emotional growth of the "whole" child, we do not know very much about the processes of psychosocial development that could influence our teaching behaviors to facilitate children's progress. According to Bressan and Weiss (1985), the social psychology of sport and motor behavior offers an excellent starting place for developing theoretically grounded strategies for building social and emotional development through physical education experiences.

The behavioral sciences focus on the behavior of human beings. *Behavior* is a fundamental term used in all the social sciences. It refers to activities that are observable by another person or appropriate recording instruments. The social sciences provide teachers and coaches with vital information for the assessment of student behavior in the motor, cognitive, and affective domains and for the planning of appropriate instructional activities and methodology to enhance a student's or athlete's performance.

Physical educators and coaches are especially interested in motor behaviors, specifically those that occur while one is engaged in sport, dance, or exercise. Teachers and coaches help people develop new skills or improve old ones.

They are also very interested in factors that can influence motor skill learning and perception. These factors vary from individual personalities to a performer's response to the effects of stress or relaxation on a given motor performance, and specific methods to motivate athletes for top performance.

As a future professional, you will begin to realize that the study of sociological and psychological foundations is an important component of your professional preparation. Whether you are the teacher or coach working with young people to develop healthy lifestyles or working in programs with individuals who need retraining, understanding the role that psychology, sociology, and motor learning play will make you more effective in your chosen career. Your future course work will include entire courses on these subdisciplines. This chapter is devoted to identifying concepts that you will encounter. Examples that illustrate the application of some concepts will also be included.

Defining Terms

As a physical education major, you should understand the language of your profession, particularly the vocabulary used to describe aspects of the discipline. Among physical educators, there are different opinions about how to use some of these terms. For example, some believe that *psychology of motor behavior* and *sport psychology* are redundant terms whereas others believe that we do not have enough knowledge to justify using the term *behavior* in the motor domain. Your understanding of these terms and your personal opinion about their use will grow and change as you gain more experience as a physical educator, but for now you should at least be familiar with these definitions.

Comparative physical education is a means of studying the similarities and differences that exist in physical education and sport in various countries of the world.

Cultural anthropology is the study of humans as individuals and the comparison and contrasting of various societies of people both contemporary and historical.

Culture is the custom, knowledge, art, law, belief, and morals that an individual acquires as a member of a specific group or society.

Motor behavior is specifically concerned with motor skill acquisition and performance. This subject consists of a body of knowledge, compiled using the scientific method, about the psychological aspects of human physical performance patterns. Thus, it may be viewed as a subfield of psychology (Sage, 1971).

Motor learning is what occurs in the brain as an individual improves his or her motor skills in attempting to accomplish a particular set of goals with precision and accuracy. The learning process consists of a variety of motor and perceptual responses acquired through practice and repetition. Eventually, the learner develops a set of motor responses into an integrated and organized movement pattern.

Perceptual motor (sensory motor) learning is the ability of the individual to receive, identify, interpret, and react properly to a multitude of external and internal stimuli (Barrow, 1977).

Psychology is a scientific field of study of complex forms of integration or organization of an individual's behavior.

Psychology of motor behavior is an attempt to learn more, and understand better, all of the psychological factors that are involved in motor activity within an individual.

Sociology is the scientific discipline that describes and explains human social organization. The size of a human group under study can range from a couple to a church congregation, a corporation, a community, or a society (Eitzen and Sage, 1978).

Sport is an institutionalized competitive activity that involves vigorous physical exertion or the use of relatively complex physical skills by individuals whose participation is motivated by a combination of the intrinsic satisfaction associated with the activity itself and the external rewards earned through participation.

Sport pedagogy is the art, science, or profession of physical education that includes formal study and research in the areas of curriculum, teaching methodology, teacher education, evaluation, organization, and administration.

Sport psychology is the scientific study of behavior in a sport or sport-related context. It is an attempt to understand the how and why underlying sport behavior. The central focus is sports for men and women of all ages and levels of competition.

Sport sociology is the scientific study of the role of sport in society.

Learning and Performance

Learning is a relatively permanent change in behavior that is reinforced through practice. Learning theories are concerned with how these changes take place and do not generally differentiate between cognitive and basic motor skills. Motor skills range from reflex behavior to complex perceptual motor tasks that require sensory integration, memory processes, motor integration, and feedback during and immediately after the pattern of movement (Sage, 1971). Essentially the same structures of the central nervous system are used in verbal learning and motor learning. A quality physical education program creates a favorable change in behavior.

Learning is different from performance. Performance can be observed. Measuring changes in performance is the method used to determine how much learning has taken place. Although performance is based on learning, there are many other variables that affect performance, such as motivation and fatigue. It is often difficult to ascertain how much performance change is due to learning or to other variables.

Learning Theories

Learning theories represent information that has been systematized and verified into principles that are relevant to understanding education and teaching its activities. Learning theories provide the guidelines that help make teaching and learning more effective. The physical education major should have a primary concern for the learning process.

There are still many mysteries surrounding the learning process, and all theories are in a state of flux because no one theory holds the answers to all questions. Theories are an attempt to organize research data into meaningful systems, but they are difficult to verify. Some new ones create new ways of looking at learning situations, but the learning process is so complicated that we may never fully understand how the human mind functions.

In contemporary psychological literature, four theories are prominent: conditioning theory, molding and imitation, cognitive restructuring, and information processing. A brief summary of each is presented here. In your professional preparation program, you will study these theories more intensively later.

Conditioning. For a long time psychologists have attempted to explain the phenomenon of learning. The conditioning theory is a classical study of behavior and is generally divided into two components known as *classical* and *operant*. Conditioning establishes a transfer or an association between an original stimulus and a new stimulus to elicit the same response. The well-known example of classical conditioning is Pavlov's work with dogs: The dogs learned to associate the ringing of a bell with the sight of food, which made them salivate. Eventually, only the ringing of the bell was needed to stimulate the flow of saliva. This was the conditioned response. The learner reacts by associating the reaction with a specific stimulus that has been followed with some type of reward or reinforcement. This form of learning involves one stimulus followed by a single response and is regarded as the basic form of true learning as opposed to instinctive behavior.

Operant conditioning, made famous by the work of B. F. Skinner, allows for even more flexibility in behavior. This conditioning permits the subject freedom to choose responses and also to choose when to respond. Reinforcement is provided when the desired response occurs. This conditioning is more concerned with the consequence of acts rather than the stimuli.

The components of the conditioning theory suggest that prompt positive reinforcement of desirable behaviors helps shape behaviors associated with affective learning. This could include emotions, attitudes, values, and motivation. Teachers of physical education, for example, should positively reinforce successful performance or personal effort by the learner.

Molding and Imitation. The theory of molding and imitation is based on the learner's observation of accurate performances according to teaching models. The learner tries to imitate or make responses from observations. Models can be real people such as a teacher, coach, or peer. Instructional media is founded on this principle and is represented in pictures, filmstrips, and videotapes.

Although this approach is often used in teaching motor skills, research has not yet confirmed that a student can learn the correct performance solely from observing a model. Complex motor skills may not lend themselves as readily to this technique as basic skills. It must also be noted that the strength (including the sex, cultural background, and status) of the model appears to be very important.

Cognitive Restructuring. Cognitive restructuring applies to more complex situations in which perception and cognitive knowledge play important roles. The learner must perceive relationships between concepts. Once this insight has been successfully applied, it can be repeated and transferred to similar learning needs. This theory does not advocate rote learning such as memorization of facts but does encourage problem solving and creativity.

A teacher using this concept designs instruction so that students associate new knowledge with previously learned skills. Concepts are arranged in appropriate sequences to encourage desired responses. This method has been used for cognitive learning, but more research is needed to examine this technique in the motor domain.

Information Processing. The advent of the computer age has triggered intense investigations into the human brain as an information processor. Scientists are comparing computer communication and information retrieval systems to the neurological pathways in the human nervous system. The ability to store, return, and retrieve information in a serial manner for varying periods of time appears to be the key to this learning theory. Though intriguing, the theory of information processing will require much more research to determine the capability of the brain as a computer.

Information processing is becoming more important every day. The amount of knowledge available to be learned and applied is growing rapidly. Computers are becoming a necessity even in the home. The ability of an individual to process and retain information accurately is becoming a basic survival skill even in the world of sport. People are performing unbelievable feats of skill, strength, and endurance. The ability to build on a basic movement vocabulary is the mark of a highly skilled athlete. An understanding of the brain as an information-processing system will provide increased levels of motor performance at an infinite pace.

ity to build on a basic movement vocabulary is the mark of a highly skilled athlete. An understanding of the brain as an information-processing system will provide increased levels of motor performance at an infinite pace.

Motor Learning

Motor learning has assumed a significant role in the teaching of motor skills and the training of highly skilled performers. The major difference between the novice and the skilled athlete is that the latter has mastered a large number of movement patterns. It is important to understand how motor skills are acquired and what factors affect learning and performance.

There are many variables that account for the speed with which learning a motor skill occurs, how skills are retained with varying practice patterns, what skill level can be developed, and what level of performance is possible at any given time. Anyone responsible for improving performance should know and understand how a skill is broken down into teachable units, how fatigue affects learning, how practice sessions should be organized and what length they should be, and how to motivate an individual to learn.

Individualized Instruction

A skilled performer is characterized as one who can produce a fast output of high quality (Sage, 1971). Smoothness and ease of movement, variations in performance, and the ability to modify motor performance are considered characteristics of the highly skilled individual. The ease with which a skillful swimmer moves through the water as compared to the beginner splashing laboriously up and down the pool reflects a sharp contrast in performance. The challenge to the teacher is to assist the novice in learning the motor skills involved in apparently effortless swimming. The novice swimmer is faced with developing a new movement vocabulary in the aquatic environment. Fear, fatigue, self-confidence, and motivation are constantly interacting in varying degrees. Individualized instruction is very important to a beginner.

Planning each swimming lesson involves much more than deciding which stroke to teach and how many laps each swimmer must swim. A good teacher will evaluate the previous class and use information from the analysis to plan the next lesson. Questions to be answered might include the following:

What new techniques could I try to reduce Sally's fear of putting her whole face in the water?

Jeremy continues to swim only with his upper torso. The stroke must be reviewed, with the leg action emphasized for this lesson.

Craig is very muscular but extremely tense. He tires after two laps. What can I do to help him relax?

Gayle performs the whip kick well but cannot coordinate the kick with the arms to achieve a smooth, relaxed stroke. How can I explain it to her so she can be successful today?

Pete's front crawl is unusual but fairly efficient. He has improved a lot and is enjoying himself. Further pressure on technique does not meet his needs. It is time to introduce a new stroke to him.

Clearly, individuals respond differently even when attempting to achieve similar skills or levels of performance. A knowledge of motor learning enables a teacher or coach to individualize learning, even in group settings, so that each participant can increase his or her knowledge and skills.

Some learning conditions are more effective than others for acquiring skills. Learning how to do a handspring, to pole-vault, or to shoot a basketball requires a lot of practice with precise motor responses. The performer's knowledge of results keeps him or her informed and motivated. Each individual brings to a new task his or her previous experiences, which will affect the development of new skills. Many motor skills have similar movement patterns that may assist in or interfere with learning another. The way one uses the wrist when playing badminton, for example, is different from the way one uses it in tennis. If these two skills are taught simultaneously, many people will have difficulty performing either one very well. However, many gymnastic and diving skills have a high carryover that facilitates performance.

The acquisition of motor skills is a very complex matter. Research has demonstrated why some traditional teaching techniques have or have not been effective, yet there are still many questions to be answered. The competent professional will learn as much as possible about motor skill development and keep abreast of the current research long after leaving the college campus.

Sport Pedagogy

Pedagogy is regarded as the art and science of teaching. This subdiscipline includes teaching methodology, curriculum design, professional preparation of teachers, evaluation techniques, and administration of programs. This area of study has been the core of the teaching profession but continues to require modification to meet rising expectations.

The literature is rich with studies on teaching methodology, class organization, grouping patterns, motor skill development, self-concept, and methods of evaluating student performance. Much research has focused on appropriate curricular activities. However, there are still many unanswered questions concerning the individualization of teaching in physical education, where physical maturation can conflict with age groupings.

Increasing teacher effectiveness has been the focal point of the discipline of pedagogy. It seems only appropriate that as professionals we acknowledge the existence of pedagogy as a discipline in its own right. Many traditional teaching methods are still very appropriate. However, new teaching methods and class organizational designs can contribute to a more effective teaching-learning experience.

Muska Mosston (1966) developed a spectrum of styles for teaching physical education, which comprised an important contribution to sport pedagogy. His spectrum begins with the teacher in control of the learning environment and ends with the student in self-directed learning. Mosston promotes independence in decision making, in seeking alternatives, and in learning. The interaction of individualized learning and the cognitive process is described throughout his spectrum. The spectrum begins with the command style of teaching, which has, unfortunately, long exemplified the teaching process in physical education. Mosston goes on to examine these other teaching styles as well: teaching by task, reciprocal teaching (the use of a partner), use of the small group, the individual program, guided discovery, problem solving, and creativity. Throughout his book, Mosston attempts to enlighten physical educators, both old and new, about successful alternatives for teaching motor skills. This work will continue to influence sport pedagogy for many more years.

Curriculum development is an important facet of pedagogy. Traditionally, the development of a curriculum in physical education has been rather haphazard and based on tradition, teacher prejudices, and seasonal changes. In their work with secondary school curricula, Bucher and Koeing (1978) advocate the systems approach to curriculum design, which provides a scientific, logical, and systematic method for preparing a program of physical education that will meet student needs. The coeducational approach to curriculum development is an important addition to pedagogy. Melograno (1979) addresses the concept of sex neutrality in physical education in his recent book. Both sexes are capable of achieving high-level performance in a coeducational setting. Physical education teachers must maintain high levels of expectations for their students. Curriculum development and teaching methodology will be an important component of your program of study.

The key to establishing the credibility of physical education as an area in which psychosocial development is formally addressed is found in linking an academic understanding of that development to an instructional theory that incorporates responsible professional practices. Effective instruction is still not well understood (Bressan and Weiss, 1985). Much research has focused only on teacher behavior. Barrow (1977) sees instruction as a dynamic interaction of observation, teacher behavior, and reaction.

Bressan and Weiss (1985) elaborated on research data to develop a cycle of instruction to promote positive experiences within physical activity. The central process is observation. Observation for competence requires focusing on a child's ability to handle the physical and cognitive demands of an activity. Observing for persistence is similar to what Seidentop (1977) described as children's on-task behavior. This includes such techniques as observing whether or not participation can be continued under varying circumstances, such as the use of task cards in lieu of direct leadership by a teacher. Seidentop (1977), through the development of systematic observation techniques, has been able to verify that "good teaching," which generally indicates direct teaching, is more effective.

If teaching behavior can be defined as either modifying task difficulty or modifying the degree and type of educational support provided to the learner, then task difficulty is a function of physical and cognitive challenge and psychosocial strategies related to the support of the learner's confidence and persistence. Deciding what degree of support to provide to children in a given instructional situation must be based on information gathered from observation.

Hellison (1987) states that if we are to make progress in clarifying and delimiting goals in each of the three domains (motor, cognitive, and affective) and in implementing goal-related strategies, the teachers responsible for these programs must assume a primary role in the curriculum and instruction decision-making process. To become the kind of decision maker needed, teachers need to study and experience different goals and strategies, to learn to problem set before they problem solve, and to develop and continually refine theory in action.

Instruction in physical education has advanced to include the development of instructional systems and multimedia packages. For example, through the use of videotape replays, knowledge of results is more precise. The future of sport pedagogy will see extensive use of computers and instructional technology to group students accurately in classes, especially in coeducational classes, according to abilities, traits, skills, fitness levels, and previous experiences. A trend is developing that will see a greater emphasis on student-motivated learning and less on teacher-induced learning. A well-developed curriculum is a prerequisite for successful motor learning and lifelong participation. Cooperation between the researcher and the practitioner is critical to the survival of the teaching profession.

Sport Psychology (Psychology of Motor Behavior)

Sport psychology covers a wide spectrum of physical activities. It attempts to observe, assess, describe, explain, and predict human behavior, its antecedents, and its consequences in a sport situation. Individuals, small groups, teams, and secondary participants (that is, spectators, family, and peers) may be involved in the quest to add to the body of knowledge concerning conduct in sport-related circumstances (Kroter, 1980).

This area of study includes the study of individuals participating in physical activities that range from relatively unstructured noncompetitive activities to highly competitive professional sports. Sport psychology attempts to help the teacher and coach understand why people behave the way they do and how the behavior affects their performances. The study of personality in sports has been a major area of concern, but information about the role personality plays in the selection of sport participation and about the effect of sport participation on personality development remains inconclusive. Alderman (1974) states that the research does not demonstrate that specific personality types are associated with high performance in particular sports.

Seidentop (1977) subscribes to the concept that sport education should be a central focus of physical education. To understand this concept, one must understand the nature of play. A person's play life is as important as any other part of his or her life; it is a vital aspect of the human experience. Play is not synonymous with child's play. We must not be afraid to suggest and defend the idea that what we offer as physical education is to teach people how to _play_ sport and dance. The task of the professional sport educator is to minimize the potential for failure in two ways. First, by carefully programming learning sequences, continuous frustration due to failure can be minimized. Second, the climate of the learning environment must be such that failure is recognized as only a momentary occurrence. Avoidance tendencies (Seidentop, 1977) can then be eliminated so that students may incorporate physical activities into their lifestyles and continue to have their lives enhanced through motor play long after their formal education ends.

As a physical educator, you should have some understanding of individual differences in level of participation, competitiveness, aggression, motivation, stress levels, and group cohesion in a team setting. The consideration of personal needs, interests, and attitudes is important in learning to treat people as individuals, whether in a class, coaching setting, sporting goods store, therapy session, or recreational program.

Sport psychology can be recognized in action in nearly every physical activity setting and in many related areas. To date, sport psychology studies have centered on the male college-age athlete. More data must be gathered to include both sexes and all age and performance levels, minorities, and special populations in sports and physical activities. The effect of youth sports on the psychological development of the child has become a growing area of research, as the roles of the coach, spectator, and parent are examined. The following shows evidence of sport psychology in several human movement professions.

Teacher
Personality of the students
Effect of competition on
    individuals
Motivation to participate
Appropriate reinforcement
    techniques
Achievement orientation
Risk behavior
Aggression
Sex-role bias
Emotional stability

Sporting goods salesperson
Sport preference
Personal ego

Coach
All of the above
Commitment and drive
Leadership
Group cohesiveness
Respect for coach
Mental toughness

Amount of participation
Type of participation
Preferred brands
Customer's personality
Salesman's personality
Drive, commitment

Health spa director
Commitment of members
Spa attractiveness
Environment
Self-concepts of individual
Preferred workout schedule (time of day)
Motivation of member
Competitiveness
Influence of others

Spectator
Commitment to a team
Level of employment
Daily tensions
Aggressiveness
Sex
Age
Personal competitive experience
Sport observing (youth, college, professional)
Respect for authority
Social involvement
Family participation
Television versus live viewing at the stadium or park

Sport Sociology

The sociological study of sport is a technique for understanding the complexities of society. Sport is an institution that provides a relevant laboratory for the study of the socialization of values and behaviors in a society. The games people play, degree of competitiveness people exhibit, types of rules, constraints on the participants, benefits or lack of benefits that groups receive under the existing arrangements, rate and type of change, and reward system in sport provide us with a microcosm of the society in which it occurs.

The subdiscipline, sociology of sport, was introduced in the 1960s. Since sport was the relevant phenomenon, no reference was made to physical education. The objective of the new subdiscipline was to understand sport per se, to identify the regularity of underlying patterns of behavior within a sport context. Early sport sociologists were more interested in identifying distinctions between play, games, and sport.

Sociological analysis does not focus on the rightness or wrongness of a situation; it simply presents the perceived reality. This can be a problem for physical educators who are used to making judgments and developing plans of action to improve a social situation. Empirical data do not always support a long-held belief—for example, beliefs related to character building through sport.

There is growing interest in some topics that may bring sport sociologists and physical educators closer together in their missions. The effect of competition is one mutual area of concern. Dubois (1986) found that children who participated in a less competitive context, in which team or individual statistics were not kept and which tended to switch players from one team to another to ensure competition balance, tended to have more fun and exhibited better sportsmanship. This finding has implications for both physical education and sport settings. Research on attrition in sport tends to support the notion that game experiences and outcome can be shaped by values inherently stressed either in the programs themselves or in the types of roles the participants occupy during their involvement (Greendorfer, 1987). This data reflects on all types of organized physical activity.

It is important to understand the role of sport in society for all careers relating to the development and use of motor skills. Teachers and coaches need to understand how sports and physical activity influence the attitudes of young people. There are many social groups in our society that influence youth, including the family, church, peer group, school, and community. A high school student from Chicago, Illinois, will probably exhibit some attitudes or behaviors similar to those of a high school student from a small rural town in Idaho; however, it is possible that there will be striking differences in their social patterns and behavior when they participate in sports.

The support of the state educational system and the local community for equal opportunities in athletic competition for boys and girls is one sociological phenomenon. Regardless of sex equity legislation, boys in some parts of the country have more opportunities for competition than girls. Some states restrict other competitive opportunities for boys, such as in volleyball, wrestling, gymnastics, and soccer. Yet many local school districts do provide a wide range of competitive sports for both boys and girls, which include but are not limited to volleyball, badminton, and water polo.

The presence or absence of certain sports in a community reflects the priorities of that community. The cost of quality education continues to rise, and funding for sports is a major issue; athletic programs are costly. However, many Americans still live in small communities, and small-town identities are strongly related to school sports. For instance, football is often acknowledged as a source of community pride and generally receives much more support. A judgment from outsiders is irrelevant to those who live in small towns and who make the decisions for their youth based on a tradition of beliefs and values.

The existence and support of professional teams in a given city or state also provides important sociological information that must be considered in the value of activities within a curriculum. Cities across the nation support different teams or sports with varying degrees of strength. Professional soccer, ice hockey, and women's basketball have received varying degrees of support in urban communities. Women's professional basketball has yet to be successful. Several teams were developed again for the 1989-90 season amid hopes for future growth.

Sport reflects our society in many other ways. Our system of social control, division of labor, ethics, and economics are important concepts. Eitzen and Sage (1978) have identified the following qualities of sport in the United States that are reflected in the larger society or qualities of society that are reflected in sport:

A very high degree of competitiveness (demand for winners)
A tremendous emphasis on materialism (athletes signing for multimillion-dollar contracts)
The pervasiveness of racism (which attitudes and actions continue to affect the play, position, number of starters, and futures of minority group members in sports)
Individuals dominated by bureaucrats
The unequal distribution of power of organizations (boards of regents, American Athletic Union, United States Olympic Committee, National Collegiate Athletic Association [NCAA], NAIA)
The use of conflict (strikes or boycotts) to change unequal power relationships in sports
Substance abuse

The sociology of sport is developing into an important area of study as a result of the unique role sport plays in American society; sport is becoming increasingly important as we become more leisure-oriented. Sports and sport-related trivia are found everywhere we turn. Much of our time is spent discussing sports, viewing sports, reading the sports page, and buying sporting goods. Major television stations compete for the right to broadcast sporting events, and the competition to televise the Olympics and major collegiate championships is stiff. In 1981, NCAA negotiated a 4-year, $263 million agreement with the American Broadcasting Corporation (ABC) and the Columbia Broadcasting System (CBS), while the young College Football Association negotiated a 4-year $180 million agreement with the National Broadcasting Corporation (NBC). This stimulated a great deal of controversy between the two organizations on the rights of televising their respective football contests. The rights to the Olympic Games of 1988 in Seoul, South Korea, were negotiated by the major television networks and won by NBC; despite poor ratings, that network still made money. NBC then pursued but lost the televison rights for the 1992 Winter Olympics to CBS.

In addition, much of our social life revolves around sports. Televised Monday night football has been a tremendous success. Originally intended to be a means of televising University of Connecticut athletics in the state, ESPN has become the nation's largest cable network providing round-the-clock coverage of sports to more than 52 million households (57.9 percent of American homes with television). Seen by 1.4 million subscribers when it began operations in 1979, ESPN is now seen in all 50 states, Guam, Puerto Rico, the Virgin Islands and 60 foreign countries. ESPN has come a long way since televising its first event in 1979: a slow-pitch softball game between the Kentucky Bourbons and the Milwaukee Schlitzes. In addition to signing the first cable contract with the National Football League in 1987, the network achieved another milestone with a 4-year contract with Major League Baseball in 1989 to carry 175 games a year (Smyth, 1989).

Athletes are the heroes of our youth. Consequently, we see well known athletes used by the advertising media to promote everything from after-shave lotion to automobiles and cereals.

Sport has completely permeated our society. Whether one supports the role of sport in society is not the point. The fact remains that sport is a microcosm of American society and reveals much information about the nature of that society.

The pervasive role of sport in society is important to all professionals in careers related to physical activity. We must understand how the concept of play and recreation has evolved into a series of highly structured sports and games, beginning with youth sports. The importance of winning and the lack of tolerance for losing or failure can be reflected in the attitudes and behaviors of students in a physical education class or of men and women in adult recreation leagues. The greater your understanding of the complex role of sports in our society and the effect it has on individuals, the more successful you will be in your chosen physical activity career path.

Anthropology

There is a close overlapping of the discipline of anthropology and sociology. Some believe that anthropology now serves as an overall science for human beings. Anthropologists are interested in evolution and genetics to help increase their understanding of the total development of the human species. Basically, anthropologists study the behaviors of human beings and their interaction with their environment. Anthropological study includes the following four areas of specialized research: (1) archaeology, (2) linguistics, (3) cultural anthropology, and (4) physiological or biological anthropology.

Cultural anthropology is one area of interest to those involved in physical activity. Researchers in the field focus on human institutions, social interrelationships among human groups, and the customs that are distinctive to each culture. They also study the behaviors humans learn and how they are modified. Humans create their culture. Culture is often described as humankind's ways of feeling, believing, and thinking, and ways that we recall them at any point in the future. A major function of culture is in providing direction to humans and their societies in our attempt to understand *who we are and what we do.* The physical educator should help the public to realize that sport, dance, exercise, and physical play are fundamental parts of American culture.

Archaeology also helps us to learn about the culture of ancient peoples through the discoveries of relics, artifacts, and buildings. This area of research provides a great deal of information on the history of physical activities and the play experience.

Physiological anthropology is the study of human adaptation through physiological responses to environmental conditions that have a strong effect on physiological functions. There are some elements of climate studies that are of interest to physical educators. One example is the effects of hot, dry climates on performance: Anthropological research illustrates that drinking large amounts of water prior to exposure to hot desert climatic conditions is not helpful because excess water cannot be stored. The lesson for coaches is that drinking small amounts more often decreases dehydration. Researchers have also proved false the myth that white people sweat less than black people. Other studies illustrated the effects of cold temperatures, high altitudes, and other physiological conditions on physical performance. These examples illustrate the vast amount of data that are available for practitioners in our profession. Physiological anthropology is an area of research that should be explored in greater depth for its possible contributions to sport science.

Although we have only briefly introduced you to the impact of the study of the various components of anthropology or human movement experiences, the importance of this area of study should not be underrated. It is one of the essential foundations of physical education.

Comparative Physical Education

In recent years, comparative physical education has emerged as a force in understanding international education. Such study is valuable because it provides insight into other cultures and helps us learn from them. For example, the movement for daily physical education in the United States came from Australia and Canada. The various U.S. coaching effectiveness programs for international levels of competition are based on programs in Canada, Australia, and the Federal Republic of Germany. Soviet methods have also changed our attitudes about high-level training and coaching. Our concept of the amateur athlete has been greatly influenced by the Soviets. The impact of Glasnost on international sport is not yet fully known.

Another important component of comparative physical education is the increasing amount of cross-cultural research, as investigators study common questions and concerns in physical education and sport. This area of study is indicative of our shrinking globe and the need to share ideas and learn from our world neighbors.

Sport and the Special Child

The learning of motor skills by children with disabilities has increased dramatically in our schools. The learning process for the learning disabled and the mentally retarded has been the subject of much research. Discussions of mainstreaming these children into regular physical education classes has aroused much controversy and many cooperative efforts.

As a result of U.S. legislation (the Education for All Handicapped Children Act, PL94-142), opportunities for these children have been mandated. Regardless of government legislation and funding, each of us in the field must recognize our professional responsibilities to meet the needs of all students. Adaptive physical education plays an important role in the development of motor skills within each individual's level of disability. One is only as handicapped as one perceives oneself to be. Sport and physical activity also play a very important role in the psychological development and socialization of these special children and adults in our society.

In your professional preparation, a course in adapted physical education will provide important knowledge about, skills suited to, and field experiences with children with various disabilities. Your ability to understand the sociopsychological needs of these special students relevant to their learning processes is important to furthering the mainstreaming of such individuals with the so-called average student or recreational participant.

Student Activities

1. Keep a journal for a week to record all contact you have with physical activity and sport. Remember to include television, radio, newspaper, cartoons, magazines, advertisements, conversation, and actual physical activity. Based on this record, do you consider sport a pervasive part of our society?

2. Observe a physical education class or coaching session and list all the sociological and psychological processes that you observe during the activity.

3. Reflect on your most recent motor skill activity. Identify the sociological and psychological concepts that you believe affected your learning and performance.

4. Describe the attributes of your most admired public school physical educator. How many of these traits are reflected in sociological and psychological foundations?

5. Go to your library and draw up a list of periodicals in the research literature that report on the sociological and psychological foundations of physical education and sport. Select one article of interest and write an abstract of it.

6. Develop a list of four or five questions on the sociological and psychological foundations that particularly interest you. Select several different people to interview and record their responses, on audiotape if possible. Compare and contrast their responses as objectively as possible. Then compare them to your personal responses.

7. Investigate the role of motivation in relation to performance.

8. Select a culture (not yours), historical and contemporary, and research it to determine the evolution of sport and physical activity.

Suggested Readings

Blair, S. 1985. Professionalization of attitude toward play in children and adults. *Research Quarterly for Exercise and Sport* 56(1):82–83.

Blanchard, K. 1988. Sport and ritual—a conceptual dilemma. *Journal of Physical Education, Recreation and Dance* Nov/Dec:48–52.

Bray C. 1988. Sport and social change—socialist feminist theory. *Journal of Physical Education, Recreation and Dance.* Aug:50–53.

Bressan, E. S., and M. R. Weiss. 1985. Relating instructional theory to children's psychosocial development. *Journal of Physical Education, Recreation and Dance* Nov/Dec:34–36.

Coakley, J. J. 1986. *Sport in society: issues and controversies.* St. Louis: Time/Mirror/Mosby.

Dubois, P. 1986. The effect of participation in sport on the value orientations of young athletes. *Sociology of Sport Journal* 3:29–42.

Edward, S. W., and S. A. Huston. 1984. The clinical aspects of sport psychology. *The Physical Educator* Oct:

Greendorfer, S. L. 1985. Sociology of sport. *The Physical Educator* 169–193.

Hellison, D. 1989. The affective domain in physical education. *Journal of Physical Education, Recreation and Dance* Aug:41–43.

Miller, D. M. 1987. Energizing the thinking dimension of physical education. *Journal of Physical Education, Recreation and Dance* Oct:76–99.

References

Alderman, R. B. 1974. *Psychological behavior in sport.* Philadelphia: Saunders.

Barrow, H. M. 1977. *Man and movement: principles of physical education,* 2/e. Philadelphia: Lea and Febiger.

Blair, S. 1985. Professionalization of attitude toward play in children and adults. *Research Quarterly for Exercise and Sport* 56(1):82–83.

Blanchard, K. 1988. Sport and ritual—a conceptual dilemma. *Journal of Physical Education, Recreation and Dance* Nov/Dec:48–52.

Bray C. 1988. Sport and social change—socialist feminist theory. *Journal of Physical Education, Recreation and Dance.* Aug:50–53.

Bressan, E. S., and M. R. Weiss. 1985. Relating instructional theory to children's psychosocial development. *Journal of Physical Education, Recreation and Dance* Nov/Dec:34–36.

Bucher, Charles, A. & Constance, R. 1978. *Methods and materials for secondary school physical education.* St. Louis: Mosby.

Coakley, J. J. 1986. *Sport in society: issues and controversies.* St. Louis: Time/Mirror/Mosby.

Dubois, P. 1986. The effect of participation in sport on the value orientations of young athletes. *Sociology of Sport Journal* 3:29–42.

Edward, S. W., and S. A. Huston. 1984. The clinical aspects of sport psychology. *The Physical Educator* Oct:

Eitzen, D. S. and G. H. Sage. 1978. *Sociology of American sport.* Dubuque, Iowa: Brown Co.

Greendorfer, S. L. 1985. Sociology of sport. *The Physical Educator* :169–193.

Greendorfer, S. L. 1987. Psychosocial correlates of organized physical activity. *Journal of Physical Education, Recreation and Dance* Sept:59–63.

Greendorfer, S. L. 1987. Psychosocial correlates of organized physical activity. *Journal of Physical Education, Recreation and Dance* Sept:59–63.

Hellison, D. 1989. The affective domain in physical education. *Journal of Physical Education, Recreation and Dance* Aug:41–43.

Kroter, M. L. 1980. Sport psychology. *Journal of Physical Education and Recreation,* 51(November/December 1980):48.

Melagrano, V. 1979. *Designing curriculum and learning: a physical coeducation approach.* New York: Kendall/Hunt, pp.27–33.

Miller, D. M. 1987. Energizing the thinking dimension of physical education. *Journal of Physical Education, Recreation and Dance* Oct:76–99.

Mourton, M. 1966. Teaching physical education. Columbus, Ohio: Merrill.

Nixon, J. E., and A. E. Jewett. 1980. *An introduction to physical education.* Philadelphia: Saunders College Press.

Sage, G. H. 1971. *Introduction to motor behavior: a neuropsychological approach.* Reading, MA: Addison-Wesley.

Seidentop, D. 1977. *Physical education: introduction analysis,* 2nd ed. Dubuque, IA: William C. Brown.

Smyth, Bob. "ESPN marks first decade with special" Press Herald, Portland, Maine Friday September 1, 1989.

9. Program Assessment and Research

Objectives

Chapter 9 is designed to enable you to:

- Understand the purpose of studying measurement and evaluation in your professional preparation course work.
- Be familiar with a variety of methods of evaluation.
- State the purpose of skill testing, fitness testing, and knowledge tests.
- Relate the difference between norm-referenced tests and criterion-referenced tests.
- Be familiar with criteria for selecting a test.

TODAY, education is well steeped in accountability. Although in the past, less pressure for testing has been placed on teachers of physical education than on those who teach the three "R's," it is your professional responsibility to be accountable for programs and the achievement of sound objectives by students at every grade level. In addition, the individual in an adult fitness program should receive scientific feedback via an appropriate evaluation tool. For this reason, evaluation is a critical component of all professionally developed movement and fitness programs. Professional physical educators must be acquainted with the tools necessary to determine whether progress toward meeting established program goals or individual objectives has been made.

What Is Measurement and Evaluation?

Measurement relates to the methods used to obtain valid and reliable data from selected tests designed to provide the instructor with information that can be evaluated. *Evaluation* is the process of determining the effectiveness of an individual's learning experience. Measurement and evaluation may relate to the total physical activity program or may concentrate on the progress made in learning a single skill or developing personal fitness. The proper collection and storage of these data provides the instructor with the information required to validate program viability and teaching effectiveness.

Using Testing Instruments

To determine whether students have met the objectives of your program and are physiclly educated, you must be able to implement a measurement program. More specific objectives as applied to the testing program in schools would be to establish grades, classify students for activity, determine present student status, measure progress, motivate students toward maximum potential, and interpret the program for students, parents, and the community. In adult fitness programs, the objectives would be similar with the exception of the grading process.

Grading Students

Instructors are challenged to assess each student's ability in class by arriving at a final grade at the end of the class, semester, or year. Measurement for the purpose of grading in physical education may range from the highly subjective to the highly objective. Unlike most areas

Evaluation provides feedback for quality student learning.

of education that offer selected material and then measure how much an individual can remember and use, physical education also involves the physical body, which readily lends itself to objective measurement.

In addition to lacking specific content material in motor skills, physical education generally lacks consistent grading methods. There are almost as many different ways of grading as there are teachers. There is also widespread disagreement among physical educators about whether grading in physical education should be the same as in other educational disciplines. The authors believe that the system used in other academic disciplines within an institution should also be used in physical education, as long as the grade is based on personal goals.

Fallacies of Grading

Grading practices are sometimes found to be educationally unsound. Some grading systems promote negative attitudes toward physical education and often have little relationship to program objectives. For example, some grading systems invest each student with 100 points or an A at the start of the program, but the student then loses points for each infraction of the dress code or other class rules. Certainly, in such a system the student will have an unfavorable attitude toward physical education and either fear losing points or give up trying when points fall below a certain level. Other grading systems allow students to receive enough points for an A if they simply dress properly and maintain good personal hygiene. These grading systems ignore the sound objectives of a developmental physical education program based on individual needs.

The professional physical educator has at his or her command enough evaluation tools to develop a philosophically sound grading plan. It is the responsibility of every physical activity instructor to formulate grading practices consistent with professionally developed principles of measurement and evaluation. Regardless of the grading system selected, it is up to each instructor to evaluate a student's ability according to accurate test scores that can be easily interpreted by students and parents and can be used as a motivational tool to encourage personal development. A system that is easily understood and encourages students to succeed or improve is usually one that is founded on measurement data reflecting progress toward stated goals.

Principles of Grading

The following principles of grading are suggested as a guide in developing your own grading system. First, grades must be determined in relation to the objectives that have been formulated—for example, the skills, level of physical fitness, attitudes, or knowledge that should be gained. There is little agreement about how much weight should be given to each of these areas, but logic dictates that each be weighted according to purposes and emphases of the program. The final grade is a total of these factors, a single index that indicates a student's total achievement.

Second, grades must have validity. The grade should be determined by the extent to which the student achieves established course objectives. Does the test really measure what you are evaluating? Ample consideration should be given to student achievement and improvement according to individual potential. The validity of most grading systems is lowered somewhat because the physical educator must sometimes measure what is difficult to measure, such as the affective domain, which often requires longitudinal assessment—that is, assessment over a long period of time. When intangibles are treated objectively, something is inevitably lost in the process.

The third principle of grading is that grades must be reliable. Evaluation tools must be consistent in measuring levels of performance with each individual or group tested.

Fourth, grades should reflect a reasonable degree of objectivity. The same basic principles should govern the grading procedure in all physical education classes in a given institution, which implies that any two instructors should arrive at the same grade for the same student if given the same information.

Finally, the grading procedure should be clearly outlined by the teacher and made known to the students. At the beginning of each instructional unit, if you ensure that students understand the evaluation process, you will help eliminate future conflict between you and your students.

We believe that learning in physical education involves the psychomotor, cognitive, and affective domains. If the program is to pursue the recognized well-rounded objectives of physical education, the grade must reflect a composite evaluation of these areas. Some physical educators believe that movement skills or fitness levels alone should be the basis for the grade. However, excellent physical performance does not necessarily indicate adequate knowledge of the activity nor does it assess a student's personal attitude, sportsmanship, or understanding of the rules, history, and strategy of the activity. Learning in physical education is both quantitative and qualitative, and the single grade earned should reflect both of these variables as they relate to the three learning domains.

A growing concern of many physical educators is the difference among students' basic motor abilities. Many students motorically will never be able to achieve status as masters or excel in any sport. Nonetheless, many physical educators continue to assign these students to classes with superior students, where they are likely to experience failure and resentment. The grading system established should test a student's progress only after determination of that student's level of motor ability, fitness, and sport skills. From these determinations, the physical educator should devise individual programs in which each student will have an opportunity to excel at his or her own level. This procedure will result in a grading method more equitable to all students and allow each to seek the highest grade. A personalized instructional program that is designed to encourage success will develop a favorable attitude toward healthful living in individuals of all ages.

Selecting a Measurement Tool

Human beings are extremely complex mechanisms and are unique in many ways. To select the program that will meet the needs of each person, measurement and evaluation techniques must be carefully applied.

An individual's initial level or baseline must first be established to permit selection of the appropriate skill or degree of difficulty that will allow one to improve. Successful performance is a great motivator and encourages continued progress. If the incorrect starting point is selected, failure is already built into the program. The starting point must be high enough to provide adequate challenge but not so high that the individual becomes discouraged. Evaluation should be viewed as a means to improve instruction once the purpose and objectives of your physical education program are established.

Another function of measurement is to evaluate how your instruction is helping you meet established physical education goals. By measuring the skill or fitness level of the individual or group, the professional is armed with data that can indicate ways to improve the instructional program. Only in this manner can skill mastery, or a positive state of physical fitness, be developed.

The following criteria should be reviewed before selecting or creating a test. Each test should

- be easy to administer,
- be fun to do,
- relate to a sport or health and fitness,
- offer immediate feedback,
- use little equipment,
- be practical in application,
- motivate participants,
- have components that are measurable, and
- relate to individual needs.

The creative professional will choose or design tests that meet these criteria and are not time-consuming or difficult to administer and score. Developing your own measurement tools based on the needs of your students is an enjoyable aspect of your professional responsibility.

Students with special needs may require more sophisticated tests. The following tests or evaluation techniques are examples of different types of measurement tools.

Norm-Referenced Tests

Many tests have established norms at the national, state, or district level. These norm-referenced tests enable you to compare the levels of achievement of members of your class to the established norms. This is an excellent way of determining levels of physical fitness in the areas of cardiorespiratory condition, endurance, strength, and flexibility. It is also a good way to compare the fitness levels of one institution against another or to group students according to established levels of proficiency. Frequency of high or low scores on this type of test will help instructors identify in their physical education program the methods of instruction or areas of emphasis that require modification.

A weakness of the norm-referenced test is that it is possible for a tested person to fail or score at the low end of the continuum, which may discourage that individual from participating in activities. A strength of the norm-referenced test is that it can challenge one to work harder to achieve a score that is comparable to the best, as indicated by the established norms.

Criterion-Referenced Tests

In contrast to the norm-referenced test, the criterion-referenced test enables the physical education instructor to challenge the abilities of students by designing a test that relates directly to the objectives of the individual or class. Tests can be developed on an individual basis to challenge the student with low-level ability to work toward achieving a higher level, as well as to incite the high-level student to strive for even greater levels of proficiency as the challenge is made more difficult.

The advantage of the criterion-referenced test is that comparisons are not made against any established norms. This enables every student to show improvement and not fear failure. Another advantage of this type of test is that it can be individualized and acts as a great motivational tool in encouraging students to continue to exercise and develop skills.

Methods of Assessment

Evaluation can be accomplished in a variety of ways. The evaluation techniques of instructor observation, motor ability tests, physical fitness measurements, developmental scales, and knowledge tests all have a place in the physical educator's repertoire. A well-developed evaluation scheme provides a clear system of accountability and verifies the degree to which program objectives are met. Regardless of the method used or the area to be measured, it is important that the time allowed for evaluation be appropriate to the activity. You should avoid letting evaluation dominate the student's learning period.

Instructor Observation

One of the most common evaluation techniques used by physical activity instructors over the years is the personal observation method. This

The sequence of motor skills required in motorically sophisticated movement such as the tennis serve make instructor observation difficult. However, the instructor who knows the basic sequence of skills can identify each aspect and suggest corrections.

approach is usually related to learning motor skills and requires a thorough knowledge of the movement to be achieved. One soon begins to understand why a sound skill base is a necessary foundation for physical education majors, since understanding and experiencing correct performance is essential to observing accurately.

To assess the current status of the learner's performance, the instructor must first view the movement skill and determine the starting level of instruction. As the learner's skills are compared to what is determined to be the correct form or proper skill sequence, corrections are made and practice continues, with the new information being processed by the learner. This type of evaluation sequence is continually repeated until the learner has corrected most faults and can successfully perform the skill.

As the learner becomes more skilled, the observation technique becomes more difficult, since the errors are not as obvious and the corrections to be made are motorically more sophisticated, such as in varsity coaching. The better the critical eye of the instructor while comparing the learner to the correct skill model, the more successful the evaluation will be.

For example, there are several critical points to observe when teaching the golf swing, which clearly demonstrates the need for a thorough knowledge of the skills to be taught (Fig. 9.1). Although the evaluation is subjective, an instructor who knows the sequence of skills, as outlined below, will be able to identify each aspect of the golf swing successfully and suggest appropriate corrections.

Figure 9.1   Observing the Golf Swing

1. **Grip**
   A. Left hand: gripped with fingers to form V between thumb and forefinger pointing over right shoulder.
   B. Right hand: not too far under shaft; V formed should also point over right shoulder.
   C. Thumbs placed on opposite sides of the shaft.
   D. Little finger of right hand overlaps first finger of left hand.

2. **Stance**
   A. Square: both feet equidistant from the line of flight.
   B. Open: with left foot a little farther from the line of flight than right foot.
   C. Closed: with right foot farther away from the line of flight than left foot.

3. **Swing**
   A. Backswing
      1. Fix eye on ball. Determine proper position of head.
      2. Start back with rotation of shoulder and hips.
      3. Keep left arm straight.
      4. Keep club head low to ground.
      5. Wrists begin to cock approximately halfway back on swing.
      6. Keep right elbow close to body.
      7. Weight is shifted from left foot to right foot.
      8. At top of backswing, left shoulder will be pointing at the ball and club will be parallel to the ground.
   B. Downswing
      1. Starts with the legs and hips.
      2. Left foot comes down flat to ground.
      3. Shift weight from right to left foot.
      4. Knees are bent to allow freedom of movement.
      5. There is a feeling of pulling from the left side.
      6. Uncock wrists when hands are parallel with ground.
      7. At the moment of impact, the ball, hands, and left shoulder are almost in a straight line.
      8. The left leg becomes firm.
   C. Follow-through
      1. The right arm is just as straight as the left was on the backswing.
      2. The head raises naturally with the pulling of the right shoulder.
      3. The grip must be firm throughout the swing.

Figure 9.1 (continued)

---

4. Stretch arms out as far as possible.
5. The wrists will begin to turn over after the arms have reached the extended limit.
6. Finish with the hands high.

4. Putting
  A. Pendulum swing.
  B. Putter blade flat on ground.
  C. Both toes parallel with line of flight.
  D. Putt ball off left foot.
  E. Keep blade low to ground.
  F. No body action at any time.

The technique of using videotape to aid in the process of skill analysis (described in Chapter 7) can be an important tool in observing every student's skill level.

General Motor Ability Tests

The capacity of an individual to perform motorically in activities that require balance, flexibility, strength, power, agility, timing, and hand-eye coordination is referred to as *general motor ability.* Motor ability tests are used to determine the general needs of the individuals or groups measured. The data collected can aid in the development of a program of activities designed to increase the abilities of the learner in the identified areas of weakness. For example, an elementary class that scores low in agility should participate in activities such as tag games or dodging activities if the program is to meet class needs. In contrast, if the class scores high in this area, limited time would be spent on games of tag and more would be spent on games, sports, and activities in weaker areas. This is not to discourage a balanced program but to ensure that the selected program addresses the areas of need as identified by the general motor ability tests.

Motor ability tests are usually highly selective in the skills they measure, because no single assessment tool can measure all of the elements of motor development. However, an instructor sometimes needs more definitive information than that received from general observation. A standardized motor ability test will provide more objective data.

An early motor ability test was developed by Barrow (1954) for college-age men (Fig. 9.2). General motor ability tests are excellent in screening

Figure 9.2 Basic Motor Ability Test

Standing Broad Jump A 5- by 20-foot tumbling mat is used for administration of this test in the gymnasium. A warm-up jump is permitted; then three successive trials are given. Scoring is the distance of the best jump measured to the nearest inch.

The 60-Yard Dash One trial is permitted and scoring is to the nearest tenth of a second.

Wall Pass A restraining line is marked on the floor 9 feet from a smooth wall. The subject stands behind the restraining line with a regulation basketball. On the signal to start, the ball is passed against the wall in any manner desired. It is caught on the rebound and returned to the wall as rapidly as possible for 15 seconds. Both feet of the subject must remain behind the restraining line and, if the ball is missed, the subject must retrieve it and return to the starting line before continuing the test. Scoring is the number of times the ball hits the wall in the 15-second time allotment.

Softball Throw The field is marked in 5-yard intervals, with football sideline markers at each interval to designate distance. A regulation softball (12-inch inseam) is used for the test. Each subject is allowed three throws, with a short run to the starting line permitted. Scoring is to the nearest foot for the best of three throws.

Zigzag Run A course is laid out as depicted below. The subject starts at the star in a semicrouched position. He or she traverses the course three times and must not grasp the standards or chairs that have been placed in the circles as obstacles. If a foul is committed, as, for example, knocking over an obstacle, a second trial is allowed. Scoring is to the nearest tenth of a second. (Standards commonly used for high jumping or volleyball supports, or chairs, or even Indian clubs may be employed as obstacles.)

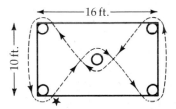

Medicine Ball Put The subject stands behind a restraining line and is permitted three successive trials in putting a 6-pound medicine ball. A distance of 15 feet behind the restraining line is designated as the area in which a run may be made up to the restraining line in performing the medicine ball put. Scoring is to the nearest one-half foot, the best of the three trials being recorded.

large groups for appropriate program development. Designing a program based on the needs of the learner will provide for greater achievement toward established physical education goals and objectives.

Skill Tests

Skill tests are specific motor ability tests designed to evaluate one's performance in a particular sport activity. Although skill tests can be used to determine the starting point for instruction, for the most part they are used as a tool to evaluate a student's progress or determine a final grade in a sport unit.

An advantage of using skill testing instead of instructor observation is the time it saves. When grouping for instruction or selecting a team, the instructor can complete initial screening in a single skill testing session that is much shorter than the time required for instructor observation. The instructor's subjective evaluation can be used to determine final grouping of students after the skill test is completed.

Administering a skill test at the beginning and end of each instructional unit can aid the instructor in evaluating student progress, program effectiveness, and teaching effectiveness. Skill tests are usually designed to represent the required motor components of skills utilized in a specific sport. Figure 9.3 is an example of a sport skill test.

Physical Fitness Testing

Physical fitness tests are used to determine strength, flexibility, and cardiorespiratory endurance. To perform a variety of sport skills successfully and live a safe and healthy life in today's society, at least a minimum level of physical fitness is required. Measuring physical fitness is the responsibility of the physical education teacher or fitness director.

There are many types of tests designed to measure strength and flexibility of selected body parts and a variety of tests to measure aerobic fitness levels—that is, the level of fitness to maintain continuous activity. The selection of a test should be based on your professional philosophy and be consistent with current research findings.

Physical Best. The Physical Best testing and education program has been developed by the American Alliance for Health, Physical Education, Recreation and Dance (AAHPERD) and is designed to motivate school-age children to improve and maintain their fitness levels. This fitness assessment and educational program includes a teacher's manual, which contains the test battery, instructions for use, criterion-referenced stan-

Figure 9.3   Russell-Lange Volleyball Test

Repeated Volleys Test   A line 10 feet long is marked on the wall at net height, 7½ feet above the floor; another line, 10 feet long, is marked on the floor, parallel to and 3 feet from the wall.

The player being tested stands behind the 3-foot line and, with an underhand movement, tosses the ball to the wall. When the ball returns, the player volleys it repeatedly against the wall above the net line for 30 seconds. The ball may be set up as many times as desired or necessary; it may be caught and restarted with a toss as at the beginning of the test. If the ball gets out of control, it must be recovered by the subject and brought back to the 3-foot line to be started over again as at the beginning.

The score is the number of times the ball is clearly batted (not tossed) from behind the 3-foot line to, on, or above the 7½ foot line on the wall. The total score from the best of three trials is recorded.

Serving Test   A court with special markings, as shown below, is prepared. Contained in each of the marked areas are chalked numbers to indicate the score value of the respective areas.

The player being tested stands behind the end line in the serving area and is given ten serves to place the ball into the targets across the net. Any legal service is permitted and a "let" ball is served over.

The score is the point value of the spot on which the served ball lands. A ball landing on a line is scored the higher value of the two areas. Serves in which foot faults occur are scored zero. Two trials of ten serves each are given, and the sum of the scores in the areas for the best trial is recorded.

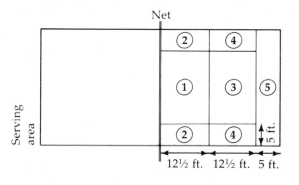

dards, awards program, and educational program kit. The recognition awards system is nonhierarchical and designed to motivate youngsters of all levels of fitness to improve their personal physical health status. The educational component features materials to aid the teacher in presenting the cognitive, psychomotor, and affective areas relating to fitness.

Fitness awards provide students with recognition for personal effort.

The Physical Best program emphasizes health-related fitness and encourages students to assume responsibility for their personal health and well-being in order to meet the demands of our current and future fast-moving society. Since the program is founded on personal goal setting, all youngsters—the physically average as well as the gifted and physically handicapped—can learn and be recognized by the program.

Health fitness standards range from 5 to 18 years of age (Fig. 9.4).

The President's Challenge. The President's Council of Physical Fitness and Sports offers The President's Challenge physical fitness and award program, designed to encourage youngsters to challenge their bodies to achieve a level of fitness considered to be outstanding. Based on national normative data, award winners must reach the eighty-fifth percentile on all five test items to meet the President's Challenge. This fitness challenge is available for youngsters age 6 through 17 years. The much sought-after Presidential Award emblem signals exceptional personal physical fitness achievement (Fig. 9.5). For those reaching the fiftieth percentile, a second award is available.

Other Fitness Tests. State professional associations, state departments of education, and other agencies have also published physical fitness tests. Many of the test items are similar in nature to those previously mentioned.

Developmental Scales

Developmental scales are used with the young child or developmentally delayed student to determine at what age level he or she is performing. Developmental scales enable the teacher to understand the level of individual ability or compare it to normal growth and development. These scales may be designed using physical, social, or emotional traits. Although children mature at different rates, these scales can serve as a guide to further testing and program development. Figure 9.6 is an example of a developmental scale for young children in the motor area, adapted from Brigance (1978).

Knowledge Tests

Evaluation is not complete without administering knowledge tests. It is important to gain an insight into the student's understanding of the principles taught in the different sports, along with knowledge of health and personal fitness. Too often physical educators focus on the skill tests

Health Fitness Standards

Girls

Age	One Mile Walk/Run (minutes)	Sum of Skinfolds (mm)	Body Mass Index	Sit & Reach (cm)	Sit-up	Pull-up
			Test Item			
5	14:00	16-36	14-20	25	20	1
6	13:00	16-36	14-20	25	20	1
7	12:00	16-36	14-20	25	24	1
8	11:30	16-36	14-20	25	26	1
9	11:00	16-36	14-20	25	28	1
10	11:00	16-36	14-21	25	30	1
11	11:00	16-36	14-21	25	33	1
12	11:00	16-36	15-22	25	33	1
13	10:30	16-36	15-23	25	33	1
14	10:30	16-36	17-24	25	35	1
15	10:30	16-36	17-24	25	35	1
16	10:30	16-36	17-24	25	35	1
17	10:30	16-36	17-25	25	35	1
18	10:30	16-36	18-26	25	35	1

Physical Best health and fitness standards for girls.

and neglect to evaluate knowledge of the subject, self-correction, strategy, or form.

Knowledge tests may be standardized or may be constructed by the teacher. The latter are most common. Each instructor designs questions to evaluate the effectiveness of his or her program and the questions are specifically adapted to his or her class. These tests are often criterion-referenced tests. To develop an exemplary knowledge test, the evaluator should:

- Make the directions clear and simple to understand.
- Avoid terms such as *should, never, all, always,* and *no.*
- Make the questions as brief as possible.

Health Fitness Standards
Boys

Age	Test Item					
	One Mile Walk/Run (minutes)	Sum of Skinfolds (mm)	Body Mass Index	Sit & Reach (cm)	Sit-up	Pull-up
5	13:00	12-25	13-20	25	20	1
6	12:00	12-25	13-20	25	20	1
7	11:00	12-25	13-20	25	24	1
8	10:00	12-25	14-20	25	26	1
9	10:00	12-25	14-20	25	30	1
10	9:30	12-25	14-20	25	34	1
11	9:00	12-25	15-21	25	36	2
12	9:00	12-25	15-22	25	38	2
13	8:00	12-25	16-23	25	40	3
14	7:45	12-25	16-24	25	40	4
15	7:30	12-25	17-24	25	42	5
16	7:30	12-25	18-24	25	44	5
17	7:30	12-25	18-25	25	44	5
18	7:30	12-25	18-26	25	44	5

Physical Best health and fitness standards for boys.

- Avoid trivial questions and ambiguous terms.
- Use a variety of questions such as recall, true and false, multiple choice, matching, completion, and essay.

Computerized Student Management

Today physical educators are expected to justify student progress and program effectiveness. A teacher, often faced with instructing 200 to 500 different students each week, must devise or utilize a storage and feedback system that will provide information to a variety of people.

Since clerical staff is usually not available for public school teachers,

A physical fitness challenge to compare your status with others.

the logical solution is to make use of the microcomputers now available in almost all educational institutions. Microcomputer programs allow teachers to manage student performance information in a reasonable time frame. Kelly (*JOPERD*, Oct. 1987) indicates this can free the teacher to devote more time to planning and improving the quality of instruction.

Kelly also describes two major categories of data base management programs that can be used by the physical educator. The generic data base program has the advantage of allowing the user to decide exactly what data will be managed; however, it requires above-average computer skills. The specialized data base programs are designed to be simple to use and to minimize the amount of expertise required of the user. Though an advantage for the computer novice, its use is limited with respect to the kind of data it can manage. The following are some questions that must be asked before selecting a program:

- Does the program match the instructional objectives of the course?
- Will the program work on the equipment available?
- What information needs to be entered and how easily can the data be entered into the computer?
- What kind of reporting feedback format does the program provide?

Figure 9.5 New Standards for the President's
Challenge Physical Fitness Award

AGE	CURL-UPS (Arms across chest) (Timed one minute)	SHUTTLE RUN (seconds)	V-SIT REACH OR SIT AND REACH (inches + / -)	ONE-MILE RUN (minutes/seconds)	PULL-UPS
BOYS					
6	33	12.1	+ 3.5	10:15	2
7	36	11.5	+ 3.5	9:22	4
8	40	11.1	+ 3.0	8:48	5
9	41	10.9	+ 3.0	8:31	5
10	45	10.3	+ 4.0	7:57	6
11	47	10.0	+ 4.0	7:32	6
12	50	9.8	+ 4.0	7:11	7
13	53	9.5	+ 3.5	6:50	7
14	56	9.1	+ 4.5	6:26	10
15	57	9.0	+ 5.0	6:20	11
16	56	8.7	+ 6.0	6:08	11
17	55	8.7	+ 7.0	6:06	13
GIRLS					
6	32	12.4	+ 5.5	11:20	2
7	34	12.1	+ 5.0	10:36	2
8	38	11.8	+ 4.5	10:02	2
9	39	11.1	+ 5.5	9:30	2
10	40	10.8	+ 6.0	9:19	3
11	42	10.5	+ 6.5	9:02	3
12	45	10.4	+ 7.0	8:23	2
13	46	10.2	+ 7.0	8:13	2
14	47	10.1	+ 8.0	7:59	2
15	48	10.0	+ 8.0	8:08	2
16	45	10.1	+ 9.0	8:23	1
17	44	10.0	+ 8.0	8:15	1

Scores are based on the 1985 School Population Fitness Survey and are the eighty-fifth percentile scores used to qualify for the award.

Some current computer programs now available are the Fitness-gram (Institute for Aerobics Research, 1984), The Physical Education Management System (PEMS) (Kelly, 1986), and the AAHPERD Physical Best Report Card (1989). See the sample student progress report in Figure 9.7.

Computer program management systems can assist teachers in evalu-

Figure 9.6   Catching Skills

Age (yr)

3   Catches a bounced 10-inch playground ball with arms and body
    Catches a bounced 10-inch playground ball with hands and chest

4   Catches a thrown 8-inch playground ball with arms and body
    Catches a bounced 8-inch playground ball with both hands

5   Catches a thrown 6-inch playground ball with hands and chest
    Catches a thrown 6-inch playground ball with both hands

6   Catches a bounced tennis ball with both hands

7   Catches a thrown tennis ball with one hand

Developmental age   •   •   •   •   •

                     3   4   5   6   7

Comments _____

ating their physical education instruction and should result in overall program improvement.

Instructor Self-Appraisal

Self-evaluation is a responsibility that professionals should face with interest and concern if personal improvement is to be achieved and maintained. True professionals will begin this process during their collegiate training and will continue to use this technique throughout their careers. A thorough, candid self-evaluation can take several forms, including a daily teaching log, where successes and failures are recorded along with pertinent comments, or a self-appraisal checklist. Figure 9.8 is one example of a self-appraisal checklist (Pestolesi and Sinclair, 1978) and (1) provides a checklist of generally accepted personal characteristics, (2) encourages the isolation of areas in which guidance may be needed, (3) provides an incentive for self-improvement, and (4) emphasizes growth through a plan for continued self-improvement.

Program Evaluation

Program development is affected by changing expectations about the functions and services rendered by educational institutions. Change should take place in the kinds of program activities that are offered.

Figure 9.7   Physical Best Report Card

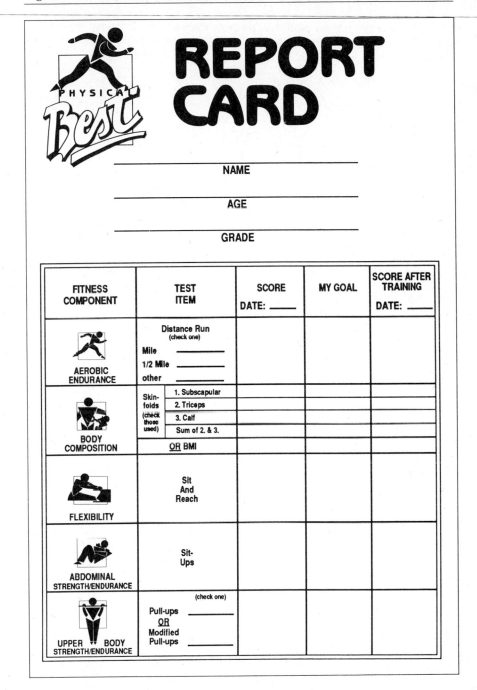

Figure 9.8 Self-Appraisal Form for Physical Education Teachers

---

Indicate your self-appraisal by placing a checkmark in the appropriate space for each item. To obtain a profile, connect the checkmarks with straight lines. To discover improvement or growth, repeat the process, using a pencil of a different color, after an interval of several months.

	IMPROVEMENT NEEDED:		
Part 1　Personal Elements	NONE	SOME	MUCH

Appearance

1. Do I always appear well-groomed before my classes—clean, hair combed, clothes neat and pressed?　(□)　(□)　(□)

2. Do I wear proper clothing for the activity the class is engaged in?　(□)　(□)　(□)

3. Do I stand erect and appear alert when lecturing to my classes?　(□)　(□)　(□)

Personal Manner

4. Do I maintain composure in the face of petty annoyances?　(□)　(□)　(□)

5. Do I feel and show a sincere interest in my students?　(□)　(□)　(□)

6. Do I inject occasional humor into my teaching?　(□)　(□)　(□)

7. Do I display confidence when presenting new material?　(□)　(□)　(□)

8. Do I feel and act enthusiastic about my work?　(□)　(□)　(□)

9. Am I as courteous to students, to co-workers, and to my superiors as I expect them to be to me?　(□)　(□)　(□)

10. Am I free from mannerisms which may be annoying or irritating to students and co-workers?　(□)　(□)　(□)

11. Do I project my voice enough that it may be heard clearly and easily by the entire class?　(□)　(□)　(□)

12. Can I speak firmly without raising my voice unpleasantly?　(□)　(□)　(□)

13. Is my voice well modulated and of good quality?　(□)　(□)　(□)

14. Do I have any speech defects which prevent clear enunciation?　(□)　(□)　(□)

15. Do I sometimes speak in a voice that is tense or "teacherish"?　(□)　(□)　(□)

Figure 9.8 (continued)

| | IMPROVEMENT NEEDED: | | |
	NONE	SOME	MUCH

Initiative

16. Do I work as industriously as I expect my students to work? (□) (□) (□)

17. Am I alert to the possibilities of enriching my teaching with new ideas and methods? (□) (□) (□)

18. Do I share ideas and methods with my co-workers and superiors? (□) (□) (□)

19. Do I initiate and sponsor extracurricular activities? (□) (□) (□)

20. Do I assume my full share of school chores and responsibilities? (□) (□) (□)

Reliability

21. Do I make sure that the information I present to my students is completely correct? (□) (□) (□)

22. Do I meet responsibilities, both those connected specifically with teaching and those which are given to me as a member of the school system? (□) (⊓) (□)

23. Do I practice regular and punctual attendance? (□) (□) (□)

24. Do I make out lesson plans and develop behavioral objectives for my classes? (□) (□) (□)

25. Can my co-workers depend on me? (□) (□) (□)

26. Do I follow directions without repeated instruction? (□) (□) (□)

27. Am I able to take care of my own student discipline problems? (□) (□) (□)

Adaptability

28. Do I adapt readily to new or unusual teaching situations? (□) (□) (□)

29. Do I adapt with reasonable ease to the various personalities among my students and colleagues? (□) (□) (□)

30. Do I have an open mind to new methods and techniques? (□) (□) (□)

31. Am I able to solve my own teaching problems? (□) (□) (□)

Cooperation

32. Do I support the accepted policies of the school without derogatory private comment? (□) (□) (□)

Figure 9.8 (continued)

	IMPROVEMENT NEEDED:		
	NONE	SOME	MUCH
33. Do I enjoy working with other teachers on committees concerned with general school problems other than education or athletics?	(☐)	(☐)	(☐)
34. Do I go out of my way to help others or to volunteer assistance?	(☐)	(☐)	(☐)
35. Am I able to work on group projects without undue concern as to who gets the credit?	(☐)	(☐)	(☐)
36. Do I participate in community activities?	(☐)	(☐)	(☐)

Quality of English

37. Can I write school reports or instruction sheets without undue concern as to their grammatical correctness?	(☐)	(☐)	(☐)
38. Do I feel that my oral English is free from grammatical errors?	(☐)	(☐)	(☐)
39. Do I phrase my lectures in terms that are understandable to the age level of my class?	(☐)	(☐)	(☐)
40. Do I give directions that are readily understood?	(☐)	(☐)	(☐)
41. Do I have an adequate general vocabulary?	(☐)	(☐)	(☐)
42. Do I feel that my regular conversation is free from errors of pronunciation?	(☐)	(☐)	(☐)
43. Do I, in my teaching, use the technical terms of my special fields readily and correctly?	(☐)	(☐)	(☐)

Part 2 Professional Elements

Subject Matter

1. Do I have sufficient mastery of the basic skills connected with the teaching of my classes?	(☐)	(☐)	(☐)
2. Do I possess adequate information relating to these skills?	(☐)	(☐)	(☐)
3. Do I have hobbies directly or indirectly related to physical education and athletics?	(☐)	(☐)	(☐)
4. Do I systematically add to my knowledge through reading and attending clinics and conventions?	(☐)	(☐)	(☐)

Techniques of Instruction:

5. Do I have a well-planned but flexible course of study?	(☐)	(☐)	(☐)

	IMPROVEMENT NEEDED:		
	NONE	SOME	MUCH
6. Do I have my instruction units logically arranged for teaching?	(☐)	(☐)	(☐)
7. Do I make adequate use of teaching devices when demonstrating or lecturing to my classes?	(☐)	(☐)	(☐)
8. Do I give adequate attention to the place of thinking in the learning process?	(☐)	(☐)	(☐)
9. Do I make an effort to introduce thought-provoking questions during class discussions?	(☐)	(☐)	(☐)
10. Do I make use of student experiences in class discussion?	(☐)	(☐)	(☐)
11. Do I conduct planned review of previous lessons?	(☐)	(☐)	(☐)
12. Do I use class progress charts to maintain student interest?	(☐)	(☐)	(☐)
13. Do I make adequate reference material available to students?	(☐)	(☐)	(☐)
14. Do I make provisions for remedial instruction?	(☐)	(☐)	(☐)
15. Do I stimulate student interest by use of school demonstrations?	(☐)	(☐)	(☐)
16. Do I plan and supervise field trips and tours?	(☐)	(☐)	(☐)
17. Do I practice privately and adequately before demonstrating activities to my students?	(☐)	(☐)	(☐)

Facility Management

	NONE	SOME	MUCH
18. Do I encourage student participation in program development?	(☐)	(☐)	(☐)
19. Do I demonstrate and teach proper sporting techniques?	(☐)	(☐)	(☐)
20. Do I inspect equipment periodically to ensure that it is safe?	(☐)	(☐)	(☐)
21. Do I have a definite system for recording and reporting accidents?	(☐)	(☐)	(☐)
22. Do I have an effective and efficient equipment checking system?	(☐)	(☐)	(☐)
23. Do I prepare for requisition time by recording equipment needs?	(☐)	(☐)	(☐)
24. Do I have a systematic plan for keeping equipment in good repair?	(☐)	(☐.)	(☐)
25. Do I keep a consistent and accurate record of students' grades and attendance?	(☐)	(☐)	(☐)

Figure 9.8 (continued)

	IMPROVEMENT NEEDED:		
	NONE	SOME	MUCH

Developing Work Habits

26. Do I impress upon students the value of training in developing physical fitness? (☐) (☐) (☐)

27. Do I impress upon students the importance of practice to improve skill? (☐) (☐) (☐)

28. Do I encourage students to warm up properly before attempting strenuous activity? (☐) (☐) (☐)

29. Do I insist that students master basic lead-up skills before attempting dangerous and sophisticated skills? (☐) (☐) (☐)

30. Do I insist that students utilize proper sporting techniques? (☐) (☐) (☐)

31. Do I encourage student reading of related material? (☐) (☐) (☐)

32. Do I consistently call attention to improper use of equipment? (☐) (☐) (☐)

Teacher-Student Relationship

33. Am I important in all dealings with students? (☐) (☐) (☐)

34. Do I create an atmosphere in which students feel free to discuss their problems with me? (☐) (☐) (☐)

35. By my own actions, do I set standards of desirable personal traits, attitudes, and habits? (☐) (☐) (☐)

36. Do students in my classes have a feeling of status and belonging? (☐) (☐) (☐)

37. Do I guide students in their activities rather than dominate them? (☐) (☐) (☐)

38. Do I commend or praise students more often than rebuke or reprimand them? (☐) (☐) (☐)

39. In the matter of discipline, do I strive to develop individual self-control rather than imposed control? (☐) (☐) (☐)

40. Do I give adequate attention to the problems and interests of individuals in my classes? (☐) (☐) (☐)

41. Is my relationship with students one of sincerity and rapport? (☐) (☐) (☐)

42. Do I go out of my way to help students who are unattractive and troublesome? (☐) (☐) (☐)

	IMPROVEMENT NEEDED:		
	NONE	SOME	MUCH
43. Do I note and make adjustments for physical handicaps of students?	(☐)	(☐)	(☐)
44. Do I welcome constructive criticism and treat it critically?	(☐)	(☐)	(☐)
45. Do I make an effort to obtain advice and assistance from my supervisor or administrative head?	(☐)	(☐)	(☐)
46. Do I make an effort to obtain advice and information from parents concerning students?	(☐)	(☐)	(☐)
47. Do I keep informed on and assume some responsibility in general civic and community affairs?	(☐)	(☐)	(☐)
48. Do I indulge in public relations regarding physical education and athletics?	(☐)	(☐)	(☐)
49. Do I subscribe to and read professional literature relating to my field of teaching?	(☐)	(☐)	(☐)

A teacher must regularly evaluate his or her program in order to check on adherence to contemporary needs and demands for physical education.

The evaluation tool shown in Figure 9.9 is adapted from the AAHPERD and identifies problem areas in programs that should be reviewed for appropriateness or improvement. The required response for this assessment is a simple yes or no. A negative response to a given question would indicate that additional study is needed in a specific area. If an affirmative response is given, the effectiveness of the program area in question would then be determined on a three-point scale, where 1 = very effective, 2 = operational, and 3 = ineffective. Once the degree of effectiveness is determined, and if changes are in order, a timeline for implementation of the changes should be established.

At the end of each school year, or at the time of a student's graduation from one program level to another, the physical education instructor should ask whether each student who experienced the program is physically educated. With a sound measurement and evaluation program, this question can be answered using objective data that will aid in the future development and improvement of teaching methodology and program offerings.

Figure 9.9 Program Assessment

Program Management
1. Are there written school or departmental policies that govern program management, instruction, athletics, and recreational activities?
2. Is there a procedure by which input from the community, faculty, and students can be utilized for program improvement?
3. Has the department investigated community position regarding physical education?
4. Is there a viable public relations program established in which all faculty members can participate?
5. Are the instructional, athletic, and recreational programs for boys and girls operating under a single administrative head?
6. Are the instructional, athletic, and recreational activities offered on a coeducational basis?
7. Have in-service training and retooling programs been established for the improvement of the staff?
8. Is the teaching load for physical education instructors consistent with other departments in the school?
9. Is there adequate clerical support to meet specific program requirements?
10. Are the instructional, athletic, and recreational programs financed through the regular school budget?
11. Are all programs in the instructional, competitive, and recreational areas for boys and girls funded on an equitable basis?
12. Is there a sound fiscal policy established that would stand up under audit?
13. Is a comprehensive medical examination required of all students participating in any aspect of the instructional and competitive sport program?
14. Does the school district or institution provide an accident insurance plan for students?
15. Is there a written policy concerning emergency procedures and safety precautions?
16. Are facilities and equipment adequate to meet the goals and objectives of a well designed program?
17. Are community facilities and natural surroundings utilized to enhance program offerings?
18. Is the faculty selection and retention process in the instructional and competitive program consistent with established procedures in other departments?
19. Are annual written faculty evaluations required, which take into consideration teaching or coaching effectiveness?
20. Is the program evaluated on a regular basis and are changes implemented?
21. Are students post tested to determine program effectiveness in relation to stated objectives?

Figure 9.9 (continued)

Instructional
1. Does the program include a student orientation concerning departmental policies and activities?
2. Are pre-tests used in ascertaining students' ability levels for appropriate grouping and program development?
3. Do the students have an opportunity to evaluate the physical education programs?
4. Is there an adequate adaptive program for the physically limited student?
5. Is there a varying formula for class size that allows for effective instruction?
6. Is there a written policy concerning grading and are the students informed of the requirements?
7. Does the program emphasize the importance of maintaining physical fitness?
8. Does the program include instruction in the values of physical development as related to optimum health benefits?
9. Is the program designed to facilitate sequential skill development for lifetime sports?
10. Does the program include opportunities for innovative instructional methods such as contract teaching or credit for prior learning?
11. Is there a school or departmental resource center available that can be utilized by faculty and students to augment the instructional process?

Athletics
1. Are there established standards for coaches required for employment?
2. Is there a certified athletic trainer on the staff?
3. Does a physician, certified trainer or nurse attend all athletic practices and contests where body contact is likely to occur?
4. Is transportation provided to athletic contests by the school?
5. Is there equal opportunity for boys and girls to utilize facilities during prime time hours for practice?
6. Are length of sport seasons and number of contests justified on an educational basis?
7. Is there a published athletic policy manual for the competitive program?

Recreation
1. Are the recreational activities conducted at times when there are no conflicts with the instructional or athletic programs?
2. Are students given an opportunity to participate in wide variety of recreational activities?
3. Is there articulation between the instructional and recreational programs where students are given instruction in the activities prior to involvement in a recreational activity?

Figure 9.9 (continued)

4. Is there adequate publicity so that students and faculty are informed well in advance as to upcoming recreational activities?
5. Is administrative time provided for the recreational director similar to competitive coaching assignments?

Research in Physical Education and Sport

The Educator's Role

Discovering new information and distributing the results of research in a scholarly way is an important responsibility of physical educators. Some educators believe that teaching and research are incompatible, but it is difficult to understand how teachers can remain abreast in their field if they do not participate in some type of research. As early as 1970, Clark stated that the overwhelming opinion on university campuses is that the most effective and stimulating teachers are those who are continually active in research: They are the ones most likely to have a thorough knowledge of and insight into their field.

We agree that active research generates interest and enthusiasm for teaching while helping the discipline progress. Physical education professionals must regularly conduct some type of research.

The Student and Research

The word *research* may be frightening to the young student of physical education. Many students fail to recognize that they have already accomplished some research in term papers and projects completed as a part of their regular class assignments. These class activities acquaint the student with the tools, techniques, and procedures necessary to conduct more advanced research.

Through the study of measurements and evaluation, the student becomes familiar with the statistical terms and techniques available, which are necessary to understand, interpret, and apply research. Some students will have an opportunity to assist professors with research projects as volunteers or graduate assistants. If such opportunities are presented to you, you should accept them, as they will help you to mature as a professional physical educator.

Areas of Research

Graduate study in physical education has a well-established research foundation. Many high-quality masters and doctoral theses consist of sophisticated research designs and contribute to the verification of or to the body of knowledge of our profession.

The broad field of physical education allows for research to be conducted in many areas including, but not limited to, biomechanics, exercise physiology, growth and development, sport management, sport psychology, sport sociology, sport medicine, nutrition, stress management, and motor development.

The future of our profession rests heavily on scientific evidence to validate, among other things, the need for physical education in an educational setting, the value of pursuing an active lifestyle for people of all ages, the importance of exercise in the workplace, the importance of youth sports and competition, and the relationship of motor development to academic achievement.

Research Designs

Early research design or method was based primarily on the laboratory experimental model. Studies in human performance have made a great contribution to the fitness and psychomotor domain. Contemporary research indicates that in addition to its biological focus, the psychological, sociological, and curricular aspects of the physical education profession will receive increasing attention.

Today's research methods are widely varied, and an increasing number of research projects are directly applicable to the teaching-learning situation.

Communicating Research

Completed research must be communicated to others in the profession for validation and support. This is accomplished in the physical education field through papers read at clinics and conferences, and through publication of articles or books by scholarly presses and professional journals. *The Research Quarterly for Exercise and Sport*, published by the AAHPERD, is an excellent professional publication. An example of a more specific research periodical is the *Journal of Sports Medicine and Physical Fitness*, published by the American College of Sports Medicine. A variety of other publications report specific research in areas such as history, sport psychology, and sport sociology.

After the research is validated, it is also the professional's responsibility to communicate this information to the general public. We must inform others of the values of our discipline. When possible, articles of general interest should be written for the daily newspapers, professionals should appear on talk shows to discuss contemporary issues, and speeches should be given to service clubs and organizations of all types. We must convince the public that there is no substitute for learning to live a healthful, active lifestyle.

Student Activities

1. Discuss how you would use tests to determine student status.
2. Investigate a high school grading system and compare it to the principles stated in the text.
3. Use the self-appraisal form and check your current strengths and weaknesses with respect to teaching physical education.
4. Take a skill test.
5. Administer a skill test to someone.
6. Take the Basic Motor Ability Test (Fig. 9.2) and compare your scores with others in your class.
7. Design a personal fitness program based on your results from the Basic Motor Ability Test (Fig 9.2).
8. Critique an article from the *Research Quarterly for Exercise and Sport* (1929 to the present) published by the AAHPERD.
9. Review and compare the AAHPERD Physical Best fitness program and the President's Challenge fitness tests.
10. Investigate computer information management systems for physical education instruction.

Suggested Readings

Bosco, J. S., and W. F. Gustafson. 1983. *Measurement and evaluation in physical education, fitness and sports.* Englewood Cliffs, NJ: Prentice-Hall.

Johnson, B. L., and J. K. Nelson. 1986. *Practical measurements for evaluation in physical education,* 4th ed. Edina, MN: Burgess Publishing.

Kirkendall, D. R., et al. 1987. *Measurement and evaluation for physical educators,* 2nd ed. Champaign, IL: Human Kinetics Publishers.

Mozzini, L., and R. A. Pestolesi. 1985. Children and youth physical fitness program management system. Reston, VA: American Alliance for Health, Physical Education, Recreation and Dance.

Presidential Physical Fitness Award Program. 1987. Washington, DC: Department of Health and Human Services.

President's Council on Physical Fitness and Sports. 1976. Youth physical fitness suggestions for school programs. Washington, DC: U.S. Government Printing Office.

Self-evaluation—a key to self-improvement. 1982. *Physical Education Newsletter*, no. 138 (June).

Thomas, J. R., and J. K. Nelson. 1985. *Introduction to research in health, physical education, recreation and dance*. Champaign, IL: Human Kinetics Publishers.

References

Barrow, H. M. 1954. Test of motor ability for college men. *Research Quarterly* 25:253.

Brigance, A. 1978. *Inventory of early development*. North Billerica, MA: Curriculum Associates: 6.

Clarke, D. H., and H. H. Clarke. 1970. *Research process in physical education, recreation and health*. Englewood Cliffs, NJ: Prentice-Hall.

Pestolesi, R. A., and W. A. Sinclair. 1978. *Creative administration in physical education and athletics*. Englewood Cliffs, NJ: Prentice-Hall.

10. Athletics Past to Present

Chapter Outline

Relationship of Athletics to Physical Education
Values of the Competitive Sport Experience
Historical Development of Athletic Programs
Women in Sport
Athletic Governance
Olympics
Sports for the Physically Challenged
Youth Sport Competition
Sports for Older Americans
Athletics and Academics
Coaching
Ethics and Drugs in Sport
Economics of Sport in Education
Extended Benefits of Athletics
Student Activities
Suggested Readings/References

Objectives

Chapter 10 is designed to enable you to:

- Understand the historical development of competitive sports.
- Describe sound policies for athletic program development.
- Develop an appreciation for codes of ethics.
- Become familiar with competitive sports for special populations.
- Understand the role of the coach in sport competition.

O RGANIZED sports not only continue to thrive as major components of contemporary interscholastic and intercollegiate institutions but also serve millions of youths in community-based programs. Competitive sports have historically played a major role in the development of the United States. For most sports, spectator attendance records continue to rise. Recently, the layperson's enthusiasm for sport was confirmed by a television viewing audience of more than 130 million for a Super Bowl professional football contest. Some holidays are centered around sport, such as the football bowl games held between Thanksgiving and New Year's Day.

Athletic competition as a part of the educational scheme has become as traditional as motherhood and apple pie. Inherent in youth is a zest for physical activity, competition, and creative adventure that can often be fulfilled or satisfied through organized sports and games. A well-planned, well-administered sports program for boys and girls can help tremendously in meeting many of the social, emotional, and physical needs of our youth. Under proper leadership, competitive sport programs at all educational levels can challenge the physically gifted student and provide expanded opportunities for other students through well-planned classification systems that involve a variety of levels of play. An institution that fails to offer a variety of competitive sport activities is depriving many students of a valuable educational experience. A professionally sound athletic program does much to promote a favorable school image and encourage feelings of pride and loyalty that are difficult to achieve in many other disciplines. There is no better way to promote the factors that enhance the total school educational program than to field successful athletic teams.

As in the past, the contemporary athlete is looked on with pride. Whether in elementary school or college, the physically gifted individual enjoys praise and support. Fans at home, in school, and in the community at large all identify with individuals who can perform at a high level of motor skill development in a competitive situation.

Relationship of Athletics to Physical Education

Ideally, competitive sport programs should be an outgrowth of the physical education instructional program. Often confused with physical education, which offers instruction in motor development, skill acquisition, and personal fitness for all students, the interscholastic competitive sport program provides challenges for the physically gifted individual, just as dramatic productions present a stage for the budding actor or actress.

Opportunities for higher levels of competition should progress from physical education to intramurals to the interscholastic level. A well-designed athletic program often serves as a microcosm of life and can be a satisfying and enriching experience for the participants. The degree to which this goal is realized is dependent on the force of outside pressures stemming from the community, alumni and resource base.

The question we must ask ourselves is: Can we maintain the positive aspects of sports competition when faced with the pressures to win, turn a profit, and attract spectator support? To obtain legitimacy, program administrators must accept responsibility for continually informing the public of how the goals and objectives of a sound competitive program fit into the educational scheme. Individuals benefit greatly from a properly conducted competitive sport experience.

Values of the Competitive Sport Experience

Skill development, physical fitness, and personal development are values of sport competition that should be emphasized in a well-designed athletic program.

Skill Development

The competitive sport program provides for concentrated skill instruction by coaches who have studied the sport at the highest level. Participants have the opportunity to become highly proficient in a sport skill that will often lead to more enjoyment and continued participation during adult life. The mastery of a sport skill often leads to greater self-confidence, individual recognition, and complete enjoyment of the activity.

Physical Fitness

Participation in competitive sports requires a high level of physical fitness. Intensive conditioning programs provide the participant with the strength and endurance to continue play over extended periods of time. Scientifically planned conditioning programs also provide a sound basis for skill development and build confidence in the student athlete's total sport performance.

Personal Development

Sports participation allows for opportunities in the decision-making process and social development. Athletes soon learn that self-control and self-discipline are required for individual and team success. Decisions need to be made that often involve personal sacrifice for the good of the team. Cooperation and respect for others through good communication techniques can lead to productive, sound social development. Relationships developed as a team member often result in lifelong friendships. There is no better arena in which to develop and test one's personal leadership skills than that of the athletic playing fields and courts.

Historical Development of Athletic Programs

What brought about today's fanaticism for sport competition in our schools? How did it begin? Why is the United States the leader in competitive sport programs at the high school and college levels? Why did we not pursue the sports club model as developed in many foreign countries? To seek these answers we must first understand the beginning stages of the American educational sport scene. Competitive athletics, surprisingly, did originate as an outgrowth of the objectives of the school system itself. Administrators, athletic directors, and coaches, who daily explain the values and relationships of a successful athletic program to the total educational scheme, cannot accept credit for its development. Athletic competitions were first organized by college students to challenge students of other colleges. There were no extensive rules or regulatory controls, and often the event was as much social as it was competitive. As these contests became more popular, the competitive urge evolved into a strong effort to win. It soon became more important to win than to play the game.

When winning the contest became all-important, high school teams began recruiting community residents to represent their school. It was not uncommon to find a coal miner, custodian, or principal playing for the school team, since eligibility rules were nonexistent. Many contests reflected the look of a street brawl rather than an athletic event. As a result of this lack of control, athletic associations were born, and athletic organization was brought under the umbrella of the educational system.

The development of college football is a good example of the evolution of a competitive sport program. Football came to America by way of the early English colonists. The first intercollegiate football game was played in New Brunswick, New Jersey, on November 6, 1869, when Rutgers defeated Princeton by a score of six to four. The contest was student-conceived and student-coached. In the early years, coaches came from the ranks of students, alumni, or friends, all of whom were unpaid. Soon professional coaches were employed based on their expertise as performers or technicians. It was only coincidental that these coaches had a high school or college education.

During the fall of 1871, the Princeton student body held a meeting, organized a football association, and elected a team captain. This football association was the first in the United States. Two years later, Yale, Princeton, Columbia, and Rutgers formed the first intercollegiate football association in New York, which was the forerunner of the numerous associations, conferences, and leagues that are now a part of the American competitive sport program.

Early Athletic Administration

Student Control

In the early years of college football, the game truly belonged to the students. They elected student captains, conducted practice sessions, established training rules, developed plays, and made all decisions. As these student-instituted programs expanded in scope and interest in them grew, it became more and more difficult for student leaders to meet the academic requirements of the collegiate institution and continue to conduct the football program.

Lack of continuity in policies and procedures was also a problem, since student leadership had a great rate of turnover. There were many difficulties in standardizing recruitment policies, eligibility, travel, and medical care. To compound the problem, during the early stage of development, many faculty viewed intercollegiate athletics as contrary to the best interests of a college education. The scope of the sport program had so increased that students could no longer effectively administer athletic competition.

Institutional Control

At the insistence of the college administrators, students were forced to establish a plan that would give more stability to the athletic program. As a result, the student athletic association was conceived, born, and directed by a graduate manager. Institutional control was exercised by an athletic committee composed of the faculty and, in some cases, developed to include alumni and students. College administrators came to view student sport programs as a necessary evil that had to be tolerated. Student-organized athletic associations were short-lived, as the need for full-time athletic administrators was soon felt. The salaried graduate manager was no longer employed to administer the program. When it was realized that financially successful alumni could be an excellent source of revenue for the athletic program, such alumni were encouraged to play an active role in athletic associations.

Student-alumni organizations soon grew into powerful corporations, which led to increased gate receipts, salaried coaches, facility construction, and recruiting campaigns. It was becoming evident that the competitive sport philosophy was expanding to include a business orientation rather than educational goals alone.

College administrators discerned the need to place athletics under institutional control and curtail the influence of outside forces. The control was initiated by appointing faculty to administer the collegiate sports program. Professionally trained medical faculty, such as Hitchcock, Sargent, McKenzie, Wood, and others, soon established the sport profession as an educational discipline. Coaches of athletic teams thus were given academic rank and were recognized as part of the educational team. At long last, the athletic program was philosophically accepted as an integral part of the total educational scheme.

Responsibility for athletics was soon transferred to a staff member of the physical education department. With this change came the burden of financial responsibility. Athletics now were truly conducted within the institutional walls.

As programs expanded to include a greater number of sports for men and women, larger institutions separated athletics from physical education. Different models were used to administer the program. Sometimes the sport program was administered separately, and sometimes it was a part of student services. Some institutions placed it directly under the president, particularly at the university level. High schools usually named a physical educator or coach as athletic director. However, this responsibility sometimes was assigned to a student activities director. In 1905, the Intercollegiate Athletic Association of the United States was established, which in 1911 evolved into the National Collegiate Athletic Association (NCAA).

While all these developments were taking place, there was a parallel change in the coaching ranks. As sport systems of play became more sophisticated and as more time demands were made on the coach, it was no longer practical to employ part-time coaches. Prominent college athletes, often graduates of the institution, were hired as full-time faculty with coaching responsibilities. In 1921, the American Football Coaches Association was founded, and coaching came of age as an established profession.

Today, competitive sport programs have gone far beyond the game of football. Prime-time television is dominated by a great variety of sporting events. Organized competitive athletic programs range from youth soccer to Monday night football. There are programs for all ages and in almost every sport one can name.

Early women's competition followed the play-day philosophy, by which many institutions sent teams to compete against each other with an emphasis on participation and socialization. Today, women's athletics are highly competitive and exciting to watch.

Courtesy California State University, Dominguez Hills

Women in Sport

Female athletes are finally moving toward equality in sports on a nationwide basis. From coast to coast, girls' and women's athletic programs
enjoy increased popularity. No longer are female athletes social outcasts,
nor is it socially unacceptable for a female athlete to be seen perspiring
and in a state of exhaustion. Many states have had strong, competitive
programs for high school girls for a number of years. Currently, these
opportunities have been universally expanded from the traditional "play-
day" approach to serious high-level competitive sport programs for all
girls and women. This change was brought about primarily by dedicated
female physical educators who perceived that as society's roles for
women were expanding in other arenas, opportunities for women in
sport also needed to be expanded.

Today, elementary schools, high schools, and colleges are heavily involved in promoting interscholastic and intercollegiate sports for
women. The female athlete has been freed from the traditional cultural
restraints once imposed on women who competed in sports. Today, female athletes are encouraged to engage in sport activities at the highest
level.

During the summer of 1972, Congress enacted Title IX, an educational
amendment that declared that no person in the United States shall, on
the basis of sex, be excluded from participation in, be denied the benefits of, or be subject to discrimination under any educational program
or activity receiving federal assistance. Whether because of the courts
and Title IX, pressure from the parents and coaches of female athletes,
the women's rights movement, or simply the joy of sports competition,
there remains little doubt that the sweeping reforms in women's athletics have created an explosion of sport programs for the female athlete. This has encouraged increased participation and has catapulted
female athletes to prominence throughout the world.

Professional sport opportunities for women are also expanding. In the
past, prize money offered to professional women golfers was nowhere
near that offered to their male counterparts. Though still not equal, the
amount offered for women's golf tournaments has greatly increased of
late. In professional tennis tournaments, prize money is offered on an
equal basis to both men and women.

There have been attempts to launch new professional women's teams
in the United States, some of which were unsuccessful for one reason
or another. However, currently a national women's professional volleyball league has been established and shows promise for expansion. In

High-level play involves intense effort on the part of the participants.

Europe, women's volleyball leagues have been highly successful and provide additional opportunities for female athletes to play this sport and earn a living.

Another indication of the growing stature of and support for women's sport is the creation of a national women's sport day, an event initiated in 1987 by the National Association of Girls and Women in Sport that honors outstanding female athletes annually. In addition, confidence in coaching ability is being displayed by professional teams who are employing female coaches for men's teams. Recently, a woman was hired to coach in the National Hockey League. Her forte is power skating, and she teaches skating techniques to newly drafted players.

Despite such advances in levels of coaching, today we face the dilemma of fewer women coaches overall for female teams. Often, male and female coaches alike do not realize the time commitment necessary for success. Year-round programs, fund raising, and other necessary undertakings may be a part of the problem. Possibly, the fast rise in women's competitive programs did not allow time for preparation and understanding of the demands of coaching. Nonetheless, today women interested in coaching may have a better understanding of these demands as they experience pressure as players and are enrolled in coaching certification curricula, which should help to reverse this pattern and increase the number and longevity of female coaches.

Sports competition for women has more of a history than that usually depicted or understood by most Americans. In ancient Greek civilizations women often engaged in fierce competition in a great variety of games and sports, including chariot racing, acrobatics, running events, horseback riding, swimming, and special competitions. Although women participated in sporting events centuries ago, modern Western cultures persisted in the myth that indulgence in competitive sports was unfeminine. The contemporary world has finally buried this myth and has transformed the invisible sportswoman into the superstar, an image she deserves.

Women today have the opportunity that was once the privilege of men alone—to experience the desirable lessons learned in the competitive sports arena. Men and women are now working together with mutual respect to open the doors to better sport programs for all through cooperation and dedication to excellence.

Athletic Governance

As a result of the inconsistencies, unfairness, and lack of continuity in the conduct of competitive sport programs at all levels, it became necessary to establish controls to ensure proper athletic administration. Sound educational principles had to be developed and adhered to if the sports programs were to be justified as a legitimate phase of the school curriculum. Athletics, when administered properly, play an important role in the total educational experience of all school-age youth in America. Participation in quality athletic programs contributes to the development of the complete person.

Collegiate athletics for men and women are now governed by the National Collegiate Athletic Association (NCAA) or the National Association for Intercollegiate Athletics (NAIA). The NCAA offers thirty-four national championships for women and forty-three for men. The NAIA offers nine for women and fourteen for men.

The creation of the Association for Intercollegiate Athletics for Women (AIAW) resulted from federal legislation passed in 1972. Title IX of the Education Amendment Act mandated equal opportunity for both sexes and served as the impetus for the development of women's athletic programs. From 1971 through 1982, the AIAW served as the governing body for women's sports. Although powerful in the development of women's sport programs, the AIAW lacked the financial and political base to maintain control over equitable competition for both sexes. (See pp. 213–214 for more details on this organization.)

The NCAA and the NAIA have similar goals and are concerned with the proper conduct and presentation of collegiate sport programs at the 4-year university and college level. The 2-year community colleges come under the jurisdiction of the National Junior College Athletic Association (NJCAA), which promotes and fosters junior college athletics on intersectional and national levels under principles that are consistent with the total educational program.

High school programs are governed by the National Federation of State High School Associations and have similar purposes in that they are concerned primarily with intersectional or interstate competitions and the general well-being of high school athletics. At the high school and community college levels, each state organization has more specific and established guidelines for competition within the boundaries of the state.

Besides the previously mentioned sport organizations, which relate to educational institutions, there have also blossomed in recent years sport organizations for various age groups from young children to senior citizens. In addition, there are national competitions for both physically and mentally challenged individuals, which are governed by various organizations.

State high school athletic associations proved to be a desirable method of maintaining interscholastic athletics as a viable phase of the total school program. State association rules and regulations guaranteed programs would be developed in an educationally sound manner. The establishment of consistent standards at the state level provided equality of competition between member institutions. However, these standards were limited to state boundaries and did not resolve differences between various rules and regulations for all interstate competitions. There was now an identifiable need to control athletics in a much broader sense. If national championships and other special promotions were to occur, then it would be necessary to develop controls at a higher level.

National Federation of State High School Athletic Associations

The first expanded organization was the Midwest Federation of State High School Athletic Associations, which came into being in 1920 when only twenty-nine states had athletic associations. The Midwest Federation was the parent organization of what was soon to become the National Federation of State High School Athletic Associations. The following statement from the National Federation handbook gives a brief history of its origin and development:

> The national organization had its beginning in a meeting at Chicago on May 14, 1920. L. W. Smith, secretary of the Illinois High School Athletic Association, issued invitations to neighboring states, and state association representatives came from Illinois, Indiana, Iowa, Michigan, and Wisconsin. The primary purpose of the meeting was to discuss problems that had resulted from high school contests which were organized by colleges and universities or by other clubs or promoters. In many cases little attention was paid to the eligibility rules of the high school associations or to other high school group regulations, and chaotic conditions developed. At this first meeting it was decided that the welfare of the high schools required that a more active part in the control of such athletic activities be exercised by the high school men through the state associations, and this control necessitated the formation of a national organization. A constitution and by-laws were adopted, and the group decided on the name, "Midwest Federation of State High School Athletic Associations." Principal George Edward Marshall, Davenport, Iowa, was elected president, and Principal L. W. Smith of Joliet, Illinois, was elected secretary-treasurer.
>
> In 1921, four states, Illinois, Iowa, Michigan, and Wisconsin, continued their interest and became charter members through formal ratification of the constitution. Largely due to their efforts, the national organization grew during the early years.
>
> In 1922, the Chicago annual meeting was attended by representatives from eleven states and the name of the National Federation was adopted. A number of college and university representatives who attended the meeting expressed sympathy for and interest in the efforts to introduce a high degree of order in the regulation of interscholastic contests.
>
> Since that time, the National Federation has had a healthy growth to its present nationwide membership. By 1940, a national office with a full-time executive staff became necessary and such office was established in September of that year.
>
> The legislative body is the National Council, made up of one representative from each member state association. Each representative must be an officer or a member of his state board of control. The executive body is the Executive Committee of at least eight members from the eight territorial sections as outlined in the constitution. Their election is by the National Council at its summer meeting.
>
> From time to time, regional conferences involving the executive officers from state associations in a given geographical section are

sponsored. Conducted on an informal basis with workshop-type meetings, the discussions cover those items which are of regional and local interest. All attending members are given an opportunity to contribute and to gain from the discussion. It provides an effective means for executive staff members to share ideas.

Annual conferences for state executive secretaries are also held. The programs for these conferences are developed by the National Federation executive secretary. This conference is directed more toward the functions of sports administrative bodies and their relationships to the interscholastic athletic program.

The National Federation was intent on coordinating the efforts of its member state associations to draft sound objectives of interscholastic competition. The following objectives were established:

1. To formulate and carry into effect policies and plans for improving high school athletic conditions.
2. To make continuing studies of the relationship of sports to the overall programs of high schools.
3. To develop, promulgate, and make uniform suitable rules and interpretations governing high school athletic contests and meets.
4. To provide programs and training for the administration thereof.
5. To develop, promulgate and make uniform suitable rules and interpretations governing eligiblity to participate in high school athletics, athletic safety and protection, and other matters relating to high school athletics and participants therein.
6. To secure proper adherence to the eligibility rules of state high school athletic associations in interstate contests and meets and to sanction such meets.
7. To cooperate with other athletic organizations in the writing of rules and in approving national or other records.
8. To provide information concerning all facets of high school athletics and, in connection therewith, to prepare, publish, issue, or sponsor all types of written, filmed, recorded, or audiovisual material in high school athletics or related subjects.
9. To engage, generally, in not-for-profit activities of an educational or athletic nature.

Today, the National Federation includes all fifty state associations along with the District of Columbia and has affiliate members including the Canadian Federation of Provinces, the Philippines, Puerto Rico, and the Virgin Islands. It is representative of more than 23,000 high schools and 10 million secondary school student athletes. The National

Federation has done much to bring credibility to the interscholastic competitive sport programs and has elevated interscholastic activities to a position of sound educational status and respect.

Minimum athletic standards have been established in areas of eligibility, interstate athletic sanctions, interstate scheduling, playing rules, equipment standards, and national records. The following ten cardinal principles were developed in cooperation with the American Alliance for Health, Physical Education, Recreation and Dance (AAHPERD) (Forsythe and Keller, 1975, p. 35).

To be of maximum effectiveness, the athletic program will:

1. Be closely coordinated with the general instructional program and properly articulated with other departments of the school.
2. Be such that the number of students accommodated and the educational aims achieved justify the use of tax funds for its support and also justify use of other sources of income, provided the time and attention which is given to the collection of such funds is not such as to interfere with the efficiency of the athletic program or of any other department of the school.
3. Be based on the spirit of nonprofessionalism so that participation is regarded as a privilege to be won by training and proficiency and to be valued highly enough to eliminate any need for excessive use of adulated demonstrations or of expensive prizes or awards.
4. Confine the school athletic activity to events which are sponsored and supervised by the proper school authorities so that exploitation or improper use of prestige built up by school teams or members of such teams may be avoided.
5. Be planned so as to result in opportunity for many individuals to explore a wide variety of sports and in reasonable season limits for each sport.
6. Be controlled so as to avoid the elements of professionalism and commercialism which tend to grow up in connection with widely publicized "bowl" contests, barnstorming trips, and interstate or intersectional contests which require excessive travel expense or loss of school time or which are bracketed with educational travel claims in an attempt to justify privileges for a few at the expense of many.
7. Be kept free from the type of contest which involves a gathering of so-called "all-stars" from different schools to participate in contests which may be used as a gathering place for representatives of certain colleges or professional organizations who are interested in soliciting athletic talent.

8. Include training in conduct and game ethics to reach all nonparticipating students and community followers of the school teams to ensure a proper understanding and appreciation of the sport's skills and of the need for adherence to principles of fair play and right prejudices.
9. Encourage a balanced program of intramural activity in grades below the ninth to make it unnecessary to sponsor contests of a championship nature in these grades.
10. Engender respect for the local, state, and national rules and policies under which the school program is conducted.

The National Federation has definitely been a guiding force in the development of interscholastic athletics. Through the National Federation, the state associations will continue to have an opportunity to develop and refine standards of secondary school competition for the betterment of the student athlete and the sound objectives of interscholastic sport programs.

National Collegiate Athletic Association

The NCAA is the governing body through which colleges and universities have an opportunity to speak and act on athletic matters at the national level. Membership is now in excess of 800 institutions, which all participate on a voluntary basis. These institutions are devoted to the sound administration of intercollegiate athletics in its entirety. The NCAA serves as the national athletic accrediting agency for 4-year institutions and conferences that are concerned with sound administration and ethical conduct of intercollegiate athletics. Through the NCAA, members have an opportunity to consider any athletic problem of regional or national interest.

The NCAA's first 85 years have been marked by phenomenal growth and expansion. The first NCAA championship was in 1921, when the Association sponsored the National Collegiate Track and Field Championship. Since that time, national championships under the auspices of the NCAA have expanded to seventy-seven, including thirty-four for women and two coeducational contests involving three legislative and competitive divisions.

Interest for developing the NCAA was based on sport safety. The flying wedge, football's major offense in the early 1900s, typified the rugged nature of the game and caused many injuries and deaths. As a result, many institutions discontinued participating in the sport and some abolished football from their intercollegiate program. President Theodore

Roosevelt summoned athletic directors to two White House conferences to urge continuation of the game: in 1905, thirteen institutions were brought together to reform the rules for playing football. On December 28, 1905, the Intercollegiate Athletic Association was founded by sixty-two colleges and universities. The association officially adopted its constitution in March 1906, and it was not until 1910 that its present name, the National Collegiate Athletic Association, was taken.

As athletics grew and postseason competitions were multiplying rapidly without control or supervision, member institutions became increasingly concerned with the scope and complexity of the many problems involving recruiting, financial aid, and general abuses in collegiate competition. The need for full-time professional leadership was clear, and in 1951, Walter Byers, who had previously served as a part-time administrator, was named executive director of the NCAA. The national headquarters was established in Kansas City in 1952 and is currently located in Mission, a Kansas City suburb. Today, more than 20,000 student athletes compete annually in NCAA-sponsored championship events in three divisions.

The purposes of the NCAA include the following:

1. To uphold the principle of institutional control of, and responsibility for, all intercollegiate athletics in accordance with the Association's constitution and bylaws.
2. To serve as an overall national discussion, legislative, and administrative body for the universities and colleges of the United States in matters of intercollegiate athletics.
3. To recommend policies for the guidance of member institutions in the conduct of their intercollegiate athletic programs.
4. To legislate upon any subject of general concern to the membership in the administration of intercollegiate athletics.
5. To study all phases of competitive athletics and establish standards, therefore, to the end that colleges and universities of the United States may maintain their athletic activities on a high plane.
6. To encourage the adoption by its constituent members of eligibility rules in compliance with satisfactory standards of scholarship, amateur standing, and good sportsmanship.
7. To establish and supervise regional and national collegiate athletic contests under the auspices of the Association and to establish rules of eligibility therefore.
8. To stimulate and improve programs to promote and develop educational leadership, physical fitness, sports participation as a recrea-

tional pursuit, and athletic excellence in competitive intramural and intercollegiate programs.

9. To formulate, copyright, and publish rules of play for collegiate sports.
10. To preserve collegiate athletic records.
11. To cooperate with other amateur athletic organizations in the promotion and conduct of national and international athletic contests.
12. To otherwise assist member institutions as requested to further their intercollegiate athletic programs.

National Junior College Athletic Association

The idea of forming the NJCAA was conceived in Fresno, California, in 1937. A small group of junior college representatives met to organize an association that had as its purpose the promotion and supervision of a national junior college sport program consistent with the educational objectives of the junior colleges. A constitution was presented at a charter meeting in Fresno in 1938 and the NJCAA was born. The initial activity sponsored by the NJCAA was track and field. The first national track and field meet, under the auspices of the NJCAA, was held in Sacramento, California, in 1939, and this continued as an annual event except for 3 years during World War II.

Although the association was founded in California, there was never any intention that the NJCAA would be just a West Coast organization. This became apparent when Trinidad College's invitation to sponsor the 1941 track meet at Denver, Colorado, was accepted. The NJCAA was fast achieving national recognition, and in 1941, teams representing colleges from east of the Mississippi joined southern and West Coast members. In 1949, the NJCAA was reorganized in a manner that divided the nation into sixteen regions. The NJCAA bulletin was authorized and published as the official organ of the association. Policies were also established for conducting national and regional events. The constitution was revised, and the organization was incorporated as a nonprofit corporation.

In 1953, the NJCAA, in cooperation with the American Association of Junior Colleges' Subcommittee on Athletics, wrote and adopted the statement of guiding principles for conducting junior college athletics. In 1954, the NJCAA obtained representation on various national rules committees and changed the name of the NJCAA bulletin to the *Juco Review*.

Another important component of the NJCAA program was developed in 1956 when football statistics and rankings became a responsibility of the association. In 1957, the NJCAA established an affiliation with the National Federation of State High School Athletic Associations and the NAIA, so that all these athletic associations might cooperate in matters of common interest.

By 1958, the scope of the NJCAA was recognized by other national organizations, and the association was asked to participate in numerous national projects. Soon, additional national championships were conceived, and expanded postseason play was available in almost all sports.

In 1975, the board of directors approved a women's division, and national championships were established in volleyball, basketball, and tennis. National invitational championships soon developed into national championships for women. In 1978, the women's division membership soared to a high of 434 members. The men's division membership stood at 565. The NJCAA is dedicated to meeting the needs of both male and female athletes and to providing them with the highest caliber of national competitive championships in a wide range of sports.

National Association for Intercollegiate Athletics

The NAIA was designed primarily for small colleges. It began as an intercollegiate basketball association, holding its first meeting in 1940 as the National Association of Intercollegiate Basketball. The NAIA continued to be involved with only basketball tournament play until 1952, when the member schools expressed a desire to expand their national championships. By 1956, the NAIA also oversaw championships in track and field, golf, and tennis. A national championship football bowl game and additional sports became available under NAIA's umbrella in 1957.

As the original NAIA grew, its influence became much more pronounced. In 1945, additional basketball tournaments known as "doubleheaders" and later as "tip-off tournaments" began in Kansas City with association sponsorship. The tip-off tournament idea spread to many parts of the country and soon was sponsored by more districts. Today, the NAIA has more than 500 four-year collegiate members and 40 affiliated conferences. National championship events have expanded to twenty-one, including nine events for women.

Association for Intercollegiate Athletics for Women

Although no longer in existence, the AIAW must be credited with playing a major role in the development and support of women's competitive programs. The AIAW was established in 1971 to provide leadership for the fast-growing women's competitive sport program. The association was dedicated to the development of standards and educational soundness in intercollegiate women's athletics. The AIAW grew out of, and soon replaced, the Commission on Intercollegiate Athletics for Women, which was created in 1967 by the Division for Girls' and Women's Sports, one of the administrative units in the American Alliance for Health, Physical Education, Recreation and Dance. The AIAW's policies and regulations were established by institutional representatives to provide equitable programs for the female student athlete and were developed as an integral part of the educational program in 2-year and 4-year institutions.

The AIAW was the catalyst in the vital effort to ensure equal opportunity in collegiate athletic programs. There were eighteen national championships for women in thirteen different sports sponsored by the AIAW. Although accomplishing much toward the development of women's sports, pressures to operate men's and women's programs under a single governing body, as well as financial limitations, terminated the AIAW's sponsorship of women's championships and governance of women's sport programs.

International Sport

Today, more than ever, sport is taking its place at the top of the hierarchy for national support from the many and varied countries of the world. Government leaders often view sport as an instrument that can promote better health and community development and provide national identity.

Developing countries are continually seeking consultation from nations with successful, established programs, inquiring about which model would best suit their countries' needs. For the most part, the interest of these developing nations is concentrated on a total program of physical education for school-age youth along with a sport training model for talented athletes that, it is hoped, will develop individuals or teams which can perform successfully at the international level.

Olympics

Every 4 years, athletes from around the world "go for the gold" in the Olympic Games. The recognition and support accrued by winning Olympic competition is sought after by the largest and smallest of nations. The Olympic movement, despite its political overtones, provides more hope for international recognition and world sport for all countries than any other single force.

Currently, many approaches are used in the participating countries to develop the athletic talent of their youth for participation in international competition. Methods range from school athletic team development programs to government-sponsored training centers. Many of the foreign government sport-training centers require young participants with sport potential to leave their homes and enter a sport institute for skill development, where national coaches work daily to mold the Olympic champion. For the most part, the United States utilizes the school setting for talent development. However, each year more and more year-round sport camps and national training centers similar to those of our foreign competitors are springing up around the country. Whatever the method, it must not be forgotten that the individual participant is of the utmost concern and that high-level athletic goals cannot be achieved by all individuals. However, a well-planned and well-designed program of sport development should keep the individual's best interest in mind and result in a positive experience for every athlete regardless of the level of achievement. We can all be winners, but we cannot all be champions.

Sports for the Physically Challenged

Today there are more than fifteen organizations involved in providing competition for physically challenged individuals. There is competition in such sports as archery, bowling, basketball, baseball, horseback riding, skiing, and track and field.

One of the most popular games that is highly organized into regular leagues is wheelchair basketball. The athletes may play the game sitting down, but they do not sweat any less for it. The action is as fast and exciting as in a regular basketball game, once you learn to see past the obvious differences.

The rules have been changed to make playing basketball in a wheelchair practical, but in no way has the game been made any easier. The baskets remain at the regulation 10-foot level and yet the players are more than 2 feet shorter than they would be if they could stand up. To compensate for the reduced mobility, wheelchair players are allowed 6 seconds in the free throw lane instead of the 3 seconds allowed able-bodied players, and the player in possession of the ball can push his chair only twice without dribbling the ball, taking a shot, or passing the ball. Other differences in the rules for wheelchair basketball are that men and women can play on the same team and there is a physical advan-

As this skier in the Second International Winter Sports Championships for the Disabled shows, the physically challenged athlete can master skills and participate in major athletic competitions.

tage foul that does not exist in any other version of the game. To equalize the physical abilities of the wheelchair teams in national competitions, the players are also classified into one of five levels according to the degree of disability. A team cannot field more than three players with minimal disability at any one time. On the court, however, the physical limitations seem to disappear, and the team focuses on the fine art of playing together as a team.

Many of the physically limited athletes who have conquered wheelchair basketball are found heading for the tennis courts to play wheelchair tennis. These athletes possess great dedication and skill as they compete successfully in games that most people without any limiting physical disability find difficult.

Physical education for the physically challenged has the same potential rewards, and goals as physical education for people without limitations. Mastering sports skills can still lead to self-confidence and complete enjoyment of a sport. Competition still provides the participant with the opportunity to develop strength and endurance. By participating in sports, the physically challenged athlete, like other athletes, learns that self-control and discipline are required for individual and team success. Social development can be enhanced through good communication techniques that emphasize cooperation and respect. The challenges and the rewards for the physical educator working with physically challenged individuals can be exciting and satisfying in many ways.

Special Olympics

One of the most successful competitive programs is the Special Olympics, a sports training and athletic competition program for mentally retarded children. Athletic competition is organized at the local, state, national, and international level. Sport in its truest sense, the Special Olympics goal is "not to win, but to try; to experience, not to conquer. No time is too slow, no distance too short to earn a ribbon, a hug, a cheer, or a sincere 'well done.' "

The first Special Olympics games were held in the summer of 1968 at Soldier Field in Chicago. One thousand mentally retarded children from all over the United States took part in the competition. Created by the Kennedy Foundation, the Chicago Park District organized a 2-day event, social experience, and celebration that involved and challenged mentally retarded children. For many of these children, it was their first time away from home, their first chance to travel in an airplane, compete in athletic events, and attend an awards banquet. These boys and girls finally had an opportunity to win a medal and experience feelings of pride and joy through their physical accomplishments.

Although competition for the mentally retarded was questioned by experts, it was soon discovered that the program was successful far beyond anyone's expectations. Today, Special Olympics are endorsed by major national agencies involved with mental retardation, and there are Special Olympics organizations in every state. These groups are concerned with year-round competition, sport activities, and training programs, and have recruited more than 100 volunteers to coach and administer the program.

Whether they finish first or last, the Special Olympics children and others in leadership roles share experiences that cannot be duplicated by any other program. There is a place for every mentally retarded person in the Special Olympics, regardless of his or her degree of disability or level of skill. After watching these children run a race, jump over a bar, swim in a pool, or throw a ball, and then step forward to receive their awards, one cannot help but recognize the importance of giving every child encouragement and a chance to succeed.

Youth Sport Competition

Competitive athletic opportunities for boys and girls outside the school system have grown tremendously since 1970. Youth sports that began with Little League and Pop Warner football have expanded to include basketball, soccer, softball, gymnastics, tennis, golf, and other sports. In many of these sports, there is a range of competition for children from 5 to 19 years old.

Millions of today's youth are crazed with the excitement of organized team play and have a special desire to wear that first team uniform. Since the work of youth sport organizations is carried out by volunteers, from peewee basketball to ponytail softball, one finds parent involvement in coaching, field maintenance, facility construction, concession stand operation, officiating, and the never-ending transportation problems.

Some abuses of a good program have been reported, but these occur primarily when a winning-at-all-costs ethnic supersedes the participation-for-all approach. Youth sport programs must be conducted under rules based on a sound philosophy of play with the welfare of the child foremost in the minds of its leaders.

Properly conducted youth sport programs provide an entry into competitive sports.

Youth sports should be a learning experience for some future super-stars as well as for those whose athletic careers often are limited to this level of competition. To expect too much from children who are at an early developmental stage is usually where problems originate. The refining of skills by a child must be carefully controlled and supervised in a manner that will be beneficial to the child's total development so-cially, emotionally, physically, and strategically. The child must be brought carefully from exploring movement potential on an apparatus or gymnasium floor to the athletic arena, where a great deal of physical proficiency and mental discipline is required to achieve success.

There is no substitute for a sound physical education base that should provide children with rudimentary strategies and tactics. In such sim-ple games as running tag, for example, a child may learn to fake a move-ment in one direction when intending to then move in another. This process of learning to outwit an opponent can be carried to the highest level of competitive endeavors. Children who are given the opportunity to play organized youth sports can later employ the strategy and tactics learned in a nonpressure situation to the automatic movements required in successful athletic competition.

There has long been controversy among parents, lay coaches, profes-sional coaches, educators, behavioral scientists, and the medical profes-sion about the value of competitive sports for the physically and emotionally immature child, but most agree that the benefits of these activities far outweigh the liabilities. If properly managed programs in-volve physically and emotionally mature children, age-group competi-tion can be a definite asset to future sport participation. With proper adult supervision, age-group activities provide outstanding opportuni-ties to use individual skills and strategy against an opponent in a com-petitive game situation.

Sports for Older Americans

Modern times have seen more physical education activities for Ameri-cans well beyond the age of 60 years. With increasing frequency, older Americans are participating in exercise classes on a regular basis. Re-cently, we have seen an expansion of the competitive sport program for seniors. Many older Americans who were athletically inclined during their high school and college years engaged in little physical activity during their 30 or 40 working years and now are enjoying competing in senior events such as the Senior Olympics. Running events have been one of the most popular activities, and finishing times in the distance races are not much greater than those of the younger competitors. Some other available senior sport activities are swimming, volleyball, softball, and basketball.

Many older Americans are replacing such traditional symbols of old age as house slippers and the rocking chair with the new symbols of running shoes, exercise bicycles, and weight-lifting equipment. Exercise programs and sports competition for those without known medical problems provide opportunities for our elderly population to obtain the benefits of regular physical activity, and to develop and maintain strength, endurance, flexibility, and balance.

Exercising regularly and participating in sport activities also helps reduce stress. Stress, a significant problem among older people, often ensues when one's spouse, relatives, and friends are no longer alive. Exercise and sport programs can do much to fill this gap of loneliness and return the individual to a healthy state by establishing new goals through competition in a variety of sport activities. Equally as important are the social benefits derived when participants partake of the friendship and socialization involved in physical activity and sport.

Athletics and Academics

The term *student athlete* is much misunderstood. To some it means an opportunity for an education through sports participation. To others it means a free ride to a degree or diploma if one is a good enough athlete. Ideally, the term should represent student learning first and athletic participation second. The main purpose of any educational institution is to provide appropriate learning experiences leading to the development of the mind. It should also include extracurricular offerings, of which sport competition and other activities may be a part.

Recently, you may have heard of or participated under the "no pass, no play" rule at the high school level. This policy varies in design by geographical area but basically means that the student athlete who fails a course or has a low grade, ragardless of grade point average (G.P.A.), is ineligible to participate in his or her sport activity for a selected period of time. This rule upholds the "student first, athlete second" philosophy. Although controversial in nature, depending on the specific rule interpretation, the "no pass, no play" policy should motivate those who wish to play to do their homework as well.

At the college level, under NCAA rules a student must be enrolled in at least 12 semester hours during the season of competition and pass 24 semester hours between seasons of competition. Also, at least a 2.0

G.P.A., based on a 4.0 scale, must be maintained for the student to be eligible to participate in a sport.

The following general rules of conduct are pertinent to academic achievement and sports eligibility at both the high school and college levels:

- A student athlete must be enrolled in an academic program on a full-time basis.
- The course of study pursued must lead toward a high school diploma or associate of arts or baccalaureate degree.
- The student athlete may not exceed eight semesters of playing eligibility.
- The student athlete must be making normal academic progress toward graduation.

Our brief discussion here of academics and athletics in no way diminishes the importance of this subject area. Coaches who believe in the true concept of the student athlete make every effort to encourage each team member to attend class, develop good study habits, and understand the relationship of education to lifelong success.

Coaching

Although coaching as a profession is discussed in Chapter 12, the coach's role in athletics is too important to overlook here. Coaches today have the advantage of completing sound professional preparation programs including instruction in such areas as coaching techniques, training programs, sport psychology, public relations, fund raising, and leadership patterns. Add to this a personal love of sport and a sincere desire to mold individuals into a team of men or women to produce a fine-tuned, precision instrument of play and you are on your way to becoming a successful coach.

Success is always one's goal, but it is not the only measure of achievement. Although difficult to substantiate, many believe that outstanding coaches do build character and teach the lessons of give and take in our modern society. However true this may be, the coach whose team or protégé wins is heralded on the first page of the newspaper sports section and goes down in history as one of sports' legends. Have you ever considered how you remember your coach as a teacher, counselor, disciplinarian, salesperson, speaker, diplomat, and organizer? Much is expected of a coach, who often fills this role only after a full day of teaching.

Many will recall one of the first coaching greats, Knute Rockne, who coached Notre Dame's football teams to an impressive 105 wins, 12 losses, and 5 ties in 13 seasons before he died in a plane crash. After 5 decades, his 0.897 winning percentage is still in the record books. Rockne's inspiring halftime pep talks remain symbolic of the profession and are mimicked by many. He had the ability to use the human voice with startling and unforgettable emphasis. A man of many talents, Rockne taught chemistry while coaching, and his scientific background aided in his personal design of uniforms and equipment to protect the human body and enhance the game. Rick Miller, one of his players, stated,

> Because Rock only weighed 155, he had to make a study of blocking angles and leverages and he was right in there without pads smacking into us, hitting us with shoulders, hips, upper arms, everything that was legal. "Come on, I won't hurt you!" he'd yell.

He prided himself in outwitting his opponents by deceiving them about the real strength of the Notre Dame team at any given moment. A contemporary journalist (Rowen, 1981) wrote years later,

> With the skyrocketing of Notre Dame out of the west, hundreds of thousands of people who had never been to college or near a campus identified themselves with the school called the Fighting Irish.

We may not all be the innovator and strategist that Rockne was, but many of today's successful coaches are cut from the same mold. Coaching still provides an opportunity for innovative, creative men and women in sports.

Ethics and Drugs in Sport

Athletic administrators in schools and colleges are proud that their sport programs are educationally based and founded on principles that are developmentally correct from the physical, social, and psychological points of view. However, the win-at-all-costs ethic often dominates and destroys sound principles of athletic competition. This is particularly true at the youth sports level or where inexperienced or lay coaches are used.

Our country was founded on and prospered because of a free spirit of competition and a will to win. Communities all over our nation have displayed their pride by posting at their city limits signs that boast athletic success, such as "Home of the 3A Basketball Champions." Fond memories of a season of glory and shared hopes of repeating that success enhance feelings of fellowship. Although there is no substitute for a winner, we must be cognizant that it is possible to win in a variety of ways. Athletes who try their best but lose the game can still be personal winners. If the athlete has done his or her personal best, deep down in their hearts is the satisfaction of giving a winning effort, a feeling of success is not soon forgotten. Wins will come for those athletes and coaches who subscribe to this philosophy.

Why, then, do we read daily about physical and psychological abuse of athletes in youth sport programs, high school athletics, and big-time college competition? Is it necessary to make under-the-table payments and provide expensive gifts to athletes as a lure to attend an institution? Does the coach have to cheat to win? One might speculate that the high visibility of sport programs and the desire to be successful could lead to pressures that might compromise a coach's principles. Can this be justified? Athletic events are evaluated more than any other program in or out of the school setting. Each day, millions of spectators are expressing their opinions of a coach's ability to recruit talent, select a style of play, or make correct decisions during competition. Alumni and booster groups are quick to criticize the coach who does not produce according to their expectations. Have we forgotten what sport programs are supposed to accomplish? Is what is best for the participant less important than what is best for the observer? Clearly, a variety of public interests should be considered, but the athlete's well-being must always come first. One cannot succumb to outside pressures at the athlete's expense.

Sound ethical practices are agreed on and used by successful, intelligent coaches. Those who win by these standards are the coaches we seek to conduct our competitive sport programs. A properly conducted sport program enhances the development of the total being and can provide a microcosmic experience of our American culture for persons of all ages.

Courtesy, respect, and understanding are fostered by adherence to sound ethical practices in all phases of athletics. Individuals who fulfill this responsibility provide the type of leadership that is associated with valid, educationally based athletic programs. Those who violate established codes of ethics should be reprimanded or dismissed from the program. Athletics must maintain an unchallenged degree of credibility in a highly visible arena.

The codes of ethics presented in this section were modified from the NCAA, AIAW, and NJCAA handbooks and are samples of sound athletic practices for selected levels of competition.

The Coach

One of the purposes of competitive athletics is to provide experiences where players have opportunities to develop socially acceptable and personally fulfilling values and characteristics. Sport programs should provide opportunities for making value judgments that will help determine desirable personal behavior. The coach has the unique opportunity to influence players in the selection and development of their personal values by setting the example through a sound competitive philosophy and behavior patterns that exemplify the highest standards of human leadership.

The coach must recognize the unique qualities and worth of each athlete and help each athlete develop confidence and cooperation through sport competition. These tasks usually are approached in stressful situations and require a maturity that is refined over the years. The coach's maturity and personal control help influence the reactions of players, spectators, and officials.

The coach also has a responsibility to provide sound teaching and training that will allow players to achieve their athletic potential. It is the coach's charge to promote sports in general through a well-developed and ethical public relations program. The actions of the coach are reflected in the public's opinion of competitive sport programs. A favorable image is critical to acquiring and maintaining public support for athletic programs.

Code of Ethics for Coaches

1. Set a good example as a coach in your appearance, conduct, language, and sportsmanship, and teach the players the importance of these standards.
2. Treat players, opposing coaches, officials, administrators, and spectators with respect and dignity.
3. Become thoroughly familiar with the rules of the sport coached.
4. Develop the ability to accept defeat or victory gracefully without excessive emotional response.
5. Coach to play within the spirit of the game and the letter of the rules.
6. Conduct practices so that all players have an opportunity to improve their skill level through active participation.
7. Stress a spirit of team play by encouraging qualities of self-discipline, cooperation, self-confidence, leadership, courtesy, honesty, and initiative.

8. Protect the health and safety of athletes by insisting that all activities be conducted for their psychological strengths and the individual's physiological welfare.
9. Employ consistent and fair criteria in judging players and establishing standards for them.
10. Treat players with respect, equality, and courtesy.
11. Emphasize the ideals of sportsmanship and fair play in all competitive situations.
12. Maintain a consistent adherence to standards, rules, eligibility, conduct, etiquette, and attendance requirements.
13. Attend sport clinics to keep abreast and informed of current trends and techniques of the sport.
14. Design practice opportunities that provide appropriate player preparation to meet the competitive situation with confidence.
15. Cooperate with administrative personnel in establishing and conducting a quality athletic program.

The Athlete

Intercollegiate athletics have evolved to provide an opportunity for the participant to develop potential as a skilled performer in an educational setting. Through sports, the athlete has an opportunity to grow physically, emotionally, socially, and intellectually. In addition, each participant has the opportunity to travel, represent one's institution, and learn the art of becoming a team member. To receive these benefits, the athlete relinquishes some individual rights to accept the policies of the program and become a member of the team.

Code of Ethics for the Athlete

1. Maintain personal habits that enhance healthful living and promote high-level performance.
2. Respect differing points of view.
3. Strive for excellence in personal performance.
4. Abide by the spirit of the rules as well as the letter of the rules throughout all games and practices.
5. Uphold all standards and regulations expected of athletic participants.
6. Respect and accept the decisions of the coach. Differences of opinion should be voiced in private.
7. Strive to learn and train to achieve one's full potential.

8. Promote favorable relations between all participants who are striving to achieve athletic excellence.
9. Exhibit dignity in manner and dress when representing one's school both on and off the playing field.
10. Respect the accomplishments of one's teammates.
11. Contribute to the effort to make each practice a success.
12. Seek to know and understand one's teammates.
13. Place primary responsibility to the team rather than to self.
14. Keep personal disagreements away from practices and contests.
15. Be grateful for the opportunity afforded by the athletic program and to assist in program development as evidence of this gratefulness.

The Administrator

The competitive athletic program provides activities for the highly skilled. Sound guidance and examples for this program must come from the chief athletic administrator. In addition to establishing policies and procedures that are consistent with the appropriate athletic governing organizations, a primary concern of the athletic director is to foster ethical practices of behavior that will accomplish and fulfill the goals of a well-designed sport program. The degree of success of an athletic program is directly related to the effectiveness of its program administrator.

Code of Ethics for the Athletic Administrator

1. Insist that players and coaches abide by the rules and regulations established by the governing bodies of which the institution is a member.
2. Promote safety by employing a full-time athletic trainer for all sports.
3. Support the athletic program, players, and coaches through personal actions and, when possible, by being present at a variety of contests.
4. Provide good facilities for practices and competition and ensure that all teams are supplied with quality equipment.
5. Seek adequate funding for the athletic program and allocate these funds in a fair and equitable manner to all sports.
6. Employ coaches who are qualified and interested in the assigned sport.
7. Inform school administrators of problems, issues, and accomplishments of the athletic program to maintain or create greater understanding and support for the competitive sport program.

8. Maintain an awareness of policy and rule changes of all athletic governing bodies.
9. Review existing policies regarding operation of the athletic program on a regular basis and recommend procedures to improve and strengthen the program.
10. Attend meetings, workshops, clinics, and conventions to maintain up-to-date knowledge of athletic administration.

Drugs in Sport

Athletes command a highly visible position in our world. They often are viewed as heroes and are looked up to by millions of youngsters and adults. A contemporary major problem in society at large is the misuse and abuse of drugs. The most specific or unique drug problem in sports appears to be the abuse of steroids. In their quest for high-level performance, some athletes turn to drugs with expectations of aiding their bodies to perform at a high level. In some cases, successful athletes turn to drugs when not prepared to cope with the public adulation that accompanies outstanding performances. Under no circumstances can drugs be justified as a means of enhancing athletic performance or dealing with the pressures of success. Drug use often impairs one's judgment and physical ability. Although steroids have been shown to improve performance in selected sports, the long term effects on the human body have yet to be determined.

As a prospective coach, one must assume the responsibility to serve as a counselor and to educate one's players with respect to the hazards of drugs, alcohol, and tobacco. Coaches who suspect the use of drugs or alcohol are ethically bound to counsel individuals or teams to seek help from the appropriate officer, counselor, or other person knowledgeable in the area of substance abuse.

The NCAA Drug Education Committee recommends that athletic departments of member institutions (1) schedule a course at the beginning of each school year on drug and alcohol awareness for all male and female athletes, (2) have in place a plan for the treatment of student athletes with drug- or alcohol-related problems, (3) encourage coaches to become more aware of potential drug-related problems in student athletes and to become an available source of support in the identification and treatment of such problems, and (4) schedule training sessions for all coaches, trainers, and team physicians as to how to recognize and work with drug- and alcohol-related problems.

Illegal drugs, alcohol and selected detrimental prescriptive medicines have no place in the athletic arena. Therefore, athletic department personnel and coaches have the responsibility to do all they can to eliminate drug misuse and abuse from their sport programs.

Economics of Sport in Education

There is no doubt that college sport programs today are big business. The role of the athletic director is as much one of a fund raiser as it is a program administrator. Concern over gate receipts and alumni and booster donations often is a first priority with respect to program responsibilities. At the college level, the cost of tuition, room, board, and books is rising every year, and many in positions of authority with regard to sport programs are electing to compete at higher levels in the hope of increasing income and spectator support. To accomplish this, new facilities need to be constructed, more coaches hired, better schedules arranged, and more equipment purchased.

A winning program enhances the fund-raising effort, and some university presidents can relate the success of their general fund raising to the accomplishments of the athletic teams. Others see no significant relationship since annual giving appears to change little if the sport program is deemphasized. Of course, much has to do with the size of the school, the school's athletic history, and the level of competition. There should be little doubt, however, that national championships afford a degree of visibility for the institution that is difficult to attain any other way and, hence, promote pride in giving. Thus, there is increasing emphasis on the economics of athletic programs.

Extended Benefits of Athletics

Few can doubt the number of benefits that athletes can accrue through a well-organized and well-developed athletic program. However, many fail to realize the opportunity a sport program offers to others in a school or community setting. Too often participation is believed to be limited to only those directly involved in playing the sport, but as a result of the numerous games and contests offered, opportunities are provided also for thousands to perform a supporting role in the sport arena.

Marching band members, cheerleaders, pep squads, drill teams, flag carriers, and dancers can experience many of the same benefits as those playing the game. Uniform dress and disciplined, patterned routines develop pride and respect through many long hours of practice. Like the

Cheerleaders, band members, pep squads, and drill teams can experience many of the same benefits as those playing the game. Patterned routines develop pride and self-respect and require hours of disciplined practice.

teams on the field, band members, baton twirlers, drill teams, and cheerleaders compete in championships at local and national levels.

Meanwhile, the "pepsters" have grown into a million-dollar pastime, supported by the sale of candy bars, flowers, and car washes. A national news release indicated that 6,000 students from around the world came together for an annual world championship involving twelve different categories of "pep arts." One competing drill team and marching band raised $160,000 through raffles, donations, and sales to travel from South Africa to the Los Angeles area, an excellent budget for any sport program. It is estimated that in California alone, 20,000 youths attend summer camps to improve their skills in the pepster arena. Although hearts can be broken if one is cut from the pep squad, for those who make it, the program promotes self-esteem, teamwork, and healthy bodies while maintaining discipline and scholarship.

In addition to the crowd interest generated by pepsters and school bands, athletics also offers opportunities for many others behind the scenes. The mathematician has the opportunity to compile statistics in all sports, and feeding this information into the computer can introduce the student interested in this aspect of sports to the world of computer programming. Art students can develop posters and flyers: Many discover that sport is an excellent subject for painting and sculpture. Students operating a concession stand at sporting events may be having their first experience in the business world. There is no doubt that sound athletic programs are an important asset to the total educational program.

Despite our awareness of the extended benefits of athletics, athletic programs continue to be eliminated in some areas of the United States. We in the physical education profession sometimes fail to publicize and promote all the favorable aspects of a broad-based program. Financial limitations should not mandate the elimination of non-income-producing sports such as tennis, golf, archery, or gymnastics if educational goals are to be maintained. Each professional in the field of athletics must take the time to extend coaching duties to include a strong public information program. What is said about athletics must go beyond the win-loss record and, if well done, will not only preserve athletic programs but will elicit public pressure to expand physical education classes, intramurals and athletic programs in order to provide these valuable experiences for everyone.

Student Activities

1. Read the daily sport page for 1 week and calculate the number of column inches devoted to (a) age-group sports, (b) high school sports, (c) college sports, (d) professional sports, (e) men's sports, and (f) women's sports.
2. Discuss the purposes of the athletic governing body at your institution and compare it to the National Federation as described in the text.
3. Investigate the written objectives of the athletic program at the institution and compare it to the NCAA objectives in the text.
4. Document how much time is scheduled for television sport programming in a week's time for both men and women. Compare coverage on cable television with coverage on major networks.
5. Compare annual attendance figures in three professional sporting events of your choice and make comparisons with the same sports at the college and high school levels.
6. Summarize one of the codes of ethics in paragraph form.
7. Watch two levels of play of any sport, in person or on television, and discuss your observations.

8. Write for information on youth sports publications from Youth Sports Press, 6801 South LaGrange Road, LaGrange, Illinois 60325. On receiving the material, discuss the type of literature available and the influence it has on the target audience (e.g., volunteer coaches, parents, volunteer officials, league administrators).

9. Read the special feature on youth sports in the March 1987 issue of the *Journal of Physical Education and Recreation*. In class, debate the suggested practices in youth sports versus what is presently practiced.

10. Investigate the "no pass, no play" rule in your area and evaluate the appropriateness of the regulation as related to athletic eligibility.

11. Investigate the Olympic movement and contrast its role in our nation and developing countries.

12. Trace the level of financial commitment to the athletic program during the past 15 years at your college or university.

Suggested Readings

American Alliance for Health, Physical Education, Recreation and Dance. 1978. *Association for Intercollegiate Athletics for Women Handbook, 1978–1979.* Washington, DC: AAHPERD.

Arnheim, D. D., and R. A. Pestolesi. 1978. *Elementary physical education.* St. Louis: Mosby.

Athletic Journal, 1719 Howard St., Evanston, IL 60202.

Forsythe, C. E., and I.A. Keller. 1975. *Administration of high school athletics.* Englewood Cliffs, NJ: Prentice-Hall.

Gallon, A. J. 1980. *Coaching ideas and ideals,* 2nd ed. Boston: Houghton Mifflin.

Jones, B. J., et al. 1988. *Guide to effective coaching.* Boston: Allyn and Bacon.

Killian, G. E. 1980. *National junior college athletic handbook and casebook.* Kansas.

Manual of the National Collegiate Athletic Association. 1989–1990. Kansas.

The National Association of Intercollegiate Athletics official handbook. 1990. Kansas City, MO.

National Federation of State High School Associations handbook. 1990. Kansas City, MO.

Neal, P. 1978. *Coaching methods for women,* 2nd ed. Reading, MA: Wesley Publishing.

Pestolesi, R. A. 1978. *Creative administration in physical education and athletics*. Englewood Cliffs, NJ: Prentice-Hall.

Redmond, G. E. 1986. The 1984 Olympic Scientific Congress Proceedings. In *Sport and Politics*. Human Kinetics Publishing.

Rowen, K. 1981. Time management of college and university football coaches. PhD diss. University of Southern California, Los Angeles.

Thomas, J. R. 1977. Youth sports guide for coaches and parents. Washington, DC: American Alliance for Health; Physical Education, Recreation and Dance.

References

American Alliance for Health, Physical Education, Recreation and Dance. 1978. *Association for Intercollegiate Athletics for Women Handbook, 1978–1979*. Washington, DC: AAHPERD.

Forsythe, C. E., and I.A. Keller. 1975. *Administration of high school athletics*. Englewood Cliffs, NJ: Prentice-Hall.

Killian, G. E. 1980. *National junior college athletic handbook and casebook*. Kansas.

Manual of the National Collegiate Athletic Association. 1989–1990. Kansas.

The National Association of Intercollegiate Athletics official handbook. 1990. Kansas City, MO.

National Federation of State High School Associations handbook. 1990. Kansas City, MO.

Rowen, K. 1981. Time management of college and university football coaches. PhD diss. University of Southern California, Los Angeles.

PART THREE

Career Paths

11. Teaching and You

Chapter Outline

Choosing to Teach
What Is Quality Physical Education?
Skills Needed by Today's Teachers
The Challenge
Student Activities
Suggested Readings

Objectives

Chapter 11 is designed to enable you to:

- Understand the challenges of teaching in multiple settings.
- Recognize the components of a quality physical education program.
- Develop an awareness for the need for people skills.
- Confirm your commitment to the profession.

I N Chapter 2, there was some discussion of the status of physical education in the schools. Although today there is greater interest in health-related issues and sports activities among the middle class in the United States, the present-day emphasis on academic reforms has not contributed greatly to improvement of our programs' image, class sizes, budgets, and facilities. Part Two of this book, which you have just completed, provides an outline of the foundations vital to quality physical education programs. It is exciting to perceive what the benefits can be to children and youth in well-designed programs that make use of effective instructional strategies and motivational techniques. There are many quality programs being conducted throughout the nation. However, you may soon discover in internship and student teaching experiences that there are varying degrees of quality.

Choosing to Teach

You probably can recall the diversity of students in your physical education classes at the various school levels. Physical education classes are often the "melting pot" of our educational system. Students from all socioeconomic backgrounds and with a wide variety of academic skills, physical fitness levels, motor development skills, and interest levels are enrolled together in physical activity. Furthermore, class size has increased dramatically in many areas of the United States owing to population growth that is exceeding growth in school budgets. Facilities, the number of teachers, and the amount of equipment are negatively affected by such growth. In many school districts taxes have not increased, so that even those districts with stable enrollments are losing money as costs rise.

As society has changed to adapt to technological advances, more leisurely lifestyles, and equitable career opportunities for men and women, children too have changed. As we have become highly mobile and as the number of single-parent families increases, the values and behaviors of young people have been altered. As a physical education teacher, you represent the epitome of traditional values for a healthy lifestyle. Can you infuse some of your enthusiasm for such a lifestyle in the children you will be expected to teach? Can you commit yourself to the unending quest for excellence in instruction?

There will be days when you will feel despair, because it will appear that no one cares—not the students, not your physical education colleagues, not your principal. The urge to abandon teaching for a coaching career, wherein your students would be selected and motivated, can be overpowering. A number of physical educators before you have decided to roll out the ball of the season and let recreation begin! After all, who cares whether students dress in appropriate activity clothing and footwear; repeatedly excuse themselves from class participation by way of a doctor's note; are consistently late for class; tire easily and decide to sit out for part of the class; are physically unfit; exclude others from active participation; make fun of other students; or are excused from physical education owing to their participation in the school band or athletics? You care! Your efforts to work toward the solution of these problems are what make you a professional.

Although the recognition may not be immediate, you will discover the future can be bright. If a job is well done, you may receive an award from the professional physical education association. An administrative change may result in more support for your efforts. A student may return and thank you for changing his or her lifestyle into a healthy, productive one. Reward yourself by knowing you have given your best to your students and to your profession.

What Is Quality Physical Education?

The term *quality physical education* is often used but rarely well understood. Since only one state, Illinois, currently requires all students in kindergarten through twelfth grade to take physical education every day (American Alliance for Health, Physical Education, Recreation and Dance [AAHPERD], 1987), few individuals can define quality physical education with any degree of accuracy. However, even though state mandates for physical education time requirements are not up to the recommended level, some individual school districts in the United States as well as schools with strong administrative support have achieved the recommended level.

According to Loughrey (1987):

No longer are faculty members content to have students engage in activities that are relatively unstructured and somewhat devoid of learning goals. The era of the bleacher teacher who rolls out the ball and then lets the students "play" is fading into history. The new breed of teachers, some fresh out of college and others with many years of successful experience to their credit, are helping to transform what is happening in school physical education programs in the United States.

Quality instruction provides students an opportunity to achieve a high level of physical education.

General Requirements for a Quality Program

According to the AAHPERD (1988), a quality program in physical education offers instruction on a daily basis to students in kindergarten through grade 12. Children at the elementary school level should participate actively at least 30 minutes each school day, and secondary students should be scheduled for at least 50 minutes per day.

In addition, a quality program means physical education is taught by credentialed specialists professionally educated in an accredited institution. A quality program should guide students through a sequentially planned program of physical fitness, motor skills, and sport knowledge and appreciation for a lifetime of health and fitness benefits.

A quality program allows students of all abilities to participate successfully by learning at their own rate and level of achievement. It also takes advantage of geographical factors and student interests to provide a variety of physical activities appropriate to the goals and objectives established.

There is no specific list of individual activities that must be covered in a quality program. The selection of activities and design of the curriculum is the responsibility of the professional physical educator and encourages individual creativity. In general, a quality program will include (1) cardiorespiratory fitness activities, (2) strength and flexibility exercise, (3) active sports, games, and dance appropriate to the ability level of the students, and (4) instruction with respect to the personal values and physical benefits of exercise as related to lifelong health and total wellness.

If presented with a quality program, students should be motivated to learn new skills, improve their fitness levels, and support physical education as an important phase of the total educational plan. "As a profession, we know what kinds of programs and the type of instruction that motivates students to learn; however, the most serious problem we face today is the continual failure of the profession to deliver what it proclaims" (Kneer, 1987). As a new physical educator, you can make a difference. Do not become discouraged if in your first job you find a program that is less than perfect. Do not allow yourself to be intimidated by experienced faculty who are still teaching in the past. Set the example by doing your job in a way you know will meet student needs and create interest in physical education. Make your classes so good and so much fun that everyone will want to follow your lead.

Other Components of a Quality Program

Quality programs also include new classes in the physical education curriculum. For the most part, traditional course work has been limited to the teaching of established goals and objectives through general sport, fitness, and dance activities. Today, many schools have developed an expanded approach by requiring a specialized course in personal fitness and healthy lifestyles.

The state of Florida was successful in requiring a personal fitness course as a high school graduation requirement (Harageones, 1987). The purpose of the personal fitness course in Florida is threefold: (1) To develop an optimum level of personal fitness, (2) to acquire a knowledge of physical fitness concepts, and (3) to acquire knowledge with respect to the significance of lifestyle on one's health and fitness. After successfully completing the course, Harageones states the students will be able to:

- Understand the components of physical fitness.
- Assess individual fitness levels.
- Understand the relationship between physical fitness activities and stress.
- Understand sound nutritional practices related to physical fitness.
- Understand health problems associated with inadequate fitness levels.

- Understand consumer issues related to physical fitness.
- Evaluate physical activities in terms of their fitness value.
- Select from a variety of dynamic activities those that will help them to improve physical fitness needs.
- Design a fitness program that meets individual needs and interests.
- Understand and apply correct biomechanical and physiological principles related to exercise and training.
- Understand and apply safety practices associated with physical fitness.
- Exhibit an improved state of physical fitness.
- Assess individual lifestyles as related to quality living.
- Exhibit a positive attitude toward physical selves and lifelong physical activity.

Experiencing courses such as this, taught in an exciting manner by enthusiastic professionals, promotes the kind of memories that encourage students as adults to vote in support of favorable physical education legislation.

Benefits of a Quality Physical Education

Quality physical education allows every student to experience success as the program becomes student-centered rather than subject-centered. Individualizing instruction to meet student needs, integrating competition as an adjunct to good programs, involving all students in worthwhile activity, and teaching the knowledge and understanding of the importance of living a healthy, active lifestyle contributes to a better overall society.

Skills Needed by Today's Teachers

Managing People

Today's physical educator needs more than the basic competencies required in most professional preparation programs. Above all, a teacher needs to like people especially young people. A great deal of common sense and an ability to apply the required course work creatively, along with growing experience, will enable the teaching professional to meet the demands of quality instruction successfully. Additionally, one does not always find that his or her physical education class is of a size equal to that in all other subjects; classroom management skills are essential if the physical educator is to avoid becoming discouraged, resorting to the "bleacher teacher" approach.

Professionals must continuously seek new ways to manage discipline, individualize instruction, motivate students, and maintain records in a variety of situations. A well-organized teacher, prepared in advance for each lesson, will be able to succeed in many different worlds. A poorly organized teacher not only will fail to meet quality program standards of instruction but can even be detrimental to the physical education profession.

Listening Skills

Do you have time for your students? Have you developed your ability to listen effectively to students' concerns within a specified time frame so that other responsibilities do not suffer? You will be working with a great variety of students in your class, many of whom have no one who shows interest in their personal concerns. Learn to be attentive to student concerns. The environment in which you work lends itself to the counselor-adviser role so important to all young people. Time

Informal conversations with teachers aid in clarifying career goals.

you spend as a good listener and your willingness to provide intelligent feedback may make the difference between a student's favorable or unfavorable attitude toward physical education and an active lifestyle.

Good listening skills also include observing students in class. Students are communicating with you through their personal behaviors. Be aware of students' reactions in class activities. Can you discern which students are learning, which are having fun in class, which have problems but are afraid to verbalize them? Become an astute observer. You can learn much about your class and the individual students.

Action Skills

A good professional does not sit back and hope matters will improve but becomes active in making improvements. Some ways to become involved are by serving on committees to improve instruction, working with groups to seek more support for physical education, and promoting legislation and political concerns for your profession. Two specific examples of professional action would be to develop a newsletter for parents regarding your physical education program and to establish a speakers' bureau for promoting physical education in your community.

The Challenge

Be persistent in your quest for support of quality daily physical education programs. Lead by providing quality instruction and by continually setting a positive lifestyle example to your students, colleagues, administrators, and community.

Student Activities

1. Visit one elementary and one secondary physical education class. Compare and contrast the situations in class size, student characteristics, class organization, quality of instruction, and general school climate.
2. Select one "who cares" issue from pages 236–237 and write a one-page response to the question. Share it with a group of classmates.
3. Describe your commitment to quality physical education in twenty-five words or less.
4. As you observe a middle school or junior high school physical education class, use your listening skills to determine the students' value of their physical activity experience.

Suggested Readings

Harageones, M. 1987. Impact of education reforms: the quality of Florida's high school physical education. *Journal of Physical Education, Recreation and Dance* 58, no. 6: 52–54.

Kneer, M. E. 1987. Where is the education in physical education? *Journal of Physical Education, Recreation and Dance* 58, no. 6.

Loughrey, T. J. 1987. Evaluating program effectiveness. *Journal of Physical Education, Recreation and Dance* 58, no. 6.

Seefeldt, V. 1987. Selling the potential rather than the record. *Journal of Physical Education, Recreation and Dance* (Sept): 42–43.

Wilcox, R. C. 1987. Dropouts: the failing of high school physical education. *Journal of Physical Education, Recreation and Dance* 58, no. 6: 21–25.

References

Harageones, M. 1987. Impact of education reforms: the quality of Florida's high school physical education. *Journal of Physical Education, Recreation and Dance* 58, no. 6: 52–54.

Kneer, M. E. 1987. Where is the education in physical education? *Journal of Physical Education, Recreation and Dance* 58, no. 6.

Loughrey, T. J. 1987. Evaluating program effectiveness. *Journal of Physical Education, Recreation and Dance* 58, no. 6.

12. Careers in the School Setting

Chapter Outline

Do You Want to Be a Teacher?
Levels of Teaching
Professional Preparation Programs
Special Credentials
Coaching Minor
Community College Articulation
Teaching Physical Education
Careers in Education
Student Activities
Suggested Readings
References

Objectives

Chapter 12 is designed to enable you to:

- Become familiar with the variety of career options in the school setting.
- Review the total curriculum required to pursue a teaching career.
- Become aware of the need to develop a variety of teaching styles for effective instruction.

TRADITIONALLY, most physical education majors pursue teaching credentials to prepare for employment in education. Opportunities in the school setting include teaching, coaching, and administration. All of these careers can be exciting and rewarding experiences for those dedicated to working with the school-age population.

Boys and girls often look to the physical education teacher or coach for guidance and counseling. Developing personal rapport with students is an important responsibility of the physical education teacher whose approach is both disciplined and informal. There is little doubt that the lives of many have been greatly influenced by the example and advice of a coach or teacher. Developing motor skills, encouraging physical fitness, and teaching the concepts of healthy living are critical to the complete education of every person.

Do You Want to Be a Teacher?

If you have any doubts about becoming a teacher, ask yourself these questions:

1. Do you want to be remembered as someone who had an important impact on many students' careers and lifestyles?
2. Do you have patience?
3. Do you enjoy being with children and working with boys and girls of varying levels of physical ability?
4. Are you willing to be creative in your teaching style by seeking innovative ways of meeting individual needs?
5. Can you make the educational experience enjoyable and meaning ful to each person in your class?

If you have given a favorable response to all of these questions, then you probably have the personality and desire needed to meet the demands of teaching in the school environment. The challenge now is to prepare yourself in a creative and enthusiastic manner to become the catalyst necessary to help young people enjoy fitness and skill development and establish a pattern of healthy living that will endure for a lifetime.

Levels of Teaching

Once you have decided to teach in school, your next decision will be to determine the age group with which you would enjoy working. The most common divisions for regular school levels, and the ones we address, are early childhood, elementary, secondary, and college. Each level is unique, but all are equally challenging and rewarding.

It is to your advantage to gain as much preservice experience as possible so that you can determine the level of teaching best suited to you. Experience at each level will help you better understand the stages of human growth and development and enable you to adjust programs appropriately to students with varying social, emotional, and maturational needs.

Early Childhood Education

Although definitions vary from state to state, we define early childhood education as preschool through the second grade. The physical educator teaching at this level must present the beginning motor experiences to children who have boundless energy and are usually successful in large muscle, gross motor activities. Bucher and Thaxton (1981, p. 203) state, "The large muscles develop more rapidly than the small muscles. Therefore, motor abilities proceed from gross motor activity to fine motor activity."

Children in this age group have a short attention span and their socialization is limited. Sensory motor programs including feeling, hearing, moving, speaking, smelling, and touching are appropriate. Cooperation activities and ball skills are limited. Children this age enjoy moving to music, and many program objectives can be reached through movement exploration activities. The basic locomotor skills of running, climbing, jumping, hopping, and skipping are enjoyed by this age group.

Elementary Education

In elementary education, grades 3 through 6, the preliminary skills that were taught in early childhood are expanded. Body control is developed, and increasing social maturity allows children to participate in games of low organization. More refined ball activities can be increased as hand-eye coordination improves. Children in upper elementary levels can play team games and are able to perform sophisticated balance stunts. Winning is important, and personal skill is looked on with pride.

Children at this level develop a greater sense of who they are. Whether they are accepted by their peers also becomes important to them. By planning activities that provide a challenge as well as an opportunity to experience success, a teacher can help the child at this age develop the self-esteem necessary for success in later years. The elementary teacher finds students wanting to improve their skills, which is clear from their growing concern to "make the team."

Junior High School Education

The junior high school level, grades 1 through 9, provides an opportunity to refine the skills introduced at the elementary level. Although there is a variance in growth and development between individuals, junior high school children are generally able to learn sophisticated sport skills. A major factor with this age group is one of motivating students to achieve their full potential.

Due to the variation in maturation, some students are still in an awkward stage and are embarrassed to perform in front of their peers. At this adolescent age, one experiences many physical, social, and emotional developmental stages, which include an awkward and gangly appearance, newly found sex drives, and a strong personal concern for peer approval. Adolescents often change their character from day to day, ranging from eager attentiveness to passive interest in school activities.

High School Education

At the high school level, students are nearing the young adult stage. Peer approval is increasingly important as individuals seek to "fit in" to the school community. Biologically, students are reaching their potential and are more aware of their personal characteristics. Physically, their growth is nearly completed, and a high level of skill performance and personal fitness can be developed.

Students at this level often make most decisions regarding their lifestyles. In many cases, this is the last opportunity to receive professional instruction in areas of health, fitness, nutrition, and sport skills.

Coaching opportunities at this level are high, as the competitive sport program is in full swing. Team games involving high-level performance and fitness activities are popular. Dance is also expanded as facilities lend themselves to the performance level. The refining-skill approach at the secondary school level demands an astute teacher's analytical eye to assist each student in achieving personal skill and fitness goals.

College or University Education

Teaching and coaching at the college or university level allows the physical educator to instruct adults. Sport and fitness activity classes and competitive athletic programs are participated in by choice. How much more adults develop is often influenced by the type and extent of physical activities in which they participate. Teaching college-age students challenges the instructor to work with individuals whose inquisitive minds have matured and whose bodies have developed more completely.

At this stage, instructors and coaches often have their demands questioned by students who want to know the significance of each activity.

Professional Preparation Programs

The professional preparation program requirements leading toward a teaching credential vary from state to state, and institutions often meet these requirements in different ways. In general, though, lower-division course work involves an introduction to the physical education profession, prerequisites to the science core, and basic skill classes in which the student learns how to perform a variety of sport, fitness, and dance activities.

Upper-division course work finds one studying the history and principles of physical education, kinesiology, exercise physiology, motor development, teaching methods, measurement and evaluation techniques, sociopsychological implications, motor skill analysis courses, and specialized coaching techniques. The sample course in Table 12.1 is typical of the courses you may find in most teacher-oriented professional preparation programs.

In addition to the requirements for a physical education major, a block of education courses must be completed to qualify for a teaching credential. The last phase of this course work finds the prospective teacher student teaching in a public school setting. This may range from a one-semester teaching experience of three class periods per day in the high school setting to a full year of residence in either a high school or elementary school. Some institutions schedule this phase of your education during a fifth year.

The student-teaching aspect of your professional preparation is an exciting and enjoyable adventure as you experiment with your personal teaching style and how it affects the learner. At this stage of your career, much of the course work required earlier in your professional preparation suddenly becomes meaningful as you apply it to make the teaching-learning experience run smoothly.

The education courses listed in Table 12.2 are typical requirements for the basic teaching credential. Some states require additional areas of study for the teaching credential outside of the major department, including health science for teachers, teaching reading, teaching English as a second language, mainstreaming handicapped students, and using computers. Many states also mandate completion of a course in their

Table 12.1 Sample Physical Education Teaching Major Requirements

COURSE TITLES	SEMESTER UNITS
Lower division	
Human Anatomy	3
Human Physiology	4
Introduction to Physical Education	2
Team Sports I (Baseball, Softball, Basketball, Volleyball)	2
Individual and Dual Sports I	3
Fundamental Rhythms	2
Aquatics	2
Gymnastics	2
Combatives	2
Team Sports II (Football and Soccer)	2
Individual and Dual Sports II (Conditioned Cross-Country and Track)	2
Upper division	
Sport and Society	2
Organization and Conduct of Physical Education	3
History and Principles of Physical Education	3
Motor Learning	2
Applied Principles of Kinesiology	3
Physiology of Exercise	3
Tests and Measurements in Physical Education	2
Behavior Problems in Physical Education and Athletics	2
Adapted Physical Education	2
Elementary School Physical Education	2
Prevention and Care of Athletic Injuries	2
Choose one	
Analysis of Aquatics	2
Analysis of Gymnastics	2
Analysis of Combatives	2
Choose one	
Coaching Track	3
Coaching Baseball	3
Coaching Football	3
Coaching Basketball	3
Coaching Lacrosse	3
Coaching Field Hockey	3
Coaching Volleyball	3
Total units	57

Table 12.2 Sample Education Credential Requirements

COURSE TITLES	SEMESTER UNITS
Adolescent Development and Learning	3
American School Systems	3
Instruction and Evaluation in Elementary and Secondary Schools	3
Curriculum and Methods in Teaching Physical Education	3
Student Teaching in Elementary Schools	6
Student Teaching in Secondary Schools	6
Total Units	24

state's history or government. For your own institution's specific requirements, check your catalog and plan to enroll in the proper sequence of classes.

Special Credentials

If you are interested in seeking special credentials, you will find that additional course work is required for certification. The astute physical education major realizes that he or she will have more opportunities in the job market if additional credentials are earned. By properly choosing electives and planning in advance, you may find little extra course work is necessary to qualify for selected special credentials.

There are many areas in education that usually require special credentials. Some may also require teaching experience or advanced degrees. Check with your state department of education or college credential office for specific credential requirements that lead to specialized physical education careers, including: adapted physical education, special education, instructing the handicapped, supervision, administration, instructing at the community college level, and coaching.

Coaching Minor

Some students may have a primary interest in coaching sports in the school setting but have little interest in teaching physical education. If this is your situation, you should consider the coaching minor as an option in your credential work. You may major in mathematics, science, history, English, or any other subject commonly taught in secondary schools and minor in physical education with an emphasis on coaching. Currently, science and mathematics teachers are at the top of the educational profession's "most wanted" list.

Large high schools generally have a need for thirty to sixty coaches for all sports and all levels and yet have only eight to twelve physical education teachers. It is important that you teach subjects you enjoy teaching, and if teaching basic sport skills to students of various abilities does not appeal to you but working with students who have a high degree of athletic ability does, the coaching minor may be appropriate for you. The coaching minor outlined in Table 12.3 is an example of what one university requires to prepare a student adequately for effectively coaching in the school environment.

Community College Articulation

If you are taking this introduction to physical education course in a 2-year community college, you should know that it is important to articulate or match your study with the requirements of the 4-year insti-

Table 12.3 Sample Coaching Minor

COURSE TITLES	SEMESTER UNITS
Required	
Scientific Foundations	4
Behavioral Problems in Athletics and Physical Education	2
Athletic Injuries	2
Fieldwork in coaching—must have course Athletic Injuries plus five other units in physical education prior to fieldwork	3
Minimum of Two Coaching Courses	
Coaching Swimming	4
Coaching Volleyball	
Coaching Lacrosse	
Coaching Field Hockey	
Coaching Football	
Coaching Basketball	
Coaching Track and Field	
Coaching Baseball/Softball	
Electives	
Electives in physical education with department approval	7
Total units	22

tution you are planning to attend. Although your college can help, you should take it upon yourself to contact the college or university to which you plan to transfer for specific course requirements.

In general, community college students will usually make the transition well if they complete the general education requirements and take anatomy, physiology, and a variety of fundamental sport skills courses.

Some institutions have skill competency levels you must achieve before enrolling in upper-division analysis classes or as a requirement for graduation. Many also allow a student to waive skill courses if that student can demonstrate proficiency at the required level. Most institutions will also accept an introduction to physical education course.

Teaching Physical Education

One of the most exciting aspects of teaching physical education in the school setting is the challenge to meet the needs of pupils at all levels of instruction. The physical education major must be thoroughly schooled in a variety of teaching styles and must be able to adjust his or her approach to the physical education lesson in a way that will affect each student in a positive manner. Continually ask yourself: Have I taught anything of use today? Am I teaching anything of interest to my students today? Am I presenting my lesson in an enthusiastic way that motivates my students to learn?

The modern professional cannot rely on the traditional command approach—where the focus is on the teacher—as the only way to present a lesson. Although still an important technique in certain learning situations, one must continuously evaluate the technique used in relation to the student's needs, abilities, and interests according to the instructional level. Gain as much early experience as you can by working in summer camps or volunteering as a teacher's aide or coaching assistant.

Teaching Style

How much responsibility an individual or group of students can assume is critical to selecting what kind of teaching style to use for that individual or group. Annarino (1980, p. 4), a curriculum researcher from Purdue University, lists the following elements as basic to the design of the physical education program:

1. What are the needs, problems, and interests of these boys and girls at the various developmental levels at which we find them?

2. What are the problems that modern American youth face in a contemporary society?
3. What are presuppositions and principles that guide us in life and education: our philosophy, our basic beliefs?
4. How does one learn? Why does one learn?
5. What are the justifiable objectives and developmental goals of our discipline?
6. What kinds of experiences not only are best suited for achieving our objectives but also contribute to growth of further experiences?
7. How are these experiences structured and sequenced in a program?
8. Which design model and instructional strategy is most appropriate for creating an effective teaching-learning environment?
9. How can results be appraised in terms of the established objectives?

Answering these questions enables the physical educator to develop a curriculum full of learning experiences that will meet the established program objectives. These elements are also appropriate for those interested in adult fitness or community programs outside of the school setting.

Teaching by Command. In teaching by command, the focus is on the teacher and the subject matter. This traditional approach to learning expects all students to respond as one to the material presented. Although simple in approach, one must be cautioned of the embarrassing situations that can arise for students who are poorly skilled and who may be singled out in front of the class for corrections. The command style is limited in its humanistic potential since individual attention to every student and opportunities for student-teacher interactions are restricted. Too many people educated in the United States have experienced only this style of teaching in their school physical education programs and, as a result, may believe that physical education is impersonal.

Teaching by Task. The task approach to learning in physical education classes is a natural adjunct to the command approach. When teaching by task, there is a transition in the decision-making process from the teacher to the student. This allows for a more individualized and humanistic relationship between the learner and the instructor.

The task sheets or listing of challenges and skills that may be self-directed can be made progressively more difficult. This facilitates instruction so that groups of students can be working at different levels simultaneously in each class. Success can now be achieved at various levels and challenges increased to motivate those who can progress rapidly.

As the teacher's role is modified to a less dominant position, more efficient use of space, equipment, and time is achieved through the flexibility of task teaching. Figure 12.1 shows a sample task sheet used for the address position in golf.

Reciprocal-Task Teaching. Reciprocal-task teaching, or peer teaching, involves the use of a partner in learning skills. One student participates in the skill while the other observes and makes corrections as appropriate to the task sheet. This system is an expansion of the individual-task approach, allowing much more interaction between students. Reciprocal-task teaching enhances the social and emotional phases of the lesson while increasing student involvement.

The instructor should stress the importance of the observer as the directions are read to the participant. The observer checks the par-

---

Figure 12.1 Sample Task Sheet for Golf

Address Position in Golf

Directions Record dates and check appropriate response for each check point for the address. Do by yourself and with your partner a minimum of five times.

	Dates									
Address (address routine)	Yes	No	Yes	No	Yes	No	Yes	No	Yes	No
1. Assume correct grip (review task sheet).										
2. Stand behind ball and sight target (choose a tree, post, etc., to act as target).										
3. Move up to side of ball; with arms extended place the club head down directly behind the ball so the club face is perpendicular or "square" to the intended line of flight.										

Figure 12.1 (continued)

	Dates									
Address (address routine)	*Yes*	*No*	*Yes*	*No*	*Yes*	*No*	*Yes*	*No*	*Yes*	*No*
4. Place your feet so the ball is opposite the center of your stance.										
5. Distribute weight evenly through feet.										
6. Relax—do not hyperextend—knees.										
7. Bend body slightly forward from hips.										
8. Relax shoulders so arms hang freely from body.										
9. Arms and shoulders form a triangle with hands as the apex of the triangle.										
10. Feel comfortable.										

Do you look like this?

ticipant's progress on the task sheet in a manner similar to the individual-task approach. If administered properly, instruction can take place on a one-to-one basis as the teacher supervises and gives suggestions while moving among pairs of students to provide necessary guidance.

Small-Group Teaching. The advantages of small-group teaching are similar to those of the individual-task and reciprocal-task approaches. More individuals are simply added to the group. Sometimes limitations of equipment or facilities mandate this style of teaching, but it is a natural outgrowth of expanded learning experiences. Once students are paired as participant and observer, other students are added as shaggers or ball throwers, depending on the activity, to make the lesson run more efficiently.

Greater responsibility and cooperation are needed within the group, for if one participant falters, the advantages of this type of teaching are lost. Small-group teaching requires added discipline, but it is primarily between peers rather than between student and teacher. Communication skills are developed as students increase their ability to organize, analyze, and adjust to achieve success. This style is particularly appropriate for large classes.

Teaching by Guided Discovery. The guided discovery technique challenges the student's intellectual ability. Teaching with this style provides students with the opportunity to invent new movements, discover what the body can accomplish, develop strategies for problem solving, compare movements with peers, inquire about technique, make decisions regarding movement efficiency, and reflect on personal technique.

When teaching through guided discovery, the instructor presents ideas by asking questions that will guide the students to the desired goal. The teacher must refrain from answering; the answer is not revealed until someone has discovered the requested movement. The teacher must continually rephrase the questions in order to progress toward the goal. Questions should be phrased so that they gradually and continually lead the class toward the desired result.

Teaching by Problem Solving. The problem-solving technique has many advantages because it assumes there is no single correct answer. Stating an open-ended question allows students to achieve success in a variety of ways. Since there are no wrong answers, each student is encouraged and motivated to participate, as positive feedback is given regardless of the response. Each student receives attention from the teacher as he or she seeks advice relating to the solution of the problem.

Teachers must ensure that problems are appropriate for this type of lesson and relevant to the experience and abilities of the students. Asking students to move across a crowded room without touching another child or to show another way to move in open space and working together with another child are examples of using problem-solving techniques when teaching how the body moves.

Instructional Design

Individualized Instruction. Individualized instruction is critical if one is to meet the needs of all pupils in class. The advantage of individualizing instruction is that it enables students to learn at their own rate and at their own level. By individualizing, you challenge every student to remain personally involved in learning skills and knowledge through motivational techniques. A greater amount of interaction between the student and instructor is built into any system that is designed to meet the needs of a particular individual through in-depth study techniques.

Contract Teaching. One example of individualizing instruction is to use contracts in physical education. This learning concept enables the stu-

Individualized instruction provides personal attention and direct teacher-student interaction.

dent to agree on a contract with the teacher that defines the learning objectives, learning activities, evaluating criteria, and other factors necessary to consummate the contract. The emphasis is on results rather than prescribed experiences. Students can proceed on their own, selecting those experiences that will fulfill the agreed-on goals. Contract teaching allows learning to develop from a variety of sources in diverse ways rather than from a single approach. This latitude in instructional design stimulates self-direction in the achievement of prescribed goals. The teacher's role again becomes to guide rather than to dominate the learning environment. Figure 12.2 shows a sample contract.

Contract teaching can also serve to reduce failure, as many contracts allow the student to repeat work until the predetermined goals are achieved. The contract may be closed or open-ended. In a closed contract, the student agrees to master a prescribed amount of information or level of motor performance. The open-ended contract allows the student to choose the learning with options to renegotiate if he or she desires to expand the project or encounters unforeseen difficulties.

There is no single way to write a contract. The process is limited only by the boundaries of the student's and the instructor's creativity. The following variables should be considered in developing or negotiating any contract for study:

1. What kind of work will be done?
2. How much work will be done?
3. How much time will be allotted for each phase?
4. Where will the work be done?
5. What learning resources will be used?
6. What kind of evaluation will be made?
7. What grade or evaluation will be received for satisfactorily completing the contract?
8. What are the consequences of not completing the work?

There are many approaches to presenting a physical education lesson that will meet the established goals of the discipline. It is each professional's responsibility to become familiar with a great variety of teaching styles and select the appropriate design for each learning situation.

Multimedia Approach to Instruction. Modern technological advances coupled with a growing concern for differences in individual learning styles

Figure 12.2   Golf Contracts

The following are contracts that you may choose to complete to earn points in the golf unit. The maximum points possible for the contract are listed next to the contract number. The contracts that have an asterisk (*) next to them are required: everyone must complete them. The other contracts are optional. Check with your instructor for due dates.

Contract 1*: 10 points
Define the following terms and turn them in to the instructor in *neat* written (typed) form.

1. Address	5. Bunker	9. Green	13. Par
2. Pivot	6. Bogey	10. Tee	14. Loft of the clubs
3. Hazard	7. Double bogey	11. Hook	15. Stroke play
4. Fore	8. Birdie	12. Slice	16. Match play

Contract 2: 5 points
Watch a golf tournament either live or on television and answer the following questions:

1. Where did the tournament take place?
2. Identify the golf swings you saw used.
3. Identify the parts of the course you recognized.
4. What new terms did you hear and what do they mean?
5. Who were the competitors?
6. What type of competition was it (i.e., match play, stroke play)?

Turn the answers to the above questions and any other comments about the tournament in to your instructor in neat written form.

Contract 3*: 10 points
Take a written quiz covering the golf material taught in class and rules and etiquette of golf.

Contract 4: 10 points
Apply the basic skills and knowledge of golf you have learned by going to a golf course or a chip and putt course. Bring your score card, signed by the course manager, in to your instructor.

Contract 5: 5 points
Play miniature golf and turn in score card.

Contract 6: 5–10 points
Go to a driving range and hit a small or large bucket of balls. Turn in receipt to instructor.

have created a media explosion in education. The multimedia approach is an expansion of the traditional audiovisual method with which most instructors are familiar. The use of computers, videotapes, motion pictures, and other materials can enhance the physical education lesson.

Some of the teaching styles mentioned earlier in this chapter are adaptable to a systems approach to instruction in which students learn at stations supplied with learning materials, both commercial and teacher-generated. Being able to watch the correct technique performed over and over again on video tape, for example, is a tremendous aid to both the learner and observer, particularly in a peer-teaching situation.

Today's instructors of physical education should learn to produce their own slides or videotapes as a supplement to commercially made materials. Viewing your instruction lesson in a learning resource center reinforces the technique presented in class. These references should be just as available in the school library as any of the supplementary materials for English or other academic disciplines.

As professionals, we can look forward to expanding the use of the media approach to teach rules, strategies, and skill acquisition techniques.

The video camera provides excellent feedback for the prospective teacher.

Careers in Education

The potential career opportunities in education are exciting, and the friends and associations made are long-lasting. As a teacher or administrator in the school system, you can have a significant impact on instructional and program success. The job you accomplish as a professional physical educator can mold our youth into adults who will continue to live an active lifestyle leading toward many years of good health and emotional stability.

Physical Education Teacher

Teaching physical education in the public and private schools is a challenging career. Guiding youth in elementary, junior high, or senior high schools toward the achievement of motor skills, physical fitness, and the knowledge and understanding necessary to develop a healthy lifestyle is a critical phase of the education process.

Teachers of physical education have opportunities to work in large

Learning computer techniques enables the teacher to use the great variety of instructional and evaluation programs available.

or small, rural or metropolitan areas. You can choose the lifestyle you prefer if you are willing to move to any area in the United States.

The teaching profession offers a security that is more permanent than many other careers. The achievement of tenure, or permanent status, offered in most school districts, is usually obtained after 4 years of successful teaching service. Although salaries range from excellent to poor, as dictated by geographical area and population base, financial contracts are limited by established salary schedules in each district or state.

A definite advantage to a teaching career in the American school systems is that one has regular holiday and summer vacations. The 2 weeks at Christmas, 1 week at Easter, and 3-month summer vacation provide flexibility to pursue other life ventures not made possible in many careers. If you enjoy working with children and young adults, the teaching profession will be an excellent career path to pursue.

Teaching—A Stressful Occupation. The teaching professional has historically been regarded as a service profession. Those who entered it received intrinsic satisfaction as a result of their work with students. Monetary rewards were never as high as for other occupations, but teachers generally believed that they made major contributions to society and were respected for their effort.

Teaching remains a very rewarding profession but is suffering, as are other professions, from the effects of a rapidly changing society. Quality teachers dedicated to their careers have never been in greater demand. Nonetheless, there are some important facts that an undergraduate physical education major must address. These include the following:

- Why are so many teachers unhappy?
- Why are they leaving their careers, even when jobs are scarce and salaries fair?
- Why are younger teachers leaving within the first 5 years of teaching?
- Why are teachers' salary increases not keeping pace with those in other professions?

Teaching is not the same as it was 25 years ago. According to Truch (1980), alienation, isolation, a sense of powerlessness, and self-estrangement help create a climate of great dissatisfaction and frustration with modern-day teaching. Some leaders in education today are attempting to resolve these problems by recommending higher starting salaries, lower student-teacher ratios, and better overall working policies.

Those students pursuing a teaching career must understand that teacher stress has been increased by the changes in the human climate of our country. This stress contributes to a decline in teacher morale. Declining enrollments, decreased school budgets, role conflicts, time pressures, inadequate administrative support, lack of self-control among children, public pressure (often unrealistic and political in origin), and an attitude that education must be all things to all people have contributed to increasing teacher stress.

Federal, state, and local school board decisions often increase paperwork that teachers must do. Declining enrollments leading toward reduction-in-force policies have also been a major contributor to teacher stress by creating job uncertainty and restricting both teacher mobility and promotions.

Students. Single-parent families and families in which both parents work may add to the stress children experience today and reduce the amount of supervision children receive. Socioeconomic problems also contribute to the stress of students of all ages. Some results of these societal conditions are student apathy, alcoholism, drug abuse, sexual permissiveness, and violence among youngsters. Suicide among teenagers is a growing problem in the United States. Alcoholism, drug abuse, and unwanted pregnancy among school-age children are increasing and even occurring in the elementary grades. The verbal and physical abuse of teachers by students is also rising at an alarming rate.

Teacher burnout in the face of such problems is staggering. The need for teachers to self-renew is much deeper than what is provided by summer vacation. The problem is massive, the challenge is tremendous, but it can be conquered. You can make a difference. This material is presented not to discourage you from teaching but to enable you to understand the situation as it exists so you will not be disillusioned.

As a recent high school graduate, you have experienced some of the conditions that can remove the joy from teaching. Some of your classmates' values and behaviors were probably in conflict with the expectations of the school and the community. Perhaps at some time in your student career, your values and behaviors also conflicted with such expectations. Nonetheless, for the person who can cope with conflicting values, who understands students' needs, who can maintain the values of the school system, and who recognizes the need for well-founded instruction, teaching can be a rewarding career. A dedicated teacher can be a significant influence on students at all levels.

The Positive Side. According to the French philosopher, René Joubert, "To teach is to learn twice." Physical education is one aspect of education in which you can develop a closer relationship with students and serve as a positive role model. Physical education classes are microcosms of society on the playing field or in the gymnasium.

Social development can be encouraged as you design your class organizational systems. The opportunities for students to cooperate with one another, develop respect for individual differences, and experience the roles of leadership and fellowship are exciting. Throughout the school year, your classes can play a significant part in the growth and maturation of youngsters.

As they learn motor skills and achieve healthful physical fitness levels, students are improving their self-concept and developing behaviors that can help them cope with an increasingly complex world. Lifetime sport skills and knowledge of physical fitness benefits will contribute to the quality of healthful lifestyles throughout their lives.

Job Facts   Teacher

SALARY RANGE: $15,000–$60,000 (9-month assignment)
GEOGRAPHICAL AREA: nationwide
EDUCATIONAL REQUIREMENTS: bachelor's degree, teaching
    certification, master's degree preferred
FOR MORE INFORMATION: campus placement service, county and
    school district offices, American Alliance for Health, Physical
    Education, Recreation and Dance (AAHPERD)

Coaching

Coaching in the school setting provides one the opportunity to work with the physically gifted student. Performing in the coaching arena is an exciting career for those who thrive on publicity and have the intestinal fortitude to endure criticism. With the strong emphasis on winning, which is an important part of our American culture, comes all the stress associated with highly competitive programs.

For those who enjoy teaching the student athlete sophisticated styles of play, game strategies, and physical conditioning levels far above the normal requirements, the coaching profession is hard to beat. Coaches usually spend many extra hours preparing their teams for a contest, and demands for speaking engagements in the community are always forthcoming and time-consuming. Although sometimes overdone, in today's highly competitive programs this time commitment is necessary if success is to be achieved.

The coach also must serve as an administrator and supervisor of the total coaching staff. This instructional group must be molded into a well-tuned unit that can conduct practices, review strategies, and work together for the betterment of the total program.

It is important that coaches follow sound ethical practices if the athletic program is to have credibility as an educationally based program. Honesty, integrity, and loyalty are critical ingredients to the coaching personality.

The coaching career provides mobility in junior high school, high school, and college. Although opportunities at each level become increasingly more limited, many coaches have achieved high salaries commensurate with their positions. Coaching assignments seldom carry adequate pay for the time spent. However, many districts that provide extra pay for coaching have increased their stipend in recent years.

The coach never knows at what point one's influence on a young life ceases. The rapport developed between a coach and the team and between teammates is an experience that cannot be duplicated in any other educational setting. The potential for molding young people into tomorrow's respected citizens through the team experience will continue to be a vital part of education's positive side.

If you approach the teaching and coaching professions realistically and are committed to young people, the possibilities are limitless. If you choose an alternate career, there are also untold opportunities for creative change and success.

Job Facts   Coach

SALARY RANGE: $15,000–$100,000
GEOGRAPHICAL AREA: nationwide
EDUCATIONAL REQUIREMENTS: bachelor's degree, teaching
     certification
FOR MORE INFORMATION: department bulletin boards, county and
     school district placement offices, AAHPERD publications

Adapted Physical Education Teacher

Working with boys and girls who have physical or mental limitations requires a patience beyond normal limits. However, the rewards gained through patiently guiding individuals to achieve at their highest potential are often much more far-reaching than those achieved in regular classes. The satisfaction in seeing the slightest improvement in motor accomplishment in a handicapped individual is difficult to surpass.

To be suited as an adapted physical educator, one must have a very positive outlook, enjoy the patient and persistent approach to learning, and be a strong motivator to enhance student development. Opportunities for positions in this field have risen in recent years, though many such positions are limited to special schools.

Job Facts   Adapted Physical Education Teacher

SALARY RANGE: $15,000–$60,000
GEOGRAPHICAL AREA: metropolitan areas
EDUCATIONAL REQUIREMENTS: bachelor's degree, special credential
FOR MORE INFORMATION: state, county, or regional district placement
    offices, college placement service

Physical Education Administrator

A career as an administrator of physical education—as a physical education supervisor, director, or site principal—usually requires preliminary experience as a physical education teacher as well as graduate course work leading to certification. Individuals pursuing this career must enjoy administrative duties and responsibilities. In addition to being responsible for curriculum development, most positions also require the administrator to administer staff development programs involving in-service sessions for the instructional staff. For those who enjoy working toward the improvement of physical education programs at all levels, administrative positions at the local, district, county or state levels provide an opportunity for creative leadership.

The duties and responsibilities of a physical education administrator closely parallel the responsibilities of a site principal. To enjoy this type of position, one must like to solve problems, be public relations–oriented, enjoy detail work, and work well with people. Every level of administration has different job requirements, but all are challenging and exciting experiences. Considering this career would influence your graduate course selection.

Job Facts   Administrator

SALARY RANGE: $40,000–$80,000
GEOGRAPHICAL AREA: nationwide
EDUCATIONAL REQUIREMENTS: bachelor's, master's, or doctorate
    degree, administrative credential
FOR MORE INFORMATION: American Association of School
    Administrators, local district personnel office, college
    placement service

Athletic Director

The athletic director in the educational setting has usually arrived by way of the coaching route. It is imperative to understand the responsibilities of the coach if one is to administer the competitive program.

Organizing the competitive program by developing sound policies is a major function of the athletic director. Confirming schedules, securing officials, arranging for team transportation, solving facility-use problems, fund raising, and representing the school at meetings are all facets of the athletic director's job.

Having general administrative ability is critical to success in this position. Maintaining productive human relations, handling detailed paperwork, and supervising the coaches and the program are all part of the job. After experiencing a coaching career, some may wish to pursue this new role with a desire to help build or maintain a total competitive program in contrast to developing a single sport.

The job is an active one that requires many hours of extra time, although extra pay often accompanies the position. If you enjoy competitive sports and like administration, you may wish to consider this option for a future career challenge.

Job Facts   Athletic Director

SALARY RANGE: $40,000–$80,000
GEOGRAPHICAL AREA: nationwide
EDUCATIONAL REQUIREMENTS: bachelor's degree, teaching credential, master's degree in administration or sport management
FOR MORE INFORMATION: *Chronical of Higher Education,* AAHPERD publications, local district personnel offices, college placement service

Student Activities

1. Visit a school and interview someone who is in one of the career positions described in this chapter. Ask about duties and responsibilities.
2. Visit an elementary, junior high, or senior high school and determine the characteristics of typical students at the level you may want to teach. Determine your preference.
3. Investigate in detail one of the teaching styles described in this chapter.

4. Review your professional preparation plan and look for options to expand your job marketability.
5. Compare teaching salaries in your area with those in other parts of the United States.

Suggested Readings

American Alliance for Health, Physical Education, Recreation and Dance. 1987. *Basic Stuff Series*. Reston, VA: American Alliance for Health, Physical Education, Recreation and Dance.

Annarino, A. A., C. C. Cowell, and H. W. Hazelton. 1980. *Curriculum theory and design in physical education*. St. Louis: Mosby.

Bain, L. L., and J. C. Wendt. 1983. *Transition to teaching: a guide for the beginning teacher*. Reston, VA: American Alliance for Health, Physical Education, Recreation and Dance.

Bucher, C., and N. A. Thaxton. 1981. *Physical education and sport: change and challenge*. St. Louis: Mosby.

Melograno, V. 1985. *Designing the physical education curriculum*, 2nd ed. Dubuque, IA: Kendall/Hunt.

Mosston, M., and S. Ashworth. 1986. *Teaching physical education*, 3rd ed. Columbus, OH: Merrill.

Pangrazi, R. P., and P. W. Darst. 1985. *Dynamic physical education curriculum and instruction for secondary school students*. Minneapolis: Burgess Publishing.

Siedentop, D., C. Mand, and A. Taggart. 1986. *Physical education teaching and curriculum strategies for grades 5–12*. Palo Alto, CA: Mayfield.

Singer, R. N., and W. Dick. 1980. *Teaching physical education*. Boston: Houghton Mifflin.

Wolery, M., D. B. Bailey, Jr., and G. M. Sugai. 1988. *Effective teaching: principles and procedures of applied behavior analysis with exceptional students*. Boston: Allyn and Bacon.

References

Annarino, A. A., C. C. Cowell, and H. W. Hazelton. 1980. *Curriculum theory and design in physical education*. St. Louis: Mosby.

Bucher, C., and N. A. Thaxton. 1981. *Physical education and sport: change and challenge*. St. Louis: Mosby.

13. Career Options in Sport and Human Movement

Objectives

Chapter 13 is designed to enable you to:

- Become acquainted with a variety of alternative career paths for the physical education major.
- Understand the need for specialized course work and job training for specific career options.
- Understand the nature of alternative career responsibilities.

S I N C E contemporary society is in a state of constant change, knowing about career mobility and career alternatives is vital to your survival as an employed professional. Those interested in the field of physical education and sports need to be aware of the social and economic forces that shape a sports and health career. Some physical education careers may soon be obsolete, the job descriptions for others may be changing, and many job opportunities are still being created. We have identified more than 100 careers that relate to the course work available in institutions of higher learning offering a physical education major.

It is our intent in this chapter to provide information on alternative career options available to professionals in physical education and sport. Too many students limit their thinking to job placement in one of the traditional teaching or coaching positions. Today, one must be aware of the many job opportunities available in and outside the school setting in order to make an informed choice regarding a professional career.

To make the study of alternative career options meaningful, you should relate each career discussed to your own personality. You should assess personal values, interests, talents, and abilities in order to obtain a clearer understanding and appreciation of the career options presented. The alternative career opportunities presented in Figure 13.1 have been grouped into a circle of spheres based on common elements of professional preparation and the employment environment. Information in the text for each career option in terms of professional preparation, employment opportunities, personal competencies, salary range, and geographical locations provides the reader with a basic description of a variety of job alternatives. Direct feedback about job satisfaction and personal descriptions can be found in the career profiles described in Chapter 14.

We believe that this material will help you develop several workable alternatives within your own areas of interest and expertise. Participation in a wide variety of learning experiences will make the human movement professional much more marketable. To know and understand a variety of alternative career options leads toward a lifetime of interesting employment opportunities and job satisfaction. Accepting this concept of expanded professional careers is the first step toward designing your personal alternative career program.

Designing the Alternative Career Program

You can choose to prepare for more than 100 careers related to the physical education course work that is available in the majority of colleges

Figure 13.1 Career Alternatives Grouped by Common Elements

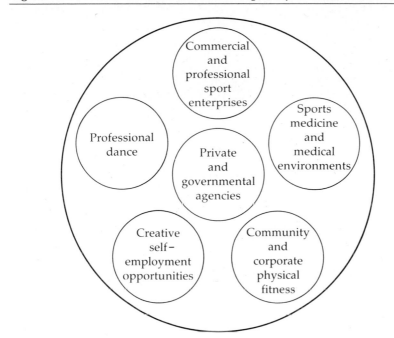

and universities. Most of the classes are offered in physical education departments, though many others are found in various disciplines in the university. Course work for many career options is a blend of interdisciplinary classes in other academic departments leading toward a program designed for a specific career path.

The fact that there is such a variety of jobs available in the field of sport, fitness, and athletics enables one to pursue the physical education major without fear of limited employment. Planning a personal professional preparation program designed to meet your individual needs and interests can be an exciting and challenging experience.

Career Options in Physical Education

More and more universities and colleges throughout the United States are developing alternative career options for the physical education major. This program option is designed to meet the needs of business and industry, public, private, and commercial health and fitness establishments, and entrepreneurial ventures.

These alternatives provide professional leadership personnel for Young Men's and Young Women's Christian Associations (YMCAs and

A knowledge of arts and crafts enhances job placement in recreational settings.

YWCAs), boys' and girls' clubs, health spas, specialized sport facilities, cardiac rehabilitation centers, and fitness programs for company employees in a host of settings. Job placement for fitness directors alone is increasing at a rapid pace because the demand for a healthy lifestyle of regular exercise is not only in vogue but has proved to be beneficial to the general wellness of the individual. The program for fitness directors is a viable option for many students who prefer to be employed in the private sector of the sports world or who desire to go into business for themselves.

The foundation for an alternative career path is basic to the program of study for physical education majors in general. One still needs to possess a strong scientific background and awareness of skills in order to understand and appreciate the difficulty and grace of a performance and the value of an activity, regardless of the setting. This approach to professional preparation is sound, as one cannot truly capture the art of movement or understand physical fitness without an adequate knowledge of the body and its motion. For example, whether one's goal is to be a fitness director or a sports photographer, the biological, psychological, sociological, and physiological concepts related to human movement should be required study in the undergraduate curriculum. From this base, one can then establish a selected program focused on a specific career.

The Double Major

Many universities provide opportunities for students to pursue a double major while working toward their bachelor's degree. This approach to professional preparation enables the student to have an in-depth understanding of the physical education profession along with another selected academic area. Some of the majors that lend themselves to this dual approach to undergraduate education are journalism, art, communications, outdoor studies, health, nutrition, special education, business management, recreation, biology, and physiology.

For those students who have selected an alternative career in the physical education and sport field, the double major provides for extended course work resulting in expanded knowledge in a second area of interest. A possible disadvantage of the double major is that it may limit opportunities for the undergraduate to enroll in elective courses outside the two major fields of study. However, the double major should at least be considered by students who have specific careers in mind and who desire a more thorough knowledge of a related field and job requirements.

The Academic Minor

Pursuing an academic minor bears some similarities to undertaking the double major. The difference is that fewer courses are required, which enables the student to choose additional electives, providing for expanded course work in a greater variety of areas. Most minors require approximately 24 semester units, in contrast to a second major, which is often twice this requirement, or approximately 36 to 48 semester units.

Obtaining a minor in a selected area of study provides the student with a second alternative for job placement. Although limited in depth in contrast to the double major, students with a minor enjoy the opportunities for elective courses that often expand their potential career options to three or four areas. If you pursue job placement in education, another academic or alternative minor field of study will greatly enhance your opportunities for employment by providing a secondary teaching area. Most of the disciplines that lend themselves to a double major approach to undergraduate study may also be pursued as a minor that is designed to enhance personal strengths and abilities in a particular area of study.

Use of Electives

The astute physical education major who pursues course work with an open mind will take advantage of the elective units available in most degree programs to prepare for a variety of alternative careers (Table 13.1). For example, a physical education major could learn more about art, photography, or business.

Table 13.1 Alternative Career Options: Sample Course Work

COURSE TITLES	UNITS

Lower Division

Prerequisites to upper-division standing in this major are the following courses which may, where allowed, also be used to meet general education requirements:

BIO	Human Anatomy and Physiology	4
BIO	Human Anatomy and Physiology Laboratory	2
PE	First Aid and Cardiopulmonary Resuscitation	4
PE	The Physical Education Profession	2
PE	Sports in American Life	2

Select four additional courses (8 units) from the following:

PE	Fundamentals of Golf and Tennis	2
PE	Fundamentals of Badminton and Volleyball	2
PE	Fundamentals of Basketball and Softball	2
PE	Fundamentals of Swimming and Track	2
PE	Fundamentals of Soccer and Football I	2
PE	Fundamentals of Soccer and Football II	2
PE	Fundamentals of Dance	2
PE	Fundamentals of Conditioning	2

Select two additional courses (or other comparative courses with consent of adviser) from the following:

BUS	Small-Business Management I	4
BUS	Essentials of Accounting I	4
BUS	Introduction to Computers and Data Processing	4
ART	Graphics Media	4
ART	Art Structure I	4
COM	Introduction to Newswriting and Reporting	4
COM	Introduction to Communications	4
	Any course selected in line with career	4

Table 13.1 (continued)

COURSE TITLES	UNITS
Upper division	
Required courses:	
PE Kinesiology	4
PE Physiology of Exercise	4
PE History and Philosophy of Physical Education	4
PE Administration of Physical Education	4
PE Prevention and Treatment of Athletic Injuries	4
Select three additional courses from the following list:	
PE Advanced Techniques of Coaching	2
PE Advanced Techniques of Fitness Evaluation	2
PE Designing Fitness and Sport Programs for Business and Industry	2
PE Promoting Fitness Programs in the Private and Commercial Sectors	2
PE Special Topics	2
Quarter units	56

Another important elective is foreign language. Bilingual persons are in great demand, and knowing a second language often opens doors to job opportunities in specialized national and international programs, which are expanding at the present time. Even within the United States, there are many regions wherein there is a great need for the bilingual professional to teach and coach school-age children or to work in a business setting.

Although one may be primarily interested in teaching and coaching in a school system, by selecting courses in small-business management, merchandise displays, foreign languages, or countless other areas, a student can prepare for a career in the commercial or private sector as well. Without additional background, students may find themselves limited in employment opportunities. The wise selection of elective courses, although admittedly less significant than pursuing a minor field of study, greatly enhances opportunities for alternative careers.

Certificate Programs

Many institutions have added special certificate programs as an adjunct to the regular physical education major. Certificate programs usually require expanded course work and can be designed in the areas of community physical fitness, athletic training, adapted or therapeutic physical education, sensorimotor activities, outdoor studies, marine or aquatic safety, supervision, and sport management, to name a few (Tables 13.2, 13.3).

Many of these programs prepare students to take examinations for national certification in fields for which an organized body exists to establish standards. Other programs are less stringent and provide the student with an institutional certificate indicating a specialization in a selected area of study. The latter approach usually requires a minimum of three additional courses in a special concentration plus a fieldwork assignment.

Special certificates provide added strength to the physical education professional's marketability. For the student who completes the required course work, opportunities for job placement are greatly increased.

Alternative Careers

In this section, we describe sample alternative careers for the student enrolled as a physical education major or in a national certificate program or a university special emphasis certificate program. These career opportunities are presented to acquaint you with some of the many job options available to you. There are few professions in which there is as much variety as in the area of human movement studies. There are numerous job opportunities for the open-minded, creative, physical education professional. A number of examples of human movement careers are also listed in Table 13.4.

Professional Athletics

Professional athletics provides tremendous opportunities for individuals from all walks of life to pursue high salaries in today's sports world. Earnings in sports for both men and women are some of the highest in our society. It is not uncommon to have a few select individuals sign multimillion-dollar contracts without ever having played a professional game. Annual salaries of a million dollars or more are frequently mentioned in the daily newspaper. However, it must be remembered that few athletes reach this level of success.

Although salaries are high, opportunities are limited to those who make it to the top-level professional teams and stay there. Since careers can be rather short, the collegiate player should always work toward

Table 13.2 Athletic Training Certificate Program Sample

The program is designed to provide the student with specialized knowledge and skill necessary to prevent and care for athletic injuries in public and private schools as well as colleges, universities, and professional athletic teams. Students may qualify under Section I of the National Athletic Trainer's Association (NATA) Procedures for Certification as follows:

1. Completed the NATA-approved athletic training curriculum requirements and have proof of a bachelor's degree from an accredited college or university.
2. Have spent a minimum of two(2) years under the direct supervision of a NATA-approved supervisor.
3. Passed an examination that includes basic principles of athletic training.
4. Have proof of one (1) year of continuous associate or student membership in NATA immediately prior to application for certification.

Athletic Training Curricular Requirements

COURSE TITLES		UNITS
Lower division		
BIO	Human Anatomy	3
BIO	Human Physiology	4
PE	First Aid (or current Red Cross card)	2
HSCI	Health Science	3
PSY	Psychology	3
Upper division		
PE	Kinesiology	3
PE	Physiology of Exercise	3
PE	Adapted Physical Education	2
PE	Prevention and Care of Athletic Injuries	2
PE	Independent Study (Advanced Techniques in Athletic Training)	3
PE	Fieldwork in Athletic Training	3
HEC	Nutrition	3
PE	Behavioral Problems in Physical Education and Athletics	3
PE	Seminar in Management Theory of Athletic Injuries or Special Studies	3
PE	Techniques of Conditioning for Sport Participation A minimum of 600 supervised clinical hours under an approved certified athletic trainer	3
CPR	(Cardiopulmonary Resuscitation) Certification	—
	Semester Units	43

Table 13.3 Certificate in Sensorimotor Therapy

The certificate in sensorimotor therapy is offered by the Physical Education Department for students who are majoring in physical education, recreation, communicative disorders, and educational psychology, or who have an emphasis in special education. It is designed to provide participants an opportunity to receive specialized training in sensorimotor activities. Receipt of this certificate indicates a proficiency in the organization and conduct of programs designed to assist children having special movement problems.

In addition to the following required courses, each student must have (1) verification that the student has specialized in physical education, recreation, communicative disorders, educational psychology, or special education, and (2) approval to take the certificate program by the Physical Education Department.

REQUIRED COURSES	UNITS
PE *Basic Movement Education* Analysis of the components of movement with application to body management, games, gymnastics, dance, rhythmic activities, and developmental skills commonly taught in the elementary school physical education program.	3
PE *Adapted Physical Education* Prerequisite: *Kinesiology* or equivalent. Organization, administration, and techniques utilized in the conduct of adapted physical education classes.	2
PE *Developmental Physical Education for Children* Analysis and participation in physical movement experiences with special emphasis placed on the study of optimum physical development of children.	3
PE *Motor Dysfunction and Remedial Physical Education* Prerequisites: *Adaptive Physical Education* or *Educational Psychology* or their equivalents. Recognition, analysis, assessment, and remediation of movement problems of the exceptional child.	3
PE *Fieldwork in Adapted Physical Education* Prerequisite: *Adapted Physical Education.* Supervised clinical experience in adapted physical education. Field training must be taken in the Institute for Sensorimotor development or approved special schools.	3
Semester units	14

Table 13.4 Human Movement Careers

Community Fitness
Fitness Consulting
Health Clubs/Spas
Weight Control Spas
Athletic Clubs
Tension Control
Human Form Engineering
Infant Development
Retirement Centers (Deterioration
    Delay)
Physical Education Extension Agents
Living Skills Analysis
Emergency Service Personnel

Public and Private Recreation
Sports Leadership
Private Clubs
Agencies, YMCAs/YWCAs,
    Boys'/Girls' Clubs
Urban Community Recreation
    (inner city)
Churches
Penitentiaries
Veterans Hospitals
Camps
Commercial Recreation
Child-Care Centers

Military Environments
Fitness Training
Sports Leadership
Coaching
Movement Efficiency

Professional Sports
Player
Facilities Manager
Sports Journalism
Athletic Training
Sports Broadcasting
Sports Photography
Sports Art

Public and Private Education
Public Schools
    Teaching Physical Education
    Perceptual-Motor Instructor

Adapted Physical Education
Mentally/Physically Handicapped
Coaching
Athletic Training
Administration
Colleges and Universities
    Kinesiology
    Exercise Physiology
    Sports History
    Sports Sociology
    Sports Literature
    Coaching Sports
    Athletic Administration
    Athletic Nutrition
    Intramural Director
    Child Development
    Motor Learning
    Motor Development

Business and Industry
Commercial Teaching: tennis, golf,
    swimming, etc.
Sports Camps: above plus team sports
Sports Design: equipment facilities,
    toys
Sports Safety Consultant: equip-
    ment, surfaces, protective
    devices (invent, test, research)
Sporting Goods/Clothing Sales
Protective Services: physical train-
    ing for police, firefighters
Industrial Recreation
Work Skills Analysis
Injury Prevention
Dance Studies

Medical Environments
Physical Therapy
Occupational Therapy
Corrective Therapy
Recreational Therapy
Play Therapy
Movement Therapy
Coordination Therapy
Emergency Medical Technician
Prosthesis Testing (work, play, living)

Table 13.4 (continued)

Rehabilitation Equipment and Design	**Professional Dance and Theater**
Movement Rehabilitation	Dancing
Movement Adaptation	Dance Production
Antigravity Movement Therapy	Body Coaching (stage movement)
Handicapped Career Education Agent	Teaching
Developmental Physical Education	Photography/Art
Visual-Motor Training	
Emergency or Disaster Specialist	**Future Environments**
Preventive Medicine	Fitness in Space
Sports Medicine Assistant	Play in Space
Rehabilitative Therapy Assistant	Movement Efficiency in Space
Handicapped Aide	Underwater Efficiency
Cardiovascular Technician	Underwater Play
Cardiovascular Rehabilitation Technician	
Electromyograph Technician	

---

a college degree as a backup for a secondary career. For the high-level performer who is dedicated to hard work and who has the desire to pursue a professional athletic career, the colleges and universities provide a showcase where professional scouts often seek talent. If you have a high level of athletic talent, you may want to consider professional sports as a viable career.

Job Facts   Professional Athlete

SALARY RANGE: $20,000–$1,000,000+ (may need a financial sponsor to begin one's career in such sports as golf or tennis)
GEOGRAPHICAL AREA: metropolitan areas
EDUCATIONAL REQUIREMENTS: bachelor's degree
FOR MORE INFORMATION: contact university or college coach, major league farm teams, AAU club sports
Professional organizations:

*American Waterskiing
    Association*
P.O. Box 191
Winter Haven, FL   33880
(813) 324-4341

Women's Jockey Association
6075 Franklin Avenue
Suite 070
Hollywood, CA   90028
(213) 705-0344

Job Facts *(continued)*

Holiday on Ice
3201 New Mexico Avenue
N.W.
Washington, DC   20016
(202) 364-5000

United States Professional
Tennis Association
Colony Beach and
Tennis Resort
1620 Gulf of Mexico Drive
Longboat Key
Sarasota, FL   33548
(813) 383-6464

International Federation of
Bodybuilders, Women's
Committee
P.O. Box 937
Riverview, FL   33569
(813) 677-5761

National Bowling Council
1919 Pennsylvania Avenue,
N.W., Suite 504
Washington, DC   20006
(202) 659-9070

Ladies Professional Golf
Association Tour
Division
1250 Shoreline Drive
Suite 200
Sugarland, TX   77478
(713) 980-5742

United States Trotting
Association
750 Michigan Avenue
Columbus, OH   43215
(614) 224-2291

Women's Professional Golf
Tour
1137 San Antonio Road
Suite E
Palo Alto, CA   94303
(415) 967-1305

Women's Professional
Racquetball Association
1 Erieview Plaza
Cleveland, OH   44114
(216) 522-1200

Women's Professional Rodeo
Association
8909 N.E. 25th Street
Spencer, OK   73084
(405) 769-5322

Women's Professional Ski
Racing, Inc.
115 East 89th Street, 1C
New York, NY   10028
(212) 427-0662

Women's Professional Surfing
International
5545 Taft Avenue
La Jolla, CA   92037
(619) 459-6294

Women's Tennis Association
1604 Union Street
San Francisco, CA   94123
(415) 673-2018

Facility Management

There are numerous types of facilities throughout the country today that provide places to compete in a variety of sports. Managing tennis clubs, racquetball clubs, and fitness and health spas has expanded the facility management business, which once was limited to opportunities only in large stadiums or sports arenas. By undertaking the study of physical education, one learns about the needs of all the teams participating and the athletes involved in a sport, while also developing a keen awareness of crowd accommodations. Added to this knowledge must be a good business sense to seek contracts for competition or events that will generate income and help make the facility financially sound. The astute facility manager can have considerable influence on sports in general by coordinating athletic contests that encourage spectator enjoyment as well as meet the needs of the competing teams or performers.

Positions of facility management are also found in large school districts or universities. Knowledge of master scheduling, concession management, and crowd control, as well as excellent organizational skills are essential.

Job Facts   Facility Manager

SALARY RANGE: $20,000–$50,000
GEOGRAPHICAL AREA: metropolitan areas
EDUCATIONAL REQUIREMENTS: bachelor's degree
FOR MORE INFORMATION: contact facilities manager in major sport complexes
Professional organizations:

Sports Management Art and Science Society
P.O. Box 8069
Boston, MA   02214
(413) 545-0621

Club Managers Association of America
7615 Winterberry Place
Bethesda, MD   20817
(301) 229-3600

World Leisure and Recreation Society
345 East 46th Street
Room 717
New York, NY   10017
(212) 697-8783

College Athletic Business Managers Association
Holy Cross College
College Street
Worcester, MA   01610
(617) 793-2571

Private sport facilities expand management opportunities.

Sports Journalism

A career in sports journalism has expanded from the traditional sport information director to include sport promotion and public relations positions that will continue to be necessary. For the physical education major who enjoys writing, opportunities in sports journalism are provided through the local newspapers and in numerous sport magazines that appear on newsstands across the United States. A writer may publish sport skill series, children's literature on sports, articles about athletic events, or fictional sport stories. The journalist with a background in sports has a broader understanding and appreciation of the degree of difficulty and level of achievement in athletic events than the person not schooled in physical education.

Job Facts   Sports Journalist

SALARY RANGE: $10,000–$75,000
GEOGRAPHICAL AREA: worldwide
EDUCATIONAL REQUIREMENTS: bachelor's degree with journalism
    courses

Job Facts *(continued)*

FOR MORE INFORMATION: consult local newspaper sportswriter, local sports announcer (television and radio), cable television, college sports information director, editors of national sports magazines

Professional organizations:

American Council on Education for Journalism
563 Essex Court
Deerfield, IL 60015
(312) 948-5840

Associated Press Sports Editors Association
St. Petersburg Times
St. Petersburg, FL 33731
(813) 893-8111

College Sports Information Directors of America
Texas A&I University
Kingsville, TX 78363
(512) 592-0389

National Federation of Press Women
1006 Main Street
P.O. Box 99
Blue Springs, MO 64015
(816) 229-1666

Photographic Society of America
P.O. Box 1266
Reseda, CA 91335

Sports Broadcasting

Today, one discovers by watching television that many sports broadcasters are coming from the professional playing ranks. For an athlete who enjoys the communications field, has a pleasant voice, and knows how to relay sports information to the listening or viewing public, sports broadcasting can be an exciting, well-paying career.

Although it is not necessary to have a physical education or athletic background to pursue this type of job, having such a background does provide greater insight into communicating the details of sports competition to the public, which an individual who has not participated in competitive sports will lack.

Job Facts *Sports Broadcaster*

SALARY RANGE: $20,000–$100,000+
GEOGRAPHICAL AREA: nationwide
EDUCATIONAL REQUIREMENTS: bachelor's degree

Job Facts *(continued)*

FOR MORE INFORMATION: consult local radio or television stations, cable television, local campus sports information director
Professional organizations:

*National Association of
    Broadcasters*
1771 N Street N.W.
Washington, DC   20036
(202) 293-3500

*National Sportscasters and
    Sportswriters Association*
P.O. Drawer 559
Salisburg, NC   28144
(704) 633-4275

Professional Coaching

Most opportunities for coaching assignments are still within the educational system. However, for those who want to work with athletes with a high level of ability and proved success, highly paid coaching opportunities are available at the professional level. Generally, the coaches who achieve this type of position began their careers with athletic assignments as high school and college coaches. The usual progression is from assistant coaching to a head coaching position, and finally, if the career is successful, one may be sought after in the professional ranks. Many have made personal contacts with head professional coaches and individuals in a sport franchise.

In pursuing a professional coaching career, the individual must be highly motivated and understand that the job is contingent on winning a very high percentage of games played and coaching a style of play that will attract paying customers. With the high salary and exceptional fringe benefit package comes increased pressure and stress coupled with a lack of job security. The time demands for successful coaching at the professional level often limit a traditional family life.

A professional coaching career is exciting, mobile and uncertain. However, successful performance brings many personal and financial rewards. If you have the personality and drive to be successful at this level, you should set goals and maintain a personal lifestyle that will prepare you to participate in this multimillion-dollar dimension of sports.

Job Facts   Professional Coach

SALARY RANGE: $40,000–$500,000 +
GEOGRAPHICAL AREA: metropolitan areas
EDUCATIONAL REQUIREMENTS: bachelor's degree

Job Facts (continued)

FOR MORE INFORMATION: contact university coach, major league
farm teams, AAU club sports
Professional organizations:

Professional Ski Instructors of   *United States Professional*
    America   *Tennis Association*
3333 Iris   Colony Beach and Tennis
Boulder, CO   80301   Resort
(303) 447-0842   1620 Gulf of Mexico Drive
                                Longboat Key
                                Sarasota, FL   33548
                                (813) 383-6464

Sports Photography

Career opportunities in sport photography are diversified. By taking a
close look at the local newsstand, you can find a tremendous variety
of sport publications. There are also opportunities to work with daily
newspapers that need photographers to cover activities for the sports
page.

Why is this a natural career alternative for the basic physical education major? By understanding the difficulty of performance, the skill
and movement required, the stress of high-level competition, or the
unique performance of the young child, the person schooled in physical education can better capture great moments in sport through
photography.

Promotion and public relations for all sport programs are necessary
to inform the public. If a picture is worth a thousand words, then sports
photography can tell much about the sport world. Students interested
in this career option may work for a sport publication or as a free-lance
photographer.

Job Facts   *Sports Photographer*

SALARY RANGE: $20,000–$75,000
GEOGRAPHICAL AREA: nationwide
EDUCATIONAL REQUIREMENTS: bachelor's degree
FOR MORE INFORMATION: contact campus newspaper, local high
school, sport magazines, local photography store; visit
photography exhibits in galleries
Professional organization:

Job Facts   (continued)

> *Photographic Society of*
> *America*
> P.O. Box 1266
> Reseda, CA   91335

Sports Art

The student with a double major in physical education and art may have the opportunity to develop a career in sports art. The demand for sports art appears to be increasing and few people understand proper movement or can capture this motion in an artistically pleasing way. Sports artists are sought after by the multitude of sport publications on our newsstands today. Sports art may also lead to a career in fashion, facility, or equipment design or design for advertising and sport promotion. Although career opportunities are more limited in this than in other areas of sport and human movement, outstanding artists may find their sculpture, paintings, and other artistic renderings in high demand.

Job Facts   Sports Artist

SALARY RANGE: $10,000–$100,000 +
GEOGRAPHICAL AREA: unlimited
EDUCATIONAL REQUIREMENTS: bachelor's degree
FOR MORE INFORMATION: contact art museums, sport publications,
    local art departments
    Professional organization:
    National Association for
        Sport and Physical
        Education
    1900 Association Drive
    Reston, VA   22091

Athletic Training

Athletic trainers have always been necessary for those in professional sports. Today, there is a growing demand for athletic trainers in educational systems as well as in amateur and professional sport. This career is open to both men and women, as athletic training rooms are no longer limited to male athletes.

Every professional sports team and every major university that conducts an athletic program employs a minimum of one athletic trainer and often has four or five on the staff. Although opportunities are still limited and many are part-time, at the secondary school level there are indications that within the next few years school systems may be required to have an athletic trainer in each institution that fields athletic teams. This much-needed service will greatly benefit the student athletes participating at the secondary school level as well as expand job opportunities for those pursuing this career.

With the emphasis on safety in sports, the athletic trainer often is responsible for supervising conditioning programs as well as determining preventive and rehabilitative activities for athletes. A major responsibility of the trainer involves taping and preparing the athlete for game competition.

The athletic trainer's lifestyle is one of flexible hours, often requiring extensive travel during the playing season. Nonetheless, the field of athletic training can be exciting for those who enjoy being with athletes and who have a sincere desire to keep athletes in the best possible condition in order to compete at their highest potential.

One can become certified by the National Athletic Trainer's Association (NATA) either by pursuing an approved program or by working under a certified athletic trainer on an internship basis for the required number of hours.

Job Facts   Athletic Trainer

SALARY RANGE: $18,000–$40,000

GEOGRAPHICAL AREA: nationwide schools and colleges, metropolitan areas (for professional sports)

EDUCATIONAL REQUIREMENTS: bachelor's degree with NATA certification

FOR MORE INFORMATION: contact NATA, local school personnel, professional teams

Professional organizations:

American Academy of Podiatric Sports Medicine
P.O. Box 31331
San Francisco, CA   94131
(415) 826-3200

American Athletic Trainer's Association and Certification Board
638 West Duarte Road
Arcadia, CA   91006
(213) 445-1978

American Physical Therapy Association
1156 15th Street N.W.
Washington, DC   20005
(202) 466-2070

National Athletic Health Association
575 East Hardy Street
Inglewood, CA   90301
(213) 674-1600

Job Facts *(continued)*

American College of Sports
   Medicine
1440 Monroe Street
Madison, WI   53706
(608) 262-3632

National Athletic Trainer's
   Association
P.O. Drawer 1865
Greenville, NC   27834
(919) 752-1725

American Medical
   Association
535 North Dearborn Street
Chicago, IL   60620
(312) 751-6529

National Therapeutic
   Recreation Society
1601 North Kent Street
Arlington, VA 22209
(703) 525-0606

American Orthopedic Society
   for Sports Medicine
70 West Hubbard Street
Chicago, IL   60610
(312) 644-2623

Strength and Conditioning Coaching

College and professional teams are now employing strength and conditioning coaches to supplement their coaching staffs. Strength development and cardiorespiratory endurance has gone far beyond the average coach's expertise. To become a specialist in this area, one must be well schooled in the sciences and be knowledgeable about a great variety of training programs. Selecting the best possible approach to team fitness or working individually with a sport-specific program is challenging and contributes greatly to successful athletic performances. Responsibilities usually include supervision of the strength training and conditioning facilities, in addition to program development. Some assignments may be on a part-time or consultant basis.

Job Facts   Strength and Conditioning Coach

SALARY RANGE: $15,000–$45,000
GEOGRAPHICAL AREA: nationwide
EDUCATIONAL REQUIREMENTS: bachelor's degree in Exercise Science
   and Biomechanics
FOR MORE INFORMATION: contact athletic department or professional
   team in your area

Professional Dancing

From a foundation in rhythmic activities in the physical education major course work, many individuals may wish to pursue additional development in the school of fine arts to achieve a major or minor in dance. For those not interested in teaching dance as their main occupation, there are many opportunities for both men and women to pursue a professional career with a dance company, in the theater, and in other entertainment arenas.

Because stage shows and dance concerts often run for only short periods, many professionals also seek opportunities in resort areas where shows are developed for audiences on a regular basis. These shows are often elaborately produced and run longer. If one is fortunate enough to secure a position in this type of show, then a dancer may stay in one place for an extended period. Others may find that considerable travel is involved as they seek to audition and obtain a job in a dance troupe.

Because many dancers audition for only a few available positions, talent and incessant determination are an essential combination in the aspiring dancer. Those who prefer to live in one location of the country often seek opportunities for teaching dance at the university and secondary school level and in private studios on a part-time basis. Professional dance can be an attractive career for those who have high-level talent and enjoy creative movement activities.

Job Facts Professional Dancer

SALARY RANGE: $15,000–$100,000+
GEOGRAPHICAL AREA: metropolitan areas
EDUCATIONAL REQUIREMENTS: bachelor's degree
FOR MORE INFORMATION: contact National Dance Association
    Professional organization:
    National Dance Association
    1900 Association Drive
    Reston, VA 22091

Sports Officiating

Sports officiating at the high school or university level is usually designed as a part-time job for individuals who have an interest in dedicating themselves to learning the rules and mechanics of sound officiating. For those who are seeking full-time employment in this area, the professional game does offer opportunities in selected sports. Professional basketball and baseball teams, for example, employ full-time officials for the length of their sports season. In contrast, professional football teams rely on part-time individuals, often from a great variety of careers, to serve as weekend officials.

The salaries for sports officiating are improving each year, and whether for the part-time or regular full-time official, opportunities for this job are great. The person interested in officiating must enjoy traveling, as he or she will have to be away from home base for extended periods.

If you are considering this career, then you should know it is never too early to gain experience and prove yourself an astute, intelligent, conscientious official at each competitive level assigned. Conference commissioners employ individuals to seek new officiating talent, and many such scouts are in attendance at the next lower level of competition to observe and make recommendations for higher-level officiating assignments. However, it is important that you take the initiative and contact college commissioners after a minimum of 5 years of high school varsity experience.

Job Facts   Sports Official

SALARY RANGE: $5,000–$75,000
GEOGRAPHICAL AREA: nationwide
EDUCATIONAL REQUIREMENTS: bachelor's degree helpful but not
    required
FOR MORE INFORMATION: contact local officials' association or the
    National Association for Girls and Women in Sport at the
    American Alliance for Health, Physical Education, Recreation
    and Dance
    Professional organizations:

*National Association for Girls
    and Women in Sport*
1900 Association Drive
Reston, VA   22091
(703) 476-3450

*National Association of
    Collegiate Directors of
    Athletics*
21330 Center Ridge Road
Cleveland, OH   44116
(216) 331-5773

*National Interscholastic
    Athletic Administrators
    Association*
P.O. Box 20626
11724 Plaza Circle
Kansas City, MO   64195
(816) 464-5400

*National Youth Sports
    Coaches Association*
1509 North Military Trail
West Palm Beach, FL   33409
(305) 684-1141

Community Fitness

Health Spa Management

The number of health spa facilities in urban communities of the United States is continuing to grow. These facilities usually provide fitness activities such as weight training along with the specialized sport facilities for tennis, racquetball, and squash. Most facilities also include hot tubs, whirlpools, saunas, or steam rooms.

To make these commercial ventures successful, many owners seek to employ physical educators who understand techniques of conditioning and physical training. These professionals can design fitness programs for the members and can present a favorable image to the business in general. The large number of facilities in each major community provides for a multitude of job opportunities for anyone interested in the area of individual health and fitness.

Most employers are seeking individuals with some knowledge of the business world who are able to present a program that can be sold in an exciting manner. A manager of a health spa must know more than just how to exercise; he or she must be able to maintain records required in a business operation, be familiar with promotional techniques, order equipment, supervise and instruct employees, and be a consultant on weight loss and nutrition. The many health spas around the nation are creating new opportunities for the physical education professional.

Job Facts   Health Spa Manager

SALARY RANGE: $12,000–$40,000
GEOGRAPHICAL AREA: nationwide, mainly metropolitan areas
EDUCATIONAL REQUIREMENTS: bachelor's degree preferred
FOR MORE INFORMATION: contact local health club or spa, national
     office of a large enterprise such as President's First Lady or Jack
     LaLanne Fitness Centers

Weight Control Spas

In the United States, we consume numerous foods that are high in calories but do little to control weight or enhance our diet. As a result of this pattern, many people fight obesity and continually seek help to reduce body weight, develop muscle tone, and improve their self-image and personal appearance.

All weight control camps need professional educators who understand exercise and how it affects the body, which area of the body will be affected by certain controlled movements, and what programs will meet individual needs. To work effectively in this area, the physical education major must also have a knowledge of nutrition and a background in psychology.

For those physical education majors who enjoy working with people having specific problems, the weight control spa offers opportunities for specialized employment. Although one will not find these spas in all parts of the country, many of them are in resort areas, nestled in attractive settings that enhance the working environment.

Job Facts   Weight Control Spa Professional

SALARY RANGE: $12,000–$40,000 +

GEOGRAPHICAL AREA: metropolitan or resort areas

EDUCATIONAL REQUIREMENTS: bachelor's degree

FOR MORE INFORMATION: visit spas advertised in local newspaper or telephone directory; write to spas advertised in national publications such as *Working Woman* and *Good Housekeeping*

Stress Management

You may want to seek employment in specialized centers for stress management in business and industry. For the physical education major who is prepared to inform individuals or companies about relaxation and tension control, job opportunities on a full-time basis or as a consultant are available.

In today's fast-moving society, the average worker as well as the executive often fight hypertension with little knowledge or understanding of methods of control. Designing relaxation programs and working with individuals who are employed in high-pressure situations is a service that many need.

Although employment in this field may be part-time, it can be developed into a full-time position as a consultant or can be an excellent adjunct to other employment in general physical education.

Job Facts   Stress Management Professional

SALARY RANGE: $5,000–$40,000

GEOGRAPHICAL AREA: metropolitan areas

EDUCATIONAL REQUIREMENTS: bachelor's degree preferred with psychology background

FOR MORE INFORMATION: attend stress management seminars; contact American Management Association; contact local

Job Facts   (continued)

hospital wellness program director
Professional organizations:
*American Management
     Association*
P.O. Box 39
Ada, OH   45810

Retirement Centers

More and more retirement centers are being constructed throughout
the country. Too often older Americans are not provided with adequate
physical activity to maintain strength, flexibility, and a reasonable degree of cardiovascular fitness. Most large retirement centers employ
professionals who are skilled in designing programs and can work with
people in developing individualized activity plans. Some programs include group activities in dance or sport leagues such as softball.

This is a rewarding area of employment as one is able to share the
excitement, fun, and satisfaction experienced by those in their retirement years. Special interest can be generated when activities that are
familiar to the client from his or her younger years are modified for the
older American. The retirement center director or instructor must be
creative in motivating members and developing a fulfilling program.

Such centers may be found nationwide, although they are more common in locations where weather is not severe in either summer or
winter.

Job Facts   Retirement Center Professional

SALARY RANGE: $12,000–$25,000 +
GEOGRAPHICAL AREA: metropolitan and rural
EDUCATIONAL REQUIREMENTS: bachelor's degree, with emphasis in
     physical education or recreation and gerontology
FOR MORE INFORMATION: contact local chapter of Association of
     Retired Persons or gerontology centers in universities; visit
     retirement communities; contact local United Way agency

Athletic Clubs

Today's athletic clubs employ professional educators in aquatics, racquetball, badminton, squash, volleyball, jogging, fitness, and a variety
of other activities. Larger clubs have a need for specialized instruction
in additional related areas, providing employment for a number of peo-

ple on a regular basis, including activity directors, fitness directors, nutritionists, and figure control specialists. Most participants in the athletic club setting are in a higher economic bracket and can afford private lessons from a professional teacher.

Job Facts   Athletic Club Instructor

SALARY RANGE: $15,000–$55,000

GEOGRAPHICAL AREA: metropolitan area or resorts

EDUCATIONAL REQUIREMENTS: bachelor's degree desired

FOR MORE INFORMATION: contact local athletic club manager; read individual sports magazines (e.g., about racquetball or tennis) Professional organizations:

*Council for National
    Cooperation in Aquatics*
P.O. Box 1574
Manassas, VA   22110
(703) 361-3288

*National Association of
    Scuba Diving Schools*
P.O. Box 1767
Long Beach, CA   90807
(213) 595-5361

*Ladies Professional Golf
    Association Teaching
    Division*
200 Castlewood Drive
North Palm Beach, FL   33408
(305) 844-2500

Motor Development Centers for Special Populations

A program that is now emerging in our American culture is the special movement education clinic for the atypical child. Activities in these centers are designed for individual or small-group instruction. Activities covered are basic movement patterns, perceptual motor skills, classroom motor activities, and basic play skills or sport, rhythms, and general fitness. A motor development evaluation is conducted first to determine specific needs and serves as a foundation for program development. From this base, individualized programs are designed to meet each student's requirements.

These clinics are designed for educationally, neurologically, or orthopedically handicapped children. In some, the emotionally disturbed or mentally handicapped child may be enrolled. It has been found that sensorimotor stimulation maximizes the developmental potential of these children.

Developmental program clinics can emphasize activities for the infant or toddler or specialize in school-age children from 4 through 16 years. Referrals to these clinics come from the medical profession, school psychologists, special education or classroom teachers, and parents.

This career option is available to students prepared in adapted physical education with course work in special education and business management skills.

Job Facts   Motor Development Center Professional

SALARY RANGE: $18,000–$40,000
GEOGRAPHICAL AREA: metropolitan area
EDUCATIONAL REQUIREMENTS: master's degree preferred
FOR MORE INFORMATION: contact local college adapted physical
    education professional

Public and Private Sport and Recreation

Public Agencies' Sport Programs

Many agencies, such as the YMCA, YWCA, YWHA, CYO, and boys' clubs, employ sport directors to develop and conduct programs within their agencies. Sport programs have become prominent in all these agencies and have expanded to include fitness programs for adults as well as youth. There is a high demand in these agencies for professionals prepared in physical education, and salaries have recently increased, becoming comparable to those in the teaching profession. A variety of boys' and girls' clubs located throughout the United States provide numerous employment opportunities.

Job Facts   Public Agency Sport Director

SALARY RANGE: $15,000–$50,000
GEOGRAPHICAL AREA: nationwide
EDUCATIONAL REQUIREMENTS: bachelor's degree
FOR MORE INFORMATION: contact local agencies; write for a copy of
    the National Vacancy List, Records Management, Division of
    Personnel, YMCA of the USA, 101 Wacker Drive, Chicago,
    IL   60606

Private Sport Clubs

With the advent of specialized sport clubs and the increased development of tennis and racquetball facilities, there is a need for private club teachers. Many private sport club members have not had the privilege of receiving lessons in particular sports in school and now seek to learn such sports for their own pleasure or to be able to participate in the activity with a friend or spouse.

Tennis, golf, badminton, bowling, and many other activities provide opportunity for employment as a private club teacher. An individual employed by a club often has other responsibilities in the organization, such as a reservation or court director, and usually must have business or club management skills.

For the individual who has had success as a player and is known as a teacher, there are opportunities to enhance a basic salary to the five-figure range. Many of the top teachers command hourly salaries of $20 to $50, depending on their reputation and expertise in the specific sport.

Job Facts   Private Sport Club Teacher

SALARY RANGE: $20,000–$60,000
GEOGRAPHICAL AREA: metropolitan and resort areas
EDUCATIONAL REQUIREMENTS: bachelor's degree
FOR MORE INFORMATION: contact local sport clubs

State Institutions

State institutions such as hospitals, penitentiaries, and work camps are now seeking trained leaders in the area of sport coaching and physical education activities. Positions in state agencies usually offer job security along with autonomy in program development. Anyone desiring these advantages must be willing to give up the higher salary potential often found in private enterprise. Although annual salaries are adequate, the range is usually found to be lower than in the teaching profession.

Job Facts   Sport and Fitness Director in State Institutions

SALARY RANGE: $15,000–$30,000
GEOGRAPHICAL AREA: nationwide
EDUCATIONAL REQUIREMENTS: bachelor's degree
FOR MORE INFORMATION: contact local and state agencies and mental
    health centers

Camps

Although most camps are seasonal, there is employment at the director level on an annual basis. For one who enjoys skiing, backpacking, fishing, nature hikes, and the outdoors in general, a directorship presents

The physical educator who enjoys backpacking, nature hikes, and the outdoors in general can become employed in a natural environment as a camp counselor, guide, or director.

an opportunity to become employed in a pleasurable, natural environment.

In addition to private camps that are sprouting up all over the United States, there is also the National Park Service, which offers opportunities for activity directors in camping facilities that provide programs for vacationers. A sport director in a camp must be willing to work with transient groups. Working with a continuously changing group is part of the fun and appeal of such employment.

Traditionally, camp salaries have been low since most include room and board as part of the workers' compensation. When one considers the high cost of living, such compensation may be found to be much higher than the actual dollar amount.

Job Facts   Camp Director

SALARY RANGE: $20,000–$30,000 (plus on-site housing)
GEOGRAPHICAL AREA: rural areas
EDUCATIONAL REQUIREMENTS: bachelor's degree
FOR MORE INFORMATION: contact American Camping Association, Christian Camping Association, Scouting USA

Business and Industry

Employee Fitness Programs

Positions for fitness directors in the business and industry setting are increasing rapidly. The value of maintaining a high level of employee fitness has been well established. Profitable companies regularly look at the effectiveness of providing fitness activities that result in increased work productivity. Employees and executives who are physically fit are happier, can relieve themselves of job stress, and can maintain a healthier employee-manager relationship. Larger companies provide facilities that include small parks, jogging trails, weight-training and conditioning facilities, and racquetball, softball, basketball, and volleyball courts.

The physical education major employed in this setting often organizes sport leagues and conducts a variety of fitness activities. The fitness director in business and industry must be able to evaluate levels of fitness, design personalized fitness programs, and manage the sport facility in which the activities are presented.

Small companies and early programs often adapt an unused room for exercise programs. Large companies with new facilities often plan the exercise area as a part of the total facility design. The work setting in such companies is usually attractive and furnished with good equipment. Salaries are increasing for fitness directors in business and industry, and jobs have been advertised to direct a national program for a large company at the $60,000 per year level. Most jobs currently offer a salary commensurate with those of the teaching profession.

If you enjoy working with adults, evaluating personal fitness levels, designing individualized activity programs, and motivating adults to participate, you should consider this career option.

Job Facts   Employee Fitness Director

SALARY RANGE: $18,000–$50,000 +
GEOGRAPHICAL AREA: nationwide
EDUCATIONAL REQUIREMENTS: bachelor's degree in exercise science; master's degree preferred
FOR MORE INFORMATION: contact the Association for Fitness in Business, directors in local corporations
Professional organization:
Association for Fitness in Business
Indianapolis, IN.

Sporting Goods and Services

Salespersons of sporting goods and services may be involved in either sales or management. They may sell directly to the customer, as in a sporting goods store, or they may travel to different cities calling on buyers or officials of athletic teams as a dealer representative. Often, salespersons of sporting goods and services become owners or managers of a store or company. Rather than actually selling merchandise, they then are responsible for the total operation of the business.

Regardless of the precise job, these salespersons deal in a variety of sport merchandise and services and are in contact with all segments of the public. It has been said that every American family has some type of sport equipment that was purchased with the assistance of a sport salesperson. The sporting goods sold range from racquets to camping supplies to golf clubs. Salespersons may also prepare bids to sell a quantity of merchandise to a single program such as community teams and school programs.

Most positions begin on a part-time basis and develop to a full-time assignment in sales or as a company representative, which usually involves travel. A sales representative often has some fringe benefits such as a car allowance and an expense account. Some salaries are also supplemented by commissions or bonuses for sales made.

If you have a sales personality—the ability to interact well with people and convince them that the product is suitable for their needs—you may consider sales as a career. If you enjoy researching product quality, setting up appointments, and talking to people, and are willing to travel, you might consider becoming a sales representative.

Job Facts   Sporting Goods Salesperson

SALARY RANGE: $15,000–$100,000
GEOGRAPHICAL AREA: nationwide
EDUCATIONAL REQUIREMENTS: bachelor's degree recommended
FOR MORE INFORMATION: contact local sporting goods stores or major
    sporting goods equipment companies
    Professional organizations:

*National Association of
    Athletic Marketing and
    Development Directors*
Athletic Department
University of Michigan
1000 South State Street
Ann Arbor, MI   48109

*National Sporting Goods
    Association*
1699 Wall Street
Mount Prospect, IL   60056
(312) 439-4000

Military Service

The U.S. military service, one of the largest organizations in the country, provides many opportunities for fitness directors and recreational leaders. For one who enjoys the military life, there are many opportunities, and the benefits of hospitalization plans, retirement plans, and other specialized services are extensive.

Not all positions in the military require subscription in the service itself. There are still opportunities for civilians to manage programs on military bases, particularly in specialized facilities such as a golf course or recreational special services. There are also opportunities in foreign countries to serve as a physical education teacher or coach on a military base in schools for children of those in service.

In some cases, there are opportunities for the college graduate to enlist in programs that provide an officer's rank in specialized procurement programs in the area of physical training and sports development. Salaries depend on the rank or government service classification.

Job Facts   Recreational Specialist

SALARY RANGE: $15,000–$40,000
GEOGRAPHICAL AREA: worldwide
EDUCATIONAL REQUIREMENTS: bachelor's degree
FOR MORE INFORMATION: contact local armed forces recruiting office
or the Department of Defense through the local post office

Private Enterprise

Child-Care Centers

In the modern family today, both parents often work away from home. As a result, there are more and more child-care centers developing all over the country. Many of these are franchised establishments, and the more sophisticated centers hire specialists to conduct or direct sensorimotor activities according to the developmental level of the children. Although the salary in these centers if often on an hourly basis, experience of this type can lead to an individual's developing a private motor clinic or institute for children.

Job Facts   Child-Care Specialist

SALARY RANGE: $10,000–$15,000
GEOGRAPHICAL AREA: nationwide
EDUCATIONAL REQUIREMENTS: bachelor's degree
FOR MORE INFORMATION: contact local independent child-care centers
or head office for franchised child-care center

Movement Therapy

Movement or dance therapy is fast becoming one of the nonteaching professions that provides excellent job opportunities. For the dance or movement person who is not interested in the performing arts, a career in movement therapy can be rewarding, as its goal is the improvement of not only the physical but also the mental health of the participants.

Those interested in dance therapy find employment in facilities for older Americans, rehabilitation centers, psychiatric hospitals, and correctional institutions. Although this profession is new in comparison to other employment for the sport and human movement specialist, the movement therapy approach to human development and good mental health has proved to be successful.

Job Facts   Movement Therapist

SALARY RANGE: $15,000–$30,000
GEOGRAPHICAL AREA: nationwide
EDUCATIONAL REQUIREMENTS: bachelor's degree with psychology
    emphasis
FOR MORE INFORMATION: contact college dance instructors, adapted
    physical education professor, therapeutic recreation specialists,
    and hospital movement therapy department

Sport Consulting

For the creative individual who enjoys going into business privately, there are opportunities to be employed as a consultant to plan and develop sport programs in schools, private clubs, camps, business, and industry. Although many administrators and managers realize the need and importance of sport or physical fitness programs, many do not have the expertise or professional knowledge needed to ensure proper application of the principles related to a healthful lifestyle. As a result, employment opportunities are increasing on a contract basis, which could enable you to become a full-time consultant to a variety of organizations.

Salaries for this profession depend on the size of the business or institution needing the service and the degree of sophistication desired by the hiring establishment. As individuals become well known for their expertise in sport consulting, salaries can be higher. Professionals interested in this career must begin with sound salesmanship techniques and learn to justify programs with accurate statistical data.

Job Facts   Sport Consultant

SALARY RANGE: $5,000–$50,000
GEOGRAPHICAL AREA: metropolitan areas

Job Facts (continued)

EDUCATIONAL REQUIREMENTS: bachelor's degree
FOR MORE INFORMATION: contact a consultant presently working
    with a local facility

Coaching Schools or Clinics

With the tremendous number and age range of participants in sports
in the United States, there is a need for developing coaching skills at
all levels. Most coaching schools or clinics hire successful secondary
or university coaches as clinicians. In some instances, coaches will have
had experience with teams competing at the international level, bringing this expertise to the participants.

There is also a need to provide coaching information and program development in other countries. Sessions can range from 1 to 6 week programs to semester or year-long activities. The length of the complete
course is based on the degree of coaching expertise requested. In most
cases, programs are designed to meet special needs for selected men's
or women's activities.

Job Facts   Instructor, Coaching Schools or Clinics

SALARY RANGE: $5,000–$50,000
GEOGRAPHICAL AREA: worldwide
EDUCATIONAL REQUIREMENTS: bachelor's degree
FOR MORE INFORMATION: contact advertised sport schools and camps

Sports Marketing

Sports marketing includes planning, developing, and executing sports-
related programs designed to build the sales or image of a product or
service. The promotion of college teams, arenas, city events, and special programs such as the Olympics' thirty-eight individual sports also
fall under the aegis of sports marketing.

Opportunities for careers in sports marketing include the promotion
of athletes, coaches, teams, colleges, and equipment. Athletes who
achieve star status, as well as successful coaches, have the potential to
earn salaries beyond that for their athletic or coaching duties. The better an individual's sports record, the greater the chance of his or her involvement in sports marketing.

A good knowledge of sports, marketing skills, and public relations
course work are the basis for this career. You may also consider the acquisition of a law degree. Professionals who manage athletes, coaches,
and special events can earn a substantial salary, usually on a percentage basis.

In addition to managing individuals and teams, there are approximately 300 corporations and numerous professional teams, all of which have sports marketing departments. Positions in this area are usually based on a fixed salary. Duties will include securing sponsorships from corporations, obtaining permits, selecting sites, securing athletes or teams, and providing promotion and advertising.

Job Facts   Sports Marketer

SALARY RANGE: $25,000 +, based on percentage
GEOGRAPHICAL AREA: nationwide, metropolitan areas
EDUCATIONAL REQUIREMENTS: bachelor's degree, law degree
    recommended
FOR MORE INFORMATION: contact *Sports Marketing News*,
    universities with sports marketing programs

Medical Environments

Physical or Corrective Therapy

If you are interested in pursuing study in the science of exercise physiology, biomechanics, or adapted physical education, your physical education major is an excellent foundation for the programs in physical or corrective therapy. Completing the certification for either option will enable you to seek employment in hospitals, private clinics, and special schools. Child-care centers, nursing homes, and retirement homes also employ personnel with such certification.

Positions are available on the local, state, and national levels. Private practice is also a possible alternative once you are certified. Many physical therapists operate sports medicine clinics, servicing high school, college, and community athletes.

If you are interested in this field of employment, it is important to maintain at least a 3.5 grade point average and to gain as much practical experience as possible. Most programs are overfull and permit enrollment of only a few students each year.

Job Facts   Physical or Corrective Therapist

SALARY RANGE: $20,000–$40,000
GEOGRAPHICAL AREA: nationwide
EDUCATIONAL REQUIREMENTS: bachelor's degree and national
    certification

Job Facts   (continued)

FOR MORE INFORMATION: contact American Corrective Therapy
Association, Veterans Administration hospitals, or local Easter
Seals Society
Professional organizations:

American Physical Therapy Association	*National Therapeutic Recreation Society*
1156 15th Street, N.W.	1601 North Kent Street
Washington, DC 20005	Arlington, VA 22209
(202) 466-2070	(703) 525-0606

Recreational Therapy

The recreational therapist is primarily concerned with bringing about
a change in behavior leading toward a favorable self-image. The recreational therapist's role has expanded from the medium of sports, games,
and nature activities to include purposeful intervention through arts,
crafts, social activities, and other special events adapted to specific needs.

The recreational therapist can find employment at the local, state,
and national levels as well as in private and public facilities for the handicapped or physically limited individual. The need for this career option
is increasing, as reflected in salaries that are comparable to those of physical, occupational, and dance therapists.

Job Facts   Recreational Therapist

SALARY RANGE: $20,000–$40,000
GEOGRAPHICAL AREA: metropolitan areas
EDUCATIONAL REQUIREMENTS: bachelor's degree
FOR MORE INFORMATION: contact mental health and mental
retardation foundations, local Easter Seals Society, drug
rehabilitation centers, or AAHPERD
Professional organizations:

American Alliance for Health, Physical Education, Recreation and Dance	*National Therapeutic Recreation Society*
1900 Association Drive	1601 North Kent Street
Reston, VA 22091	Arlington, VA 22209
(703) 476-3400	(703) 525-0606

Entrepreneurial Opportunities in Sport

Do you enjoy the responsibility of creating and implementing your own ideas? Can you manage the stress that emanates from the requirements of successful performance to achieve financial gain? Are you ready to assume the risk of a business-oriented venture for the sake of a potentially unlimited profit? Do you have the enthusiasm and drive it takes to persevere? If you have answered yes to these questions, you may be ready to travel into the world of the entrepreneur.

Next you will have to determine whether you are planning to become a full-time or part-time entrepreneur. If you are already teaching or coaching or preparing yourself for a career in education, you may want your business venture to be limited to a part-time, summer, or school holiday time frame. A word of caution is appropriate here. The full-time teacher or coach who wishes to engage in part-time entrepreneurial endeavors should always place his or her contracted position in education at the top of the work priority list. It is one's professional responsibility to execute the demands of one's teaching or coaching position with dedication and enthusiasm. A person's educational career should not take a back seat to a part-time salary-supplement business.

If you are investigating the opportunities for a full-time entrepreneurial pursuit in sport and physical education, then the limits are few. The professional should be bound only by the rules of integrity, honesty, and ethical behavior in the process of redirecting one's career designed to meet the needs of our modern society. In addition, there must be the willingness and strength required for long hours of day-to-day management and an almost fanatical commitment to a quality service or product.

To start a business takes a great deal of hard work, long hours, self-sacrifice, and a total commitment to the effort. To succeed, one must be willing to be more demanding of one's time than most employees would ever consider being. Have you made a decision yet? Are you considering one of the many and varied entrepreneurial opportunities in sport and physical education? The following are samples of successful entrepreneurial efforts.

Mobile Fitness and Health Risk Appraisal

Do you possess the scientific knowledge and ability to test adults and have access to a van and a computer? Can you prescribe an individualized program to aid adults in the reduction of coronary heart disease risk factors? One successful entrepreneur who started alone in his mobile fitness and health risk appraisal venture now has six employees and has contracted with seventeen school districts to offer this service to classified staff. The service qualifies under the school district's benefit program.

The health enhancement programs offered are in the areas of general fitness levels, cardiorespiratory functions, weight reduction, and smoking cessation. Testing includes the fitness components of cardiorespiratory endurance, flexibility, body composition, and blood makeup, along with a family health history. The average fee per staff member is $150.00 for this service.

This business opportunity could be expanded by adding other fitness components in the areas of muscle strength and muscle endurance. It might also be developed to include school-age children, credentialed staff, or older adults in retirement centers.

Personal Fitness Instruction

In highly populated areas or where celebrities abound in the entertainment or business world, the job of a personal fitness instructor is a viable entrepreneurial option. Many celebrities or executives wishing to enhance their fitness levels prefer the individualized personal approach to exercise programs in the privacy of their own home or office. Many do not have the incentive or time to go to a health club on a regular basis. If you have the ability to evaluate, plan, prescribe, and execute a fitness program for adults and are willing to travel from site to site, this may be an exciting career option to pursue. There is a minimal investment in equipment, no overhead and, for the most part, an attractive environment in which you work.

Fees for this service range from $40.00 up to $150.00 per session. Based on the number of clients who subscribe to your program, the business can be either a full-time or a part-time venture. In selected areas, the business could grow to a company that employs a number of professionally trained fitness instructors.

Personal Coaching

With newspapers sporting headlines of collegiate athletic scholarships and multimillion-dollar professional contracts, many parents seek the aid of a private coach to develop and refine sport skills in their children. In addition, some athletes, both amateur and professional, wish to receive personal coaching on a regular basis. In sports such as swimming, diving, tennis, ice skating, track and field, and other selected activities, opportunities are available to work on a one-to-one basis with the athlete.

If you like to coach on an individualized basis or are stimulated by high-level performance, then this careeer may be for you. However, the job opportunities in this arena are not as readily available as in other entrepreneurial ventures. Nonetheless, the lifestyle can be very attractive if you are working with a celebrity on a full-time basis. Part-time personal coaching opportunities often are created by parents who wish to provide their children with extended coaching expertise.

The private coach must be willing to travel and be on call at almost all hours, depending on the needs of the individual athlete. Salaries range from hourly wages for private instruction to a full-time salary for one employed by a professional athlete.

Sport Tours

Airlines have made it possible to travel the world for much lower fares than in the past. In the area of sport tours, the entrepreneur can plan, coordinate, and administer a variety of activity tours throughout the world.

A popular trip for adults is a golf or tennis tour. Many individuals who like to travel also enjoy participating in a sport activity as they see the sights either abroad or in the United States. Sport tours are becoming more popular every day, and often a sport tour will appeal to an individual who otherwise would have little interest in traveling.

Youth soccer is growing by leaps and bounds in the United States. It is a challenge for youngsters to play against teams from other parts of the world. Soccer tours can be designed not only to enhance the experience of the youths participating in the sporting events but to provide tour opportunities for the parents as well.

This type of business can be begun on a part-time basis. Choose your sport and organize a tour for travel and summer income.

Computerized Skill Analysis Centers

It is not uncommon to see at one end of a golf driving range a small building that houses a video camera and a computer. Computerized skill analysis is here to stay. For the professional interested in biomechanics, this program could be developed for a variety of sports and offered not only to the general public but to athletic coaches for enhancement of skill development.

Computer analysis intrigues most individuals and also serves as a permanent record to evaluate progress. A follow-up videotape on instruction could be a part of the package offered the individual. Golf driving ranges, sporting goods stores, sport facilities, and sport fitness clubs would be appropriate sites for this service.

A professional with interest in one of these areas, coupled with a knowledge of computers, has endless opportunities for program development in computerized skill analysis.

Sports Products

Are you inventive by nature? Have you discovered a better product for sports competition or skill instruction? Who could better design sports clothing or sports equipment than a professional who is well-schooled in the various sport activities?

If you have a product you have made yourself and have successfully tested, consider going into business for yourself. Successful business ventures by professional physical educators include sport clothing lines, equipment storage carts, protective athletic mats, and sport timing systems, to name but a few. Some biomechanical engineers have been employed by shoe companies to develop running shoes.

Look around at the sports products you have been using for years. You may find a potential business opportunity waiting in the wings.

Futuristic Environments

A creative physical education major today must dream of the future and imagine job opportunities that may involve conducting sport and fitness programs in space. It is not too early to be thinking about developing activities in the weightless state as well as pursuing sport activities that may be conducted in a limited area. In addition to the space activities, we may also find ourselves involved in underwater movement efficiency programs.

The individual with an interest in space or underwater sport programs who seeks out training and information that may not appear appropriate now may well end up a pioneer in one of these specialized programs in the near future. You should never overlook an opportunity to take a course, complete an independent study project, or pursue avenues of instruction that lead toward program development and knowledge in the futuristic environment. Who knows what the salaries may be? One can be assured that a pioneer in this field will not be underpaid.

Opportunities in physical education extend to other environments and may include conducting sport and fitness programs in space. Here the flight crew of the first Space Shuttle orbital flight train for movement in zero gravity as they learn to don and doff their life support systems.

Job Facts   Position in a Futuristic Environment

SALARY RANGE: unlimited

GEOGRAPHICAL AREA: worldwide

EDUCATIONAL REQUIREMENTS: bachelor's degree to doctorate

FOR MORE INFORMATION: contact university academic counselor to discuss available programs (for example, the Underwater Training Program at Temple University)

Comments

In this chapter we have discussed just a few of the many career opportunities available in our field of study. Through initiative and drive, new services and products will be made available to the society. It is better to place professionally educated individuals in these sport and fitness ventures than to allow the opportunist who is not professionally sound to take advantage of a growing interest in the sports and fitness boom.

If you have the appropriate personal and business qualities, enjoy having control of your own destiny, and have an entrepreneurial spirit, then go for it! The reward of conceiving an idea, struggling to bring it to fruition, and seeing it work and expand is an enjoyable, fulfilling, and profitable experience.

As you can see, there are tremendous opportunities for job placement for the person with a physical education background. The many alternatives in course work and specialized programs available today should be considered carefully with regard to your interests and abilities. Many students later find themselves managing their own business or involved in an alternative career that was not even considered at the beginning of their professional preparation program.

Although one's first job may be difficult to find, there is no limit to the potential career opportunities the well-prepared physical education major will have. While you must carefully select specific courses to enrich your education, you must exercise caution so as not to exclude important training that, if avoided, could later restrict your career development. Recognizing that there are other possibilities for careers in addition to teaching and coaching can help you realize how important and exciting physical education is in our changing world. Chapter 14 will help you understand more about the variety of careers available by providing personal accounts of physical education professionals.

Student Activities

1. Make an on-the-job visit to a person with a physical education background who is working in a nonteaching career. Interview the person and make a report, using the following model:

Model Report of On-the-Job Visit

Kim Allen
Introduction to Physical Education
Baker/Pestolesi

Sports Custom Design

To whom I spoke
 Corrine Stoly from Just for Fun.
How she became interested in custom designing
 Went out to purchase a tennis dress and found them to be too expensive, so decided to make and design her own. After much investigation and disappointment, found the dress would cost $140.00. From there she decided to make tee-shirt dresses, but was disap-

pointed in the way the demo turned out. She finally hit on something big: tee-shirts with unusual sayings on them and panties with sayings for wear under tennis dresses. She next found someone to do the embroidery on the panties and print the sayings on the tee-shirts. Corrine took some samples to Palm Springs and the people flipped over them. From then on she couldn't keep enough on hand.

Salary

After the first month of business she was making $2,000 a month — as she said, enough to support a family.

Suggested training

Background in business, accounting, designing, and fitting, and a lot of *determination*.

What exactly is Just for Fun?

Corrine purchases the tops and bottoms, hires someone to put the designs on the garments. Then Corrine fills orders and sends them out. She is the middleperson.

If you are interested in this line of work, Corrine suggests you be ready for a great deal of work and definitely have a lot of determination.

2. Sit behind the scenes to observe a specialized sport and human movement career, such as sports broadcasting or hospital therapy. List the pros and cons of your visitation experience with respect to your personal career goals.

3. List identifiable alternative career personnel mentioned in publications such as *Sports Illustrated*.

14. Career Profiles

Objectives

Chapter 14 is designed to enable you to:

• Gain first-hand career information from professionals.

THIS chapter provides a personal commentary from physical education professionals working in a variety of careers. While you read these brief autobiographies, consider what preprofessional experience you need, how much career mobility you would have, what the responsibilities of the job are, and what career preparation is suggested by each professional. From these personal comments you should better understand the attractiveness of selected job opportunities and how individuals often are steered toward an exciting career by professional and personal contacts as well as by their choice of preprofessional courses. It is the authors' hope that this introduction to some professionals will provide you with a better insight for planning your own career path.

Regardless of the career choice made, all of these professionals emphasize the importance of effort in one's academic preparation and the achievement of good grades. These profiles should be reviewed with attention to your personal lifestyle expectations, career objectives, and assessed character strengths.

Carolyn McDonald
Director of Health, Racquet, and
Recreation
Health and Racquet Club at Grand
Traverse Resort
Acme, Michigan

Education
Associates Degree, Hotel/Motel
Management, Michigan State University
Associates Degree, Physiology/Allied
Health, Ferris State College

Professional Experience
Four years' experience in the hotel business.
Ten years' experience in health and fitness.

Personal Background in Sports and Physical Education
Cross-country and downhill skiing. Modern, jazz, ballroom, and aerobic dance. Parasailing and boating. Reading, knitting, and gourmet cooking.

I've always been active in sports and exercise and for 8 years owned and franchised my own aerobic workout and gyms. While working at the Los Alamos Scientific Laboratory in the occupational health field, I had the privilege of working on diet, training schedules, and flexibility workouts with three of the marathon hopefuls for the 1980 U.S. Olympic Team. It was shortly after that I started training and studying exercise physiology.

Business Development

In 1980, I started my own exercise company called "The Sweat Shop" and shortly thereafter franchised it. With my education in Hotel/Motel Management and my health and exercise background, moving into the resort/health club setting was natural.

The club where I work serves both the community, as a private, full health club, and the resort, as an amenity for the guests as well as recreational entertainment for convention groups. It's a delicate balance but extremely manageable. The majority of convention work is done during the summer and on weekends, and the private club members use the facility more during the week and in fall, winter, and spring. Consequently, the club sells a 9-month membership that begins in September and runs until the end of May.

Current Responsibilities

As Director of Health, Racquet and Recreation, I oversee the areas of the Racquet Sports Manager (United States Professional Tennis Association certified professional as well as having a degree in Professional Sports Management), Fitness/Aquatics Manager (minimum of bachelor's degree in Exercise Physiology), and Control Desk Manager (bachelor's degree in Business Management, with a Recreation minor), Ski Center Manager, Beach Club Manager, and the sales staff. All of these areas serve hotel/convention guests and private club members. I am completely responsible for all budgets and budget projections.

Career Satisfaction and Future Prospects

This type of business is on the cutting edge of growth for both the resort and health club business combination. In order for a fully equipped, full-service health club to really flourish financially and be able to deliver the type of customer service and expertise that the public has come to demand, the club must merge with a hotel or resort to offset overhead expenses. By the same token, the discriminating resort/hotel/convention guest demands a full-service health spa/club as an amenity. This becomes a creative way to serve both the community and the resort/hotel business.

I've had a tremendous amount of fulfillment in being one of the first to make a profitable business out of health/exercise and sports training and then being able to watch it grow into a necessity in the resort business. The most career satisfaction has been watching lifestyles change from a watching to a doing society.

Suggestions to Students

A degree with an emphasis in an area of physical education is important. For my type of position, education and experience in the Hotel/Motel Management field is critical due to the integration of both resort guests and the community.

A resort business offers a variety of opportunities aside from the directorship. For instance, the Racquet Sports Manager plays an important role and needs an advanced degree in Professional Sports Management. The Fitness/Aquatics Manager has a varied program that requires a degree in Exercise Physiology.

Flexibility in the workplace is critical. Programming needs change with the clientele and the seasons. A resort attracts many personalities that one has to support. Your work hours are varied, and weekends are high-use times.

Salaries vary with the responsibility and area of the country.

Personal work experience in a resort environment would be beneficial to determining whether you would like to pursue a career in this arena.

Our resort offers a diversified range of internship programs. By working with Grand Traverse Resort's diversified range of programs, an intern will get a working understanding and knowledge in all areas of planning, implementing, and evaluating programs. The intern will also help in expanding our existing programs by developing innovative ideas that will enhance current offerings. Other major areas in which the intern will participate include facility maintenance, control desk operations, running a fitness facility, and scheduling convention groups.

Dianna Coughlin
Owner
Fitness by Dee
Ogunquit, Maine

Education

B.S., Western Kentucky University, 1968
M.A., Western Kentucky University, 1974

Professional Experience

YMCA Senior Director

YMCA Healthy Back Instructor Trainer, 1974–1979

YMCA Advanced Fitness Specialist Training at Oral Roberts University, 1978

International Trainer of Feelin' Good (childhood fitness program), Spring Arbor College, 1986

IDEA certified, 1986

Maine Emergency Medical Technician

Maine Instructor, American Heart Association Cardiopulmonary Resuscitation (CPR)

Substitute Teacher, Sacramento School District, Sacramento, California, 1968–1969

Substitute Teacher, Rome City School District, Rome, New York, 1970–1974

Fitness Director, Rome Family YMCA, Rome, New York, 1974–1979

Assistant Professor, Department of Physical Fitness, Jackson Community College, Jackson, Michigan, 1979–1985

Fitness Director, Body Designs, Inc., Kennebunk, Maine, 1986–1987

Owner, Fitness by Dee, P.O. Box 1887, Ogunquit, Maine, 1987 to present

Personal Background in Sport and Physical Education

I was active in college sports but was never a spectacular athlete. In 1974, I got hooked on fitness running. Between 1974 and 1984, I completed eight marathons; two were "ultimate" running events, totalling 34 miles. In that time and to date, I have logged thousands of miles and stayed relatively injury-free.

I cross-country ski in the winter, jump rope, bench step, and look for ways to cross-train so I can remain "fresh" to teach my classes.

Current Responsibilities

Local resorts refer tourists interested in classes to my facility. This enables vacationers to continue their fitness programs.

As a community health facility, fitness can be built into a lifetime endeavor. My facility offers a more individual approach for someone who does not feel inclined toward group participation. Health club facilities with more group-oriented programs refer to me.

Career Satisfaction and Future Plans

Owning a facility offers many challenges and keeps satisfaction high. There are always different ideas with which to experiment so you can stay involved in the creative process.

Future plans are to direct heavily into the self-care concept and away from aerobics. Becoming involved with the medical community and offering classes in stress and nutrition are among specific goals. Expansion into nearby communities is another area of concentration. Contacts have been made and contracts are being drawn to begin this project.

Suggestions to Students

I think it's very important to have a strong sense of self; which comes with deliberate "internal" work. Owning one's own business is very time-consuming and carries with it an enormous amount of responsibility. If you aren't a stick-to-it type of person, you won't make it.

I believe it's important to get a wide variety of experience in order to develop where one's interests gravitate within the profession. My 5 years in the YMCA were the most valuable. They taught me how to work hard on low pay and still find enjoyment. It also brought out my strong desire to serve people and make a difference in their life.

It would be helpful to get additional training in first aid. A good course in business management, advertising, and public relations would also be beneficial. The most important of all is to *read*. Always continue educating yourself.

You need investment capital or investors to start your own business. I spent 12 years working for others before going on my own.

Have a facility that offers variety. It is not easy to sell fitness. You need a lot of direction so that if one thing doesn't produce, something else can be tried.

It is important to understand what has happened to the aerobics movement. Many people with less education than those of you reading this book teach aerobic fitness. This is *not* helpful to our profession. It makes it difficult to make a living at just teaching classes. Much more has to be included. When you teach with a degree, don't sell yourself or your business short. Do a professional job and stick with it.

Salary

Population base is going to determine one's salary. A large city would command greater income than a small town. Some larger fitness clubs can pay $50,000 to $100,000 per year. With experience and good programming, one can expect $25,000 to $40,000 if willing to put in the time necessary to build the reputation.

Professional organizations are very important but can be costly for the self-employed. After researching what was available, I chose IDEA because it best met my needs.

I subscribe to *Physician and Sports Medicine, American Health, Family Health,* and *Running Times.* The more reading you can do, the more knowledgeable you remain in your profession. It's not always possible to subscribe to all pertinent publications. It's a matter of finding what best meets your needs.

Kermit Daniels
Elementary School Physical Education
 Teacher
White Elementary School (K–5)
Houston, Texas

Education

B.S., Physical Education and Biology,
 Prairieview A & M University, Texas,
 1970

Professional Experience

Taught both social studies and physical education in an elementary
 school, 1970–1971
Decided to teach only physical education and accepted a transfer to full-
 time physical education with a split-school assignment. Taught

physical education 3 days per week at one school and 2 days at another elementary school, 1971–1972

Accepted a transfer as a single-school elementary physical educator at White Elementary School, 1973

Personal Background in Sport and Physical Education

As a youngster, I grew up in a rural community in Texas. I attended the same school for 13 years, kindergarten through twelfth grade. My father taught fourth grade and my mother taught high-school English in the same school. My father also drove the school bus, and consequently I never missed a day of school. I enjoyed school and really never considered anything but teaching as a career.

As a kid, I played a lot of sports—baseball, football, basketball, and track. My school was too small for a football team, but my friends and I played a lot together. I loved sports! I knew all the baseball players and their averages. I read all the sports magazines I could get my hands on and watched all the sports possible on television. I dreamed of becoming a professional player, but I gradually grew to understand reality—I was too small to make it.

In college, I played baseball. When I first graduated I wanted to coach baseball. However, all the positions I applied for included being an assistant football coach. I did not have that qualification, so I decided to teach full-time at the elementary level and have not regretted this decision.

Current Responsibilities

I am responsible for the entire physical education program for all students at White Elementary. My class periods are 30 minutes long, and I meet ten to twelve classes a day. My schedule is varied during the day with different grade levels and I enjoy it.

Career Satisfaction and Future Prospects

Elementary physical education is where the important movement fundamentals are taught. I really enjoy seeing children accomplish new skills and having fun. I have never missed a day of teaching because I feel so good about my job. I am really dedicated to the kids.

I obtain a lot of self-renewal when I work with my students on preparations for our annual Field Day. Field Day includes a track meet and carnival, and many parents attend. I enjoy meeting parents and sharing their child's accomplishments with them.

I know I won't get rich as a teacher. However, my wife also teaches and we get along really well. Summer vacations give me a chance to explore other careers as a part-time experience, my family and I can travel, and I really enjoy the amount of time I can spend with my two children. I am very family- and church-oriented, and my job provides me with the time needed to enjoy both.

I plan to remain an elementary physical educator. I cannot see myself in a suit and tie every day as an administrator, nor do I really want the additional responsibility and time commitment of such a position.

Each state and local community has its priorities and budget concerns. The Houston Independent School District is committed to providing physical education instruction to all elementary students, and it is anticipated that this commitment will continue. However, there will probably continue to be more jobs in the larger cities than the suburban areas for the next several years.

Suggestions to Students

As soon as possible in your college years, take a course in elementary physical education or get out in the schools and observe professionals working with elementary-age kids. It would also be wise to become involved with a variety of age groups by coaching Little League teams or working in community recreation programs.

I believe that children have changed. Television has had a great impact by affecting their attention span. Children do not listen as well and expect to be entertained. The increasing mobility of society creates situations where children change schools so often and sometimes several times in the same school year. Children also know more at younger ages, although socially and emotionally they are about the same. It is important to work with children and experience these things before deciding that teaching should be your career.

My entire educational experience, including college, was in all-black schools. I never taught white children until I got out of college and started my first job. Earlier contact would have been helpful, but I don't dwell on the differences. If you know what you are doing and teach the individuals, you'll do fine. There appear to be more jobs in minority areas, and it would be helpful to gather some experiences with other groups as a student. If you love people above all, that's what makes the world go 'round.

It's important to remember that teaching is not easy. There is more to it than merely teaching the subject matter. Elementary teaching is a great opportunity to teach personal habits, interpersonal relationship skills, and responsibility for self.

Salary

Salaries vary across the nation. Each state has a minimum salary scale, and local boards of education decide how much their districts can afford to pay teachers. The current starting salary in Houston for a teacher with a bachelor's degree is $19,000.

Maria Carmen Reyes
Junior High School Physical Education
   Teacher and Coach
Fleming Junior High
Houston, Texas

Education

B.A., Physical Education, Pan American University, Texas, 1978

Professional Experience

Taught physical education in LaJoya, Texas, 1978–1979
Taught physical education in Mercedes, Texas, 1981
Began teaching seventh grade physical education and coaching, 1981

Personal Background in Sport and Physical Education

As a child, I liked sports, and my sister and I did a lot of running together. I had a brother who played football and ran track, and we would go and watch him compete. While I was in high school, we did not have any varsity teams for girls. As a result, we were very competitive in physical education classes.

I wanted to be a better physical education teacher than the one I had. She would just sit around a lot and wasn't very involved with the girls. I wanted physical education to be what it should be for students.

I did not have much money and had to work a semester before I could enter college. I had to work and carpool, so I still did not have the opportunity to play varsity sports. However, I really enjoyed college and had thought of pursuing a counseling degree, but I wanted to be closer to students and did not want all the paperwork of a counselor.

Current Responsibilities

I teach seventh grade coeducational physical education at Fleming Junior High School. I also coach volleyball and track.

Fleming Junior High is close to being an all-black school. At first I had some difficulty with some students, but I never gave up and I feel things are going more smoothly. The major difference between my rural student teaching experience and teaching in the big city is not so much the ethnic differences as the effects of the differences in socioeconomic status that exist in the city and the fast pace of life.

At first I felt unsuccessful and believed that I was not helping the students. I decided to become more familiar with the neighborhood the school served. I spent some time exploring the community and gathered important information on the type of homes the students came from, socioeconomic status, and leisure-time activities. In my classes, I make sure that I mix the students up so that their socioeconomic differences [aren't] so noticeable.

I have had to serve as a consistent role model and have to be firm with the students . . ., the girls expect a good coach. I feel that I have established good rapport with my athletes. Despite my lack of competitive experiences, I feel competent. I do not feel that you need to be an ultrajock in order to be a good coach.

Career Satisfaction and Future Prospects

I came to Houston to have different experiences as a teacher. I feel that I have learned a lot. My current job is very challenging and I believe that I have adapted well, but it has been discouraging at times being so far away from family and friends.

In a few years, I plan to return to south Texas and teach in a rural community. I know I will return as a different person and have a different perception of the problems that rural youth face. It has been a great experience to leave my hometown and have such a different personal and professional experience. I believe that I will be a much better teacher when I return.

I enjoy helping students and working with them as a teacher and coach. Students need to learn to deal with people as individuals and learn more about their own capabilities. I am happy teaching and coaching and plan to continue this career.

There will continue to be a need for quality physical education teachers. Athletics for both boys and girls are increasing in quality and quantity at the junior high level. Students at this age need special people who can perceive the changes they are undergoing and the pressures that exist in the schools to participate in socially acceptable behaviors.

Suggestions to Students

As a physical education major, you need all the experiences with a variety of children that you can obtain. Volunteer or work part-time in places where you never thought you would be. Observe a variety of teachers and coaches. You will learn a lot about different teaching and coaching styles.

Physical education teachers in the junior high schools are expected to coach. It is important to have some experience in coaching situations before you graduate.

Teaching is really hard. There is a lot of pressure in today's schools and you need to be able to handle it. You are a role model and need to practice what you preach. When working with junior high youngsters, you will need a lot of patience and humor. It is important not to be too sensitive to criticism from kids. Your level of expectation has to be realistic. You need to understand the perceptions of students and their problems, but do not get too involved.

To be a good physical education teacher is challenging but very rewarding. As a junior high coach, you will work long hours for minimal financial compensation, but there are a lot of rewards as a coach helping a team to improve.

Salary

From $15,000 to $40,000. Teacher salaries are the same at all levels. Coaching salaries do vary, depending on the grade level and sport involved.

Douglas Richard Todd
High School Physical Education Teacher
Artesia High School
Lakewood, California

Education

B.A., Physical Education, and Secondary Teaching Credential, California State University—Long Beach, 1980
M.A., Education, California State University—Dominguez Hills, 1984

Professional Experience

Assistant Track Coach, West Torrance High School, Torrance, California, 1979–1983

Substitute Teacher, Torrance Unified School District, 1982–1983

Science Teacher, Artesia High School, Lakewood, California, 1984–1988

Head Cross-Country and Track Coach, Artesia High School, 1988

Physical Education Teacher, Artesia High School, 1989

Personal Background in Sport and Physical Education

I have enjoyed sports and games for as long as I can remember. I played every sport offered in junior high school, and in high school I played football and ran track. I competed on a community college track team for 2 years and really enjoyed myself.

When I began thinking about a career, I knew I wanted to do something associated with athletics. My original plan was to become a physical therapist and work in sport rehabilitation. However, while waiting to be admitted to the physical therapy program, I started coaching at the high school level and really liked what I was doing. I also came to the realization that trainers or therapists can't coach because most of their work is during the teams' practices. As a result, I switched to the physical education major.

Current Responsibilities

I teach four periods of physical education at the high school level. Three of my classes are all ninth graders, and the other is made up of tenth graders. All are coeducational. My fifth class is made up of the members of the pep squad (cheerleaders, flag twirlers, and song leaders); class time for this group is devoted mainly to the practice of their routines. A certain amount of time is devoted to physical fitness.

In addition to my physical education classes I coach boys' and girls' cross-country and track and field. All of my coaching is done after school for extra pay.

Each physical education teacher is also responsible for locker room supervision, line duty, and facility upkeep.

Career Satisfaction and Future Prospects

Overall I am very satisfied with my choice of career. I love coaching and working at the high school level. The teaching is challenging and fun but can be frustrating at times. The negative perception of physical education that the students sometimes bring with them is hard to deal with. I am fortunate in that the majority of the teachers in my department are committed to developing a sound physical education program and take their teaching seriously.

The hours one has to work in teaching are ideal. Between my two coaching seasons, I am off and heading for home by 3:00 P.M. on most days. This is an added benefit of teaching that I never thought much about before I became a teacher. Being involved with physical education and especially athletics affords me the opportunity to become personally involved with the students much more than when I was a classroom teacher. When I first started teaching, this involvement didn't seem like any big plus or minus. After teaching a few years now, I find that I really enjoy keeping in touch with former athletes and students. This is a most satisfying part of my job that I never thought much about before.

I wish I made more money teaching. One of the frustrations in education is that to make more money one has to move into administra- and thereby leave the classroom. At the present time, I enjoy my teaching and coaching too much to leave it.

I believe physical education will remain in our public schools. I don't see the *mandatory* year's requirement increasing, but because of public awareness, I do not feel it will be cut back further.

Suggestions to Students

Full-time, tenured high school physical education jobs are hard to come by. Most of the people I know who are teaching now, myself included, got into the schools through coaching. Being able to coach is a major plus. Being able to coach two or three sports a year really helps to get your foot in the door.

A second suggestion is to obtain an academic minor that is taught in high school. Currently, math or science are the most desired areas of expertise, but one must be willing to teach anything. Since receiving my teaching credential, I have taught world and U.S. history, health, driver's education, math fundamentals, pre-algebra, physical science, and physics.

A third consideration is to make yourself visible and participate in all aspects of high school life. I run the clock at football and basketball games, attend school plays and choir performances, work the wrestling matches, and have been a freshman, sophomore, junior, and senior class adviser. I have also served two terms on our school site council. If the time comes to cut back on staff, the more you do, the better your chance of staying.

Another suggestion is to begin coaching now while in college. High schools are always looking for assistants. You will not only gain experience but also find out whether this is really what you want to do in life.

Don't expect to be hired into physical education right away. First, do a good job in the classroom. Let your principal know that you would like to move into physical education and develop a relationship with the people in the department. Have lunch with them, talk to them during your conference periods, and so on. It is not always your qualifications that get you a job. People want to work with people they like and know.

Show a personal commitment to physical fitness. When I go out on my runs at school, I make sure I go past the principal's window every so often.

The principal, in most cases, runs the school. He or she hires, fires, and places people. Therefore, I would send résumés and make phone calls to principals rather than district offices.

Be adaptable. Don't complain about your small coaching budget or your need for your own classroom or desire for an athletic period. Take what you are given, do a good job with it, and prove yourself even though conditions are less than ideal. Very few people get everything just the way they would like. Education is no exception. Once you have done your job well, you can approach an administrator with your requests and, in my experience, you will be given help.

If you want a job quickly, find a district with an increasing enrollment. Go where new homes are being built. If a district is closing schools because of a decreasing student population, you are probably wasting your time looking there. If you are open and adaptable and willing to work hard, I believe that there are jobs to be found in the public schools.

Salary

A first-year teacher in my district with just a bachelor's degree will make $21,278. A teacher who has taught 10 years and has a master's degree will make $35,129. The pay scale tops out at $40,195. A head coach makes approximately $1,500 per season, while an assistant coach makes $1,100 per season.

Elizabeth Blake Stack
Adaptive Physical Education Teacher
Tustin Unified School District
Tustin, California

Education

B.S., Physical Education, California State
University, 1972
M.A., Art, California State University—
Fullerton, 1976
Adaptive Physical Education Credential, California State University—Long Beach, 1988

Personal Background in Sport and Physical Education

I decided to be a physical education teacher when I was in high school. I followed that educational path and taught for 6 years in a junior high school. Besides teaching physical education, art, home economics, and student leadership, I coached volleyball and tennis and was athletic director and activities director. My teaching career came to a sudden halt when I was laid off due to falling student enrollment. At that time, I became disillusioned with the teaching profession since seniority was the only criterion used to determine layoffs. My teaching record could not be considered, and it seemed that I had become nothing but a number.

I spent the next 3 years successfully working in the business community. However, I chose to stop working when our first child was born with Down's syndrome. From his birth, I began to focus on his development, and I became his teacher. By the time he was 6 months old, I called the local university to see what course work I would need to be qualified to teach adaptive physical education

Our local school district needed an adaptive physical education teacher for a summer session, and at that time the completed credential was not required for summer school. I applied since I wanted to experience teaching in this area before I committed myself and my family to my becoming a full-time college student again. I enjoyed the experience, went back to college, and received my adaptive physical education credential a year later.

Current Responsibilities

I teach 2 days per week (by choice) at an elementary and a junior high school that share the same site. I have between 20 and 24 students. I am responsible for conducting assessments, writing goals, attending IEP meetings, and seeing each student twice weekly. I develop individualized lesson plans, depending on the student's needs. On occasion, I work with the student's medical team. Some students are involved with Special Olympics. I have coached one sport and help the students train for others.

Career Satisfaction and Future Prospects

I know that I have made the right choice. I am able to work part-time while our children are still young. I enjoy the range of ages (3 to 18) that I work with and the diversity of their disabilities. I feel constantly challenged. I can be involved in extracurricular sports if I choose. Having few students at a time to work with is a distinct pleasure. I love seeing the difference I make in someone's life. Imagine sharing the joy of a student's first ride on a bicycle when she is 18 years old!

The Education for All Handicapped Children Act (PL94-142) has provided for the services of adaptive physical education teachers. I feel that there will always be a need for our positions as long as the funding is available and parents voice their desires. The number of students who need our services has increased over the past years, and this trend will continue since many more "at risk" babies are being born.

Suggestions to Students

Look for opportunities to experience an area of interest before committing a lot of time, money, and energy.

Check out the geographical distances that must be traveled. I am lucky that my schools are on the same site. Many adaptive physical education teachers spend a great deal of their day in the car.

Become knowledgeable about all aspects of the disabilities. Read, read, read!

Become a resource for your students. Find out what the community offers and what is available for those with disabilities. Don't let the walls of the school confine you or them.

Salary

An adaptive physical education teacher is paid the same as a regular teacher ($18,000 to $50,000 per year). If personal use of your car is required, then a mileage wage is paid in addition to the base pay. I am currently paid two-fifths of a regular contract per year. Work is usually available during the summer for extra pay if you desire to do this.

Charlene E. Thomas
All Saints' Episcopal School (Boarding School)
Director of Physical Education, Recreation,
  Activities and School Administrator
Vicksburg, Mississippi

Education

B.S., Physical Education, Mississippi
  University for Women, 1963
M.A., Physical Education, Mississippi Col-
  lege, 1989

Professional Experience

Taught physical education and coached track, volleyball and tennis,
  Vicksburg Public School, 1963–1971
Supervise five physical education teachers; teach and serve as one of
  five school administrators, 1971 to present

Personal Background in Sport and Physical Education

As a student, I never had physical education or played a varsity sport.
I was a cheerleader and in the school band. You could say I'm a "people
person" because I really enjoy people, so when I went to college all I
knew was that I wanted to work with people. My college counselor was
head of the Physical Education Department. She really guided me into
this profession. (We still keep in touch.)

I wanted to learn and experience everything I could because I had a
lot of catching up to do since I was not an athlete or sports person. I
really enjoyed my college experience—learning so many things, participating in activities, and sharing ideas with my classmates. In the
summertime, I worked in camps and city recreation programs to get
other related experiences. After deciding to become a P.E. teacher, my
goal from the very beginning was to be the best teacher I could be, just
like my professor.

Current Responsibilities

I direct the physical education, recreation, aerobics, and activities program at all Saints' Episcopal School. I also teach one class from among
the following: volleyball, nutrition, fitness, camp counseling, or beach
volleyball.

There are five physical education instructors on the staff, plus six to eight other teachers who work in the aerobics and contracted activity program after school. I supervise and direct this program. I also serve on the school administrative staff—one of five members—which makes decisions involving every aspect of student life.

Physical education at All Saints' is a carefully planned sequence of learning experiences designed to fulfill the needs of every student in a variety of areas—growth, development, behavior, health, and play. The extensive variety of the program through individualized activities in physical education, recreation, and competition allows each student to select from a broad range of courses (pickle ball, traditional sports, fencing, project adventure, etc.).

I feel it is the right of every child to be physically educated, that every boy and girl should learn at least one lifetime sport and should get started early thinking about physical activity as a part of his or her lifetime plan. Personalized learning and the individual's development of a positive self-concept are hallmarks of a quality program.

Career Satisfaction and Future Prospects

Physical education was not required for students at H.V. Cooper High School, my first teaching job. Out of a population of 150 girls, 140 elected to take the class. . . . Sixteen girls out of that physical education program chose to teach physical education as their career. After 8 years at Cooper, I went to build a program at All Saints' School. With much excitement, the work effort began in a nonregulation basketball court gym located in the basement of one of the buildings. A creative program was designed based on the needs of the students and their interests. Under my direction but with total support from the headmaster, faculty, staff, and students, the following evolved:

1. Initiation and development of a selected coeducational physical education program which now has six physical education teachers for a population of 181 students grades 8 through 12.
2. Initiation and development of a comprehensive coeducational intramural program with 100 percent participation.
3. Direct involvement with planning, raising money, and construction of a physical education center (gymnasium).
4. Created a physical fitness trail and a grass track and developed a program for both the low-risk and high-risk activities in a Project Adventure Ropes Course (the only one in Mississippi).

5. Designed a comprehensive physical education curriculum for instruction; a contract activity program to enhance the physical education program; an aerobic program by which for 3 days per week every student walks, jogs, runs, rides a bike, or attends an aerobic workout for thirty (30) minutes, in addition to the required physical education period.

All this was possible because of a commitment to excellence where students, faculty, and staff have a sense of belonging, assurance that there is a place where they can win . . . that winning is not everything but the effort is. After all, teaching is guiding a student from where he or she is to where he or she might be.

There will continue to be a need for *quality physical education teachers*. Remember the words of William H. Danforth from his book *I Dare You:* "Some leaders are tall men, some are short men, some are men from the country, some from the city. Some are men with college backgrounds, others are men whose only schooling was "Reading, Riting and Rithmetic," some are geniuses, some are pluggers. Each man is a distinct personality . . . no two come from the same environment but they have one common attribute. That is *energy*."

I appeal to you to strive to be the best in your profession. If you don't have the energy to be the best, then develop the energy.

Good teachers will have students in physical activities. Not-so-good teachers will have students in line, choosing teams, waiting, and managing.

Degrees do not make teachers. It's what teachers are doing that makes teachers.

The twenty-first century will care for leaders with vision, energy and a commitment to excellence — accept the challenge!

Suggestions to Students

Motivation for excellence is the key. My motivation is to be an effective teacher has come from several areas. I'd like to share a few:

1. Staying involved *professionally* by sharing ideas, keeping "in tune" with current methods of teaching, participating in school life and community, reading, studying, attending workshops and conventions (local state and national level), and furthering my education

2. Gathering support of school officials, other teachers, parents, and students

3. Constantly "telling the story" and often being amazed that there is so much going on, so much to do, and that we really are teaching, modeling, and preparing our students for lifetime activities
4. Being patient by planning, working, waiting, and allowing programs and ideas to develop
5. Receiving encouragement, support, and recognition from local and state colleges
6. Maintaining a high energy level, a commitment and dedication to excellent teaching for *all* students
7. Not being content with a good program but always striving for new ways to improve

Being an effective teacher means accepting the fact that we all have strengths and weaknesses, and in order to be a "winner" we must have high expectations, accept the responsibility of teaching for excellence, and seek attention to or feedback on what we are doing. One last thought: I've never lost sight of how important it is to be excited and "fired up" about what I was doing, whether it be a how-to lesson or participation in the event or activity—and believe me, I can get fired up!

Salary
Boarding school salaries are from $12,000 to $35,000. Teacher salaries will vary from state to state and according to the job description.

Freddie Elaine Thompson
Junior High School Physical Education and
    Dance Teacher
Henry Clay Junior High School
Los Angeles, California

Education
B.A., Physical Education, Wichita State
    University, Kansas, 1968
M.A., Administrative Academy, California
    State University—Dominguez Hills (in
    progress)

Professional Experience
Physical Education and Dance Teacher, 1968 to present

Personal Background in Sport and Physical Education

I have always enjoyed sport activities both as an observer and as a participant. Although I had a sister who excelled in track and a brother who excelled in basketball, I was just an all-around sport buff. Throughout junior and senior high school, I participated in physical education activities, both in the regular program and after school. By the end of my senior year, I had accumulated enough service points in the school athletic program to receive a letterman's necklace, one of the highest recognitions given to female students at the local level. I also received many medals for my accomplishments in sports during my high school years.

On the artistic side of physical education, I participated in the dance program. I began taking dance classes while in junior high at the local YWCA. I was fascinated with modern dance and tap. While in eighth grade, my friends and I persuaded our new physical education teacher to form an after-school dance club. Although she admitted to us that she was not experienced in this area, she allowed us to establish one. Little did I realize that the foundation for my future career was being laid. I continued participating in dance throughout high school and college.

By the time I reached high school, I had made up my mind that I was going to be a physical education teacher. I never wavered from this decision. In retrospect, I believe that my junior high school teacher played a very important part. She was so innovative and deeply involved herself with her students. She made physical education fun and challenging. She served as my second role model, my mother being the first.

And what a role model my mother was! She did not have it easy. Being a single parent, she raised five children. She helped one daughter finish nursing school and helped send me through college. This was done by pooling our finances and obtaining a series of small scholarships, government loans, and matching grants. At graduation in May 1968, I stood with my mother, each holding one end of my diploma. I was the first member of my family to earn a college degree.

Current Responsibilities

I teach physical education in an urban school setting, grades 7 through 9. My daily teaching schedule consists of two periods of regular physical education, two periods of adapted physical education, and one dance class. I serve as a mentor teacher for my region and as the after-school youth services coordinator. I have also served as the physical education department chairperson.

Over the years of teaching at Clay Junior High, I have witnessed changes in our school population from a multimix of white, black, and oriental to a predominantly black and Hispanic population. I have experienced the change from teaching all girls to coeducational classes. Both situations have been challenging and added a new dimension to my growth as a teacher.

As a teacher, I believe that one must be a firm and consistent disciplinarian as well as "practice what we preach." I continue to strive to build good rapport with my students, encourage them academically, and serve as a positive role model. My students are made aware of my involvement with the mentor teacher program and with my professional responsibilities that take me away from them several times during the school year.

Career Satisfaction and Future Prospects

The following have been satisfying to me in my career:

1. Sharing in my student's accomplishments.
2. Sharing my expertise with my colleagues.
3. Being a positive role model.
4. Learning that my former students have chosen to become physical education teachers or dance educators or have excelled in sports.
5. Being invited to speak at various conventions, conferences, and workshops.
6. Being active in my professional organizations.

The future for physical education is bright. However we must all be outspoken advocates for quality daily physical education in grades K through 12. When that occurs, many more jobs will be available in our area of expertise. Our future is in our own hands.

Suggestions to Students

As a physical education major and future teacher:

1. Visit many schools in a variety of community settings, observing a variety of teachers and coaches.
2. Be firm and consistent in your teaching and yet open to change.
3. Have a sense of humor.
4. Teaching requires patience—make sure your expectations of students are realistic.
5. Attend as many in-service workshops, coaching clinics, and dance workshops as possible to enhance your teaching.

6. Join and actively participate in your professional organization at the local, state, and national level.

Salary

Salary begins at $25,000 to $50,000 and is based on completed course work and years of experience above the minimum requirement. Coaching positions receive a yearly stipend depending on the sport. After-school activities, such as sponsoring a sport or related program, pays from $8.89 to $10.44 per hour.

Teresa D'Anza and Larry D'Anza
Owners/Partners (with another couple)
Sport-About
Albuquerque, New Mexico

Previous Experience

Larry: Marketing educator
Teresa: Administrator for a public agency

Personal Background in Sport and Physical Education

Along with our other partners, we have participated in a variety of sports throughout our lives. It was this interest that brought us together as potential partners. Our diverse sports interests, such as one partner's love of skiing, strengthens our overall marketing in a community that has multiple resources for school sports, organized youth leagues, and family recreation environments.

Current Responsibilities

Each of us is an owner/manager. Our sporting goods store is different because a portion of our business is the actual manufacturing of garments. We produce custom-made uniforms for teams such as baseball and softball teams and cheerleader squads. This was our key to going into business. We felt we could offer our community something they were unable to get elsewhere. Each owner/partner has clearly defined areas of responsibility, and if something isn't clearly defined, then we define it.

Business Expectations in Sport

If you are the sole owner of a business, you have to have a dynamic personality. There is so much that you have to learn and be able to do, plus there is a lot of time involved. Since there are four owners in our business, it has made it easier for all of us. This does not mean to imply that it has been easy, because it definitely has not. Our varied educational backgrounds and personalities have helped.

We believe that anyone expecting a large salary when first beginning a business is courting failure. The odds are against large salaries unless you have a very large bankroll with which to start. Three of us had jobs when we began our business and are still employed outside our business. The fourth partner is paid a minimal salary of $1,000 per month. If we had all given up our jobs and tried to live off the business when we first opened in 1985, we would have failed. We needed every penny we generated in sales to put back into the business for buying products, advertising, and other expenses.

In the early period of opening a business, you give every minute to that business. You don't think the business can function even one-half hour without you. Eventually, you will be willing to spend more time outside of your store. However, at least one of our owners is at our business at least 90 percent of the time.

Career Satisfaction

There are endless possibilities in store for us. The key is knowing the right time to make major changes such as attempting to grow, changing direction, moving to a new location, and so forth. We have seen lots of what appear to be very successful businesses decide to expand and, within a year, they are bankrupt. We have hopes of becoming extremely successful but are planning for this business to fly high before we do anything else. We are anticipating that beginning in 1990 we will be able to get some financial gain for ourselves from our business.

Suggestions to Students

1. The key to making your business successful is knowing how to market your product. Marketing alone is not the answer. A student would

do well to pick up some human resource classes as well. Your business is only as good as the employees who represent you to your customers. Knowing how to educate, motivate, and keep these employees satisfied is critical.

2. Work-related experience in a job similar to that which you plan to enter as a career is helpful.

3. If we were to select one personality trait necessary for this career, it would be flexibility. However, you must also be optimistic and hardworking, have tough skin, and be able to communicate well.

4. If you own your own business, it's important that you take the time necessary to manage your business. You cannot try to save money by doing everything yourself, including working the retail store, and then have the time to manage. We made a commitment to hire the appropriate number of employees necessary to run the store and allow us the time to manage our business.

5. Financing the purchase or the start-up costs of a business requires investment capital. There are many possibilities, but as an entrepreneur you will need financial assistance.

6. Read *The E Myth—Why Most Businesses Don't Work and What To Do About It* by Michael E. Gerber (Ballinger Publishing Company, Cambridge, Massachusetts, 02138).

Salary
Salary potential is unlimited.

Ali Swofford
Owner and Vice President for Sales and
    Marketing
Ladies First Sports Fashion, Inc.
Knoxville, Tennessee

Education
B.S., Physical Education, Oregon State
    University, 1971
M.A., Physical Education Administration,
    University of Southern California, 1972
Ph.D., Physical Education Athletic Administration, University of Southern
    California, 1973

Professional Experience

Playground Director, Water Safety Instructor, Program Director in recreation department during summers, Inglewood, California, 1967–1971

Graduate Assistant, University of Southern California, 1971–1973

Assistant Professor, Texas Woman's University, 1973–1975

Women's Athletic Director, University of Nebraska, (first full-time women's athletic director), 1975–1977

Founded Ladies First, 1977

Current Responsibilities

Ladies First is a manufacturer of women's athletic uniforms, warm-ups, and coaching apparel. The company was founded by myself and Harold Finley. Throughout my career as an athlete, coach, and athletic director, I never felt that there was a manufacturer dedicated strictly to the women's market. There was not enough style, enough attention given to patterns and fit, or enough input on the needs of the female athlete. As a result, Harold Finley and I decided that Ladies First could and would be such a line of products. An extensive business plan laid the foundation for financing and developing the company. The operation now involves more than sixty people on either commission or hourly payroll. Our sporting goods network consists of more than 500 accounts.

Business Expectations in Sport

It takes a lot of hard work, long hours, self-sacrifice, and total financial commitment to start your own business. Owning your own business does mean that you are your own boss. However, in order to succeed you must be willing to be more demanding of yourself than any employer would ever dream to be. At times your business must come before even your family.

I travel to trade shows, softball shows, coaches' clinics, national tournaments, meetings, and any other engagements that might benefit and promote Ladies First. As a result, I may be on the road 2 weeks, home 2 days, gone again for 10 days, and so forth. This may sound exciting, and at times it is; however, problems such as laundry, paying bills, spending time with people you care about, and having time for yourself are prevalent.

As for financial compensation, again sacrifice is the word. Suppliers must be paid, employees must be paid, and there are taxes, insurance, utilities, phone bills, and so forth. Then what is left can be your salary or you can put a good deal back into your business to help it grow. Of course, since you want your business to grow, you re-invest your monies into the business. Within a few years, one hopes, the financial picture will change.

Career Satisfaction

In the aforementioned paragraphs, I have painted a rather grim picture of starting one's own business. This was intentional. No one should go into a situation with stars in their eyes. However, the reward of conceiving an idea, working and struggling to develop it into reality, be accepted, work, and grow is awesome. The feelings of accomplishment are unparalleled. I do not believe these same feelings can be reached when working for someone else or for an organization. It is that inner feeling that overcomes the many sacrifices necessary and in the end brings about the statement, "If I had it to do over again I would make the same decision and again try to make my dreams reality."

Suggestions to Students

If you are interested in starting your own business, experiences and course work in finance, production, planning, personnel selection, product selection, marketing, pricing, advertising, cost analysis, bookkeeping, and receivable financing are highly recommended. You should seek help from the federal government (Small Business Administration), local people already in the same type of business, libraries, trade associations, retired persons from the field, chambers of commerce, and banks.

As an employer looking for new salespeople, these are some characteristics that I look for: a pleasant personality, knowledge of both athletics and garment construction, sincerity, and hardworking attitude, the ability to be a self-starter, and evidence of being responsible.

When looking for employees in product design, I look for knowledge of athletics, knowledge of commercial design, the ability to design a uniform that not only looks good but is functional, innovativeness, the ability to be a self-starter, cost-consciousness, knowledge of new fabrics, ideas about new methods of construction, good pattern-making skills, flexibility, and the ability to deal with customers who wish to design.

Salary

Salary ranges in these positions vary ($12,000 to $100,000) depending on experience in product design and the amount of sales for commissioned sales representatives.

Stan Mintz
Executive Fitness Director
Fluor Corporation
Irvine, California

Education

B.A., Physical Education, California State
University—Northridge
M.A., Physical Education (Administration
and Motor Performance) and Health and
Safety Education, California State
University—Northridge

Professional Experience

I taught physical education, driver education, and driver training for 5 years at Beverly Hills High School and 1 year at Victor Valley High School; coached varsity baseball and varsity football for 4 years at Beverly Hills High School and 1 year at Victor Valley High School, and also coached varsity baseball at Los Angeles City College for 1 year. I also worked 1 year as a physical therapy aide. Since 1979, I have been Executive Fitness Director at Fluor Corporation.

Personal Background in Sport and Physical Education

While attending college, my career objective was to teach and coach in the California school systems. I was fortunate in securing a position at Beverly Hills High School and enjoyed working with secondary-level students and athletes. I was always interested in physical fitness and motor development and attended a National Conference for Fitness Directors in Business and Industry to learn more about employee fitness programs. As a result of contacts made at this conference, I was offered a job as a fitness director in a company setting. This experience confirmed my interest in adult fitness and led to my current position as Executive Fitness Director for the Fluor Corporation in Irvine, California.

The teaching and coaching profession prepared me for my current position in important leadership areas necessary to run an effective and successful program. These include organization, communication, education and, most importantly, motivation. Physical therapy gave me experience working with my clientele who have had strokes, polio, joint operations, bypass surgery, and an assortment of "weekend warrior" injuries.

Current Responsibilities

As Executive Fitness Director, my responsibilities include the following:

1. Manage the operation of the Executive Fitness Center, including maintenance of equipment, purchase of supplies, and supervision of people
2. Provide direct continuing exercise information and supervision to individual executives with appropriate consideration of medical limitations
3. Develop plans and programs to maximize benefits for the fitness center
4. Keep informed of the current state of the art and maintain appropriate liaison with fitness-related organizations

Suggestions to Students

My major concern in interviewing prospective individuals is in the area of leadership qualities. Keys that I look for in an interview are: Is the person self-confident? Is the person extroverted? Is the person physically appealing? Is the person concerned for the individual? These keys, I have found, have a direct correlation with communicating, educating, and motivating.

For a career such as mine, I would suggest the following course work:

Anatomy and physiology
Human performance laboratory experience
Exercise physiology
Kinesiology
Care and prevention of athletic injuries
Public speaking
Weight training
Administration of physical education
Hands-on experience

Salary

Assistant staff: $16,000 to $28,000
Director: $22,000 to $45,000

Carmen O. Ness, H.S.D.
Vice President and Director of Government
   Relations, Managed Care Development
PacifiCare Health Systems
5995 Plaza Drive
Cypress, California 90630

Education

B.A., Physical Education with a minor in
   Biology, Buena Vista College, Storm
   Lake, Iowa, 1950
M.A., Physical Education, State University
   of Iowa, 1953
H.S.D., Health and Safety, Indiana University,
   Bloomington, Indiana, 1957

Professional Experience

Teacher, Football Coach, and Track Coach, Teacher's High School, Cedar
   Falls, Iowa, 1953–1955
Assistant and Associate Professor, Health and Safety, California State
   University—Long Beach, 1957–1962
Director of Athletics, Professor of Health Science, Central Missouri State
   University, Warrensburg, 1962–1964
Professor and Chairperson of Health Sciences, Western Illinois Univer-
   sity, Macomb, 1964–1968
Professor and Chairperson of Health Sciences, University of Utah, Salt
   Lake City, 1968–1970
Director of Postgraduate Education, University of Utah Medical School,
   Salt Lake City, 1970–1972
Dean, College of Health Related Professions, Wichita State University,
   Wichita, Kansas (directed fourteen health education programs),
   1972–1975
Associate Executive Director, Family Health Program, Fountain Valley,
   California, 1975–1978
Vice President of Marketing, HMO Concepts and California Health Plan,
   1978–1982
Vice President and Director of Government Relations, Managed Care
   Development, PacifiCare Health Systems, and Executive Director,
   Pacific Review Service, 1982 to present

Personal Background in Sport and Physical Education

My early experiences as an athletic coach, professor of health sciences, and college administrator were extremely important to make the transition from the academic world to business. The primary difference between business and academia is that while a professor, I was rewarded for mastering a body of knowledge and being effective in communicating this information to students, whereas in the business world, management gets paid for achieving satisfactory results from a business or management unit.

Current Responsibilities

PacifiCare Health Systems is a major health maintenance organization that provides health care to approximately 400,000 members in California, Oregon, Oklahoma, and Texas, with annual revenues of $650 million. Current responsibilities include government relations, product development, utilization management, and cost containment, which includes working with selected medical groups to improve management of quality health services.

During the last 3½ years, I served as Chief Executive Officer and Founder of Pacific Review Services, a subsidiary company now providing nationwide health care utilization management for 475,000 members. The program currently provides utilization management for Hartford Insurance Company, Columbia General Insurance, ITT Corporation, and numerous other companies. We are growing 15 to 20 percent annually. Health care management is an extremely dynamic industry, in which hard work, management skills, and human relations are extremely important.

Career Satisfaction and Future Prospects

Most of my career satisfaction has come from developing health programs and business units into successful entities. I personally feel stimulated by the dynamics of the business world, where opportunities are plentiful and the environment is ever-changing. The feelings of accomplishment are not much different from that of teaching, coaching, or academic administration, but the financial rewards are significantly improved.

Health and physical education majors could find many opportunities in the health care system. Health benefit programs are starting to require positive lifestyle changes in Americans in order to lower the cost of health care to corporations and individuals. Creative, hardworking, competitive, and flexible individuals could not only be stimulated by this environment but be amply rewarded financially.

Suggestions to Students

You should enjoy working with people and putting in long hours, if necessary, to establish and maintain a program.

Take elective course work in management and business.

Do volunteer work in a medical environment (clinic, hospital, health maintenance organization, etc.).

Keep your career objectives open.

Salary

Salaries vary depending on geographical location and job responsibilities. The range for a position of this nature is from $50,000 to $150,000. In addition, fringe benefits such as car allowance and other expenses are negotiable.

Bob Marley
Head Athletic Trainer
Houston Baptist University
Houston, Texas

Education

A.A., Southwestern Iowa Community College, Creston
B.S., Northwest Missouri State University, Maryville
M.A., Michigan State University, East Lansing

Professional Experience

I served as a student trainer at Northwest Missouri State University while studying toward my B.S. degree. I was certified by the National Athletic Trainer's Association (NATA) as an athletic trainer (ATC) the summer after graduation.

I was awarded a 2-year graduate assistantship as an athletic trainer at Michigan State University and worked with football, basketball, baseball, and track. Then I earned my M.A. in physical education with an emphasis in sports medicine. I assisted in teaching the laboratory portion of the undergraduate course of Care and Prevention of Athletic Injuries.

I was hired directly from Michigan State by Houston Baptist University as the Head Athletic Trainer and became licensed by the state of Texas as an athletic trainer (LAT). In 1987, I was named the male Teacher of the Year. I became a certified strength and conditioning specialist (CSCS) through the National Strength and Conditioning Association (NSCA) in 1988.

Personal Background in Sport and Physical Education

Like almost everyone born and raised in Nebraska, athletics became very important to me at an early age. Outside of my parents, my junior and senior high school coaches were the most influential people in my life. Professional athletes and coaches were my role models. After playing football and basketball, I got involved in athletic training my last 2 years of college. I jumped in with both feet and haven't regretted a minute of it.

I was very fortunate to have worked as a student trainer under an excellent head trainer in college. He took time to answer all my questions and teach me the intangible parts of training. He did everything possible to help me succeed. I feel it is very important for a student trainer to feel comfortable with the head trainer supervising him or her.

Current Responsibilities

I am responsible for 200 student athletes in fourteen intercollegiate sports at Houston Baptist University. As the head trainer, my duties are to provide for the care, treatment, and prevention of injuries and illnesses sustained by the athletes. I must work closely with the team physicians and other health care professionals to provide preparticipation physical examinations, first aid, evaluations, rehabilitation of surgical and nonsurgical injuries, and referrals to other providers. I am also responsible for the drug education and testing program at our institution. I teach kinesiology, care and prevention of athletic injuries, and weight training classes in the physical education department. All faculty members at Houston Baptist must also advise students as to what classes to take in order to attain their particular degrees, and I advise fifteen to twenty students per year.

I am responsible for filing the insurance claims for medical bills that arise from athletic injuries to the student athletes, and this probably requires the greater portion of my time.

In addition to my position as head trainer, I also serve as the strength and conditioning coach. This involves developing and administering tests and programs to improve the strength and conditioning levels of our athletes.

Future Prospects

Because of our society's infatuation with sports and fitness, the need for qualified athletic trainers will continue to grow in the future. High schools and sports medicine or rehabilitation clinics are the two areas where the most growth is being seen. Corporate fitness is a relatively new area for trainers and is increasing its demand for trainers. Professional teams have one or more trainers on staff, although this is a tougher area in which to become involved.

Suggestions to Students

In order to be a successful trainer, you must be flexible and willing to work long hours. I suggest you start by becoming a student trainer in high school to best prepare yourself for a college position. It is always a wise idea to visit several colleges you are interested in attending and to talk with the student trainers. They can give you the best sense of whether that school is the best for you. I feel it is important to investigate college student trainer positions early in your senior year of high school if you are looking for some type of financial aid in return for working as a student trainer.

If you are planning to become a certified athletic trainer, you will need to work as a student trainer under a certified athletic trainer for a minimum of 2 years prior to taking NATA's certification examination. Some states also require you to be licensed by that state in order to work as a trainer.

When I recruit a student trainer at Houston Baptist University, I look for loyalty, honesty, dependability, an eagerness to learn, experience as a high school trainer, above-average grades, leadership abilities, good communication skills, a friendly personality, and good common sense. These are traits most head trainers want in their students, and individuals that can display these characteristics will be rewarded with scholarships and other financial aid.

Suggested course work for athletic trainers includes the following:

Required
Human anatomy
Human physiology

Physiology of exercise
Applied anatomy, or kinesiology
Psychology
First aid and cardiopulmonary resuscitation (CPR)
Nutrition
Adapted physical education
Personal, community, or school health
Basic athletic training
Advanced athletic training

Recommended
Physics
Pharmacology
Histology
Pathology
Organization and administration of health and physical education
Psychology of coaching
Coaching techniques
Chemistry
Tests and measurements

Salary

Assistant trainer: $13,000 to $20,000
Head trainer: $18,000 to $40,000

Linda Kempfe
Outdoor Education Teacher
Houston, Texas

Education

Teaching Certificate, All-Level Certification,
  Texas A&M University, 1973
B.S., Health and Physical Education, Texas
  A&M University, 1973
M.S., Health and Physical Education, Texas
  A&M University, 1976

Professional Experience

Camp Counselor and Horseback Instructor for seven summers at Camp
  Olympia, Trinity, Texas

Elementary Physical Education Teacher in the Northeast Independent
  School District, San Antonio, Texas

Aerobic Dance Instructor in the Northeast Independent School District;
  YMCA Camp Cullen-Wilderness Trip Camping, Trinity, Texas; and
  Outdoor Education Center Teacher, Houston Independent School
  District, Trinity, Texas

Personal Background in Sport and Physical Education

I was raised by parents who believed being outside and being physically
active was most important. As a child, I was introduced to wilderness
camping and all the recreational aspects that go along with it. It instilled
an appreciation for the outdoors, wildlife, and our environment.

I was active in all sports and developed a special interest in animals,
especially horses. College summers were spent with a recreational camp
supervising counselors and campers. I became involved in the horseback program and worked to increase my knowledge concerning their
health and physical fitness.

After graduating with a B.S. in Health and Physical Education, I taught
elementary P.E. for 2 years, then made the decision to go back for a
master's degree. This is where I found a lot of freedom in the course
work. I was able to pick up courses in recreation, forestry, animal
science, and wildlife biology.

My decision to change to outdoor education came when I realized that
I could fulfill all my interests working for an outdoor education center.
My interests include being surrounded by nature, teaching, and work-
ing with students and animals while using the outdoors as a classroom.

Current Responsibilities

I am employed for the Houston Independent School District's Outdoor
Education Program located near Trinity, Texas. I am the resource teacher
at the Model Farm Program. My responsibilities include the selection
and development of activities that are safe and educational. They also
allow plenty of hands-on experiences. However, my major responsibility is to teach both staff and children the various activities within this
program.

Career Satisfaction and Future Prospects

One of the rewards of working in an outdoor education program is the
teaching environment in which one works. Within this environment
you can apply the basic concepts in a more practical way. An outdoor
educator can use the environment as a tool for relating the students'

experiences to each and every discipline. The children you work with are active and interested because it holds so many mysteries for them. An outdoor educator has the responsibility of making the students aware of their importance and role toward the total environment. The satisfaction of giving students information and hands-on experiences makes me feel I have contributed to our Good Earth.

People today have a growing interest and concern for our environment. In the past years, there has been a trend to clean up the environment and save our natural resources. This has opened the door for outdoor education because the basic concepts of our natural environment can be taught at all levels. As long as there is a concern and interest for our environment there will be outdoor education programs.

Teaching the basic concepts outdoors offers unique educational opportunities. It extends and enriches classroom curricula while offering more hands-on, multisensory, and discovery experiences. Students as well as teachers can develop the appreciation needed for our environment while working for an outdoor education program.

Suggestions to Students

There are usually structured programs to follow for a physical education major. Most of the time a student may select electives that could strengthen areas of interest. Outside experiences during the school year and summer are important so that interest areas are developed. Programs working with children, nature, and animals are among several that will best prepare you for a later teaching assignment at an outdoor education center.

Salary

Certified outdoor education teachers are paid on the same salary scale as classroom teachers in a school district ($15,000+). The salary of outdoor educators in a private facility will vary depending on the number of months employed, number of children served, amount of administrative work, and the funding source ($12,000 to $25,000+ plus room and board).

Donald Bingham
Corporate Director of Health and Fitness
Greater Boston Young Men's Christian
  Association
Cambridge, Massachusetts

Education

B.S., Northeastern University, Boston,
  Massachusetts
YMCA Certification, Springfield College

Professional Experience

I worked 7 years as a first-class lineman for a power company before pursuing the career I really desired. I was married with three children, and the decision to go to college as a full-time student was a family commitment. As an undergraduate, I worked my way through school as a mason and a carpenter. These skills now help me with my maintenance responsibilities at the YMCA. I was employed after graduation at the YMCA in Brockton, Massachusetts. During my 10 years there, I worked my way from Assistant Physical Director to Fitness Director, Program Director, and eventually to Director of the Fitness Department. In 1975, I became Executive Director of the New London, Connecticut, YMCA. In January 1982, I assumed the position of Corporate Director of Health and Fitness at the Greater Boston YMCA.

Current Responsibilities

As Corporate Director of Health and Fitness, I am responsible for the staff leadership of the health and fitness programs in all branches of the Greater Boston YMCA and the direct supervisor of all facets of the program at the central branch. The position requires technical expertise in the development and delivery of health and fitness programs and services, budget management, facility management, understanding organizational dynamics, hiring and supervising staff, and experience in working with professionals in related health fields.

Future Prospects

I believe that the future in the YMCA holds a great deal of potential. I also believe that some jobs have yet to be designed. For example, a career as a health counselor may become quite common. This person would set up a practice that would deliver counseling and lifestyle skills to a clientele that depends on the counselor for preventive health needs to take a load off the medical community. This position may become identified as "risk factor analysis" or "lifestyle counseling."

Suggestions to Students

If you are interested in a career with the YMCA, I suggest that you consider the following:

1. Examine your personality—especially how you feel about people and how you get along with others.
2. You will need to be a role model consistent with your job. If you are counseling people about cardiovascular risk factors, you cannot be a smoker, overweight, and unfit.
3. You need to be neat and clean or you won't go far.
4. As an undergraduate, take advantage of all opportunities. Volunteer experiences in the community will give you some insight into related YMCA/YWCA work.
5. The work hours in the YMCA are not always convenient as you have the opportunity to respond to the needs of people. However, you can set your working hours dependent on your program responsibility, and your family can join you.

When I hire employees, I look at an applicant's work experiences and college background. I am interested in the type of electives that people choose to complement their education. I look for people who have a good track record in dealing with others. I can always teach them to be a technician. Other items that I look for are applicants who are trim, well groomed, confident in their abilities, sincerely acknowledge personal limitation, and who have an honest concern for people.

Salary

YMCA salaries are competitive with teaching and private health clubs and spas.

Beginning: $15,000 to $18,000
Aquatic program director: $13,000 to $16,000
Corporate assistant fitness program director: $17,000 +

Tony Donatelli
High School Physical Education Teacher
   and Coach
Uxbridge High School
Uxbridge, Massachusetts

Education
B.S., Physical Education, Boston University

Professional Experience
Elementary Physical Education Teacher, Wallingford, Connecticut, 1958–1961
High School Physical Education Teacher and Coach, Uxbridge, Massachusetts, 1961 to present

Personal Background in Sport and Physical Education
As a high school athlete, I participated in football, basketball and baseball. After high school, I joined the navy. It was during my experience with the navy that I decided to pursue a career in physical education. The officer in charge of physical training made a strong impact on me.

Following graduation from Boston University, I accepted a position as the elementary physical education instructor for the Wallingford, Connecticut, schools. At that time, they had ten elementary schools. I taught in two schools per day in order to cover all ten each week.

At the end of my third year, I received a call from the athletic director at my alma mater in Uxbridge. I accepted his offer to return to the high school to teach and coach. I have never regretted returning to my hometown and spending the rest of my educational career here. Throughout my tenure, I have continued to learn new activities to improve my classes so that they are enjoyable and that the students feel they are learning. I have also coached all our major sports and put on gymnastic shows for the community. We are a small school so the sports offerings are limited to football, basketball, and baseball.

I have stayed in Uxbridge because I really enjoyed the staff within the entire school. Kids have not basically changed. I have enjoyed working with youngsters that I have known all their lives, as well as their parents. I did not stay for money but for the enjoyment of teaching. When I began to coach, I spent 3 to 4 extra hours per day at school. As I became more experienced, I was able to reduce that to about 2 hours per day.

When I retire, I hope that my former students can say that (1) I was fair, (2) I cared about all of them, and (3) I avoided using physical education class as a way to coerce boys into playing athletics. I believe that you can be a friend to your students as well as maintain their respect.

Future Prospects

I believe that physical education is in crisis. We are suffering from a lack of identity. The coeducational program is part of the problem. The need has not been accurately defined or appropriately placed in the total picture of the physical education program. During my years of teaching, we have not progressed in importance to the general curriculum. If I hadn't had such a long tenure within my school, my program could have suffered some serious setbacks.

Suggestions to Students

We need strong people who are willing to work with the legislators to keep physical education a mandatory curriculum requirement. We need to make physical education classes enjoyable and relevant to daily life. High school programs need teachers who have a variety of skills and who are open to learning new activities. High schools of our size do not need specialists but generalists who can teach a wide variety of skills.

As a teacher and as a person, the best advice I can give is:

Be yourself.
Be fair.
Be consistent.
Do not compromise your principles to be liked by students. Students
    can easily detect a phony.
Make sure you like teenagers.

Salary

Base salaries vary from state to state. Most states begin at $16,000 to $18,000 per year plus additional monies for coaching.

David E. Yanai
Head Basketball Coach and Physical
    Education Professor
California State University—Dominguez
    Hills
Carson, California

Education

B.A., Physical Education, California State
    University—Long Beach, 1967

Professional Experience

Head Baseball Coach and Teacher (math), Fremont High School, Los
    Angeles, California, 1967–1969
Head Basketball Coach and Teacher (physical education), Fremont High
    School, 1969–1976
Head Basketball Coach and Teacher (biology), Gardena High School,
    Gardena, California, 1976–1977
Head Basketball Coach and Professor (physical education), California
    State University—Dominguez Hills, Carson, 1977 to present

Personal Background in Sport and Physical Education

As a youngster I participated in a variety of sports, deriving many enjoyable experiences. These positive experiences were due mainly to the
excellent coaches for whom I played and the fine people I met as a young
athlete. These coaches and people exemplified the best in sports and
athletics, and it is without doubt that these experiences are what influenced me to select teaching and coaching as a profession. I have never
regretted that decision.

Current Responsibilities

My responsibilities at California State University—Dominguez Hills are
twofold. First, as Head Basketball Coach, I am responsible for developing a competitive and respected basketball team. This involves being
in charge of recruiting, fund raising, scheduling, and the management
of resources. My second area of responsibility is that of an instructor
in the physical education department. I have a teaching load of three
classes in the fall, three classes in the winter, and six classes in the
spring.

Career Satisfaction and Future Prospects

The teaching and coaching profession has been very good to me and has allowed me to provide a very comfortable living for my family. But beyond the comfortable living, I feel the true reward in coaching is the satisfaction one derives in seeing young people develop into positive young adults. We as coaches not only teach technical aspects in a specific sport but have the opportunity to teach proper attitudes in fulfilling their needs of future interests. It is a great feeling to know you had some influence on a young person making a success of himself or herself. My philosophy has always been and always will be to move young people in a positive direction through the athletic experience.

Because we live in a society that is very sports conscious and athletics oriented, we will always have the need for good coaches and teachers. Certainly, the job prospects of the near future are as good as ever with the expansion of more teams and sports, especially in the area of women's sports. If you have the educational qualifications and are willing to be totally dedicated and willing to make the necessary sacrifices, then I say the future looks very bright.

Suggestions to Students

I believe there are a number of qualifications that you must possess or obtain if you are to go into coaching as a profession. First, you must obtain the educational background (credentials and degrees) necessary to obtain teaching and coaching positions. Second, you must obtain as much technical knowledge as possible through reading updated literature, attending clinics, and speaking to other coaches in your profession. Third, it is helpful that you observe good health principles and develop an acceptable standard of motor skill. Last, and perhaps most important, I believe you must have a genuine concern for the young people you teach or coach.

Salary

Salaries range from $25,000 to $100,000 and up. College coaching positions can be very lucrative if one includes extra benefits such as appearing on television shows or having housing and transportation provided.

Bobby Pope
Sports Information Director and Associate
   Vice President of University Relations
   and Development
Mercer University
Macon, Georgia

Education

B.S., Health, Physical Education, and Recreation, Georgia College, Milledgeville, Georgia

Professional Experience

Reporter, WMAZ Radio Television, Macon, Georgia, 1964–1970
Sports Director, WMAZ Radio Television, 1970–1977
Account Executive, WMAZ Radio Television, 1977–1985
Sports Information Director, Mercer University, 1980 to present
Associate Vice President, University Relations and Development, Mercer University, 1985 to present

Personal Background in Sport and Physical Education

As a student in high school in Thomaston, Georgia, I participated in football and track. While in college I played tennis but was never the "big" athlete. However, I loved all aspects of sport and enjoyed following team statistics with sports broadcasters. I decided that I wanted to be associated with the sports world in the capacity of providing information to others.

Current Responsibilities

As Sports Information Director, I am responsible for all the public relations activities of the athletic department. I supervise the development of all brochures and am responsible for all photography. I serve as the school liaison for all the media: newspaper reporters, radio broadcasters, and television reporters. I occasionally fill in as radio announcer for games. As needed, I develop additional public relations programs.

Career Satisfaction

There is a great deal of satisfaction working with young people. It is exciting to see them strive for their goals even if they do not become league champions. I am one who believes the experience is the key, while winning and losing are secondary in the final analysis.

The potential for extended liaisons within the college community is exciting. My position has evolved to being the information director for the university as well, as the Associate Vice President for University Relations and Development.

Suggestions to Students

There must be a great deal of time invested when working in the area of sports information. It necessitates some travel with the teams, attendance at home athletic events (I broadcast local radio coverage), and paperwork in the development of sports brochures and compilation of statistics. This requires doing a lot of work at home.

I feel the best way for any individual to learn is through on-the-job experience, and I would strongly suggest internships. For additional information, I recommend that you contact the following sports information directors:

Claude Felton, University of Georgia, Athens, Georgia
Mike Hubbard, Auburn University, Auburn, Alabama
Joe Dier, Mississippi State University, Starkville, Mississippi

Salary

Salary varies tremendously with the size of the school, division of the NCAA to which the athletic department belongs, number of sports offered, budget, location of the school, and alumni support.

Denise Katnich
Co-Owner
A-Plus Body

Education

University of Arizona, Tucson, 1975–1977
B.A., Physical Education (emphasis in adult
    fitness and physiology of exercise),
    California State University—Long Beach,
    1977–1979

Personal Background in Sport and Physical Education

A former nationally rated gymnast, I've had a positive attitude about physical activity since childhood. I competed in the 1974 Junior Olym-

pic Invitational in Mexico City. I was ranked fifth in the all-around competition and second for the United States Team. I also ranked ninth in
the nation at the 1976 Collegiate Nationals. Traveling throughout the
country, I was offered twenty-one scholarships and chose the University of Arizona.

Current Responsibilities

With the understanding that physical fitness is essential to good health,
I am dedicated to the teaching and promoting of all aspects of physical
education. As co-owner of A-Plus Body, I direct and operate a full spectrum of health and fitness activities for eleven various businesses, hospitals, and private health enterprises throughout southern California.
Health and fitness activities include the following:

1. Aerobic Workout—cardiovascular conditioning
2. Fitness Over—designed for those older than 40, overweight, or over-
   due for exercise
3. Body Revival—especially designed exercises to keep muscles and
   joints in working condition for the senior adult
4. Pre- and Post-Natal Conditioning—exercises to keep flexible and fit
   for an easy labor and quick recovery
5. Stress Reduction/Healthy Back—program to relieve tension through
   stretching and relaxation techniques
6. Physiological Tests—fitness testing such as body fat composition,
   vital capacity, heart response to exercise; evaluate, design, and instruct individualized exercise program
7. Stretching Clinics—prerun stretching and motivational warm-ups for
   participants in 10 K marathon

As a result of my work in fitness programs for the aging, I was appointed
to serve as a consultant and clinician in 1981 on the President's Council on Physical Fitness and Sport. My services included lectures, demonstrations, and training programs. I am involved with the National
Conference on Fitness and Aging, in which I have designed an exercise
program for senior citizens.

Career Satisfaction

While my basic premise is to teach people in the mechanics of exercise, I strive to motivate and encourage "every body" so that they enjoy
all the benefits that exercise affords. This is very rewarding to me.

Suggestions to Students

Keep all alternatives to your professional career open. During my undergraduate years, operating my own business never entered my mind.

Salary

$20.00 or more per hour.

William "Ed" Ratleff
Former Professional Basketball Player,
  Houston Rockets
Assistant Men's Basketball Coach
California State University—Long Beach
Long Beach, California

Education

B.S., Physical Education, California State
  University—Long Beach, 1981

Professional Experience

Professional basketball player for five seasons with the Houston Rockets
  of the National Basketball Association, 1973–1978
Assistant coach of women's basketball at California State University—
  Long Beach, 1979–1980
Assistant coach of women's basketball at University of Southern California, 1980–81
Head coach of women's basketball at California State University–Long
  Beach, 1981–82
Assistant basketball coach of men's team at California State University–Long Beach, 1982

Personal Background in Sports and Physical Education

As a child, I grew up in Ohio. I lived my first twelve years in a small
city outside of Dayton named Bellefontaine. This is where I learned all
about winning and losing. I played baseball from the age of six until
college. When I was twelve, my mother remarried and our family moved
to Columbus, Ohio. I continued to play baseball, but when I was a seventh grader basketball entered my life though my mind was set on being
a pro baseball player. My future changed from baseball to basketball
after I entered high school. I attended Columbus East High School. . . .

Our record there was seventy wins and one loss. Basketball had now moved in front of baseball.

I entered Long Beach State University in 1969 and finished my college career in 1973. In 1972 I played on the Olympic team. After my eligibility was completed in 1973, I was drafted in the first round by the Houston Rockets. Professional basketball was an exciting career with many rewards. The salary was excellent and it took me to all parts of the United States. However, after much success as a player I injured my back and my career as a professional basketball player was over. I am glad I had an alternate career to turn to when this occurred.

Current Responsibilities

I assist in player recruiting, development, and team management. I also teach physical education classes. I plan to get our players more involved with their school work. A major problem is that athletes often do not complete a program leading to a degree. This is something I would like to change. It is something that will take time and hopefully can be accomplished in the near future.

Career Satisfaction

I have coached women's basketball for three years and feel it has been a most valuable experience. Moving into men's basketball coaching is a challenge and what I have always wanted. Someday I hope to become a head coach somewhere—who knows, maybe even at my alma mater.

Suggestions to Students

Keep an open mind to all your coaches and teachers. A student should remember that there is more than one way to teach. College coaching is tough because it is not enough to help your players grow to be nice young men and women. The team must win in order for the coach to keep his job. The pressure is always there.

Future Prospects

There will always be a need for coaching at all levels and the prospect looks good for those willing to dedicate themselves to many hours of hard work and who enjoy working with the physically gifted.

Opportunities in professional sports are limited to a select few. If you are fortunate and have the talent, it is an exciting career. However, playing time may be terminated quickly by injury or new player personnel. One should always have a back-up career.

Current Salaries

Professional Athlete: $30,000–$1,000,000 +
Coach: $15,000–$50,000

Student Activities

1. Identify a professional in the school setting. Visit for a day. List the career responsibilities as you see them. How well do they match up with your career objective?
2. Visit a local professional in a nonschool environment. Discuss the job or position according to your lifestyle expectations.
3. List all of the physical education career-related professions that exist in your community.
4. Develop a list of career-related experiences (volunteer and salaried) that are available to enrich your undergraduate experience.

15. Selecting a Career Path

Chapter Outline

Career Objectives
Self-Assessment
Career Differences
Course of Study
Branches of Your Career Path
Personal Marketability
Student Activities
Suggested Readings

Objectives

Chapter 15 is designed to enable you to:

- Determine your personal strengths.
- Discover your personal accomplishments.
- Develop your career objectives relevant to your personal strengths and interests.
- Select a course of study that will maximize your potential.

YOU should now begin to develop plans for your career path. The longer you wait to examine your career objectives and design a realistic path to follow, the greater are your chances of missing potential opportunities in the human movement profession.

Your career path should be designed to provide you with opportunities to analyze your skills and interests as they relate to your career objective. The earlier chapters in this book have given you an overview of our multifaceted discipline. Each component will be examined further in your course of study as a physical education major. However, you will also have the chance to study more extensively those components that are more attractive to you or appear more relevant to your career path.

It is important to remember that a career path is based on your skills and interests but should remain flexible to adapt to changes in your future. The longer you procrastinate in developing a career path, the greater the chance of missing good opportunities because you have not properly prepared yourself. In the previous chapters, discussions concerning the influence your future occupation will have on your lifestyle and the explanations of the foundations of physical education have provided a conceptual framework for the development of your career path.

Career Objectives

Where do you want to be in 10 years or 20? At retirement, on what accomplishments would you like to look back that reflect your strengths? You should already be able to cite at least five accomplishments. You might say, "But I haven't achieved anything yet!" However, everyone has had many experiences throughout life in which they have been successful. The settings for these accomplishments could include, but are not limited to, your home or school, social, church, or community activities, work, or athletics. How you believe others perceive you and your achievements is not important. What is important is the way *you* feel about what you have done.

When you have done something well, enjoyed doing it, and were proud of it, you maximized your strengths. Your past accomplishments illustrate your strengths in action and are important in planning your career path. List your five best accomplishments and the information requested for each accomplishment in Table 15.1. Consider your unique accomplishments. The core of the self-assessment process is identifying the strengths that created your accomplishments. Referring back to Table 15.1, the strengths illustrated by the results of the team cap-

Table 15.1 Personal Accomplishments

CONDITION BEFORE YOUR EFFORT	ACCOMPLISHMENT (WHAT YOU DID)	SPECIFIC RESULTS	STRENGTHS
Example			
Apathy on the team.	As team captain, I held team meetings without coaches and pulled the team together.	Majority of players put forth greater effort; we won 50% of games.	
1.			
2.			
3.			
4.			
5.			

tain's efforts could include perception, problem solving, organization, leadership, persuasion, or empathy.

Review the strengths that contributed to your five accomplishments. If you examine them closely, your strengths will probably cluster in several areas. These areas are the important ones to match up with an appropriate career path. If your strengths cluster around planning, persuasion, and being empathetic, teaching may be part of your career path. If management, marketing, and challenge are major strengths, then managing or owning your own health spa, racquet club, or sporting goods business may be branches of your career path worth considering. Can you think of any other suggested career choices that could be added to the list in Table 15.2?

In developing your career objective, you need information. This information is obtained from self-assessment, advice, course work, and professional experiences. Before going any further, from your readings to date and general perceptions of your career and lifestyle needs, write down your current career objective. This objective will be used as a reference for further self-assessment and career path development. For example, your career objectives may be to become an athletic trainer for a professional team in 10 years or to be a specialist at a major university in the field of perceptual motor development of young children in 15 years. Your career objective must reflect you, not someone else's plan for you.

Table 15.2 Personal Strengths and Careers in Human Movement

STRENGTHS	SUGGESTED CAREERS
Analysis	Teacher, coach
Perception	Scientific researcher, sports psychologist, professional sports scout
Observation	Teacher, coach, judge
Problem solving	Coach, sports club director, department chairperson, administrator
Planning	Teacher, coach, administrator
Organizing	Equipment manager, recreation supervisor
Clerical ability	Athletic director, sports statistician
Management	Director of physical education, health spa, or tennis club
Leadership	Coach, department chairperson
Administration	Director of YMCA, YWCA
Creativity	Teacher, coach, administrator
Imagination	Sportswear designer, teacher
Codification	Coach, athletic director
Artistic ability	Sports artist
Homemaking	Health food store staff; sportswear designer
Agriculture	Greenskeeper
Building	Pool designer
Operation	Camp director
Persuasion	Player agent
Marketing	Sporting goods salesperson
Arbitration	Sport lawyer, athletic administrator
Relating	Umpire, sports information director
Exploration	Sports business, sports tour guide (golf, skiing, tennis, fishing, hunting)
Challenge	Wilderness school teacher
Recognition	Professional athlete
Sympathetic demeanor	Athletic trainer, physical therapist
Empathetic demeanor	Coach, health spa director

Your career objective should include your skills and interests, your lifestyle expectations, your prospective professional contributions, and your retirement expectations. For the young, retirement seems far away and irrelevant. However, retirement from one career to pursue another is occurring often, and people are retiring earlier in life. It is projected that by the year 2030, more than half the population will be 40 years old or older. Early retirement at that point will be the norm, not the exception.

Self-Assessment

Assessing one's strengths and weaknesses is the key to finding the best match between one's unique qualities and an appropriate career path. Our real strengths equal our abilities plus our interests. Self-assessment is a positive process that should continue throughout one's lifetime to help determine when it is time to modify or cease our work routine.

In determining your best fit in the career marketplace, accentuate the strengths that you currently have as well as the strengths you have the potential to develop further. Remember that your attitude is extremely important. Ask yourself: "Where can my skills contribute the most to the profession? How can I use my skills and interest in sports to help others and still earn a good salary?" Avoid the negative! Never say to yourself or others, "But I can't do that" or "I'll never be able to learn enough to qualify for that position" or "Only the lucky land those jobs!"

People who have a realistic perception of their strengths, accept themselves as they are, and plan accordingly to maximize their potential are the ones who reap the rewards of a satisfying career. You have the opportunity to be such a person if you begin the assessment and planning process now.

Everyone has abilities—those things that we do and do well. We also have interests, those things that we find exciting or enjoyable. Most importantly, we all have personal strengths, abilities that are motivated by our interests. Our strengths are those things that we do well and enjoy doing, which make each of us unique.

To develop a career path, it is necessary to determine your strengths. This is best done by first considering those achievements in your life that have provided personal and career-related satisfaction and benefit to yourself and others around you (teammates, family, fellow workers, employers). Accomplishments improve as a result of your attitude about your work.

Reexamine the career objective you just developed. What strengths (abilities plus interests) are needed in your career objective? Do the strengths you discovered in your personal accomplishments match the strengths needed in your career objective? If these strengths appear closely related, you may be on the right path for your unique strengths, career objective, and lifestyle expectations. If there is a large discrepancy between your assessed strengths and your career objective, reexamine your career objective to see if there are some alternative but related career options that would maximize your strengths. This is an opportunity to redirect yourself to a more appropriate and satisfying career. Do not be discouraged. Remember the student teacher who completed 4 years of course work only to discover as a student teacher that she did not have the patience to work with children all day, day after day.

An important step in career planning is to get advice. Take your list of accomplishments and strengths to your adviser, to a career counselor, or to other professionals in related careers, and actively listen to their perceptions of you and your strengths. Someone may suggest an alternative that you have yet to consider but that might be an appropriate match for you.

Career Differences

Careers differ in three major ways. First, the actual work involved varies from rote tasks to creative experimentation. The actual work is directly related to your abilities or potential to develop those abilities. Second, the unique rewards of a position vary intensely, from the joy of seeing a child in a wheelchair score his or her first two points in a basketball game to an athletic administrator making a $40,000 or more annual salary. The rewards are symbolic of your interests and motivation in your work. A third difference is the type of co-workers with whom you associate both on the job and in leisure activities. Those whose careers revolve around children have personalities and motivations that differ from those in sport businesses and adult fitness clubs. Competition, recognition, and status vary in sport-related occupations and influence the working environment. Your career path should be designed to optimize your personal needs concerning the actual work involved, unique rewards, and the type of co-workers you prefer.

Course of Study

Thus far, you have developed a career objective that includes personal professional contributions and lifestyle expectations. You have recognized your five greatest accomplishments and have listed the personal strengths that supported your accomplishments. Then, you compared your career objective with your assessed strengths. Following this, you obtained advice from significant professionals and personal acquaintances to further your career path expectations.

The career path is not designed to lead to only one goal at the end. As Figure 15.1 shows, the path should lead to many career options. It is designed as a continuing journey that provides alternatives which maximize your potential. As you plan your coursework with your ad-

Figure 15.1 Planning a Personal Career Path

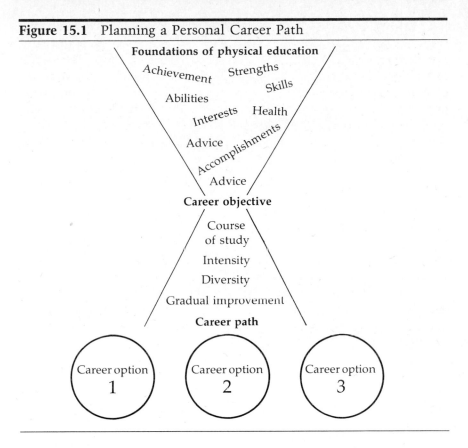

viser, explore as many options as possible within the framework of your college or university. Every institution has a set of general education requirements and a department that determines the criteria for course work in the physical education major. Owing to the vastness of the discipline, the opportunity to take electives is often limited but varies from institution to institution. You and your adviser should work together to develop a course plan that provides the following: (1) intensity in at least one area, (2) diversity to accommodate change, and (3) gradual improvement as a young professional.

It is important to develop higher skills in at least one area that exemplifies your greatest strengths and interests. Perhaps specializing in teaching dance is your major objective; however, if dance is your only skill, you may be severely limiting yourself. The ability to teach or coach several different activities may increase your marketability. You may

Working closely with an adviser can assist you in achieving your educational goals.

decide that you would like to specialize in teaching and coaching at the secondary level to develop high levels of skill. Then, to maximize your potential, you might select some basic business courses that would help you transfer your sport skills to the business sector. Change in careers is less stressful if you plan your undergraduate years well. The third dimension is to plan for gradual improvement in all areas. It is impossible to learn in your undergraduate course work all that you will need for a lifetime. Additional diversity or specialization may occur in graduate school or on the job. Extracurricular experiences during your undergraduate years can contribute significantly to professional development. Attending conferences, classes, and workshops also can contribute not only to an increase in skills and knowledge but to an awareness of current affairs in the profession. Perhaps most importantly, through such activities you will meet other professionals who may influence your career path. Volunteering to assist in related career opportunities or part-time jobs in coaching, recreational agencies, and business will gradually improve your professional awareness and growth.

Branches of Your Career Path

As you begin to travel the path toward your career, you will discover many branching paths leading off to either side. You will have to make a decision every time you reach such a fork in the road. The outcome for divergent paths will not always be the same. Opportunities will present themselves only if you have the proper credentials. The successfully designed career path will provide you with the credentials for several careers. Once the opportunities exist, you will have to decide whether to pursue the alternative. The ability to make choices is becoming increasingly important to obtaining lifelong career satisfaction.

Personal Marketability

The more you have to offer an employer, the more marketable you will be. You want to be the solution to someone's problem or need. Your marketability as someone's solution is the product of careful planning and hard work.

The next few chapters will explore in greater detail careers in physical education and sport. After studying these chapters, remember to review your career objective. A new alternative may match your abilities and prove very interesting. Your objective should be flexible enough to include several options for your assessed strengths. As you read the chapters about careers, read with an open mind and explore the possibilities that await you in our exciting profession. Career planning is fun and should remain fun throughout your career.

Student Activities

1. Select a partner. Answer the following questions and exchange written responses. Give each other advice regarding career choices based on the other's written responses.
   a. List five factors, activities, or responsibilities that you believe should be included in your ideal career.
   b. In your latest course work, activity, or work, what did you do best and enjoy most?
   c. What activities give you the most pleasure when you are not at work?
   d. In what part of the country do you plan to pursue a career?
   e. What is the annual salary you are expecting for your job?

2. Write your career objective, accomplishments, and strengths. Review them at the end of the semester and note any changes in your perception.

Suggested Readings

Fordham, S. L., and C. A. Lest. 1978. *Physical education and sports: an introduction to alternative careers.* New York: Wiley, pp. 63–78.

Keen, S. 1981. Lovers vs. workers. *Quest 81.* Sept: 14–17.

Roth, P., et al. 1981. Great teachers remembered. *Quest 81.* Sept: 25–30.

Seahill, J. L. 1988. New P.E. career options—time for assessment. *Journal of Physical Education, Recreation and Dance* May/June: 62–64.

16. Professional Responsibility

Chapter Outline

Membership Goals
American Alliance for Health, Physical Education, Recreation
    and Dance
Special Membership Organizations
State Coaches' Associations
National Intramural and Recreational Sports Association
American College of Sports Medicine
Association for Fitness in Business
President's Council on Physical Fitness and Sport
Personal Professional Factors
Public Relations and Public Information
Student Activities
Suggested Readings

Objectives

Chapter 16 is designed to enable you to:

- Develop an attitude of professionalism.
- Become familiar with the national professional organizations
  for physical education.
- Be aware of the variety of special interest associations and
  agencies within the physical education profession.

P ROFESSIONALISM is an assumable trait of the true educator or activity director. Whether one is involved in health, physical education, recreation, dance, athletics, safety, business and industrial fitness, or other creative ventures, it is important to maintain a tie and give support to the appropriate professional organization.

Today one can choose from a variety of organizations, many of which support the same concepts or have shared interests and responsibility. These questions always arise when considering a membership in a professional organization: Should I join? Which one should I join? Can I afford to join? What will it do for me? As a student, your choice is simple. The question should be, "How can I join a student organization for professionals?" Professionalism is an attitude that you should begin to develop while still a student. Students should want to become members of an appropriate professional organization and learn as much about their future career as possible.

The professional student is one who reads journals regularly, attends conferences, volunteers to help at conventions, and participates in local professional programs. The values of these experiences cannot be underestimated. The students who become members and are truly committed to their chosen profession are provided with opportunities to meet leaders in the field, to obtain the latest information regarding research in their area, and to see how such information can be applied to practical situations. Through professional contacts, the fire of enthusiasm is kindled in the aspiring professional.

However, professionalism is more than becoming a member of an organization. This first level of involvement shows minimal support and provides the member with publications that can offer the latest information on material presentation, position statements, and professional meetings. The second level of participation should find one attending clinics, conferences and conventions where an interchange of ideas can take place and questions can be asked of those making presentations. The third level of professional involvement is to serve the selected organization actively as a conference presenter or office. This level provides an opportunity to express personal concerns, relate research, and serve the profession in the highest manner. Many well-known leaders in selected fields of study are commonly found among the office or founding members of professional organizations.

Membership Goals

Your first step now is to join your student organization. If your institution does not have an active student organization, take the initiative by seeking an enthusiastic faculty sponsor with whom you can work toward developing an active unit. This will satisfy your need to belong and become a part of the profession. It is your responsibility to meet this minimum requirement in the early stages of your college career. If you are uncertain about how to achieve this goal, consult your faculty adviser. Only in this manner will it be possible for your name to appear on future rosters as a leader in your chosen field. Once you become employed in the field, you should become a member of the appropriate local, state, and national organizations and become involved in special professional groups that reflect your job responsibilities and personal interests.

American Alliance for Health, Physical Education, Recreation and Dance

The American Alliance for Health, Physical Education, Recreation and Dance (AAHPERD) is a nonprofit organization representing professionals in physical education, sports and athletics, health and safety education,

National headquarters of the American Alliance for Health, Physical Education, Recreation and Dance (AAHPERD), Reston, Virginia.

recreation and leisure services, and dance. Today's AAHPERD has as its members more than 40,000 teachers, administrators, researchers, coaches, students, and others.

The AAHPERD was founded in 1885 as the Association for the Advancement of Physical Education. This original organization was initiated by a group of approximately 60 men and women who were called together by Dr. William G. Anderson, M.D., a faculty member of the Adelphi Academy, Brooklyn, New York. The first president of the organization was Edward Hitchcock, M.D. Vice presidents were Edward P. Thwing, Ph.D., Miss H. C. Putnam, and D. A. Sargent, M.D. William Anderson, M.D., was the secretary, and Professor J. D. Andrews was treasurer.

The organization later became known as The American Association of Health, Physical Education and Recreation, and later still as The American Alliance for Health, Physical Education and Recreation. *Dance* was added to the title in 1979.

Alliance Associations

The following are the major associations within the Alliance.

- National Association for Sport and Physical Education (NASPE)
- National Association for Girls and Women in Sport (NAGWS)
- American Association for Leisure and Recreation (AALR)
- Association for Research, Administration and Professional Councils and Societies (ARAPCS)
- Association for the Advancement of Health Education (AAHE)
- National Dance Association (NDA)

Alliance Objectives

The AAHPERD provides a framework for the growth and development of its six national associations, including information-sharing dialogue and debate and research application. The Alliance encourages professionalism by increasing the knowledge base and promoting quality programs in health, physical education, recreation, dance, sport, and research. The objectives of the organization are to:

- increase public understanding of the contributions that Alliance disciplines make to an improved quality of American life;
- provide members with the opportunity for professional growth and with support in the development and operation of their programs;
- promote the development of standards of evaluation to maintain the quality of professionals and programs represented by Alliance disciplines;

- encourage research that enriches the scope and depth of Alliance disciplines, and provide avenues for dissemination of new research findings; and
- focus attention on Alliance issues and concerns by serving as a professional resource for federal, state, and local governments and by informing members of public policy decisions that affect the profession.

Alliance Benefits

In addition to its objectives, the Alliance provides many professional benefits to its members. For example, the *Journal of Physical Education, Recreation and Dance* is published nine times yearly. This outstanding journal brings to its Alliance members articles on current material, new methods of instruction, trends in the profession, and new instructional materials. The journal includes such features as book reviews, the latest information on instructional products and supportive equipment, news updates, and information on Alliance events.

The *Journal of Health Education* is published six times annually and features articles for elementary through college educators working in the schools and community in the field of health. The *Research Quarterly of Exercise and Sport* is the primary research publication, designed to apprise professionals in physical education, athletics, and sport of the latest research and information regarding all aspects of the profession.

A new publication titled *Strategies* is currently being developed. It is designed to allow more opportunities for transmitting practical information on program ideas specifically for teachers of physical education.

The Alliance publishes a monthly newspaper, *Update*, that affords the entire membership a view of the latest news, legislative information, and Alliance developments. This publication also includes a section on job opportunities in selected disciplines addressed by the organization. In addition, *Update* provides the members with conference information at the district and national levels.

Alliance Services

AAHPERD national and district conventions, in addition to regional, state, and local conferences, provide many opportunities for members to visit with colleagues, hear outstanding speakers, and view the latest materials and equipment from a variety of manufacturers who display items in the exhibit area. The annual national convention has registered as many as 10,000 professionals.

Six hundred exhibitors display health, fitness, and sport products at the AAHPERD National Convention.

The AAHPERD has expanded its service in the areas of both professional publications and media materials. Presently, more than 400 titles, including some of the best literature in the field, are available through the AAHPERD office or at the National Convention Alliance Book Store. In addition to these services, members can take advantage of group insurance plans, job placement services, consultant services, leadership opportunities, and other selected activities, such as special travel and membership discounts.

For more information on the American Alliance for Health, Physical Education, Recreation and Dance, you may write to the AAHPERD at 1900 Association Drive, Reston, Virginia 22091.

Alliance District Organizations

The AAHPERD is also divided nationwide into six districts—eastern, southern, central, midwestern, southwestern, and northwestern. These districts have basically the same purposes as the national organization and are composed of a group of states that elects officers, has annual conventions, and serves the local state members by helping to meet their selected goals and objectives. Through the district organization, leadership opportunities are provided for a large number of individuals who are dedicated to serving the profession and providing programs and services in a more localized setting.

Through this district plan, representatives have an opportunity to present concerns from the various parts of the United States and such subsidiary territories as Guam, Puerto Rico, and the Virgin Islands. During semiannual Board of Governors meetings, one held at the Alliance center in Reston and one at the site of the national convention, each district has direct input into national organizational concerns.

Membership in the national organization also provides membership in the district associations. There are no special fees since funding for the district associations comes directly from the national organization and district conventions and special projects.

State Associations

Although state associations are not as directly related to the AAHPERD as are the district organizations, they have similar objectives and provide services to their state membership. Most state associations do not require national membership, but any reimbursement from the national association to the state associations is based on the number of professionals who are members of both organizations.

As in the national and district associations, state association members are professionals in health, physical education, recreation, dance, and athletics. The state organizations are usually nonprofit and are dedicated to improving the quality of life through sound programs in health, physical education, athletics, dance, and leisure and movement activities.

As an example, California's state association's aims are as follows:

- To support, encourage, and provide guidance for personnel in the state as they seek to develop and conduct school, community, and other programs in health, physical education, athletics, recreation, and dance.
- To improve the effectiveness of health, physical education, recreation, athletics, and dance programs.
- To increase public understanding and an appreciation of the importance of these fields through a strong public relations program.
- To encourage and facilitate research in each of these fields.
- To hold conferences and meetings to enhance the effectiveness of the organization and coordinate and support selected activities in the area of health, physical education, recreation, and dance.

- To produce and distribute information and disseminate research to the state membership.
- To conduct special activities that will be of service to its members.

State organizations provide many opportunities for the aspiring professional to associate with leaders in the field and contribute to the development of health, physical education, recreation, and dance programs leading toward fulfillment of a healthful lifestyle.

Special Membership Organizations

In recent years, additional professional organizations have developed in line with special interest groups. For those wishing to specialize, membership in these organizations can supplement membership in more general associations and provide information through conferences and special programs in selected areas of study such as fitness, sports medicine, intramurals and coaching.

State Coaches' Associations

Many states have professional organizations that relate specifically to coaching responsibilities. Some are general in nature and seek membership from coaches of a great variety of sports. Others are specific to a sport and limited to the promotion and development of programs in a single coaching responsibility. These associations usually sponsor such activities as clinics and coaching workshops about specific aspects of competitive sports. At these sessions, one can learn about the defensive techniques used by a state high school championship football coach, for example, or learn of creative styles of offense from another successful mentor. As diagrams and patterns of play are illustrated on the chalkboard, coaches attending the session plan how this may help their teams climb the ladder of success.

The members of coaches' associations help promote interest in sports, review and make recommendations for possible rule changes, establish standards for coaching ethics and, in general, support sport competition on a sound basis for the benefit of the student athlete.

The following code is a sample of philosophical statements developed by a football coaches' association and can be adapted to general use for all sports.

Purpose   This Code of Ethics has been developed to protect and promote the best interests of the game and the coaching profession. Its primary purpose is to establish approved ethical and professional practices. Its secondary purpose is to emphasize the value of football and to stress proper functions of coaches in relation to schools, players, officials, and the public.

The welfare of the game depends on how coaches live up to the spirit and letter of ethical conduct. Coaches unwilling or unable to comply with the principles of the Code of Ethics have no place in the coaching profession.

This Code should be studied regularly by all coaches, and its principles should always be followed. Violation of the Code should be reported to the Ethics Committee.

Code of Ethics

1. The coach should never place the value of winning above that of instilling the highest desirable ideals and character traits in the players. The safety and welfare of the players should always be uppermost in the mind of the coach, and they must never be sacrificed for any personal prestige or glory.

The late Paul "Bear" Bryant, coach at the University of Alabama, brought credit to himself, his institution, and the game of football. The welfare of any game depends on how well coaches live up to the spirit and letter of ethical conduct.

2. Both the letter and spirit of the rules must be adhered to by the coach.
3. A coach should not make demands on a player that will interfere with the player's opportunity for achieving academic success. The function of the coach is to educate students through participation in the game of football. This primary and basic function should never be disregarded.
4. A coach should promote good sportsmanship. Any coach who permits or encourages the use of unsportsmanlike tactics shall be considered guilty of the most serious breach of football coaching ethics.
5. For a coach to address, or permit anyone on the bench to address, uncomplimentary remarks to any official during the progress of a game, or to indulge in conduct that might incite players or spectators against game officials, is a violation of the rules of the game and must likewise be considered conduct unworthy of a member of the coaching profession.
6. Resolving professional problems should be discussed within the profession and not in the press.
7. All institutional, conference, and state athletic regulatory body rules pertaining to recruiting shall be strictly observed by coaches.
8. Coaches' actions and behavior should at all times bring credit to them, to their institution, and to the game of football.

The gathering together of coaches from all sections of the state or corners of the nation provides an outstanding opportunity for those in attendance to discuss coaching systems, training programs, and other concerns with the best in the profession.

National Intramural and Recreational Sports Association

In 1950, Dr. Willard Wasson, a professor at Dillard University in New Orleans, along with other interested directors, formed the National Intramural Association. The purpose of the organization was to stimulate professional growth, exchange ideas and information, and to promote, publish, and conduct research on intramural sports. There was great cooperation with other interested agencies such as the AAHPERD, the National Association for Physical Education and Higher Education, and the National Collegiate Athletic Association, since many sessions on intramural activities were presented at the annual conventions of these organizations. As the Association grew, so did the kinds of services requested, and the name was changed to the National Intramural and Recreational Sports Association (NIRSA) in 1975.

Interest in intramural sports is still growing, and expanded programs now have active student support since many facilities now directly address intramural sports rather than the needs of only the athletic program. This new emphasis on sports is providing opportunities for a large number of students to participate in competitive activities. Many programs and facilities are in operation 24 hours per day to meet student demands.

American College of Sports Medicine

In recent years, sports medicine has developed into a highly sophisticated profession that integrates science, medicine, and education. The purpose of sports medicine is to protect the human being from the stresses of competitive sports and fitness activities through the application of sound medical, scientific, and educational principles.

The American College of Sprots Medicine was founded in 1953 and in its brief history has made an enormous impact in solving problems stemming from sports participation of individuals of all ages. It is the only professional organization in the United States that observes sport through the eyes of both the scientists and the medical professionals.

The College states that its objectives are (1) to promote medicine and other scientific studies dealing with the effect of sports and other physical activities on the health of human beings at various stages of life, (2) to cooperate with other organizations, physicians, scientists, and educators concerned with the same or related specialties, (3) to arrange for mutual meetings of physicians, educators, and allied scientists, (4) to make available postgraduate education in fields related to these fields, (5) to initiate, promote, and correlate research in these fields, (6) to edit and publish a journal, articles, and pamphlets pertaining to various aspects of sports, other physical activities, and medicine, and (7) to establish and maintain a sports medicine library.

For the most part, these goals have been accomplished or initiated, and interest in the area of sports medicine continues to grow. Expanded areas of research include interdisciplinary study of growth development, and aging, injury rehabilitation, environmental effects, psychological and sociological concern, injury prevention, diet and nutrition, and safety and protective measures.

Sports medicine is fast attracting professionals in physiology, sociology, psychology, and medicine to pursue the study of sport participation as an additional important phase of their specific discipline. By teaming together, these professionals are enhancing sport participation for all.

Association for Fitness in Business

Today or currently, business and industrial firms have expanded their services to employees by providing physical fitness activities in a variety of settings. Some companies have developed their own sport and exercise facilities, whereas others make use of existing programs offered through public and private agencies in the community. Initial efforts began with employers protecting their training and development investment in company executives by reducing the risk of heart attacks through executive fitness programs. The bottom line in the business world is the profit-loss figure, and current research has confirmed that employees increase productivity, decrease absenteeism, and experience improved job satisfaction when in a state of good health and physical fitness.

In 1974, a group of thirty-seven individuals representing business and industry founded The American Association of Fitness Directors in Business and Industry in cooperation with the President's Council on Physical Fitness and Sport. Today, the organization has changed its name to the Association for Fitness in Business (AFB) and boasts a membership of more than 5,000. Professional membership is open to individuals employed by a company or organization as a fitness director, supervisor, coordinator, or instructor of a physical fitness program operated by the company or organization for its employees. Physical fitness careers in the business setting include exercise test technicians, exercise specialists, recreation specialists, and program directors.

The following purposes and objectives were developed to define the goals of the AFB:

1. To provide a professional organization to support and assist in the development of quality physical fitness programs in business and industry.
2. To create an increased awareness of the importance of initiating and maintaining a high level of physical, emotional, and mental health among employees.
3. To cooperate in a national program of physical fitness and sports with the President's Council on Physical Fitness and Sport and other similar purposes and objectives.
4. To recommend qualifications and professional standards for fitness directors and other professional personnel in business and industry.

5. To encourage and provide support for in-service training activities and programs on continuing education for fitness directors and other professional personnel in business and industry.
6. To stimulate active research and to compile and disseminate research information regarding the effects of physical fitness programs.
7. To provide leadership in physical fitness and health for the profession.
8. To serve as a clearinghouse for information and services pertaining to physical fitness programs.
9. To develop operational, administrative, and educational material for physical fitness programs in business and industry.

Continued and expanded interest in employee fitness programs has made the AFB one of the more needed and fastest-growing professional organizations in the United States. The following topics selected from an AFB conference program illustrate the relationship of the physical education profession to special membership groups:

• Marketing Health Promotion within the Corporation
• Corporations: The Fit Will Inherit the Turf
• A Lifestyle Model: A Theoretical Model for Employee Lifestyle Programs
• Principles of Exercise Testing and Prescription
• Interval Training for Health and Fitness
• The Musculoskeletal System: Injury Recognition, Treatment, and Prevention

Although the return on investment for setting up fitness programs may not be immediate, those employers who offer physical fitness and health enhancement programs for their employees will reap the benefits of curtailing spiraling health care costs and improving employee job satisfaction.

President's Council on Physical Fitness and Sport

Each professional should always seek to cooperate with and support other groups or agencies involved in developing sport and fitness programs. Although not a professional membership organization, the President's Council on Physical Fitness and Sport (PCPFS) has much to offer in support of health, physical education, recreation, and dance programs for all ages.

The PCPFS was established in 1956 as the President's Council on Youth Fitness. The original council was developed in response to public concern over the poor physical condition of our American youth. Newspapers referred to our young boys and girls as the "marshmallow generation," and a national magazine compared the fitness of American youth and European youth by running a story titled, "The Report that Shocked the President."

President Eisenhower was dismayed by the low endurance and strength test scores across the nation and called the President's Conference on Fitness of American Youth in June 1956. This meeting led to the development of a national fitness program with White House leadership. President Kennedy changed the name of the program to the President's Council on Physical Fitness in 1963, and in 1966 President Johnson added the word *sports*. The Council's charge was now expanded to encourage a program of fitness for all ages and included sports participation as a major physical fitness activity. Since the program's initiation, seven presidents have strongly supported the PCPFS in its effort to make our country a strong and healthy society through physical fitness and sports activities.

In September 1981, the PCPFS held the first National Conference on Fitness for the Aged in Washington, D.C. This conference confirmed the value of exercise for the aged as research studies consistently verified the favorable physiological effects gained through physical activity. Only a few years ago, a person reaching 100 years of age made the headlines in daily newspapers. Today, America boasts more than 14,000 citizens who are older than 100 years. Many elderly persons who had resigned themselves to a sedentary lifestyle have been "reborn" to social, emotional, and physical activity through appropriate exercise.

The PCPFS has been exceedingly successful in making America aware of the importance of physical activity in establishing credibility by recruiting outstanding athletes, politicians, researchers, corporate businesspersons, and participants of all ages to support program activities. This small government agency may be among the most important operations in the federal scheme; under effective leadership, it has been a major catalyst in changing the American sedentary lifestyle.

The PCPFS plays an active role in promoting school physical education programs, conducts pilot fitness projects for people of all ages and occupations, and presents physical fitness and sport clinics throughout the United States. More than 6 million boys and girls have earned the Presidential Physical Fitness Award since President Johnson established the program in 1966. This program is now available to Americans of all ages. One of the major strengths of the PCPFS has been its ability to generate ideas and organize programs with financial support from the business sector.

Personal Professional Factors

Professionalism goes much further than participating in professional organizations. Although membership and leadership at this level does much to promote continued interest in one's professional area of study, there are many other factors that contribute to a professional image.

A favorable attitude toward other disciplines in the schools, personal grooming, displaying a breadth of academic interest, and concern for being prepared and updating instructional techniques are some points worthy of discussion and review by the new as well as the experienced professional.

As a professional in the field of health, physical education, recreation, and dance, you have a responsibility to present an image that reflects the purpose and goals of the discipline. Such factors as dress, personal grooming, weight control, and state of fitness should be beyond reproach when viewed by the layperson or student.

The day of the obligatory jacket and tie for men and dress for women may be gone, but sloppy jeans, beat-up shoes, and messy hair have no place in the professional's attire. Many have worked for years to eliminate the sweatshirt-and-whistle image, and each future professional should build on this foundation by presenting a favorable picture. Appropriate dress for activity is important; however, when attending meetings or in public relations settings, good sense should prevail. Clean, well-kept clothes that are appropriate to the event, should be worn.

Proper weight and good posture are necessary traits of those in our field. We cannot all be perfect body types, but whether stocky or slim, one can and should present oneself as healthy and physically fit. If you do not practice what you preach, how can you appear credible to your students, community or group participants?

It is important to be able to speak before audiences in an intelligent and effective manner. Many times physical educators are expected to address both small and large groups. Good written expression should also be practiced because of the many required reports.

The professional should make every effort to establish relationships outside of the gymnasium. Visiting or sharing a meal with teachers from other disciplines can squelch the "dumb jock" image. To the surprise of many, they find out we can recite poetry, play musical instruments, discuss world politics, and appear intelligent when confronted with questions about areas other than sports. Developing relationships with different audiences can strengthen and promote our professional image.

Another important trait is to support other school and community activities. Offer help to the drama teacher, volunteer for the school carnival, or work with the art teacher. The return on your investment will be in the form of much-needed help at your track meet or supervision at your sport contests. Program support must be nurtured.

Finally, we must display a sincere desire to work with people. This can be accomplished by preparing lessons to meet the needs of all the class participants. Your students must feel they are accepted before effective learning can take place. Individualized instruction, contract teaching, and instructional learning packages are here to stay. There is no place for the uninspired in our field. You must be well-prepared, enthusiastic, and convinced you are in the best profession available.

Whether as coach, teacher, or fitness director, your image must stand up to the established standards of the true professional. Being an initiator, a leader, and a creative force are proven traits of strong professionals in our field of study. Following this pattern will ensure community and institutional support and nourish continued growth for all programs leading toward the achievement of a healthy lifestyle.

Public Relations and Public Information

Although the American public has never before been so concerned with health and participated so much in physical exercise, one still hears about the erosion of public school physical education requirements, expanded class sizes, and other factors that thwart the development of skills required for a vigorous lifestyle. For the most part, few physical educators have been directly involved in promoting and publicizing what physical education can do for individuals at all levels of instruction.

The student of physical education needs to be aware of the importance of public relations, basic political skills, creative promotional concepts, and marketing techniques. The professional physical educator has a responsibility to promote physical activity as a way of life and must be able to explain the values of a sound program to a diverse public within the educational institution and the surrounding community. Professional physical educators have traditionally been skilled in teaching and coaching sport activities and working with people but have not usually been aware of the need to explain, in a systematic manner, the results and the value of their teaching. The public that decides whether physical education is supported financially, maintained, expanded, or decreased cannot make intelligent decisions without a clear understanding of the physical education curriculum and its value to all people.

There are many environments for effectively promoting physical education, and it is the physical education teacher's responsibility to take advantage of each available opportunity. Physical education teachers must seek to promote their programs through shopping center demonstrations, talks to service clubs, special youth demonstration teams, class performances, and other selected activities that will let the public know what constitutes a good instructional program.

Many leaders in the community did not have an opportunity to experience a well-designed, quality physical education program and must be made aware of the favorable changes in today's classes that do meet the needs of all participants. Each instructor must be willing to write effective news releases for distribution to the local news media and make time to speak on television and radio shows at every opportunity.

This approach requires professional knowledge of the values of all aspects of a good program and the ability to communicate these objectives clearly to the lay public. The National Physical Education Public Information (PEPI) Project, developed through the AAHPERD, has developed for the public many promotional materials about physical education. These materials answer such questions as "What is a good physical education program? Why is it important for my child to have physical education in school? Is it true that good physical fitness and motor activities will help my child learn better? What does physical education contribute to making my child a happier, better-adjusted person? What does physical education do to help my child get along with others?" These and other concerns of the public must be intelligently addressed if support for physical education programs is to be received.

The National Physical Education Public Information (PEPI) Project, developed through the AAHPERD, created this logo to identify the promotional material it publishes to keep the public informed about physical education.

Each professional should prepare an outline of answers to some of the questions that parents and the general public commonly ask about the physical education curriculum.

For example, the answer to the first question might be that a good physical education program involves personalized instruction for all school children, beginning in early childhood. It should start with basic motor development activities and culminate with instruction in high-level, lifetime sport skills and a personalized and physical fitness regimen. Through individualized instruction, each child should realize a positive self-image, achieve physical and mental health benefits accrued through fitness activities, and develop intellectually through a body that is physically fit. A good physical education program is for everyone, not just for the gifted athlete.

The professional physical educator should always have at hand his or her responses to such questions and should make this information readily available and promote it on a continual basis in his or her own community. Check with your state, district, or national professional organization for materials already developed and rework them in your own style.

The physical education team must have the initiative to develop an aggressive attitude to maintain a continuous and dynamic public relations program. As a professional, one cannot afford to respond only when under attack. Make it a point to let the right people know about the good job you are doing. Take advantage of all possible opportunities to promote a professional career that contributes to our nation's health and well-being.

Student Activities

1. Investigate the goals and purposes of your state professional organization.
2. Visit a school and report on your observations of professional attitudes. (Taking photographs may be hazardous to your health.)
3. Discuss appropriate and inappropriate dress for various situations.
4. Develop a plan for communication with teachers from other disciplines.
5. Investigate new instructional techniques for your teaching or coaching specialty offered at clinics, workshops, or conferences.
6. Make a presentation at a professional conference in the student sector.

7. Develop a public relations plan to promote health, physical education, recreation, and dance programs.

Suggested Readings

American Alliance for Health, Physical Education, Recreation and Dance. 1985. *Journal of Physical Education, Recreation and Dance* 56, no. 4 (centennial issue). Reston, VA: American Alliance for Health, Physical Education, Recreation and Dance.

Heinz, A., and E. T. Turner. 1983. Building a successful major's club. *Journal of Physical Education, Recreation and Dance* 54:55–60.

17. Steps to Obtaining a Career Position

Chapter Outline

Refining Your Career Objective
Goal Setting
Your Professional File
The Résumé
How People Get Jobs
Interviews
The Job Offer
Student Activities
Suggested Readings

Objectives

Chapter 17 is designed to enable you to:

- Refine your career path search.
- Distinguish between myths and facts about résumé writing.
- Begin to develop a professional résumé.
- Understand the importance of advice interviews.
- Prepare for a job interview.
- Better evaluate a job offer in relation to your professional and personal strengths and interests.

I F you are confused and undecided about which career path is for you, take heart. This is natural when you are presented with alternatives and possibilities that you may never before have considered. On enrolling in an institution of higher education, it is appropriate and timely to explore opportunities to the fullest extent to discover your own potential and to learn what your institution can do to aid in your career development.

In Part One of this text, you were introduced to physical education as a discipline and a profession. The concept of career exploration by first examining your goals and objectives and then developing a healthy attitude were stressed. The influence of your lifestyle preferences and personal attributes on your selected career path were also discussed. Part Two presented an overview of the foundations of physical education and coursework that, as a physical education major, you will encounter in your course of study. In Part Three, we have already introduced a variety of self-assessment techniques, career overviews, and personal profiles of professionals in the field. This chapter should help you refine the career path search by showing you techniques of interviewing and résumé writing.

Refining Your Career Objective

As one assimilates additional information related to career goals and becomes involved in a variety of professional experiences, career objectives are refined. The course work you pursue in your major program of study may help you cultivate new interests and skills that can be added to your list of strengths and perhaps lead to development of a new career objective. New professional experiences such as joining your state and national associations of health, physical education, recreation and dance will also help clarify your career aspirations.

On a national scale, economics and preferences for a certain geographical climate are shaping career objectives in a dynamic way. One must also be in tune with the political climate and current events so as to modify career plans continually to avoid being a victim of "future shock." What you have read throughout this book, discussed in class, or experienced outside of class must constantly be integrated into the person you are as you follow your career path.

Goal Setting

As discussed in Chapter 3, it is important to set reasonable, attainable goals for your career and personal life. These goals should not be viewed as hard-and-fast plans for your life. Rather, goals should be based on a reasonable assessment of your strengths, interests, and lifestyle expectations *at the time they are set;* these goals may change as you grow as an individual and a professional.

If you have a long-range goal that will require a great deal of work to achieve, and if you have the ability to recognize and capitalize on opportunities to attain goals, greater flexibility in short-range goals is often advantageous. The timely return to graduate school or membership in a new professional organization are examples of flexible short-range goals that may open doors to your career objectives sooner than you expected.

Achieving goals does not simply happen to the lucky individual. Planning for, working toward, and recognizing opportunities are key elements to achieving professional success and happiness in most careers. This applies not only to individuals pursuing alternative careers or a midlife change in career but also to the person whose long-range goal is to positively influence the lives of youths as a teacher or coach. Short-range goals such as taking on additional course work, participating in professional associations, and attending workshops and conferences are vital to maximizing your continued success in meeting the needs of changing youth throughout the decades of your career.

On whatever career path you direct your energies, self-assessment of goals, job performance, and career satisfaction is important and should be undertaken frequently. Review the career objective that you developed in Chapter 11. After reading the chapters on careers, are there any modifications that need to be made to your objective? What short-range goals can you develop for this year and during your undergraduate years that will help you work toward your career objective? Some possible goals might be (1) to maintain at least a 3.0 grade point average in all course work, (2) to take at least two elective courses in the communications or business departments, (3) to volunteer as a coach of a youth sports team, (4) to become active in the student government association on campus as a means of learning about working within an organization, and (5) to graduate with a major or minor that will ensure qualification for at least two careers.

Complete Figure 17.1 by filling in your career objective (personal strengths and lifestyle expectations) and short-range goals. Remember, these are tentative and will most likely change to some degree, but it is important to identify where you feel you are now and put it in writing. Once you can verbalize some of your career thoughts, then further exploration and planning can occur in a meaningful sequence.

Figure 17.1   Career Objective and Short-Range Goals Chart

Career Objective (25 words or less):

_____

Goal #1

_____

Goal #2

_____

Goal #3

_____

Goal #4

_____

Goal #5

_____

Goal #6

_____

Your Professional File

As an emerging professional, you should develop a personnel or placement file. Your institution's placement office is a good place to visit
early in your college career. The services provided by these centers are
varied; they can offer you assistance with such tasks as career planning,
résumé writing, job interviewing, and further testing for career aptitude
and graduate school. Plan now to visit your institution's placement center. Get acquainted with the people who operate the center. It is often
helpful to select a career counselor with whom you can develop and
maintain a professional relationship throughout your college years. If
you begin early to develop a placement file with semester transcripts
and professional letters of recommendation, it will prove very helpful
as you explore career possibilities.

As you develop an official placement file in your institution, it is a
good idea to keep a personal copy of that file handy, including dupli-
cates of transcripts and personal letters of recommendation. Your file
should be updated annually with a new professional résumé and new

letters of recommendation from various professors or employers. Remember to discard old résumés and recommendations that do not reflect your current professional development. Maintaining an updated placement file and personal résumé may allow you to capitalize on a professional opportunity.

Letters of reference are important to prospective employers and generally provide more information about you than a transcript. Many institutions have developed special forms for you to distribute to selected individuals for completion. In addition to these forms, letters of reference on personal or business stationery can be a good addition to your file because letter writing gives a person more flexibility in responding. Start accumulating such letters now. You need merely three or four good letters from a variety of people that will reflect your academic ability, personal talents and skills, volunteer or paid work experience, and personal character. (Avoid compiling too many letters since prospective employers and graduate school administrators will not wade through a sheaf of papers.) Good references mght be provided by current or former teachers, coaches, employers, or your minister, pastor, or rabbi. Be selective when asking people to write a reference for you. Remember to solicit references from people who know you well and whom you believe will recommend you strongly and positively. A letter of reference from a well-positioned but barely familiar source (for example, a university department chairperson) will probably be only ordinary, one in which the writer states exactly what is known about you but does not highlight your unique strengths. The individual who writes a letter of reference is putting his or her professional accountability on the line.

Remember to ask for reference letters that describe your character and abilities in a manner that can be directed to a variety of possible employers. Asking for a letter that appeals to a wider audience can help you avoid repeatedly asking the same individual for a reference. It takes time to write a thoughtful, well-developed reference letter, and you may not be the only person requesting such assistance. Be sure to allow the individual enough time to prepare a good reference letter for you. Some placement centers require confidential versus open letters of recommendation, whereas others may give you the option. A confidential letter is better for the receiver of the reference, but you had better be certain when you approach the writer that he or she will write either a favorable letter or none at all. Finally, as soon as the reference letter has been completed, send a note of appreciation to the letter writer for his or her consideration and effort.

The Résumé

Myth versus Reality

The résumé is a tool often abused by individuals searching for a job that fits their career objective. Most people place too much emphasis on the résumé. At conferences, conventions, and job fairs, you can identify these individuals by the stack of résumé copies they are indiscriminately handing out to all prospective employers and at every interview. Such job seekers have succumbed to the following ideas (Career Management International, 1977):

1. The quality and length of the résumé determines whether an individual will be granted an interview.
2. The résumé is the employee's first contact with the prospective employer; therefore, it carries a lot of weight.
3. Without the résumé, an individual cannot be successful in securing or changing positions.

These are myths perpetuated by many authors and employment agencies, as well as by individuals who serve in an advisory capacity to job seekers and who are unaware of research data. In most instances, the following are true:

1. A résumé should seldom be longer than one typed page because people neither have nor take the time to read more and because you should be able to depict yourself accurately on one page.
2. The short résumé may be used to respond to advertised positions. A more detailed résumé is prepared for a specific position and is more effective when delivered in person.
3. The résumé is not as significant in the job-hunting process as people are led to believe. Employers rarely hire people because of their résumé alone. Employers hire people they like. In education, the appropriate teaching credentials and first impression at an interview are often more important.

By applying these principles, you set yourself apart from the average applicant. During an interview you want to present yourself well and maintain dialogue with the interviewer. As an applicant, you want to avoid interviews in which the interviewer merely reads your résumé rather than talks with you. If you adopt the preceding principles about the résumé's importance, you will focus on assessing the prospective employer's needs so as to gather pertinent information and design a résumé targeted to those needs. The informational interview is a critical tool for such assessment. By using this tool, you establish a credible reason for a second interview — to bring back the résumé — and you flatter the employer because you think enough of the opportunity to do something special.

Preparing the Résumé

The first part of the résumé is critical. This is because the interviewer will not read any more than the first few lines if there is nothing interesting to be found. Place your personal information, such as legal name (nicknames are unprofessional), mailing address, and telephone number, in the upper right-hand corner (Fig. 17.2). To indicate that the résumé was prepared specifically for this employer, put the employer's name and firm or school district under *Prepared For* in the upper left-hand corner.

The next step is to write an objective in response to previously determined needs. Be sure to use descriptors that fit your assessed strengths. For education, state only the college, degrees earned, and year graduated. List further training only if it is relevant to the stated objective. Do not list a summer school, workshops, or conferences. The reader is mainly interested in your degrees.

Place the words *Related Accomplishments* in the center of the page. Review your objective and select for presentation no more than three strengths from your previously defined list of accomplishments. Your list of accomplishments should be updated annually so that you have considered your current strengths for a résumé or interview. The strengths selected should correlate with your objective. Expand on each accomplishment to support each strength, but be brief.

For your employment history, list no more than three recent positions. If this is your first attempt at securing a full-time position, it is appropriate to list part-time, summer, and volunteer positions. Remember to state briefly the duties you performed for each position. Do not list any salaries previously earned or salary desired for the future unless your employer requests such information.

Under *Personal Information*, include whatever you feel is necessary. Generally, it is best to avoid putting your height, weight, marital status, spouse's name, and so forth. Put association memberships and awards only if they are relevant to your objective.

The sample résumés in Figures 17.2 and 17.3 provide general guidelines for a résumé that you can develop to fit nearly any prospective employer's needs. This format has been successfully used in many professions and is appropriate for education.

It is important to remember that delivering your résumé, unless you

Figure 17.2 Sample Résumé A

PREPARED FOR:	ROBERT R. DOE
James Kerr, Personnel Director	101 Main Street
Denver Public Schools	Yourtown, State 99999
	(555) 555-4173

OBJECTIVE   *Physical education teaching and coaching,* where experience in working with children, ability to communicate enthusiasm for learning, and success in motivating young people will contribute to the district's educational program.

EDUCATION   B.S., Ohio State University, 1984.

RELATED ACCOMPLISHMENTS

WORKING WITH CHILDREN   The number of young boys on the YMCA's swimming team doubled within 1 year due to the change in philosophy of competition and demonstrated interest in each youngster.

COMMUNICATING ENTHUSIASM FOR LEARNING   Created unique physical fitness program for junior high school students, and students elected to take it over several other course offerings. Students had reading assigments, training schedules, and dietary modifications. The success of their work was measured by scientific tests, and the positive results encouraged other students to participate.

MOTIVATING YOUNG PEOPLE   Members of the swim team spent 2 days each month teaching handicapped youngsters to swim. Successful in encouraging swimmers to extend themselves to meet the needs of others.

EMPLOYMENT HISTORY   *Coach.* Yourtown YMCA. Responsible for developing the swim team for boys and girls. Coached more than fifty swimmers. (1980–present)

Teacher. Forest Friends Montessori School. Volunteered to develop and teach a preschool movement education program. (1981–present)

PERSONAL   Member of American Alliance for Health, Physical Education, Recreation and Dance.

were asked to bring it to the interview, is one way to reinforce your first personal contact with a prospective employer. As a follow-up tool, the résumé should be delivered in person, during a second interview if possible. The second interview reinforces your interest in the position and allows you to remind the employer that you are more than

Figure 17.3 Sample Résumé B

PREPARED FOR:	SHELLY S. SMITH
Mark Lardgren	909 Anywhere Street
Fitness and Recreation Director	Yourtown, State 00001
Tenneco, Inc.	(714) 555-4080

OBJECTIVE   *Adult fitness programs*, where experience in developing adult fitness programs, stress testing and monitoring cardiovascular patients, and success in motivating people will contribute to a corporate employee fitness and recreational program.

EDUCATION   M.A., University of Maryland, 1978.
B.A., Oberlin College, 1976.

RELATED ACCOMPLISHMENTS

DEVELOPING PROGRAMS   Received a grant to start a program at a hospital, and within 1 year had twenty-five patients actively participating in the program. Persuaded administration to permit implementation and donate some space.

CONDUCTING TESTING PROGRAM   Conducted treadmill stress testing with a team of cardiologists, and monitored the exercise prescription of fifteen patients. Developed personal exercise schedules and instituted a training program for interns to assist in the program.

MOTIVATING PEOPLE   Encouraged patients to continue with the program when initial progress was slow. After 2 years, 85% of the patients were continuing their own fitness program.

EMPLOYMENT HISTORY   *Fitness Director.* Presbyterian Hospital, Lansing, Michigan. Responsible for developing and implementing an adult physical fitness program for cardiovascular rehabilitation patients. (1978–present)

PERSONAL   Member of American Sports Medicine Association.

information on paper. Another personal contact can make a big difference in securing a desired position.

How People Get Jobs

The methods for finding the appropriate job to match an individual's career path have become very sophisticated. There are many placement agencies and personnel-related businesses that seek out the employer as well as the applicant. The credibility of agencies, personnel offices in companies and schools, and newspaper advertisements varies immensely. It is as important to learn the method of job seeking that will best suit your career objective as it is to learn about common misconceptions and mistakes found in the process.

There are many methods available to an individual seeking employment. Educators are primarily involved with a formal process of obtaining an application, sending the application to the appropriate school district, and forwarding placement files and teaching credentials, followed by a formal interview. However, this process is not always fruitful, and educators can learn job-seeking skills from other professional arenas including business and industry.

According to one study (Granovetter, 1974), more than 74 percent of the professionals who had recently found jobs became employed not because of advertisements or employment agencies but because they took the initiative to build on personal contacts (including relatives, friends, and friends of friends) to make themselves known to potential employers. This is known as *networking*. For the physical education professional who is interested in teaching or an alternative career, this informal method of building on personal contacts is an excellent one. Personnel agencies are intermediaries between the applicant and the employer. The job descriptions they provide are usually rigid, and some of the best applicants are often screened out and never given the opportunity to meet face-to-face with the prospective employer. Remember that being able to have dialogue with the individual who is doing the hiring is important. Newspaper advertisements are firm descriptions, and many, many people usually respond to such advertisements. Again, your telephone call or letter of application is probably one of hundreds and is easily ignored. You need the opportunity to present yourself in person before you can illustrate your unique qualities as the best solution for the employer's needs.

The informal method is founded on the premise that personal contacts are very important in connecting people with jobs. Better jobs are found by knowing individuals who can provide information on the location of available positions and the appropriate contact person. This method relies on the job seeker's awareness of individuals who are known personally by family and friends and on his or her ability to capitalize on the opportunity to contact such individuals.

This method does not imply that the only qualification for a position is who you know. Employers are searching for persons who can meet the standards for a given position and will hire only qualified individuals.

However, the introduction of an applicant by a successful colleague can open doors that normal screening procedures often close. Communicating your career objective to people you know and sharing it with successful others that you meet personally may afford you the opportunity you need. You may be remembered when a position opens.

Career opportunities in physical education and sport are numerous and varied, but so are the applicants. You will not be alone, and personal contacts will prove very helpful. Examples of information that contacts can provide include the following:

Teaching
Where there is a position open
Knowledge of someone leaving a position
Employer's special skills needs (for example, coaching)
Referral to appropriate contact person
Personal introduction or reference

Business and industry
Where there are companies that have or are interested in developing
    adult fitness and recreation programs
Where there are private fitness clubs that are hiring

Your determination to reach your objectives can set you apart from the competition as you strive to attain your goals.

Sports medicine
Which medical facilities conduct or are interested in developing well-
ness programs
Where there may be athletic training positions open

Interviews

Advice Interview

An advice interview is just what its name implies—an interview to obtain advice. It is important to talk to successful people in a variety of
careers for advice on your career alternatives. Your career decision is
one of the most important that you will make in your life. The more you
can share your personal strengths with others and gather their perceptions of your career possibilities, the better decision maker you will be.

Advice interviews can begin now and should continue throughout
your career. Who do you know? We all know many people, some very
well and others only in passing. Any one of these people may be aware
of a career position that would be just right for you. Develop a list of
people with whom you could discuss your personal assets and current
career objectives. Your list may include physical education and sport
professionals but also should be expanded to include successful people
in business and industry and service-oriented professions. A church or
community agency can be a valuable resource. When you finish your
list, you will be surprised at the number of contacts available to you.

Before contacting an individual you would like to meet, you should
write a letter of introduction. Write about who you are and what you
are planning to do. Remember to tell the person from whom you want
advice that you do not expect him or her to hire you or offer you a job.
Make it clear that you are writing because he or she is a successful professional and you would like to make an appointment to solicit advice on
a career. The letter should also indicate that a telephone call will follow to confirm an appointment, and specify the day you would like to
call. Show respect for the person's time by informing him or her that
you need only a brief meeting at a mutually convenient time.

Remember that approach letters are powerful tools in your career
search. Write them thoughtfully and often. Always follow up an advice
interview with a thank-you letter.

Preparing for the Job Interview

Two of the purposes every interviewer has in mind are to evaluate an
applicant's personality and to learn facts about background, personal history, and attitudes. To do this, some interviewers try to create pressure

or stress situations and generally encourage applicants to expose them-selves. There are no pat answers for questions. Your answers must be worked out carefully and intelligently. To help create the best impression and minimize the difficulties resulting from careless answers, remember these points:

- Listen to the question. Understand exactly what is asked. If you are unsure, request clarification.
- Take time to think through all facts that should be used to answer the question.
- Use positive information to answer the question directly and suc-cinctly. Discuss only the facts needed to satisfy the question so that you do not open areas of difficulty. Be truthful, but it is not neces-sary to offer unsolicited information that could detract from the im-age you are creating.
- Seek to focus and refocus attention on your strengths and related ac-complishments. Stress their future use in the position being discussed.
- Be observant of personal interest hints in the interview setting, such as a golf trophy or a photograph on display. A brief statement about the subject may assist you in establishing rapport with the interviewer.

When you successfully apply positive answers, you can control the situation and satisfy the interviewer's need to determine (1) whether you exhibit a consistent interest in a specific vocational area or career objective, (2) whether your employment history, education, and other development show application of your energies, (3) whether your em-ployment history shows progress, achievement, maturity, and respon-sibility, and (4) if you lack the specific background desired, whether your experience includes some of the same activities for which you are being considered. Remember that you always want to present the best possi-ble image consistent with the truth. Practice your interviewing skills using the sample questions presented here:

1. Why do you want to work here?
2. Why do you want to get into this field?
3. What did you like least in your last job? (could include part-time work, volunteer work, or student teaching)
4. Tell me about the best (and the worst) boss you ever had.
5. Tell me about the hardest job you have ever performed.
6. If you could have your choice of any job, what would you do?

7. If you were choosing a person for this job, what kind of individual would you select?
8. How do you spend your spare time?
9. Tell me about your health.
10. Tell me about your greatest disappointment in life.
11. Are you considering other positions at this time? How does this one compare with them?
12. Just what does *success* mean to you? How do you judge it?
13. What is your philosophy of education? (for position in education)
14. How do you feel about discipline in a school? (for position in education)
15. Everybody likes to criticize. What do people criticize about you?
16. What else do you think I should know about you?
17. If you feel you have any weakness pertaining to the job, what would it be?
18. What salary would you consider?
19. What type of performance assessment do you think is fair?
20. What is your philosophy of competition?

The Job Interview

The job interview is very different from the advice interview. You are now being interviewed for a specific position. Before you go on a job interview, you should find out as much about the school district, corporation, business, or organization as you can. Make sure that you arrive several minutes early for your interview. There are usually publications available for you to read while you wait.

Very few offers are made at the first interview. Your priorities at this interview are to secure a second interview and learn as much as possible about the interviewer's needs. When you give the interviewer information, make sure it is positive and relevant to the employer's need. Some helpful points to remember include the following (adapted from Career Management International, 1977):

1. Be personable. People hire people they like. This has been proved time and time again. Qualifications for the position are obviously important, but a less qualified individual may be hired because of his or her enthusiasm and positive attitude.

2. Orient your interview and job objective toward the type of position for which the school district or company is recruiting. Be enthusiastic, confident, and ambitious, but as controlled as the situation de-

mands. You should project a well-conceived image of yourself for a given position.

3. Worn suits, frayed shirts, and shoes with holes in them are a liability, as is excessive makeup. Bow ties, shaded glasses, and dress that is out of the ordinary are becoming somewhat more acceptable, but most people will do better by dressing conservatively and trying to appear as relaxed, neatly groomed, and successful as possible.

4. Underplay your need for a job, and always use a soft-sell approach.

5. Maintain your professionalism at all times. If your dignity is abused, then politely close the interview and go on to better things. Never apologize for your liabilities.

6. When the interviewer has only briefly covered a subject of interest, you should not hesitate to ask him or her to expand, define, or describe in more detail.

7. If a situation begins to stall, you can always raise questions about any subject by merely asking who, what, when, where, and how.

8. Protect the confidence of your past or present employer. Any breach in this area will quickly lessen your opportunities as the potential employer may assume that someday you will do the same thing to him or her.

9. Avoid placing anything on your interviewer's desk. This is forbidden territory, and the interview can end very quickly if you invade it.

10. Do not drum your fingers, look at your watch, or exhibit other signs of nervousness or impatience.

11. Avoid talking about race, religion, or politics unless it is relevant.

12. Avoid revealing to the interviewer any salaries you have made with past or present employers. This weakens your negotiating position.

13. Avoid being restrictive about location preference. Try to remain as open as possible, pursuing opportunity first and location second.

14. Do not dwell on questions about school district or company benefits, vacation policies, and so on. You can get the details later.

15. Get a business card from your interviewer, if possible, for future contacts and also in order to write him or her a thank-you letter.

16. Project confidence, but do not imply that you can work miracles.

17. Do not permit your time to be arbitrarily wasted at a job interview by people who have the time to interview but not the authority to hire you. However, do not lose the opportunity for a potential advice interview.

18. Avoid naming your references until the very end of the interview.

19. Above all, be yourself and you will be successful. Do not try to be what someone else wants you to be.

Job interview techniques should be practiced. Your institution's placement center has career counselors who can help prepare you for interviews. If possible, arrange to be interviewed and videotaped. Then you can see how you look and analyze your verbal responses to questions and your presentation of your strengths and accomplishments. With practice, you can learn how to relax and establish rapport with your interviewer.

Once again, every job interview requires a thank-you letter. The desired outcome is that an opportunity to return to deliver your résumé or have a second interview will develop.

The Job Offer

Successful interviews lead to job offers. To evaluate such offers you will need certain basic information that may not be volunteered by interviewers. Your lifestyle expectations must play an important role in your decision. If you are interested in an active social life and the fine arts, a position in a rural community 200 miles from a large city may not match your needs. There are several items to consider about the job itself, including the job description, personnel, the history of the school district or company, the surrounding community, and what compensation you would receive.

Job description	What are the specifications for this position? Are the duties and responsibilities described clearly? What does "other duties as assigned" really mean?
Personnel	Who are the people with whom I will work? What is the leadership style of the principal or boss? What are the personality traits of my co-workers?
History of the school district or company	How long have they been in existence? How large are they? What are their facilities? What types of in-service programs are offered? What is the turn-

	over rate of teachers or employees? Is there room for upward mobility in the system?
Community	Where can I get information on housing, cost of living, religious and social organizations, schools, libraries, and recreational facilities?
Compensation	What is the salary being offered? What fringe benefits are available? Is there a periodic assessment or performance review? What are the prospects for salary increases?

Finally, you want to decide whether this offer matches your career strengths and career objectives. Can your personal lifestyle needs be met? Are you jumping at the first offer because you are afraid it will be the only one? Should you wait and see what other offers may appear? Employers respect your right not to make an immediate decision. If a response is needed quickly, tell the employer that you need to think about it and will be sure to call the next morning. Do not be pressured into accepting a job about which you are not enthusiastic or cannot see as an opportunity to grow. A follow-up interview may be needed to resolve the last few questions.

Your undergraduate years should be full of rich and varied experiences so that you will be able to make a choice when you reach the job-offer stage. Take the time to analyze each offer carefully and examine the future potential of each position. Remain flexible and confident that you are the solution to someone's need. You can begin by practicing these skills as you investigate part-time and summer employment. Advice interviews can and should be practiced often. The more you develop job-seeking skills, the more effective you will be when trying to secure the first full-time position of your career.

Student Activities

1. Complete the chart in Figure 17.1. Discuss your career objectives and goals with another student.
2. Begin developing your personnel file.
3. Using the examples in Figures 17.2 and 17.3, write your first résumé.
4. Seek an advice interview and report your experience to your class.

5. If you have a career placement center, practice role playing in the applicant and interviewer situation. Videotaping the practice interview can help in evaluating your skills.

Suggested Readings

Bolles, R. N. 1982. *What color is your parachute? A practical manual for job hunters and career changers,* rev. ed. Berkeley, CA: Ten Speed Press.

Career Management International, 5353 West Alabama, Suite 203, Houston, TX. (Series of seminars and brochures, 1977.)

Coordinated Occupational Information Network, 1230 West Wooster, Bowling Green, OH 43402. (Brochure, 1978.)

Granovetter, M. S. 1974. *Getting a job: a study of contacts and careers.* Cambridge, Massachusetts: Harvard University Press.

U.S. Department of Labor, Bureau of Labor Statistics. 1982–1983. Occupational Outlook Handbook, Bulletin 2200.

18. Future Perspective

Chapter Outline

Keep Yourself Current
Graduate Course Work
Selecting a Graduate School
Administrative Internships
Self-Renewal
Your Future
Student Activities
Suggested Readings
References
Resources

Objectives

Chapter 18 is designed to enable you to:

- Value the importance of self-renewal.
- Develop a realistic yet positive view toward career opportunities in physical education.
- Pursue your career path with professional dedication and personal enthusiasm.

"ONE day, a global network of smart machines will be exchanging rapid-fire bursts of information at unimaginable speeds. If they are used wisely, they could help mankind to educate its masses and crack new, scientific frontiers" (*Newsweek*, June 30, 1980). The future is difficult to comprehend in a world that moves through each day at a frightening pace. How often at the end of a day do you find yourself wondering where the time went? And when New Year's Eve comes around, where has the old year gone? The old adage that time passes more quickly as we age may be replaced by the phenomenon of increasing technology. There will continue to be vast increases in the quantity of material to be learned, synthesized, and applied. Computers are beginning to control facts and predict the application of facts, but the human element will continue to influence the intangible decisions that cannot be computerized. Despite stringent accountability practices in education and business enterprises, the need to maintain a human focus has never been more apparent.

Your physical education career has the potential to progress with future trends and assist individuals in their pursuit of personal growth, performance, fitness, and satisfaction. You can be an important influence on others because of the nature of your career and your unique value as a professional who cares about the health and lifestyle of others.

Keep Yourself Current

Education is a continual process. It does not end with the completion of a degree or credential program. In today's world, technological advances are so rapid that refresher courses are needed on a regular basis. The professional in the field of sport, physical education, and fitness has a responsibility to progress with the times. A true professional leads the way by seeking new information and implementing new techniques and procedures rather than relying solely on the traditional. Attending clinics, workshops, and conferences should be a way of life if one is to keep pace with new trends in the profession. However, in-depth study and clear understanding of selected subject areas is best accomplished by pursuing advanced course work in graduate school.

Some believe universities do not offer updated course material presentation. However, universities can and should be leaders in professional study. Institutions with enthusiastic, dedicated faculty will protect their programs by maintaining this position.

Graduate Course Work

One should view graduate study in several ways. To some, advanced study is preparation for upward mobility in one's field. In higher education, such mobility may be in the form of specialized teaching assignments, promotion, or preparation for administrative responsibilities. Graduate study may also be viewed as a means to progress in one's current position. As one develops into a better practitioner and meritoriously warrants advancement on the salary schedule, one also becomes a more valuable asset to the organization.

Another benefit of graduate work is that it can present opportunities to prepare for career changes. A physical education generalist may, for example, pursue specialization in computer science, public administration, or communications. As a result of this preparation, doors may be opened to positions in the business world, other disciplines, or other departments related to physical education.

The discipline of physical education has evolved from a general area of study containing a broad base of information to a series of smaller subdisciplines, each with its own body of knowledge. This fragmentation has led to a variety of content areas in which graduate students are forced to specialize. Obtaining a specialist's degree appears to be the most desirable path to follow. To decide which specialty area to pursue, some information on employment opportunities would be helpful. Specialist degrees lend themselves to employment in higher education.

Koslow and Nix (1988) undertood the task of tabulating the number and type of higher-education job opportunities from the *Chronicle of Higher Education* advertisements as there is no centrally compiled list of employment opportunities relating to physical education. Their findings are listed in Table 18.1. These data highlight the need for individuals with coaching abilities or training in the areas of exercise physiology or teacher preparation. In most cases, an ability to teach in additional areas of physical education was considered desirable. However, few job descriptions were for generalists. Without analysis of the supply of qualified individuals for these positions, one can only speculate on the degree of competition for college-level positions.

Selecting a Graduate School

Once you have made the decision to enroll in a graduate program, several key questions must be answered: Which institution should I attend? Should I be a full- or part-time student? Can I afford to return to school at this time? What financial support is available?

Table 18.1 Number and Percentage of Job Opportunities in Higher Education as Related to Year and Area of Specialization

JOB CATEGORY	NO. OF JOB OPPORTUNITIES				OVERALL JOB OPPORTUNITIES (%)			
	1984	1985	1986	Total	1984	1985	1986	Total
Physical Education/Coaching	39	69	41	149	17.8	21.5	20.3	20.1
Exercise Physiology*	31	57	41	129	14.2	17.8	20.3	17.4
Teacher Preparation*	32	39	22	93	14.6	12.1	10.9	12.5
Generalist	19	33	11	63	8.7	10.3	5.4	8.5
Chair/Director	15	23	9	47	6.8	7.1	4.5	6.3
Activities Specialist	16	19	23	58	7.3	5.9	11.3	7.8
Athletic Trainer*	7	16	3	26	3.2	4.9	1.5	3.5
Kinesiology/Biomechanics*	16	15	15	46	7.3	4.7	7.4	6.2
Adapted Physical Education*	6	7	13	26	2.7	2.2	6.4	3.5
Motor Learning/Motor Control*	9	9	6	24	4.1	2.8	3.0	3.2
Aquatics Specialist*	12	8	3	23	5.5	2.5	1.5	3.1
Sport Management	4	7	6	17	1.8	2.2	3.0	2.3
Psychology of Sport	4	5	6	15	1.8	1.6	3.0	2.1
Administration*	3	5	0	8	1.4	1.6	0.0	1.1
Statistics/Measurement*	1	5	3	9	0.5	1.6	1.5	1.2
Motor Development*	1	2	0	3	0.5	0.6	0.0	0.4
Miscellaneous	4	2	0	6	1.8	0.6	0.0	0.8
Total	219	321	202	742	100.0	100.0	100.0	100.0

*Specifies subdisciplines within the area of physical education.
R. E. Koslow and C. L. Nix, "Employment Opportunities in Physical Education Higher Education: 1984–86," *The Physical Educator*, Fall, 1988: 121–123. Reprinted with permission.

When selecting an institution some things to consider are location, reputation, and cost. Each profession is unique and decisions must be made that are appropriate to each person's situation. Ask your counselor, colleagues, and former college professors for suggestions. They often have contacts that can help you. Through your own readings you should also become familiar with the leaders in selected areas of study. Students study under people rather than programs so make sure you are getting the best instructors available in your field.

If your current institution offers a graduate studies program, this may be an appropriate opportunity to examine the coursework and programs offered. In some institutions, the graduate faculty and undergraduate faculty are the same. In other schools, some faculty teach more at the graduate level than at the undergraduate level. As you examine your institution's graduate program, you may find that you will already have taken undergraduate courses with some of the graduate instructors. Whether or not you would wish to take additional graduate courses from the same professors would depend on your degree program objectives plus the quality of instruction.

The quality of graduate professors within degree specializations is very important. Publishing excellence and professional contributions of college professors are indicators of graduate program quality. It is becoming more important to visit graduate schools in order to make the best choice regarding your degree plan. Graduate schools also differ in the quality of facilities and research support. Most advanced degrees require various types of laboratory work, including exercise physiology, kinesiology, and motor learning. The quality and quantity of laboratory equipment and computer support available at an institution is important. Research also requires a comprehensive professional library to support your efforts.

If your situation permits, pursue a graduate or teaching assistant position. These usually involve a financial stipend or tuition waiver that will allow you to relocate. Moving to a different environment and studying under leaders with different philosophies can broaden your understanding of the field. Obtaining a degree from an institution in another area of the country may enhance your résumé also.

If you are already employed as a teacher, check your institution's policy regarding sabbatical leaves. You may qualify for paid leave that will allow you to continue studying and researching. If there is a university nearby, you may be able to commute and attend on a part-time basis. Above all, never assume that your education is complete.

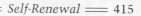

Graduate study provides opportunities to participate in research projects.

Administrative Internships

Another option to consider is an internship as a way to experiment with various job responsibilities. Participation as an administrative intern may reveal whether you have interest and ability in this area. Such an internship may become available when you are a graduate student or after you become employed. It is also important to discover whether you are suited for administration; if not, you can return with new enthusiasm to teaching or whatever other career you select. Be certain to investigate all aspects of future graduate work before making your career decision.

Self-Renewal

Today people in all professions are experiencing increased levels of professional burnout. Burnout is a state of physical and emotional exhaustion. It is important to recognize the symptoms so you can design a personal stress-prevention program. According to Truch (1980), research has shown that responsibility for people always causes more stress than responsibility for things. For example, teaching is susceptible to this kind of occupational stress.

Symptoms of job burnout include a feeling of constant tiredness, sleeplessness, depression, and a run-down feeling. Frequent colds, headaches, and dizziness are experienced. It is difficult to participate in a physical education class or get excited about a student's performance when you are uncomfortable and out of sorts much of the time. A teacher's reaction to students or an employee's reaction to a boss can be extreme; angry outbursts or sarcastic remarks can permanently damage a relationship between a teacher and student or among colleagues. Persons in alternate physical fitness careers in the business world experience stress related to customer sales, fluctuating health spa enrollments, and job security that depends on sales figures. Careers in community service are stressful when decreasing budgets and lack of community support occur. As a professional, you can reduce or alleviate some of the symptoms of burnout or stress:

Administrative intern reviews computerized registration printout with department chair.

- Schedule a mental health break. Do something on a weekend that is novel and completely unrelated to your professional work.
- Attend a workshop or clinic to learn new skills—for example, to learn new teaching, coaching, or training techniques.
- Take a trip during a vacation period and experience a different lifestyle or culture. The United States is a highly diverse nation and offers many opportunities for self-renewal.
- Take a leave from your business or a sabbatical from your campus for professional study, research, or travel.
- If you are a coach, consider taking a season or a year off. Try coaching a different sport.
- A career change could give you a needed change of pace. It could be temporary or may develop into a new attitude about life.

Whatever profession you choose, the more responsibilities you earn, the more stress with which you will have to deal. How you handle stress will be an important factor in determining how much pleasure you derive from your career.

Your Future

Your personal goals and career path developed during this course should be reviewed as you continue work toward your degree. As you complete each year of study, this review will either confirm that your education is progressing in the right direction or suggest that you should change your goals as your knowledge and experience grow. A more thorough study of selected course work in your professional preparation program will increase your knowledge of and enthusiasm for your potential career as well as clarify your personal goals.

It is our hope that you have enjoyed reading this text and that we have played a small part in helping you to understand your profession and to select a career path. By providing an overview of the physical education profession, we have attempted to give you a realistic approach to developing professional and personal goals that will lead to continued success. Your dedication and enthusiasm can create an exciting future.

Student Activities

1. Attend a parent organization meeting in a school and a nonschool setting. Attempt to identify parent concerns.
2. Attend a board of education meeting. Attempt to identify concerns that could affect physical education or athletics in the future.

3. Attend a city council or town meeting and identify issues that affect community health, recreation, and the environment.

Suggested Readings

Truch, S. 1980. *Teacher burnout and what to do about it.* Novato, CA: Academic Therapy Publications.

References

Koslow, R. E., and C. L. Nix. 1988. Employment opportunities in physical education higher education: 1984–86. *The Physical Educator* Fall: 121–123.

Resources

H & F Career Resources, P.O. Box 471, Bloomfield Hills, MI 48303.

Index

Q-R